# An Introduction to Land Tenure in Sub-Saharan Africa



Written by a scholar-practitioner with over four decades of experience, this book is an accessible introduction to land tenure and its implications for African development.

The book carries a clear warning: intensifying conflict over land across Africa is not the growing pains of a positive evolution in land tenure, but a problem that can only get worse without the state's recognition of customary tenure systems when undertaking tenure reform. The author reviews Africa's experience of evolution in customary land tenure and the often-difficult experience of the new nation in land tenure reform, including the failure to prevent further loss of land by rural populations and the unwitting contribution of some reform elements to that loss. The book has a broad reach across many countries in Africa and many different types of land, including farmland, pastures and rangelands, and forests. It is complemented by insights from a variety of disciplines to provide an accessible but nuanced introduction to a topic not well understood even in some development circles. While it focuses on Africa, the book is highly relevant to many countries of the developing world that have a common heritage of colonialism and dualistic systems of land tenure.

This book will be of great interest to students, scholars and practitioners wanting to understand the role of law and land tenure in African development.

**John W. Bruce** is a scholar-practitioner who has worked on land policy and law in developing countries for over 50 years. He served as a Peace Corps Volunteer legal advisor to the Ministry of Land Reform in Ethiopia and has worked for the Ford Foundation in Sudan and the World Bank, where he served as Senior Counsel and Senior Land Tenure Specialist for the Rural Development Department. He holds a PhD from the University of Wisconsin-Madison, where he was later African Program Coordinator, and then Director of the University of Wisconsin-Madison's Land Tenure Center, an interdisciplinary center of excellence on land tenure in the Global South.

## Earthscan Studies in Natural Resource Management

**Governing Natural Resources for Sustainable Peace in Africa**
Environmental Justice and Conflict Resolution
*Edited by Obasesam Okoi and Victoria R Nalule*

**Capacity-Building and the Water-Energy-Food Nexus**
Rethinking Integration in the Asia-Pacific
*Maureen Papas*

**Governing the Palm Oil Industry**
Perspectives from Southeast Asia and Latin America
*Edited by Patrick O'Reilly and Helena Varkkey*

**Researching Institutions in Natural Resource Governance**
Methods and Frameworks
*Edited by Fiona Nunan*

**Sustainable Management of Cordyceps**
Supply Chains and Resource Management Policies
*Edited by Jiping Sheng and Ksenia Gerasimova*

**Reimagining Resources and Community Development**
Lessons from Newfoundland and Labrador
*Monica Gruezmacher, Kelly Vodden, Brennan Lowery, Amy Hudson and Kristof Van Assche*

**An Introduction to Land Tenure in Sub-Saharan Africa**
Dualism, Reform and the Roots of Conflict
*John W. Bruce*

For more information about this series, please visit: www.routledge.com/Earthscan-Studies-in-Natural-Resource-Management/book-series/ECNRM

# An Introduction to Land Tenure in Sub-Saharan Africa

## Dualism, Reform and the Roots of Conflict

**John W. Bruce**

Routledge
Taylor & Francis Group
LONDON AND NEW YORK

earthscan
from Routledge

Designed cover image: Getty Images

First published 2026
by Routledge
4 Park Square, Milton Park, Abingdon, Oxon OX14 4RN

and by Routledge
605 Third Avenue, New York, NY 10158

*Routledge is an imprint of the Taylor & Francis Group, an informa business*



*British Library Cataloguing-in-Publication Data*
A catalogue record for this book is available from the British Library

*Library of Congress Cataloging-in-Publication Data*
Names: Bruce, John W. author
Title: An introduction to land tenure in Sub-Saharan Africa: dualism, reform and the roots of conflict / John W. Bruce.
Other titles: Earthscan studies in natural resource management
Description: Abingdon, Oxon; New York: Routledge, 2026. |
Series: Earthscan studies in natural resource management |
Includes bibliographical references and index.
Identifiers: LCCN 2025043091 (print) | LCCN 2025043092 (ebook) |
ISBN 9781032759715 hardback | ISBN 9781032759692 paperback |
ISBN 9781003476429 ebook
Subjects: LCSH: Land tenure—Africa, Sub-Saharan | Economic development—Africa, Sub-Saharan
Classification: LCC HD966 .B778 2026 (print) | LCC HD966 (ebook) |
DDC 333.73/130967—dc23/eng/20250923
LC record available at https://lccn.loc.gov/2025043091
LC ebook record available at https://lccn.loc.gov/2025043092

ISBN: 978-1-032-75971-5 (hbk)
ISBN: 978-1-032-75969-2 (pbk)
ISBN: 978-1-003-47642-9 (ebk)

DOI: 10.4324/9781003476429

Typeset in Times New Roman
by codeMantra

**This book is dedicated to that remarkable first generation of African scholars of land tenure, who in their courage and persistence under often difficult conditions have helped us understand better the land tenure systems of their countries and to appreciate what Africans value in their land and property rights systems. I have had the privilege of meeting and working with some of them: Okoth-Ogendo and Shem Migot-Adholla from Kenya, Issa Shivji from Tanzania, Kisamba Mugerwa from Uganda, Dessalegn Rahmato from Ethiopia, Sam Moyo and Mandi Rukuni from Zimbabwe, and Ben Cousins from South Africa. Their dedication and strong sense of purpose should inspire today's new generation of African land tenure experts.**

# Contents

# Foreword

Those who know John Bruce know that he values what he's learned from "the field" over any academic credentials or positions he has held. His scholarship on land tenure was not developed in offices or Range Rovers. Rather, it is rooted in deep appreciation of the knowledge of ordinary people, travels on mule back, sharing meals in villages, walking the landscape and learning the local language. In short, by working with respect and appreciation at the village level and with a curious mind, he opened himself to understandings that have so often been lost on those who arrive in rural communities laden with theories and assumptions.

His work is also rooted in the research and writing of African land tenure scholars. Their work has informed his own, and much of his work has been co-authored with them.

He began with a degree in law and then joined the Peace Corps where he served as a Peace Corps Volunteer legal advisor to the Ministry of Land Reform in Ethiopia, returning to do doctoral research on the future of customary land tenure systems in the Tigray region. For 12 years he was the Director of the University of Wisconsin-Madison's Land Tenure Center, an interdisciplinary center of excellence on land tenure in the global south. Under his leadership the Center became the go-to place for scholars of African land tenure.

It is no surprise that John Bruce has long been a towering scholar-practitioner in the field of land tenure in the global south and African land tenure, in particular. His argument that tenure under customary systems is not inherently insecure or non-accommodating of investment is a major contribution to the field. He is also known for his skepticism concerning the cost-effectiveness of systematic title registration as a strategy for reform of customary land tenure and his conviction that traditional communities have shown remarkable ability to change their customary land tenure systems to meet their needs.

John Bruce's insightful, pathbreaking work is taught in classrooms around the world and used globally by scholars. As a practitioner he has influenced land policy and tenure reform in numerous countries. He is known for his intellectual generosity, attracting young scholars to the field of land tenure, while helping experienced practitioners appreciate how tenure issues impact their own work.

In this book he rigorously analyzes the historical and present-day dynamics of African land tenure in a way that is accessible to the layperson while challenging many of the ingrained conventional wisdoms that often dominate the thinking of experienced scholars and practitioners. It is an extraordinary contribution to the field. Only John Bruce could have written it.

Louise Fortmann
Professor Emerita
University of California, Berkeley
June 2025

# Preface

I arrived in Addis Ababa with four other young American lawyers in the rainy season in 1968. We were all recent graduates of very good law schools, but with little experience. We were volunteers in President John F. Kennedy's Peace Corps, recruited in response to a request from Ethiopian government agencies for legal assistance. Ethiopia's first law school had opened but had not yet graduated its first class. I believe there were at that time only two university-trained Ethiopian lawyers in the country.

I was assigned to the Imperial Ministry of Land Reform and Administration. In those years Ethiopia's land tenure system was an important front in a struggle to reform or destroy an old and deep-rooted imperial order. Ethiopian colleagues in the Ministry allowed me to share their experience of field studies, foreign consultant visits, legislative drafting, long and sometimes heated discussions of land reform, and ultimately, disappointment. Reform proposals prepared in the Ministry were sent to Parliament by the aged Emperor Haile Selassie I. However, when it became clear that polarization of the legislators would make passage difficult, the emperor took the advice of senior members of the nobility and withdrew the proposals. It was a failure of will that led directly to the seizure of power by leftist army officers in 1974 and the 1975 land nationalization and reform proclamation.

During my time with the Ministry, my curiosity about customary land tenure was ignited by what I observed during a Ministry field trip to northern Ethiopia. What I saw there, in Tigray Province, was inconsistent with much of what I had read about African customary land tenure in the literature. This led to three years of doctoral field research in Tigray and work with the Ministry as a United States Agency for International Development consultant. Ultimately, it led to a lifetime of work on land tenure. My jobs over the years have given me the opportunity to do further research on land tenure, consult on land policy and projects, and teach land law and tenure in many places and to a considerable variety of audiences.

When I first began work on land tenure issues, those in the United States with much expertise on those issues might have fit into a microbus; of course there were more in Europe, given its African colonial experience. Today there are many hundreds of people with that expertise, and an increasing percentage of them are Africans. Much has changed in our understanding of the roles played by land tenure over those years. The field has exploded into dozens of specializations and developed impressive new disciplinary and technological dimensions.

Unfortunately, what has been learned about land tenure over those decades is not being passed on very effectively to new generations of those working in development. We rely heavily on universities to transmit such knowledge between generations, but only a handful of exceptional faculty members, usually with personal experience in rural Africa, are teaching courses on or related to land tenure and property rights and development. They are in different disciplines. The subject, in part because of the interdisciplinary approach needed to teach it well, is still seen as exotic and has never been mainstreamed. The vast majority of university students, even those with an interest in development, never encounter the topic. Later, if they work in developing countries, they may stumble upon land tenure issues in the course of their work. If they do, they often want to dig deeper and get better grounded in the field, but they find there is limited introductory material available. Much of the recent literature on land tenure consists of highly specialized academic studies, often driven by disciplinary concerns and presented in language that those outside the discipline find challenging.

I have written this book in the hope of addressing those needs. It is written not just for students but for practitioners, advocates, implementers, planners and policy makers. I would hope others would find it useful in training and teaching related courses. Many of the chapters in the book tell stories of specific experiences in particular places, chosen both because context is so very important in dealing with land tenure and because they make some points of broader applicability. While the book reflects insights from recent academic research, its purpose is not the systematic exploration of that body of knowledge. It is rather to tell some stories about what has happened to land tenure in Africa over the years and suggest some ways of approaching that material that help us understand better the important issues facing African policy makers.

It begins with an introduction to the concepts of property rights and land tenure, then explores how culture and land use patterns combine to shape land tenure systems. It examines the ways in which land tenure systems change, from evolution to reform, and reviews and assesses the land tenure reform experiences of the continent's new nations and the dilemmas which face their policy makers today. It covers issues that are academically controversial and politically sensitive. I have tried hard to be even-handed in stating the evidence for different positions, but by the end of the book, most readers will have realized that I am critical of much of current land policy in Africa, believing it is still grounded in misconceptions about customary land tenure originating from the colonial era.

This is the sort of book I wish someone could have given me when I joined the Ethiopian Ministry of Land Reform and Administration in 1969, professionally well-prepared but painfully ignorant of land tenure, governance and administration in Africa. After 50 years, I remain fascinated by its complex and powerful interactions with social and economic institutions and development processes. I hope the book conveys, along with information and analysis, some small sense of why those who work on land tenure find the work both enjoyable and compelling. Progress has been made toward better land tenure rules and institutions in many countries, but in many others dysfunctional and unjust systems remain in place, and efforts to reform them face stubborn opposition. There is much to be done, and some of that work is urgent. The stakes are daunting. Getting land policy, law and implementation wrong can impose a terrible cost in the form of deprivation and conflict. Getting them right can open doors into fuller, more abundant lives for rural people.

John W. Bruce
Alexandria, Virginia
March 2025

# Acknowledgements

This book draws on lessons learned from many colleagues and friends over decades. I thank many of them below but have certainly forgotten to include others, for which I apologize, and I can only thank in the most general terms the farmers, elders and officials from whom I have learned so much.

- My thanks to the Ethiopian and Eritrean colleagues who helped me to understand the importance of land tenure, in particular my former colleagues in the Ministry of Land Reform and Administration, who received me with a warmth and acceptance I find remarkable even today: Tamrat Kebede, Alemante Gebre-Selassie, Teame Beyene, Zegeye Asfaw, Haile-Leul Getahun, Fisseha Ezaz, Nega Wolde-Kidan, and the minister who sponsored my research in Tigray, Belai Abai.
- Colleagues and students at the Land Tenure Center of the University of Wisconsin-Madison, both the experts on land tenure in Latin America such as Peter Dorner, Bill Thiesenhusen, Marion Brown, David Stanfield and others, and in particular those who worked with me in building the Center's Africa Program: Don Kanel, Jim Riddell, Steve Lawry, Mark Marquardt, Peter Bloch, Dick Barrows, Carol Dickerman, Mike Roth, Mark Freudenberger, Greg Myers, Jon Unruh, Louise Fortmann, Kent Elbow, Doug Stienbarger, Rebecca McClain, Frank Place and Anna Knox.
- United States Agency for International Development professionals with whom I was fortunate enough to work over the years, in particular Lane Holdcroft, Tom Mehan, Gloria Steele, Joan Atherton, Keith Sherper, John Lewis, Ian Cohen, David Atwood and Pam Stanbury.
- My former land tenure colleagues from my several years at the World Bank, in particular Jorge Munoz, Wael Zakout, Mika Torhonnen, Shem Migot-Adholla, Klaus Deininger, Nora Dudwick, Frank Byamugisha and Li Guo.

I very much appreciate the assistance of my old friend, He Daofeng, a pioneer and practitioner of private philanthropy in China, for his covering a large part of the costs of editing and text preparation that an author must assume. A special thanks also goes to those friends and scholars who have read and commented upon the whole or parts of the manuscript for this book: Louise Fortmann, who was also kind enough to write the Foreword; Nora Dudwick, an anthropologist, now retired from the World Bank; Michel Roth, an economist and former colleague from the Land Tenure Center; Steve Lawry, a land policy expert and again a former colleague from the Land Tenure Center, and my late son-in-law Scott Deacle, head of the Economics Department at Ursinus College. Their thoughtful comments have made this a far better book. Any mistakes remaining are entirely my fault. I am very appreciative of the contributions of Anna Knox and Rebecca McClain, land tenure researchers and consultants, former Land Tenure Center staff, who helped with editing, research and preparing some of the text boxes and figures, and in the case of Anna Knox, co-authored the chapter on gender and tenure. Caroline Reed provided support on finalizing citations, while Chris Heidenrich worked on the indexing process. I am especially grateful to our friend Shufang Zhang, an old friend of my wife and myself, for voluntarily contributing her time to word processing for the book. I can not express enough gratitude to Serena Watkins of Taylor & Francis for her remarkable patience as this book came slowly to completion.

This book would not have been possible without the generosity of several friends and former colleagues, including Joan Atherton, Meg Bruce, Sarah Bruce, Shao Bruce, Kent Elbow, Louise Fortmann, Mark Freudenberger, Allan Hoben, Susana Lastarria-Cornhiel, Steve Lawry, Mark Marquart, Scott McCormick and Katie Rick, Frank Place, Mike Roth, Alemante Gebre-Selassie and David Stanfield. Their donations were crucial to getting the book over the finish line when resources dwindled.

Finally, my thanks to my wife, Zongmin Li. I am grateful for our discussions as land lawyer and land economist over the years, and especially for her support during the years I worked on this book, including a good deal of time I should have spent with her and the family.

# Acronyms and Abbreviations

| | |
|---|---|
| AU | African Union |
| AUC | African Union Commission |
| CBWM | community-based wildlife management |
| CFS | UN Committee on World Food Security |
| CLDMC | Community Land Development and Management Committee |
| CLS | customary land secretariat |
| CNRF | National Commission on Land Reform |
| CPA | cattle post area |
| CSO | civil society organization |
| CTV | Centro Terra Viva |
| DFID | Department for International Development |
| FAO | Food and Agriculture Organization of the United Nations |
| F&G | Framework and Guidelines on Land Policy in Africa |
| FIDA | Lesotho Federation of Women Lawyers |
| IIED | International Institute for Environment and Development |
| ILO | International Labour Organization |
| LAP | Land Administration Project |
| LGS | African Union Land Governance Strategy |
| LLA | Liberian Land Authority |
| LTRP | Land Tenure Regularization Program |
| MCC | Millennium Challenge Corporation |
| NGO | non-governmental organization |
| NTFPs | non-timber forest products |
| SDI | Sustainable Development Initiative |
| STR | systematic titling and registration |
| TGLP | Tribal Grazing Land Policy |
| TPLF | Tigray People's Liberation Front |
| UNDRIP | United Nations Declaration on the Rights of Indigenous Peoples |
| USAID | United States Agency for International Development |
| VGA | village grazing area |
| VGs/VGGT | Voluntary Guidelines on the Responsible Governance of Tenure of Land, Fisheries and Forests in the Context of National Food Security |

# About the Author

**John W. Bruce** is a scholar-practitioner who has worked on land policy and tenure reform in Africa for over 50 years. He graduated from Columbia Law School in 1968 and spent the next ten years in Africa. He first encountered land tenure issues as a Peace Corps Volunteer legal advisor in Ethiopia's Ministry of Land Reform and Administration and later conducted doctoral research on indigenous land tenure reform in Tigray Province. In Sudan, he taught Property at the Faculty of Law at the University of Khartoum and managed the Faculty's Customary Law Research Program. He returned to the United States to join the staff of UW-Madison's Land Tenure Center (LTC), an interdisciplinary research institute working on land and property rights in the development context, He was hired to develop an Africa Program at an institution most of whose prior international work had been on Latin American land issues. He built a staff with African expertise and with them developed and supervised research programs under funding from the United States Agency for International Development and elsewhere, and taught courses and seminars on Property Law, Community Forestry and African Land Tenure. After nearly two decades at the LTC, including two terms as Director, he was recruited by the World Bank as a Senior Counsel and specialist in land tenure. At the Bank he worked on land issues in investment project design in Africa, China and Southeast Asia. Since retiring from the World Bank, he has consulted widely for developing country governments and development agencies. In 2014 and 2015, resident in Beijing, he taught a graduate seminar on Global Land Tenure Trends as a Visiting Professor at Renmin University. Bruce retired from consulting in 2017 after seven years as principal legal advisor with Liberia's Land Commission, from the planning for and creation of the Commission through expiry of its statutory term. He holds a BA in international relations from Lafayette College, his JD from Columbia Law School and his SJD from the Law School of University of Wisconsin-Madison. He lives with his wife, Zongmin Li, in Tyson Corner, Virginia.

# About the Book

Most countries in sub-Saharan Africa came to independence with at least two systems of land law, applicable to different land state law, created by the colonial power based on its own land law for colonists, indigenous laws associated with particular communities, clans or ethnic groups. The broad consensus among new African governments was that nation-building required dualism (statutory law/customary land tenure) to be replaced by a nationally uniform statute-based system managed by government rather than traditional authorities. Reform has proven more difficult than expected on a surprising scale. Roughly 70 years later, despite new tenure reform laws and donor-funded programs, 75–80% of Africa's land is managed by communities under customary land tenure. Reforms were not successful in building national unity. Ethnicity is an increasingly important, openly acknowledged factor in a divisive political scene, involving struggles for control of land access. An important factor in civil wars and state failure, conflict, including violent conflict, is growing. Policy failure on this scale requires explanation. The author examines the African experience with land tenure reform to understand why results have been so disappointing, asking if assumptions about land tenure and legal dualism on which those programs were based were flawed.

# Introduction

Land is the platform on which almost all human development occurs. It plays many roles. It is a productive resource, the source of livelihoods and the food that sustains us. It is also social space, the physical foundation of families, clans, towns, cities, regions and nations. It is a source of great beauty and spirituality, of great gardens, shrines and sacred forests. It is real estate, a commodity bought and sold in financial markets. It is sought by many for competing purposes. It is power. People need land and are empowered if they have it. If they do not, and must depend on others for land, it gives those others power over them. Conflict over land is all too common and intensifies as populations grow and land becomes scarcer.

This book introduces readers to the variety of systems of land rights and obligations, called systems of land tenure, and how they have evolved in Africa, both under colonialism and then especially in the half-century and more since independence. It examines how the terms on which people get and hold land influence the way they use it, and the different roles land tenure plays in development. It asks how we have come to the current position, which involves considerable conflict and confusion. A number of factors contribute to that conflict and confusion; this is a time of rapid change in land use and land rights, driven by a variety of factors but most dramatically by a sudden growth of pressure for change from overseas. As a result of the global food crisis, around 2006 international demand for the relatively cheap land and labor of developing countries peaked dramatically. Africa has been the continent most affected. Governments driven by a need for hard currencies from export revenue have handed out—and are still handing out—extensive tracts of land to investors under concessions. The land for these concessions, while legally government land, has been occupied and farmed by locals under their customary land tenure systems. That land, the basis of their food security and holding the graves of generations of family members, has been taken from them with little or no compensation by their governments and given to foreign investors and, increasingly, to domestic urban-based elites.

This experience has drawn attention to how vulnerable Africa's small farmers are under existing law. That vulnerability is not an accident, but a part of Africa's colonial heritage. In almost every African country, people obtained and held their land through two discrete and quite different systems of rights in land. The two systems apply to different areas of land. One system is a statutory law imported from Europe by colonial governments. That system applies in areas of the country carved out by colonial governments from the land under customary systems for colonization. In former "settler colonies," it includes significant areas of the best farmland, but in other colonies it is largely limited to urban and peri-urban areas and scattered towns and plantations. The other system of land rights is African customary land law and consists of the country's land tenure systems of the nation's diverse ethnicities, its indigenous systems which prevailed prior to the colonial period and still govern access to and use of the majority of land today. This is a collection of diverse, often quite local, systems of indigenous origin. In some countries customary land rights had no recognition under state law and so were unprotected by that law, while in others they received weak recognition but little or no protection from the law of the state. The general historical pattern in this matter has been some recognition of customary rights in the early colonial period, decreasing in the heyday of colonialism and then decreasing still further due to broad nationalizations of all land declared after independence in many African nations.

Today, the land once held by colonists or others from the colonizing country on western tenures is now held largely by Africans, usually members of an educated elite that soon succeeded the departing Europeans in positions of power and influence. That land in urban areas is still in most instances held under the law imported from Europe during the colonial period, usually in private individual ownership or on long-term leases under the protection of the state's law. The customary land of Africa's small farmers, in contrast, are usually state-owned under the statutory law of the state. Investors seeking to acquire land have targeted land under customary land tenure systems because they offer large open tracts of less intensively used land and because the rights of the people there lack legal protection under national law.

The largely uncompensated appropriation of the customary land of smallholders and herders for investors is easily recognizable by most of us as an injustice on a major scale. In defense of their actions, most governments assert that their actions are legal—the state owns this land, either from the colonial period or as a result of the socialist land nationalizations in the years following independence. The moral problem posed by this assertion of state ownership had arisen earlier. In the context of major infrastructure projects that required resettlement of large numbers of people, the World Bank attempted to address the issue by providing for resettlement costs and urging governments to provide land elsewhere for those affected. That compensation was, however, rarely adequate to compensate the household for the inconvenience and loss of other opportunities involved in the removal. Now, given the scale of these takings in the Land Grab, and given there is little direct development aid agency involvement in land takings for concessions, that humanitarian assistance is unavailable to those displaced from concession land.

The Land Grab is fraught with potential for future conflict. In Liberia, the country in which I have been able to watch the Grab most closely, there is no issue with greater potential for violence and civil war in the near future. Violence over land is growing and, as discussed in this volume, not just in relation to concessions.

It is dualism that set up this tragic situation. This dualism of land tenure systems has been for generations the most important structural feature of African land tenure. Its key role was to facilitate a smooth and inexpensive (to the colonial power, that is) shifting of land from Africans to European colonists. As time went on, it provided a critical part of the legal support for a broader economic dualism, whose purpose was to advantage European farmers. In the process, it disadvantaged Africa's small farmers. Today, it is still performing that function for the colonists' successors in influence and power. Tenurial dualism has continued into our day. There are still two bodies of land laws operating in the same social space, in this case the nation. How is it that this dualism of land tenure persists, so many years after these countries gained control over their own destinies? How is it an influential factor even now, continuing to affect land policy decisions? To answer these questions, we need to focus less on the fact of dualism and more on how the two systems interact to produce lasting impacts, including the resultant patterns of investment in infrastructure and technology and the development of an impersonal market in land rights. We need to understand who benefited from dualism during the colonial period and who benefits from it today.

Finally, we must ask how the handling of dualism and pluralism has contributed to the growing conflict over land. The conflict around concessions is just one highly visible example of growing struggles for land, complicated by legal confusion and accompanied by violence. If things continue on the same trajectory, millions of African smallholders seem likely to lose their land in the next 20 years, if not to concessions to international firms, then to national investors following in their path. Change is inevitable, and investment in agriculture is desirable, but why do so many rural people need to lose their land in the process, receiving little or nothing in return for centuries of good husbandry? Can fragile states withstand this level of individual and social trauma? Don't there exist other, arguably fairer options for rural transformation, options both in terms of land tenure choices and change processes? If so, why have African governments not opted for them?

While the appropriation of smallholder and herder land is a painful part of this picture, there is also reason for serious concern over the failure of most African countries to attain stronger national unity by the attempted imposition of uniform national land tenure systems. These are hard issues and no solution will work in all countries. They require difficult choices because land plays so many roles in our societies, and if we ask land to perform a new role, this can change or undermine the performance by land of another valued function.

This book has four parts:

Part I, "Property Rights and Land Tenure," reviews the history and actors of the establishment of legal dualism in Africa. It examines customary land tenure, both its norms and institutions, which will be less familiar to most readers than western forms of land tenure. It indicates what is meant by "land tenure," "property rights," "legal dualism," "statutory land tenure," "customary land tenure," "security of tenure," and *de facto* and *de jure* tenure, as well as how these concepts have developed and changed over time. This is a field with a specialized terminology, much of it borrowed from other disciplines, with other terms invented as needs arose. It is also an area in which words are freighted with connotations from decades of prejudice and political correctness.

Part II, "Change in Land Use and Land Tenure," looks at how different tenures tend to be associated with different land uses. One of the major contrasts between customary and statutory land tenure is the variety of customary land tenures. This is because customary land tenure is local, heavily affected by the culture of the community concerned and also by the land uses in that community. Within a given culture, land use is probably the main determinant in variability of customary land tenure. In the long term, culture itself is shaped in part by land use patterns. This part focuses on the process of change in statutory and customary law, a major point of contrast between the two. It looks at how customary land tenure systems in Africa have evolved and changed, as new opportunities or problems present themselves and land users respond, or fail to respond, with needed legal changes. Land tenure systems are usually changing, part of global processes of change and development. Are those changes in tenure going nowhere in particular, or is an evolutionary pattern clear? Given that customary tenure shows considerable variety, does that experience under different systems converge at some point? Is there a natural path into an inevitable tenure future, as some believe, and if so, can policy take nations off that track and down a different road? Is there a price that must be paid by doing so?

Part III, "Land Tenure Reform," considers the experience of national governments and international agencies that have launched and supported policies, programs and projects which have sought to change Africa's land tenure systems. The chapters in this part are classified according to the tenure patterns they sought to create. As you go through those reform experiences, it will become obvious that across the board, whatever the objective of the reform, implementation has been a major challenge. This is the longest part in the book, looking in some detail over 16 country reform experiences, considering questions such as the objectives of these reforms, by whom and why were they initiated, and how far have they succeeded? What is lost and gained by the reforms? Who are the winners and losers? Who was to benefit from them, and who did benefit from them? Where the results have been disappointing, is it because of weak implementation or because we are operating on some long-standing assumptions that are flawed? This part concludes with a chapter that specifically addresses a subset of tenure reform programs, those addressing women's lack of access to and security in land in their own right, and a final chapter that attempts to identify some common points in the continent's diverse experiences with the reform of land tenure.

Part IV, "Land Tenure Futures," is a single chapter, stating some conclusions. It makes a number of points about land tenure reform in general that are important to bear in mind in planning future reforms. It emphasizes the potentially very broad implications of the Great Land Grab after 2007. These developments have shaken the foundations of agricultural development policy and land policy. They have placed in question a long-standing consensus among African governments and international and bilateral donors in favor of a smallholder-based development policy, and may quite rapidly create a newly variegated tenure landscape with radically different farm sizes, scales of production and agricultural technologies associated with different tenures. While there may be potentials for coordination, my concern is that these may be overwhelmed by continuing instability and conflict over land fueled by a deep resentment of massive dispossession, growing inequality and landlessness. Given the diversity of existing patterns of land tenure on the continent and the diversity of national political contexts in which they exist, this chapter does not propose generalizable solutions. It instead imagines a number of tenurial futures for African countries, in the hope that these can inform the deliberations of the emerging generation of African land tenure researchers and policy makers.

# Part I

# Property Rights and Land Tenure

# 1 Property Rights and Land Tenure

## Land Tenure or Property Rights?

In her book on migrant cocoa farmers in Ghana, Polly Hill referred to "That awe-inspiring subject 'land tenure'" (Hill, 1997, p. 138). In dealing with African land tenure, especially customary rights, analysts have often felt more comfortable using an older term, "land tenure," rather relying on the more familiar "property rights." This is because property rights in the western model are more strictly about rights. Reform of land law in the western world has focused on eliminating obligations that once came with those rights. In customary systems a right to land is usually part of a more complex relationship between the member and the land-providing community, involving both rights and obligations. The term "tenure" means "the terms on which a land is held." It comes out of feudal England and was used for property institutions that involved both rights and obligations.

## Creating Property

How do property rights originate in the first place? Today it's hard to find land over which there are no property rights, in part because most modern constitutions provide that any land without an owner is the property of the state. In the past, this was not the case. Property rights have expanded with the expansion of human settlement and cultures into largely uninhabited regions. How and why does property in land arise in these regions? Different cultures and ideologies have their own answers to these questions, creation stories that seek to not just explain but to legitimize property. Peasant cultivators in West Africa explain that rights in land arise from first clearing and cultivation of the land. They refer to a parcel as "land of fire" or "land of the axe." Ethiopian farmers in the northern highlands traditionally recited long genealogies to connect them with ancestors who took possession of and farmed their land centuries ago. Often in these stories, culling land out of a state of nature for the first time created a property right. In many parts of Africa tree-planting, a significant investment, creates or is seen as evidence of a property right in the land held by the planter. Explanations of property in land by early European economists were not very different. Locke considered that property rights in land arose from a farmer mixing his labor with the soil. Property creation stories

DOI: 10.4324/9781003476429-2

often cloak darker realities. Many land rights arise from conquest and taking land by force. Conquering peoples bring with them their own property justification tales and superimpose them, obscuring the stories of the generations who held the land before them.

Scholars have differed on the usefulness and morality of property in land. "The magic of property" asserted Arthur Young in his book, *Travels in France During the Years 1787–1789*, "turns sand into gold" (Young, 1912). Classical economists such as Adam Smith agreed more cautiously. The French anarchist Proudhon declared property to be theft. Marx concurred, particularly regarding land, the most fundamental of resources. John Stuart Mill, who was comfortable with the idea that people could own things they made for themselves, felt that property in land was more of a reach, since no one creates land. In the end, he decided that property in land was justified by its usefulness (Becker, 1977).

Property rights are clearly useful. They prevent a free-for-all over land with attendant conflict and violence that no society can afford. The appropriateness of particular property rights in a particular society and economy is debatable. Such rights seem to arise when land users seek to establish control over land that allows them to exclude others. They convince others, by persuasion or power, to recognize the right of exclusion. When land is plentiful, it may be sufficient to have rights in a valuable resource on the land rather than "land" more generally. For example, in colonial New England, settlers found that the local Native Americans, with plentiful land, had property rights in scarce resources such as stands of sugar maples, not in land generally (Cronon, 1983). First Nations in Canada could initially extract animal skins from the forests without property rights, but this changed as needs evolved. In the vicinity of Quebec, members of the First Nations trapping for the colonial fur trade developed property rights in "land" when uncontrolled hunting decimated key species and threatened their trade. At that point their communities began to recognize claims to large areas of land so that right-holders, protected against hunting by others, could manage animal populations within their properties sustainably (Gettler, 2012).

## Tenure Origins

To understand the origins of their own English property rights, British scholars have looked to the Middle Ages. In Europe, the idea of private ownership was established early. The Romans had a concept of private ownership quite like that in western market economies. With the collapse of their empire around 400 AD most of the peoples of Europe reverted to tribal custom. A system of land tenure and governance called feudalism gradually emerged on the Continent. In 1066 AD a Norman conquering army brought it to England. They systematized the feudal system there to a level not known elsewhere, developing the Domesday Book, a national tax cadaster showing all landholdings in England. The King's courts early assumed responsibility for development of a national Common Law, a task greatly facilitated by their tradition of judicial law-making. Box 1.1 explains the nature of feudal tenure and how it has been changed over time by the English judiciary.

**Box 1.1 Feudalism and Tenure Reform**

From the Norman Conquest in 1066 AD, society in Britain consisted of a descending set of relationships from the Crown through great lords to lesser lords and down to men of substance, based at each level on a set of mutual rights and obligations concerning land and its use. A subject who received a grant of land tenure had a right to land (a "fief," the larger ones were called), and they were small principalities. The grantee was entitled to protection from his lord. In return, the grantee owed his lord specific duties, a certain amount of fodder for the lord's cattle or a lamb for the lord's table every third month and, in time of war, service in the lord's army. A description of the tenure in which land was held would normally include the type of service and its duration. There existed standard limitations, named sets of rights and obligations for a specified duration (for his life, or that of his heir), and these constituted a "tenure." For example, a man might hold land in knight service for his lifetime.

Look at that framework of land grants and the relationships it created, and you are looking at the structure of governance. The power behind the system was access to land, as fundamental a need in England of that time as in today's Africa. The land and the mutuality of rights and obligations provided the glue that held the nation together (Baker, 2019).

My property text in law school went on to briefly discuss how medieval English judges by their decisions simplified the land tenure system of England over the centuries. That reform has stripped the tenures of their attached obligations or monetized them, leaving only the rights. While individuals holding land still have obligations to their neighbors and society in general regarding their land, these are no longer built into tenures and depend upon the existence of those tenures for their legal authority; today, they exist by virtue of other laws and, especially lately, regulatory laws. As the obligations fell away, limitations in terms of time did so as well, and today most ownership is alienable, inheritable and devisable, and therefore perpetual except where there is an absence of heirs. The owner may change but the property right carries on. In England and its territories, the Crown still "owns" the land but in a largely symbolic manner. The obligations of the landholder to a feudal superior are gone. The terms for this reformed tenure are "fee simple absolute" suggesting the absence of obligations and conditions. When people in Britain say they own their land, they mean very much the same thing as an American or a Frenchman would mean. Ownership in western law is today simply a property right; and there is no longer the old feudal sense of mutual rights and obligations. The current concept of ownership in western law owes more to the French reformers who eliminated France's feudal remnants, with much greater dispatch than the English, during the French Revolution. The ending of the *complexum feodal* was a priority of the revolution, and it was abolished in the "August Decrees" enacted on August 4, 1789. They provided for a bold return to the Roman law concept of land ownership, and the Napoleonic Code of 1804 relied heavily on Roman Law for its provisions on real property rights (Constantinoff, 1951). The forms of land law that colonial regimes brought to Africa were the results of these reforms. They were mainly about rights, not obligations.

European history's relevance is threefold: (a) while feudal and African customary land tenure are very different, the feudal example illustrates the power of land as a strong generator of social solidarity and cohesion in Europe. It plays a similar role in indigenous land tenure systems in Africa and other parts of the global south; (b) one element of feudal tenure is shared by some African customary systems: a sense of mutuality involving rights and obligations; (c) the meaning of the term "tenure" has changed over time as African indigenous systems have evolved from older models of mutual rights/obligations toward less conditional, more individual rights in land. It has come to mean "the terms of which land is held."

## Land Tenures in Africa

As the British Empire expanded, its scholars and a few officials sought to understand the land arrangements of colonized peoples. Drawing on their own experience of tenure as combinations of rights and obligations and finding it appropriate, they wrote of "Irish land tenure," "Indian land tenure" and "African land tenure." There is a critical distinction between the mutual rights and obligations of feudal tenure in England and that of customary land tenure in Africa. In European feudal society, no subject had a right to tenure. Tenure was granted by the feudal lord as a distinction, in connection with a position in the feudal hierarchy. Most of the rural population were peasants farming on commons or the land of tenured holders. In African customary tenure members of the community (or at least most male heads of households) had a right to a share (not necessarily an equal share) in the community's land and so members (at least male heads of households) are as a birthright automatically involved in a tenure relationship with their community. The patriarchal nature of African land tenure systems limits that broad access, at least that of direct access, to men, though women have access to use some land through their husbands under the customary law regarding marital relations.

While there are differences between western property rights and African customary land tenure, there is one familiar element: mutuality of rights and obligations, in less hierarchical settings, in tenure relationships between peasant and a landholding lineage, or clan, or village. Land access was based on membership in the land-providing community. The communities were defined by common ancestry and/or a common area of residence. Members had a *right* to a share in land that the community controlled. The member was obligated to perform certain tasks and duties as a member of the community. Land birthright is central to African land tenure systems today. In other land policy contexts we struggle to reduce landlessness and provide the poor with at least the modest land they require for their food security. In Africa, they have land access and yet prevailing concepts of tenure reform in the international development agencies call for increasing marketability of land rights to those outside the community, undermining that birthright concept and community cohesion. It is odd, and we try to understand why this is the case in Part III on land tenure reform.

In discussions of African customary land rights, the term "land tenure" is used regularly. Most working in this field refer to any right in land as a "tenure." That very broad usage obscures an important element in the original meaning of "tenure" (the mutuality of rights and obligations with respect to land), but the broad usage of the term seems unlikely to change. Its use should serve as a reminder that obligations as well as rights are involved in land tenure. Those aware of the background need to seize the opportunity to make this point essential to understanding land's role in community, belonging and identity in African societies.[1]

## Land Tenure Systems in Africa

A land tenure system is simply all the tenures used by a community, working together. Western tenure systems have several tenures, from ownership to short-term leases to permits. African land tenure systems also have multiple tenures having their own names. Those names can come from the use of the land. For instance, a tenure for land growing vegetables might well be called "vegetable land," short for "the terms on which land for growing vegetables is held," or "common pasture." The name might also reflect the destination of the production of the land, as in, "land for the support of the land fertility priests."

Rights and obligations are part of the normative side of the land tenure system. The primary factors shaping land tenure systems are cultural values and land use systems, with land use reflecting the potential of the community's land and available technologies. New technologies can change land use and in turn create pressures for changes in rules. Cultural values tend to be a stabilizing and homogenizing influence on rules of tenure within a society or ethnicity. Land use differences account for local variability. If you visit an African community engaged exclusively in rainfed cultivation of sorghum, then an otherwise very culturally similar community which is engaging in riverbank recessional cultivation, you can expect to find important differences in how land tenures are defined and land is allocated.

Land tenures in African customary systems have their particular roles to play, as indicated in their naming. Ideally, they complement each other and work together well, though sometimes they serve purposes other than what we might expect, and even surreptitious purposes that the community considers inappropriate. Box 1.2 on the roles of short-term tenancies and possessory mortgages in highland Ethiopia offers an example.

**Box 1.2 The Roles Tenures Play**

A tenure type may play different roles in different tenure system contexts and even within the same tenure system. In my own experience, in Ethiopia, those who planned the land reform that followed the 1974 Revolution found it difficult to appreciate the usefulness of short-term leases. Their experience with such tenancies had been in the context of the large estates established in the south of the country after the conquest of the south by the Empire. Those estates were lands taken from local peoples and allocated to the victors and members of the nobility after conquest. The lands were cultivated by local tenants on smallholdings on annual leases, usually on a sharecropping basis. The system was widely regarded as exploitative. It was more like serfdom than a contract. After 1974 large holdings were broken up and redistributed by peasant associations among their members. In northern Ethiopia, most farmers had farmed their own family smallholdings under a customary land tenure system known as *rist*. Under that custom, short-term leases had always been allowed, serving useful purposes.

Initially, tenancy of any kind was outlawed under the national reform law. It took some years to convince government that short-term leases had at least two valuable roles in a smallholder agriculture. First, it allowed a farmer who was ill, or whose oxen were ill, to lease out a parcel of land on a short-term lease and get some rent income from it until he and his oxen were recovered. Second, after women were approved in some provinces to receive land of their own under the reform, many of them asked for divorces and moved to towns to find jobs. They leased their land to someone who still lived in the village and used the rent to supplement their modest incomes in town. Today, the law has been changed and short-term leasing is allowed.

A tenure may also perform a role of dubious legality. A form of mortgage was practiced traditionally in northern Ethiopia that is rarely seen in western legal contexts. It is a "possessory mortgage." Under Civil Law it's called a contract of *antichresis* and treated as a pledge. In such a contract, a lender does not ask the borrower for interest on a loan, as is usual in the case of mortgages. Interest on loans was traditionally prohibited as usury by Orthodox Christianity practiced in the northern highlands. Instead, the lender receives possession of the land that the landholder is offering as security for the loan. Its production belongs to the lender and serves as interest on the loan, and the land remains with the lender until the loan is repaid. This is not a very satisfactory borrowing arrangement if the borrower has only one piece of land, and no other way to earn the money to repay the loan. Fragmentation of holdings is common in the highlands, so a borrower might easily have several parcels of land and could in theory pay off the loan with the income from another parcel. In practice, the borrower often never repays the loan.

The borrower under such a contract is often someone who wants to leave the home area for a job in the city or another region of the country. He is avoiding a prohibition under custom of selling land of his community. The lender simply holds onto the parcel and the loan is never repaid. Whether and when the lender will be confronted about his right to the land will depend in part on whether or not the lender is a member of the landholding community from which the borrower held the land.

Tenures, rights and obligations are all normative, but what about rules governing behavior and providing a basis for making decisions about allocation of land? Some observers remark that these are not like the western idea of law, just rough and vague principles, epigrams rather than the precise, carefully worded and wordy legal texts of western legislation. I have heard Africans who were acknowledged community experts on the rules of their customary law say that this was generally correct. In Tigray Province of Ethiopia, I studied a community in which land was allocated by elders (see Chapter 11). Its basic principles of allocation could be stated as follows: (1) Inherited ancestral land belongs to the people and all residents have a right to share in it, while nobles have their right to a share in the tax revenue from the community. This is clearly a message to officials: Hands off our land! (2) All sons and daughters inherit land equally from their parents. (3) Every member of the community should have as much land as s/he is able to farm. (4) Every member of the community should have as much land as s/he needs for his/her family.

The first establishes an important parameter. The second and third are most interesting because they are manageable in times of land abundance, but land scarcity brings them into tension. The elders understand that they must find compromises that honor both principles when making decisions in particular cases. Such proceedings involve long, wandering discussions of factors that might make one decision or another appropriate. In the end a situation-specific solution is arrived at by people who know the local situation well. My sense is that it often produces a more satisfactory result than a very specific rule covering a wide range of situations, the application of which sometimes produces bizarre results. The matters covered by the elders in such a discussion benefit from their considerable knowledge of earlier land relations among those now involved, their family histories and likely heirs, the land they now hold, their position in the community, their family's ability as farmers and the health of their plow oxen. Sometimes they include considerations that puzzle us as outsiders, because their relevance escapes us. In framing remedies in such proceedings under custom, there is great flexibility in allocating penalties and rewards to the parties, as compared to the "winner take all" decisions in modern courts. In other cases, a customary disposition simply does not comport with our notions of justice. We think of justice requiring that everyone should be treated in the same way, but a village society may feel that people of different statuses deserve to be treated quite differently.

## An Organizational Dimension

There is an organizational dimension to a tenure system as well. A coherent description of what goes on concerning land in a community or nation requires talking about the chiefs, elders and other traditional authorities who usually govern the land of the community, their roles in their community and their interactions with the state and its officials. Those authorities have responsibilities that differ considerably from one ethnicity to another, and from one land use system to another. Common roles of traditional authorities include articulating the rules of the land tenure system, managing processes of change in land tenure system rules, managing the allocation of the land to community members, and mediating or deciding disputes over land. Their roles have been key in debates over the future of customary land tenure: the extent of their cooptation and manipulation by colonial governments; the expansion of their role in governance of land under custom; the authenticity of customary land tenure (given such manipulation); and the political and policy consequences of the attack mounted on their authority by many African governments in the years after independence. The situation differs from place to place, but they still retain considerable influence in land and other matters and were at independence seen as a challenge to the centralized governance that many of the governments of the fragile new states considered necessary.

The chapters that follow discuss how and why the European colonies in Africa chose to create to parallel and very different land tenure systems on a racial basis for their European and African subjects, how the customary land tenure systems of Africans were regarded and dealt with by the colonial governments and courts, and the nature and implications of dualism, especially the potential for mischief created by dualism.

## Note

1 In my observation, discipline has an effect on whether one uses "land tenure" and/or "property rights." Social scientists (anthropologists, sociologists, geographers) use "land tenure." Lawyers and surveyors working within their own national system tend to use "property rights"; those who work in international development may use "land tenure." It seems odd to speak of property rights not recognized by law, perhaps because the "right" wording suggests the claim is legally valid. Many agricultural and institutional economists use "land tenure" regularly, as do other economists that have worked in the global south. Most other economists use "property rights."

## References

Baker, J. (2019). Real property: Feudal tenure. In *Introduction to English Legal History* (5th ed., pp. 241–266). Oxford University Press. https://doi.org/10.1093/oso/9780198812609.003.0013

Becker, L.C. (1977). *Property rights: Philosophic foundations* (1st ed.). Routledge.

Constantinoff, J. (1951). French law of property and its proposed revision. *Tulane Law Review*, *26*(1951–1952), 475–490.

Cronon, W. (1983). *Changes in the land: Indians, colonists, and the ecology of New England.* Hill & Wang.

Gettler, B. (2012). Money and the changing nature of colonial space in northern Quebec: Fur trade, monopolies, the state, and Aboriginal peoples during the nineteenth century. *Histoire sociale/Social History*, *46*(92), 271–293. https://doi.org/10.1353/his.2013.0057

Hill, P. (1997). *The migrant cocoa farmers of southern Ghana: A study in rural capitalism.* LIT Verlag Münster.

Young, A. (1912) *Travels in France during the years 1787–1789.* G. Bell and Sons, Ltd.

# 2 The State's System of Statutory Rights

## Customary versus Statutory

Are both customary and statutory norms governing land "law" in the sense we care about? They are, in the sense that they are the normative tools used by society to ensure compliance by its members with the rules regarding land access and use. They differ in how they compel compliance. While they do so differently, they do so effectively enough. In this "how" we find the most important differences between customary land tenure systems and the law of the state. Their processes are very different: how they make rules, how those rules acquire legitimacy and authority, and how they evolve over time. These processes, the initiatives under laws enacted by the state and the development of custom in indigenous communities, are happening simultaneously over the same territory. They are happening on quite different scales: those of the state at a national level, while those of community are limited to the area of the community. The differences and the issues they pose today should be understood in the light of a century or two of interaction among them under colonialism. They influenced the nature of colonial administration, and they themselves have been influenced and affected by colonial practices. Especially in the early period when colonial legal frameworks were being established, it is the law of the state that is doing the work of creating dualism.

## Legally, Europeans Saw Africa as a Blank Page

In the 17th and 18th centuries a European country dispatched settlers and troops to an area of the world in which none of the political entities had developed into nation-states. International law in Europe had just finished enthroning the nation-state as the sole actor in a world of multiple states, the embodiment of law and power, and holder of a monopoly of force and coercion, exercised to ensure the rule of law. To Europeans, the smaller political units they found in Africa looked like the units out of which the European nation-states had been created. They had limited reach in terms of authority and power. Today we are aware of more large entities, kingdoms and federations, with networks and coordination among them for good natural resource management. The exceptional nation-state that was respectable by the European standards was Ethiopia, which had an empire of its own and a Christian Emperor.[1]

DOI: 10.4324/9781003476429-3

In Europe, if one country conquered another, the law of the conquered country remained in effect until specifically repealed, as did property rights. This was not the rule applied in most colonial contexts in Africa. Europeans were reluctant to admit that the law or custom of the inhabitants amounted to real law. Africa's polities were not real states, they reasoned, and so did not have real law. What they had was custom, unwritten, and not as clear, cogent or enforceable as law. They were in fact small nascent states, not unlike those small polities in Europe whose gradual and messy assembling into much larger units gave us the current world of nation-states. European interaction with Africa might have stimulated that process if it had continued to develop through trade, avoiding conquest. Instead, European military conquest and colonization of Africa put a stop to the evolution of these potential states, creating colonies that became nation-states a century or more later without going through processes that would have rendered them better integrated and more stable (Joseph, 2003; Davidson, 1992; Miller & Stitz, 2021).

The dismissal of the public institutions and law of these polities meant a new colony was, from a legal viewpoint, a blank slate. Britain, France and the other colonizing countries filled colonies with their own law. British colonial lawyers used the Hong Kong Ordinance to create the Ghana reception statute of 1876. It empowered the courts of the colony to resolve disputes arising there according to the English common law, the doctrines of equity and statutes of general application. Further, it reserved to Africans the legal rights they had held under customary law, which was to be applied to their cases except if it contradicted the law of the colony or, more generally, "doctrines of justice, equity and good conscience." The Ghana statute became the model for the exception statutes of other British African colonies. The "exception" stated here for application to Africans of "native" law and custom covered 99% of the population and land of the Gold Coast Colony of the time. It also marks the beginning of the dual land tenure system (McAuslan, 2000).

## Building Dualism

The basic legal framework was in place for two tenure systems in parallel: the customary system, covering the vast majority of land, and the statutory system, applied to modest amounts of land under European control. While all colonies came to independence with dual systems of land law, what came next depended on whether the colony was a settler colony or not. The settler colonies were farmer colonies which appropriated and reallocated considerable land, mostly in eastern and southern Africa and largely in British colonies. Several times they moved as much land into western land tenures as did the more trading-oriented colonies, most French colonies, most in West Africa.

In the colonies that did not attract settlers, trade was the main economic activity promoted by colonialism. Labor rather than land was the focus for law-making and reforms. Colonialism came into societies where African models of slavery still flourished, and in which forced labor was a tool used by traditional authorities and even early colonial governments. The colonial governments enacted labor codes and found that indigenous labor issues were entwined with other relationships: lineage, pawning of persons, kinship, clientage and tenancy. Labor opportunities were also closely connected to access to land (Roberts & Mann, 1991).

If land acquisition in a colony was to be substantial, the colony would from the outset begin to make new laws and rules to reinforce or take advantage of the emerging dualism. New legislation was soon put forward dividing the land into three or four legal categories. In a British colony such as Kenya this might include Crown Land, Reserve Land and Trust Land. Land occupied by Africans fell into the Trust Land category. Other categories also had African inhabitants. Most were gradually resettled in more thinly populated Trust or unclassified areas. Key laws were a Crown Lands Ordinance, affirming the right of the colonial state to take land from African communities for purposes of the colony, and the Reserve Land Act and Native Lands Trust Ordinance. They covered land inhabited and farmed under customary land tenure by Africans but ultimately legally vulnerable to taking for the colonial enterprise. Land was regularly taken from African communities for European settlement and the displaced African landholders resettled on more remote, less attractive land. Areas governed by western law grew at the expense of land under customary land tenure (Meek, 1949; Okoth-Ogendo, 1991). In crowded areas of southern Africa and parts of Namibia, the African population was gradually cleared from large areas of the country and packed into small resource-poor "homelands," most of which were no more than labor reserves. In some areas of South Africa today, the present government is struggling with the results of resettlements in which succession of tribes or other groups were settled into the same "homeland" (Beinart, 2012).

The basic purpose of having two land laws was so that one did not have to treat everyone the same way. Two systems of land law did not require a policy behind them. At the time it must have seemed the only possible arrangement.[2]

Settler colonies went on to enact laws and regulations intended to benefit colonial agricultural production. They either sought to privilege European farms generally to ensure their success or barred African farmers from use of facilities and services provided to European farmers by government. In Kenya the Coffee Marketing Board excluded small producers from its export programs on the grounds that the smallholders did not clean and prepare their coffee properly for processing. All the European producers were large landholders. To support farming, the government waived import taxes on imported farm machinery. In the early years of the colony, Africans did not own much petrol-powered farm machinery (Meek, 1949; Okoth-Ogendo, 1991).

## Controlling Land Access

Colonial governments sought to maintain control over landholdings across the boundaries of indigenous and settler economies. Provincial governors implemented this control. Any person from the European areas, including both Europeans and Africans living there in connection with their work, was prohibited from residing and acquiring land there, except with the written consent of the governor. Even with consent, one could only lease land. Consent was rarely given. In the early days of the colony land acquisition was usually to establish trading posts. Sales of African land to outsiders were not allowed under customary land tenure. The government supported the traditional authorities on implementation of this customary rule. No African who resided in the African areas could reside in a European area except in connection with a work permit. Government needed labor from the African areas to work on the European commercial farms; to encourage this, colonies' administrations made them pay hut taxes and schoolbook fees. Fees had to be paid in cash, which pressured Africans to seek employment on the European commercial farms and receive wages in cash (Meek, 1949; Opoku, 1974; Roberts & Mann, 1991).

The Africans could not overnight follow European law, and the colonists did not want to live under "native" law and custom. The British colonists did not aspire to an integrated society so creating legal dualism must have seemed entirely natural. Having two bodies of land law opened up possibilities. You didn't need to treat everyone the same way. It meant that land rights could be developed differently, perhaps in complementary ways. If the colonial power could keep these two economies separate, it could manipulate them, controlling what moved between them. In particular, the colonial power could control the flow of labor, and it could control land values. Land still farmed by Africans would eventually be needed for further expansion of the European area, and it would be easier to manage that transfer of land if Africans did not realize that their land had value and that its value was growing. It could be kept relatively inexpensive by the colonial power supporting traditional authorities in enforcing customary rules that such land should not be sold (Okoth-Ogendo, 1991; Meek, 1949).

The dual economies took shape over time, as the product of both decisions by government and other developments beyond the control of the colonial government. The two sides of the dual economy were the same, in that each involved a legally defined area of land and the economic activity in that area. But they are also different. On the European side, the landholders are part of one society with its various components, from the colonial officials down to the farmer, people who knew each other and had a shared language, law and values. On the other side, Africans spoke different languages, and different communities held different values and notions of authority. Moreover, the jurisdiction of the European area extended over the nation, while those of the areas under custom fell within the jurisdiction of a European dominated area, either at national or some lower level.[3]

The African population was isolated from dealings with Europeans, except along lines of interaction established for reasons of colonial policy. Separation was consistent with general policy: let the Africans go about their business, undisturbed, until it was time for them to give up their land and be resettled.

## Native Law and Custom in the Colonial Courts

There is one more element in the reception of foreign law that should be considered: the mandate that the disputes of the Africans be dealt with under their own law and custom, but only if it was not contrary to law or "justice, equity and good conscience." In French colonies, the colonial administrations were not much concerned with the future of African law and custom. The French solution was to suppress practices judged backward, albeit gradually, and eventually replace them with French law. The core of French law on property rights was the chapter of the Civil Code on *propriétés immobilier* (immoveable property, the Civil Law equivalent of real property under Common Law), supplemented by more recent enactments, often regulatory in nature but in some instances containing reforms of the property law, all to be read and understood in the light of the *jurisprudence* (the judicial practice) of the French courts. The basic problem, insisted radical reformers, was that land tenure under African custom was in some general sense "communal," which to them suggested a lack of incentives for improvements.

In France's colonies, assimilation was the policy, but realistically, the African inhabitants could hardly be expected to live under French law. Instead, French inhabitants of the colonies had the "*statut civil français*" and were governed by French law, while Africans had "*statut personnel*." An African could become a French citizen and have access to the French courts. Non-citizen subjects (the vast majority of African inhabitants) of a French colony could not take their cases to the French courts. This meant that there were fewer changes in the customary rules by the judicial system. Where change was made, it was through legislation or by administrative action. Senegal was an exception in that its African subjects were all citizens, with access to the French courts (Opoku, 1974; Roberts & Mann, 1991).

In the British colonies, there was a constant interaction between custom and western ideas of law, particularly "equity and good conscience" under the English system.[4] The British, relying to a greater extent on indirect rule, were more willing to integrate chieftainship and custom into the legal system. Africans could not be citizens, but their land matters were governed by the customary tenure of their home area, and they could take their disputes to British courts. They might in some situations and colonies do so directly, in others on appeal, deciding questions of law and fact. The colonial government's main involvement in the evolution of African law and custom was through the courts. They relied on a variety of sources for information about what they called "native law and custom," including precedent (where available), text and theses such as Evans-Pritchard's *The Nuer* (Evans-Pritchard, 1940; Johnson, 1982) in southern Sudan and Lloyd's *Yoruba Land Law* (Lloyd, 1962) in Nigeria, on the testimony of chiefs and other traditional authorities, and on panels of assessors. The judge on appeal had very limited authority to affect the findings of fact in such a case, but he could reverse decisions appealed on matters of law. As Common Law courts, they had ideas about how to deal with unwritten law. The majority of law on land in England was not in legislation, but in the holdings of the courts that had heard land law cases. The law was shaped by their decisions. Even where there was conflicting evidence as the rules evolved, judges still needed to rule. They could not send litigants home without a decision. It was their responsibility to adjudicate cases and they had been trained to make law where this was necessary to do so (Woodman, 1969; Roberts & Mann, 1991).

**Box 2.1 Mapping Law/Mapping Reality**

I first taught a course on African Land Tenure at the University of Wisconsin-Madison in 1982. The Law School was not interested, but the College of Agriculture and Life Sciences listed the course for three credits. I had worked in Ethiopia and Sudan, and I had a good grasp of the land tenure situation in those countries and a few others whose land reforms had been widely discussed, such as Kenya and Tanzania. My understanding of the situation in the 50 or so other countries in Africa was pretty sketchy. I decided I should work up a map of land tenure in Africa for the class. A student, Doug Stienbarger, actually prepared the map. Blue was the color we chose for state-owned land, green for land owned under customary systems, red for land in private ownership, and brown for what I called "collective land." I'm not entirely sure what I meant the last to cover.

I started with the countries I knew best. Ethiopia was easy. I could identify most areas as owned either by individuals privately or under customary systems, which were fully recognized as law by the Ethiopian Civil Code. Happily, the land in those two categories existed in large blocks and could be shown relatively easily, if approximately, on the map. Sudan was more complicated. In 1970, just a few years before I arrived in Sudan, Nimiery's Sudan Socialist Union government abolished customary land tenure: land held under custom and for which no formal title existed was declared owned by the state. The areas of land held under formal title were limited to irrigated holdings along the Nile in northern Sudan, registered in the "settlement" that sought to settle rights to land in an area after the British and their Egyptian partner retook Sudan from the Mahdists at the end of the 19th century. The rest of the country was under customary land tenure, which in the case of Sudan was an amalgam of custom and Islamic rules in relation to land. In effect, 95% of this vast country was nationalized.

Should Sudan be all blue, as state land? Hardly anyone noticed nationalization, least of all the Sudanese who continued to farm and graze the land under customary rules. At the Law Faculty of the University of Khartoum, the Sudan Customary Land Tenure Project funded by the Ford Foundation continued to gather material that could be used for teaching customary land tenure. The land tenure provisions of the 1970 law were hardly enforced and have subsequently been repealed, restoring the legal recognition of customary land tenure. But in 1982, custom was still a legal nullity, so what should be shown on the map? Shouldn't it show not just the formal legal situation (state ownership) but also the actual dominance of customary land tenure? How? Green stripes on blue? Recalling the influence of Islamic Law on both customary and statutory law in much of Sudan, I began to feel a little desperate. I decided to get on with some of the simpler country systems, but after trying a few more countries, I realized that such complex situations were very common and even more complicated than my Sudan case. It became laughable when we tried a small country like the Gambia. Just not enough space. It seemed our project had developed needs well beyond our modest graphic skills and we had to go back and start over.

In the end my students received two tenure maps of Africa, one *de jure* (legal and largely blue) and one *de facto* (actual and largely green). I had no idea how dramatic the contrast would be. While the state claimed the ownership of most land in Africa, the management of rights to that land was largely in the hands of the local traditional institutions administering it under customary land tenure. My legal map was legally accurate but, in terms of what was happening on the ground, largely aspirational: the situation as the state wished it to be rather than the country as it was. The *de facto* map was the normative reality on the ground, in the lives of the people.

A foundational principle of English law, the doctrine of precedent, was applied to native law and custom. The decisions of the senior colonial courts and the English superior courts became precedents, which should in most cases be followed, to ensure the same justice for all. The Privy Council in the case of Angu v. Attah (1916, PC '24–'28, 43) (cited and quoted in Korang, 2015, p. 93) sets out how a decision concerning customary law became a precedent:

> As is the case with all customary law, it has to be proved in the first instance by calling witnesses acquainted with the native customs until the particular customs have, by frequent proof in the courts, become so notorious that the courts will take judicial notice of them.

Finding customary law was handled in the same manner as a British court might find law in another country, as a matter of fact. A court was usually free to note any point of law, but since European judges did not have any background in customary law, customary rules had to be proved as a fact, with evidence. Moore (2000) defines law as a process. This is particularly true of customary land tenure. Handling the litigation among Africans was challenging because customary law often changed without much formality or publicity. It could be difficult to confirm whether a change in the rule had occurred and if the change affected the entire tribe or only a portion. These courts set about a process of unification of the case law of England as received in Sudan and the holdings of senior courts of Sudan, creating a common law of Sudan, a body of precedent that included the "customary land tenure" of the many tribes or other ethnic groups in the country. That process was not an attempt to restate customary law in court decisions, but rather a strategy for dealing with those portions of it that were problematic in some sense, often because they were inconvenient for the policies and plans of the colonial administration.

This became the main colonial government policy for managing the coexistence of European and African law. The colonial courts and those in England on appeal had the power to both decide what customary law was and to verify that it was not contrary to law or "justice, equity and good conscience" and so fit to become part of the court-recognized customary land law of the colony concerned. There was no "Plan for the Implementation of Dualism in Eastern Africa." The judges did not have a reform program to guide them. Still, their decisions could be appealed to Britain's highest court, the Privy Council in London, which provided supervision of the empire's courts. As Chanock (1991) has pointed out more recently, this law-making process of British courts was subject to the political objectives and cultural attitudes in colonial society. Their holdings on land law tended to be aligned with colonial land policy, especially as they affected the relative interests of colonial governments and their subjects.

Building a Common Law on land for an African country is an ambitious and impressive undertaking.[5] For large, important tribes or other groups, and in particular the sedentary groups, disputes were sufficiently frequent to build the body of coherent case law. But for smaller and more remote groups and for pastoralists, it was difficult. No one knew when the next case relevant to a contested point of law would arise. If a party asserted that custom had changed, it was not always easy to tell if this had happened and often difficult to determine how broad the spread of change was geographically. The work of these judges had its limitations, but they did develop a body of reasonably consistent case law and that body of law has had a major impact on African law and custom. Many Africans today see some institutions and rules as traditional that in fact have been shaped by holdings of British courts. The task of making the system work effectively has not become easier with the passage of time. In the growing list of post-conflict countries, registries and court records have burned and law library collections have been looted. Replacing the published material will be possible but challenging; unpublished material may be gone forever. Reviving the process for getting opinions published and circulated among courts will take time. Judges may have been away from their courts for years. Today, digitizing offers protection against such losses of data, but it is only now becoming available for these purposes in many post-conflict countries.[6]

## The "Customary Land Tenure" of the Courts and the Village

"Customary land tenure" is that which is practiced by community members and their neighbors, rules and practices often captured by outsiders, mostly anthropologists, who have studied them. There is however another "customary land tenure," that of Chanock (1985) and the courts: a customary land tenure that has diverged to some extent from the customary land tenure as it continues to exist in the practice of local communities.[7]

The customary land tenure of the courts has legitimacy conferred by the state, while the customary land tenure of the villages depends for legitimacy on the social legitimation provided by the communities following it. Customary land tenure of the villages is itself changing, in some cases due to holdings in the colonial courts, but also for reasons that had nothing to do with colonial government's preferences (for example, the spread of the idea that land could be sold and that the two interact constantly with one another). They are fundamentally different in another sense as well: the custom of the village is just the custom of the village, but the custom of the courts is the law of the land. The law of the state, so dominant legally, feels remote and unreal if one is in the village, talking to villagers and trying to understand what impact customary land tenure will have on a proposed development initiative. However, when one returns to the capital, the customary land tenure of the courts is the reality with which ministry planners must deal. Both need to be taken into consideration.

In the following chapter, customary land tenure is discussed in a variety of contexts. As suggested earlier, this requires understanding not just another system of law as we know it, but a different kind of law, with which many of us trained in the western legal tradition have little familiarity.

## Notes

1 To understand how Europe's industrial revolution allowed that continent to dart ahead of Africa in nation-building and the impact of that development on European attitudes toward Africa, I recommend the story of a Portuguese embassy to Ethiopia led by Father Francisco Alvares in 1520. It is the story of a visit from the representative from one Christian kingdom to another, largely free of the condescension and prejudice that marked European attitudes toward Africans in the centuries that followed (Beckingham, 2017). The Conference of Berlin, at which the European powers parceled out Africa among themselves, suggested standards that excluded other Christian nations from the process. Nevertheless, Italy was not restrained long by Ethiopia's impeccable credentials as a Christian nation-state (dating from the 4th century AD). Its northernmost province, Eritrea, was invaded and colonized by Italy in 1889.

2 I was very interested in McAuslan's paper on legal dualism and legal pluralism (2005). I had been unclear, I realize now, on the precise relationship between pluralism and dualism. I had an overall positive impression of pluralism because of some positive associations (diversity, tolerance, multiculturalism) but was not clear on where legal dualism fit into the larger scheme of pluralism. McAuslan cautions us not to imagine dualism, two rather than more bodies of land law in a polity, as benign. Instead, he stresses, it is a policy tool whose principal purpose under colonialism was to provide a legal basis for colonial land takings from the African people, a pernicious role. That is true, and I profited from reading the article, but I am still inclined to think of it as an example of a negative use of pluralism. There are others. (See de Lemos [2020] for a good review of the uses of the term in the development context.) As a result, I try to look more carefully at any case of two or more land laws in a polity. Having been used to dualism as old and fading policy in the African context, I was amazed to find it in play in China when I moved there in 2013 (Bruce, 2017).

3 Anthropologist Sally Falk Moore (2014), in an article devoted to trying to get authors to use the term "pluralism" more selectively, suggests that use of the term "legal dualism" for this situation is objectionable. Dualism, she considered, should not be used except in the case of two systems of law. The term did not capture the situation of one community with customary law subsidiary to a colonial administration and its regime of statutory law. She preferred to refer to the community under custom as a semi-autonomous social field. The term conveys more than "dualism," but "dualism" is well established for *de*

*jure/de facto* situations and will continue to be used in this context, hopefully using Moore's phrase to define the term. Dualism might then be defined as a state and a community within the state, each of which have their own land law, the law of the community being subsidiary to the law of the state.

4 The proceedings of the African Conference of Local Courts and Customary Law (1963) is an excellent and detailed report on the experience of British courts with customary land law in Africa. It was obviously intended as a hand-off report to a new generation of university-trained lawyers.

5 Mustafa (1971) gives perhaps the best sense of the hope and some of the uncertainties affecting the project of creating the common law of an African nation. Mustafa is a Sudanese legal scholar whose works deal with constitutional and land tenure issues, and he is a member of that first generation of African land tenure scholar.

6 See Joireman (2011). The devastation of land records systems in these cases is often appalling. My own experience has involved studies and consultations in post-conflict contexts in Mozambique, Rwanda, Liberia and Uganda. I have watched the search for volumes of the land register in Uganda, hidden at rural sites to protect them (intentionally avoiding concentrating them in the capital, Kampala). I have seen small boys selling peanuts on the streets of Monrovia, Liberia in screws of paper torn from land registers and the volumes of reports of cases decided by the courts. It was there that I bartered for legal material I needed. I copied a copy of Liberia's land registration regulations held at the University of Wisconsin Land Tenure Center. I traded it with a private attorney in Liberia who held the only surviving copy (or so we thought at the time) of the land registration act itself.

7 See, in the same vein, Snyder (1981) on the creation of customary land tenure for Senegal and Klug (1995) in South Africa.

## References


Beckingham, C.F. (2017). *The Prester John of the Indies: A true relation of the lands of the Prester John, being the narrative of the Portuguese embassy to Ethiopia in 1520, written by Father Francisco Alvares*. Volumes I–II. Routledge.

Beinart, W. (2012). Beyond "homelands": Some ideas about the history of African rural areas in South Africa. *South African Historical Journal, 64*(1), 5–21. https://doi.org/10.1080/02582473.2012.642225

Bruce, J.W. (2017, March 20–24). *Land tenure dualism in China: How the dichotomy between state and collective ownership of land has shaped urbanization and driven the emergence of wealth inequality*. [Conference paper]. World Bank Land and Poverty Conference, Washington, DC, United States.

Chanock, M. (1985). *Law, custom and social order, the colonial experience in Malawi and Zambia*. Cambridge University Press.

Chanock, M. (1991). Paradigms, policies and property: A review of the customary law of land tenure. In K. Mann & R. Roberts (Eds.), *Law in colonial Africa* (pp. 63–66). James Currey.

Davidson, B. (1992). *The Black man's burden: Africa and the curse of the nation-state*. James Currey.

de Lemos, M. (2020). Legal pluralism and international development: Introductory notes on the dialogue between the two concepts. *Humanities and Rights Global Network Journal, 2*(1), 190–233.

Evans-Pritchard, E.E. (1940). *The Nuer: A description of the* modes *of livelihood and political institutions of a Nilotic people*. Clarendon Press.

Johnson, D.H. (1982). Evans-Pritchard, the Nuer, and the Sudan political service. *African Affairs*, *81*(323), 231–246.

Joireman, S.F. (2011). *Where there is no* government*: Enforcing property rights in common law Africa*. Oxford University Press.

Joseph, R. (2003). Nation-state trajectories in Africa. *Georgetown Journal of International Affairs*, *4*(1), 13–20.

Klug, H. (1995). Defining the property rights of others: Political power, indigenous tenure and the construction of customary land law. *The Journal of Legal* Pluralism *and Unofficial Law*, *27*(35), 119–148. https://doi.org/10.1080/07329113.1995.10756461

Korang, D. (2015). Ascertainment of customary law: A question of law or of fact or both? *Journal of Law, Policy and Globalization*, *38*(93), 93–95.

Lloyd, P.C. (1962). *Yoruba land law*. Oxford University Press.

McAuslan, P. (2000). Only the name of the country changes: The diaspora of "European" land law in commonwealth Africa. In C. Toulmin & J. Quan (Eds.), *Evolving land rights, policy and tenure in Africa* (pp. 75–96). IIED/DFID/NRI.

McAuslan, P. (2005). Legal pluralism as a policy option: Is it desirable, is it doable? *UNDP–International land coalition conference "Land rights for African* development*: from knowledge to action"*, Nairobi, October 31st –November 3rd, 2005. www.undp/drylands

Meek, C.K. (1949). *Land law and custom in the colonies*. Frank Cass & Co.

Miller, R.J. & Stitz, O. (2021). The international law of colonialism in East Africa: Germany, England, and the doctrine of discovery. *Duke Journal of Comparative and International Law*, *32*(1), 1–59.

Moore, S.F. (2000). *Law as process: An anthropological approach*. LIT Verlag Münster.

Moore, S.F. (2014). Legal pluralism as omnium gatherum. *Florida International Law Review*, *10*, 5. https://dx.doi.org/10.25148/lawrev.10.1.5

Mustafa, Z. (1971). *The common law in the Sudan*. Oxford University Press.

Okoth-Ogendo, H.W.O. (1991). *Tenants of the crown: Evolution of agrarian law and institutions in Kenya*. ACTS Press.

Opoku, K. (1974). Traditional law under French colonial rule. *Verfassung Und Recht in* Übersee/*Law and Politics in Africa, Asia and Latin America*, *7*(2), 139–153.

Roberts, R. & Mann, K. (1991). Law, property, labor and authority in colonial Africa. In R. Roberts & K. Mann (Eds.), *Law in colonial Africa* (pp. 3–58). James Currey.

Snyder, F. (1981). Colonialism and legal form: The creation of "customary law" in Senegal. *The Journal of Legal Pluralism and* Unofficial *Law*, *13*(19), 49–90. https://doi.org/10.1080/07329113.1981.10756258

Woodman, G.R. (1969). Some realism about customary law: The West African experience. *Wisconsin Law Review*, 128–152.

# 3 Customary Land Tenure

## The Recent Reassessment of Customary Land Tenure

What are the characteristics of African systems of customary land tenure? Much of the thinking on this topic through the 1960s remained stuck in misconceptions from the colonial era. Customary land tenure was often described as a roadblock that negatively affected investment in agriculture and development. Governments in the years after independence concluded that the solution was replacement with "modern" laws. By "modern," they meant a contemporary system of tenure based on capitalist (private, individual ownership of land) or socialist (state or community ownership of land) norms. It is only now, after a disappointing experience with replacement reforms, in analyzing why they have proven so hard to implement, that we have begun to understand more fully what African peoples valued in their customary land tenure systems.[1]

Most customary land tenure systems have important positive aspects, and some directly contradict what colonial land administrators thought they knew about customary land tenure:

1. These systems are local, not decentralized but actually local, exhibiting a surprising capacity for autonomous rule-making and problem solving.
2. They are flexible and have demonstrated their ability to adjust to meet new needs and provide security in what is often an otherwise uncertain environment. They sometimes change basic rules but also generate contractual solutions.
3. They often had a hierarchy of chiefs and other traditional authorities that penetrated deep into rural society, an inexpensive system with which "modern" systems of local governance found it difficult to compete in terms of presence and cost-effectiveness.
4. The tenure systems are customized to local needs, reflecting the experience of generations living in a locality, and show a remarkable variety of arrangements, not just between major ethnic groups but in detail, from one community to another.
5. They use access to land as a basis for systems of social organization that build strong links among members, playing on the importance of land to survival and identity and often providing land as a birthright to all or most members of the community.

DOI: 10.4324/9781003476429-4

6. Because of the many roles customary land tenure systems play in Africa's rural communities, they are embedded in local society so deeply that imposed reforms run a high risk of affecting local society in unexpected ways, including major negative impacts.
7. Those systems, often as a matter of custom, discriminate against classes of persons with respect to access and use of land, the most renowned being that patrilineal systems provide women no birthright entitlement to land, such that women's only access (sometimes a right) to land is through their husbands, fathers or brothers.

This last characteristic is common to most customary land tenure systems, and by today's standards, it is by far the most concerning and becoming increasingly detrimental as the instability of marriages and families grows as a consequence of development processes.

I have become increasingly concerned over the years that our mainstream development institutions have largely failed to capitalize on the positive elements of customary tenure in land policy development. Land tenure reforms to date have largely been framed based on incorrect assumptions about the nature of customary land tenure systems, exaggerating the problems associated with them and failing to utilize their positive potentials in reform programming. Reformers have failed to understand their value to those who live under them. They underestimate their capacity for resistance and resilience in the face of replacement reforms and broader economic forces. Development powerhouses have failed to mine their remarkable complexity for ideas about how to move forward. Broad rethinking of perceptions of customary land tenure, its relation to and its potential to contribute to development processes in Africa is needed.

Some clearly misleading characterizations, generally negative toward customary land tenure, are so built into the vocabulary of our policy discourse on land tenure that even those aware of this problem find themselves struggling to manage the problem in their own writing.

## Other Common Characterizations

*Customary?* A number of authorities have shown there are problems with using the words "customary" or "traditional" in describing the land tenure systems of Africa's indigenous people (Platteau, 2000).

"Customary" suggests systems with authority established by long use and rules obeyed almost automatically due to long repetition of compliance. Customary land tenure is often obeyed with little conscious reflection on the rule or the reasons for it, in the way I don't drive across my neighbor's lawn to get to the street, though it would be convenient. It takes time for new rules to acquire this "customary" feel.

Chauveau (1998) defines a customary system of land tenure in more substantive terms as "a system of authority based on anteriority[2] and alliance, in which access to resources depends on social belonging and the rights are allocated—and sometimes renegotiated—under the auspices of land management institutions."

Lavigne-Delville (2007, p. 35) cites Chauveau (1998) and adds, "Current tenure arrangements can be said to be customary in so much as they remain essentially based on these principles (even if important changes may occur in the rules, authorities and concrete rights held by the resource users)." A complication is that some elements in customary law have originated as colonial impositions but have become customary (embraced and legitimated by the community concerned). My inclination is to continue to consider them "customary," and I am comfortable using the term even where major changes take place in substantive rules, so long as the system is legitimated and internalized by members of the community.

Finally, application of the term "customary" is not wrong so much as incomplete. What is missing is that, as Knight (2010) notes, customary land tenure is "contemporary," the land tenure currently practiced and often preferred by rural communities across Africa. What needs to be done about these terms and the misleading impressions their use creates? I probably use "customary" in this book more often than any other adjective, but where appropriate, I use the terms "contemporary customary land tenure" or "contemporary custom concerning land."

*Traditional?* It is true that most custom involves practices developed gradually over time that are often of considerable age, but those systems are not frozen in time. Customary land tenure is flexible and responds to new needs. Its unwritten nature facilitates this. These systems have evolved and are still evolving. Evolution involves both success and failures, leaps forward and dead ends. It is not difficult to provide examples of how customary tenure has changed, for better or worse. Part III of this book is devoted to stories of such change.

Not all customary land tenure systems are old. Even today new customary land tenure systems can develop quite quickly, in a generation where needed, for example, by ethnically mixed groups settling in the pioneer zones of Senegal's *ferlo* (Golan, 1990, 1994) or settlers relocating inside forest and game reserves in Uganda as a result of land shortages and government policies encouraging clearing land for agriculture (Aluma et al., 1989). Such communities can cobble together a consensus on land access and rights quickly, in a decade or two, and these are very soon customary land tenure.[3] Wily (2008) reminds us that these systems exist today, serving real needs of real people, and so are in fact *contemporary*. In discussions about land tenure, "traditional" is best reserved for norms where the age of the rule or institution is relevant.

*Informal?* The term "informal" is a term that was originally applied to occupants of land without a legal claim in urban contexts, people who once would have been called by the pejorative term "squatters." Extension of the use of the term "informal" to customary land tenure systems is seriously misleading, because in those cases there is a claim of right, even if the state would not recognize it. That sense of right is a powerful factor in determining how a landholder will respond to a threat to that land.[4]

In more recent times, it is common for land policy analysts to write of customary land tenure as "informal" for customary land tenure systems, a term which in this context does not mean disordered or casual but only that customary landholders hold their land outside the "formal" legal system of the state. They must then forgo some opportunities and protections provided by law. They often hold the land outside the formal system, advocates of formalization suggest, because they are unaware of or unable to access opportunities and advantages under the state's legal system. Their abstaining from or actively evading those opportunities instead reflects their estimate that the asserted advantages do not apply to them or that they are outweighed by their disadvantages. They may feel that accepting the state's system for land would have real costs in terms of forfeiting social capital in the community and in particular in the family.

Customary land tenure is better thought of as an *alternative formality* to national law on land, the normative system of a non-state polity socially legitimated and managed by community institutions, with all that implies in terms of power and vested interests. Failure to recognize this contributes to the underestimation of the strength of customary land tenure systems and the failure of initiatives to change or replace those systems as expected. From the viewpoint of national law customary tenure is legally subsidiary to national law. That may not make a difference in contexts where implementation of national law has little reality on the ground or lacks social legitimacy.

*Enforceable, and so law?* In his poem, "Recessional," Rudyard Kipling, Britain's "poet of empire," describes the challenges his British "tribe" faces in ruling "lesser tribes without the law."[5] Like many Englishmen of his time, he assumes that the empire's conquered peoples do not have rules worthy of being called "law." Law was seen in the colonial era as one more light the empire could bring to the "Dark Continent." When it became impossible to deny that these cultures had their own complex normative systems and rules governing access to and use of land, those rules were characterized as "customary," in the case of land, as "customary land tenure." "Customary" was accurate in one sense. It correctly conveyed that customary land tenure was something habitual. It also implied that it was something less than law: less enforceable than law and more dependent on comity and good manners for compliance. Kipling's contemporaries in the colonies were sure it was very much a lesser law (if law at all) than the law of the state with all the majesty and power of a Crown behind it. In Europe, popular accounts of African custom tended to highlight aspects that struck readers there as odd or repulsive,[6] some of which were rejected by British colonial courts as "contrary to law, equity and good conscience."[7]

For western readers, "custom" does not suggest enforceability. In western jurisprudence, the distinction between custom and law is important. Compulsion (the monopoly of the state) can be exercised at a lower level of social organization only if delegated to an institution at that level by the state. Law is compulsory, and therefore a monopoly of the state, while custom is not. Since law is the monopoly of the state, custom is not enforceable. Calling indigenous systems of land tenure "customary" is misleading for western readers because it suggests lack of enforcement. Africans recognize that some norms are enforceable by society, and some are not. When I asked an elderly gentleman with whom I dined one evening in Mochudi in Botswana about the concept of "law" in Tswana custom, he mulled over the word "law" for a moment or a moment before answering: "Law … law.

... Yes, I have heard about it. It is what you must have when people no longer have good manners."

The question of enforceability is an important issue because in western jurisprudence, enforceability has been the essential requirement for a rule to be considered law. It is the reason why western jurists have hesitated to consider African custom as law. Most African land tenure authorities find that too narrow a gate. It does not serve well in African circumstances. The line between enforceable norms and norms that cannot be enforced is not the bright line that western legal theory expects. A rule may be enforceable in one context but not another, or against one person and not another. Not all people are "equal before the law" under custom. In fact, rather than in theory, this is also the case under western legal systems, whether by law, corruption or lack of financial resources for litigation or enforcement.

Most key norms in customary land tenure meet this classic western requirement. They are usually enforceable not by the state but by sub-state communities such as villages, clans and lineages (Moore, 1986). Their enforcement methods range from familiar forms such as action by a tribal constabulary and imposition of fines to less familiar forms including organized community censure, shunning, trial by ordeal and supernatural sanctions (Moore, 1972). In Liberia, I once huddled with awed villagers in a hut in the night as costumed "spirits," garish and threatening, ran howling through the darkened alleys between the huts. They were showing the spirits' displeasure with an offence against community rules and with the village and its head for not dealing with the matter more firmly. Those demonstrating were members of a secret society in the village.[8] This form of enforcement and the one described in Box 3.1 may be open to objection for other reasons, but in my own experience they are remarkably effective in obtaining compliance. However effective they may be in the rural village context, enforcing customary rules in less socially cohesive contexts would require rethinking enforcement tools and strategies.

**Box 3.1 A Customary Formality**

A typical norm in customary systems is that people should keep their word. This has been extended to contracts regarding land, so long as they are consistent with custom. This transaction concerns the lease for ten years of a plot of land held under custom on a terraced mountainside in southern Tigray Province of Ethiopia. This is valuable land, small by most standards but substantial by local standards. Care is taken to ensure that there will be no confusion. There are to be witnesses, not just to the contract but to the location of the land and the turnover of the land to the man leasing it.

Two ten-year-old boys, unrelated to the parties to the transaction, have been chosen by the local chief to witness the transaction. The principals meet at the parish church in the morning, high on a mountainside overlooking the land concerned. The contract is recorded in a few lines on a page torn from a student's spiral notebook. A priest from the parish church is given the paper for safekeeping. The owner of the land has purchased a new set of clothes and even shoes for each boy at the weekly market the day before. Now he gives them to the two and they don them. The boys are excited, but the seriousness with which the adults are behaving quiets them.

The owner points down the mountain to the location of the parcel concerned and several geographic features are noted that would help them locate the parcel from this viewpoint. Then the group walks down to it on a series of rocky paths. The boys are reminded that they must remember the details of the parcel. The names of the owners of the land adjacent are noted. The lessor again recites the brief terms of the lease, and then the parties walk the boundaries of the parcel with the boys, pointing them out to the boys and suggesting how they should remember them. The boys promise that they will witness as to the location of the land and the nature and terms of the agreement if it should ever be questioned.

The group then goes to a nearby traditional stone and thatch hut, where a meal has been prepared for the boys. There is more grilled goat meat than they would normally eat in months. The shoes they received earlier are of leather, locally made. They are the first shoes they have ever owned other than rubber sandals made from salvaged truck tires. They put on the old clothes they wore on that day and folded their new clothes so that they will not get soiled on their long walk home. It's a memorable day.

One hopes that the long-debated question as to whether custom is "law" in the western meaning of the term is over, though it seems to resurface from time to time.[9] In this book I will use the word custom or customary to indicate norms that are usually respected in community, without asking whether the norm is reliably enforced, which may have more to do with context than the nature of the norm or rule itself.

*Embedded?* Ben Cousins (2007) of the University of Western Cape in South Africa argued that it was essential to approach land tenure reform within the idea of embeddedness of customary land tenure systems of society and culture. Customary systems of property rights are tenure systems, based on mutual rights and obligations among members of a community defined by common descent or residence with respect to land. As such, they generate a wide range of social obligations between members of the community over land, which connect with larger complexes of rights and obligations generated by other non-legal rights under the rules of the community. Essentially, tenure systems are entwined with the entire societal structure and the rules governing it, such that trying to replace them threatens the unraveling of a whole system.

*Flexible? Diverse? Complex?* I've been struck by a number of aspects of customary land tenure as my opportunities to see it in operation have expanded. This chapter has discussed some of them already, including their capacity to evolve to meet new needs. They change more easily than I had once imagined. Such change has been amply documented. Because it is unwritten, custom changes more easily than if it were in the form of a text, sometimes quickly, at other times in a more gradual evolutionary fashion. What changes it? A wide range of factors from new markets, new technologies, new faiths, politics, war, climate change, etc. The list is long. It may help to remember that it is those factors that might require a change in land use that are likely to push broad changes in land tenure (see Part II, whose overall theme is evolutionary change in land tenure).

It was not a surprise to me that there are a significant variety of customary tenure systems since the connection with ethnicity is clear in the literature. The sheer extent of the diversity (the number of ethnic groups, the extent of the differences not just between but within ethnic groups, and even between neighboring villages) took some time to sink in. When it did, I found the implications for policy development and organizing a tenure reform alarming. The complexity of customary systems was also a surprise. I had a notion that normative systems evolved toward greater complexity. This is not necessarily the case as regards land tenure and property rights. I suspect that customary land tenure systems are complex because they perform so many roles in the community societies and economies.

*Simple?* These customary systems may or may not be legally recognized by the state. They are well known to community members and "socially legitimized" by the community's commitment to them (Allott, 1952; Bennett & Vermeulen, 1980).[10] They have developed incrementally, sometimes slowly, sometimes more quickly, reflecting changes in needs and values in the communities concerned. In some societies, the rules of customary land tenure are quite specific. There are individuals who are recognized as especially knowledgeable about them. In other cultures, one is dealing with less specificity and structure. Those who have studied such cases write of "a loosely ordered … repertoire of norms" and "rare systematization" (Cotula, 2007, p. 10, citing Bennett [1985] on the Merina of Madagascar and Comaroff and Roberts [1986] on the Tswana of Botswana). In some cases not all individuals are "equal before the law." Some community members may have statuses that make it inappropriate or unlikely that a rule will be applied against them as opposed to other community members. In some cases, stories and even myths are used to convey certain rules. This means that descriptions of a customary land tenure system, however well done, need to be approached with caution a generation later; some rules may have changed or become more or less mandatory.

**Box 3.2 A Few Basic Certainties about Rights**

Madison, WI, circa 1980: My family and I have just moved from Khartoum, the capital of Sudan, to Madison, Wisconsin, where I'm starting a job at the Land Tenure Center at University of Wisconsin-Madison. My two daughters, both under seven, have been playing barefoot in our backyard. The soft green grass is a luxury after years in dust-dry Khartoum and the spiky, brown grass in much of the yard in our home there. In their play, my daughters cross an invisible line between our yard and that of an elderly neighbor lady. She has been watching her new neighbors from her back steps, and now she leans toward the girls, shaking her finger at them, and intones, "Property, property!" It is not very neighborly of her, but she is asserting one of her rights of ownership: the right to exclude others. I am struck by how utterly confident she is of her right. She doesn't have to think about it. It is part of her culture. I realize that in spite of the differences between customary land tenure and western real property rights, the way most people think about them is not so very different: a few basic certainties, firmly held, about how they have a right to be treated with respect to their land.

*Communal or community-based?* There are other common characterizations of customary land tenure that are less than reliable. Customary land tenure systems are often characterized as "communal." Colonial administrations were quite happy to consider the land as communal property since it could provide a basis for the colonial state asserting (as the successor of the formerly autonomous land-owning communities) ownership of the land. Perceptive observers (e.g. White, 1958) have long raised questions about how far this is accurate. There are certainly communal elements in those tenure systems, for example community-owned and managed resources such as communal pastures and forests.[11] There is also a community interest in its land more generally, less than ownership but more similar to territoriality, a distinction generally not made in customary contexts.

A rural household will often hold several parcels of land. Some will be under different tenures with many rights resembling those of private ownership: The household or members of it may have: several small parcels used for rainfed grain production; a plot along the river cultivated through recessional agriculture; and an area in a community pasture where a pregnant cow can be tethered to graze in season. Tenures tend to vary with the customs of the community and land use. Sometimes the name of the tenure is taken from the use, being described as "river land tenure" for recessional cultivation of riverbanks as the water recedes at the end of the seasonal rains. If the production is for some purpose other than household use, it may be held under a tenure named to indicate this, for instance a *waqf* under Islamic law to support a mosque. It is these tenures that may be "communal" or "individual," not an entire customary land tenure system.

A list of tenures and an indication about whether each tenure is communal or individual does not give you an adequate sense of a tenure system in this respect. It is hard, even when examining a single customary system, to assess the balance between the individual and the communal. As in so many areas, context matters. Africans exhibit a strong sense of responsibility to ancestors, progeny and their community, but also have a strong sense of their personal right to the land of the community that they have held for generations. Such a customary holder will, when he feels his land threatened, stand and shout "This land is mine!" with as much passion as any freehold landowner. In Ethiopia's northern highlands, fathers told their sons: "Even the smallest piece of family land, you must defend with your life." Responses regarding the nature of these rights receive answers which are conditioned by the identity of the questioner and context. If the audience is an outsider, or if a community resource is the topic, the answer often has a strong communal tone. The gates are closed so that only the walls around the community and its land resource can be seen. If instead the conversation is between members of the community competing for land, or otherwise concerns a member's holding, the personal right is on full display, flags flying.

It is critical to understand that "customary" does not mean "communal." Custom is the *system* under which land is held, and communal is the *way* in which *some* of that land is used. Knight (2010, p. 24) argues, citing Wily (2005, p. 6) that:

> Customary domains are territories over which the community possesses jurisdiction and often root title. … [W]ithin the domain, a range of tenure arrangements typically apply. These include estates owned by individuals or families, and estates owned by special interest groups in the community [such as] ritual societies or women's groups. This is not to be confused with 'properties' which are owned by all members of that community in undivided shares, often the larger or remoter pastures, forests, woodlands, swampland and hilltops … these are Common Properties, defined by virtue of membership to the group, and a group whose composition may change over time.

Whereas "communal" can be legitimately applied to specific tenures, it should not be used to classify tenure systems, even where communal ownership and management is a large part of the system. Wily (2005) holds that "the heartland of customary land law is simply that it is community-based law, devised and upheld by the community." Community-based would be more accurate. This book will continue to use the term customary land tenure but it will also sometimes use the "community-based" terminology, including "communities of residence" and "communities of descent."

*Identity? Entitlement? Birthright?* Customary land rights are also determinants of identity. Membership in a land community is an attribute by which people in rural Africa identify themselves. "I am a son of Tselim Haramat," a man from Agame in Ethiopia's Tigray region will say, referring to the small village where he was born. A man of the village in good standing will be described as a *balabat*, suggesting a man of good repute. Literally, a *balabat* is "a man with a father," a descendent from the first settlers and so a landholder by right.

Identity and its relationship to entitlement to land are important elements that these customary tenure systems have in common but not adequately highlighted in discussions of their characteristics. These systems have both individual and communal elements, all community-based. A community holds the land and has through its traditional institutions the authority to administer and enforce the customary land tenure system. A clear response to the question of whether the community "owns" the land is often hard to obtain or is shaped by the responder's ideas of advantages to be gained under national law by his response. The community takes different forms, often part of larger, nested systems of social organization. The institutions and authority over land may be vested in one or another of the levels of the traditional hierarchy. Custom provides that membership in that community means that he has *a right to a share in the community's land.* These are land entitlement systems. This characteristic strongly distinguishes them from land right systems in market economies, where no such entitlements exist.[12] This is not to suggest that there is no landlessness or rights deprivation in these communities. Women's lack of direct rights to land is a glaring example. There are certain groups believed to have occult powers, such as blacksmiths in West Africa, who are barred from land ownership under custom. But one does not find significant numbers of male heads of households who do not have rights and control over land.

In lineage-based systems, a person who establishes membership in a lineage by proving descent has a right to a share in the land of that lineage. Anthropologists such as Hoben (1973) in his classic on the Amhara of Ethiopia have explored land rights in what he and others call descent corporations and explain different levels in corporateness. In the case where residence rather than descent is the basis for community membership, membership carries with it a right to a share in the land of that community. This is fundamental to these systems. It constitutes one important element in a foundational tenure institution involving mutual rights and obligation by the individual as a member of the community. It provides access to land to their members as a birthright and also imposes, as obligations of membership, limitations on behavior and duties to the community.

I have found in talks with local officials that taking land away from a customary holder with such a birthright is difficult to contemplate. The idea of a member without land is practically inconceivable. In Swaziland, in my own experience, one could not punish a lineage member by taking away their land. They would also need to be exiled from the community. This might be the case if a villager had profoundly offended the community or even had prospered beyond the chief. Such a villager could be accused of witchcraft and exiled, his land taken by the chief initially. The chief would assert a right to reallocate it, but there was often a claim for the land by another lineage member.

Consider the profound importance of membership in a land-owning community. A man gives his loyalty to the group and receives in return not just a piece of land, but a right to land not just for himself but for his descendants, a transgenerational right that will benefit future generations. The right is a birthright, a blood right and cannot easily be lost. In a number of rural communities in Africa I have asked elders and chiefs: What if a man who holds land of the community sells it? Is he still a member? Can he get new land from the community? They struggle with the question, and I realize that thinking of the tenure relationship as a bargain misses the point. Without land from the community the member would not be who he is. Compared to his birthright, perpetual and so extending to his descendants, fee simple ownership would seem to him a brief, fragile thing. This is a feature which has rarely been considered in terms of the economic incentives it would generate for good husbandry and conservation of land resources.

**Community Authorities**

In pre-colonial Africa, the community members with responsibility for managing and allocating the land of the community were a part of a broader system of community governance. Many of these local authorities had responsibilities extending beyond land matters. Early anthropological studies in Africa reflected colonial administrators' need to understand the political side of these societies, including the role of land and the institutions involved in its management. These varied from case to case. They might, depending on the land tenure system, exercise functions such as performing ceremonies necessary to the fertility of the land, allocating or reallocating landholdings, ratifying intra-family land dispositions, deciding or mediating land disputes, and representing the community in disputes with neighboring communities.

The tasks that might need to be addressed vary according to the nature of the land tenure system and contextual factors. In societies with very valuable natural resources, such as the irrigable land of the Lozi along the Zambezi River in western Zambia, a hierarchical system of social control of land reminded some European researchers of feudalism. At the other extreme, one finds cases with less special land resources and especially where land was still plentiful where it was difficult to identify the institutions with significant roles in relation to land. In other instances, the presence of many community leaders in unfamiliar roles (e.g. rain priests and earth priests) confused colonial administrators and led to mistakes in choice of officials as "chiefs" for their system of indirect administration (Colson, 1975; MacGaffey, 2013).

During the colonial period, the most important element in changing these institutions was their incorporation by the colonial powers into their systems of indirect rule. But as Delville (2007) reminds us, much of the change in the local institutions responsible for local governance of land and natural resources takes place through less obvious socio-economic processes. (See his table of institutions and contexts (p. 35) to get a sense of how increasingly complex the institutional landscape of rural Africa has become over the years.) In some countries, a variety of regional organizations have a planning and coordination role in managing land resources in their territories and traditional institutions at village level have been joined by a variety of committees, often established by donor-funded projects. They then dissolve or continue a shadowy half-life after the project is over and its funding no longer available.

At independence, the colonial powers bypassed these "traditional leaders" to turn power over to a new generation of educated and westernized leaders, whose education taught them that "traditional" was a negative descriptor. They resented the compromising role many traditional leaders played during the struggle for independence. They came to power convinced that traditional leaders were destined for "the trashcan of history." In the years that followed, it became clear that their subjects had not resented the role their chiefs had played to the same extent. New leaders understood the awkward position that traditional leaders' official positions in the colonial system of indirect rule had placed them and understood the need for them to compromise. Davidson (1992) notes that if the colonialists had ended their incursions in Africa 50 years earlier, they would have turned power over to these traditional authorities. By the time independence arrived, liberalism had taken hold in Britain that demanded an educated leadership. The new leaders were jealous of the power inherent in traditional authorities' control of land and increasingly apprehensive about the potential challenge to their own newly acquired authority.

During the 1960s and 1970s, most of these regimes sought to break the hold of traditional authorities over land, at least their authority to allocate or reallocate land. They sometimes purported to abolish or phase out customary land tenure or customary law in its entirety. New elites were concerned with the power of traditional authorities. This is a major thread running through this book's Part III on land tenure reform.

The new states lacked staff and funds to make things happen in the rural areas, except in those countries which attained independence through mass political action. There were only a few of these, such as Guinea Bissau. When it came to state administrative authority, the tribal authorities had been shown the door. Most had gone quietly, while still exercising many of their traditional powers over community-based land. Even as they enacted new land tenure reforms, new states were not equipped to train and build the local staff necessary to take over land administration functions. Disappointment with implementation of reforms grew over the 1970s and 1980s. By the 1990s recognition dawned on outsiders that customary land tenure structures and institutions, including traditional authorities, were still governing most of the rural land in almost every country in Africa. Implementation of reforms was instead being overtaken by evolutionary change. Bruce (1993), Place and Migot-Adholla (1998) and Platteau (2000) questioned whether the reforms were cost-effective or really needed, given the proven ability of customary institutions and custom to adjust to address new needs. Some argued that these more gradual reform scenarios could benefit from reinvolvement of such local authorities in local land management. Bruce and Knox (2009), discussing cost-effective decentralization, indicate opportunities for officially reinvolving the local authorities in reforms. A number of recent land tenure reform programs have sought to rely on these authorities, including those in Uganda, Mozambique and South Africa. These are discussed in detail with other reform models in Part III of this book. After 2000 new arguments for replacement strategies have been put forward. The donor community remains committed to expensive land registration programs seeking to replace customary land tenure.

Depriving traditional authorities of their authority over land has led to chiefs moving into other roles with respect to government. In some situations, they become opponents of governments and their reform programs. In Zambia, an effort by the government with the support of the African Union (AU) and aid agencies, including the United States Agency for International Development (USAID), the World Bank and UN-Habitat, to reform the way land under custom is administered sought reforms to promote transparency and accountability. The reform policy would create new local government agencies with a role in administering government land. Traditional leaders rejected the reforms, convinced their purpose was to undermine their role and endanger their existence. In 2018, the traditional authority representatives stormed out of the meeting being held to validate the new land policy (Chitonge, 2018). Berry (2017) discusses in depth such instances of resistance.

In the case of tenure reform programs that seek to replace customary systems through registration of titles in western forms of land tenure, Honig (2017) notes that those in communities with "strong customary privilege" (i.e. strong entitlements to land under custom, such as lineage) have less interest in titling while those with low customary privilege have more. This is consistent with findings by other researchers. In his research in Nigeria, Meyers (1991) found that those who most needed the protection of titles were those who acquired customary land under questionable circumstances: simple illegal purchases by outsiders to land-grabbing by powerful officials. Myers mentions military officers who were concerned whether they would be able to hold onto land after a change of regime and wanted titling and registration to protect their rights. Honig (2017) discusses those within the local communities who feel disadvantaged, reminding us that customary land tenures systems create winners and losers. This is a potential wedge issue, as noted by Chitonge (2018). In Zambia the government sought to present itself as the protector of the poor in the customary system. Honig (2017) notes that it would be very difficult if not impossible to impose a system of western tenure over the level of opposition he observed. Chiefs (and community members) understand that these replacement reforms transfer the control of local community land to the state. He suggests that governments focus on creative reforms targeting the "low customary privilege" members of the communities, using the customary system itself to improve their land access and security of tenure. Women are an obvious example.

Part III shows other patterns of interaction between chiefs and officialdom, including building new informal systems of land governance and collaboration between official and traditional authorities to achieve common goals. This often includes personal enrichment by providing rich and influential outsiders access to land under custom. Delville et al. (2023) analyze such a situation in Senegal. Networks of actors in new informal systems of local governance have considerable strength because they include actors on both sides of the divide between national government and local authority in the rural areas.

There is obviously no general answer to the question of whether and to what extent rural local leaders can play a useful rule in the future. It will depend in part of the nature of the traditional leadership institution, the local history of conflict or cooperation between national and local leaders, how ethnicity is configured in the country, the membership of national and local elites in different ethnic groups, the different levels of power at national and local level, and the options of the leaders as they see them.

When it comes to reforms of tenure one important factor is the reason for the resilience of old forms of leadership and institutions. If it is based simply on the power of those institutions, they may be more vulnerable to appeals and promises by the national government. If they are valued because their communities trust them more than the national government to deliver social and other goods, including tenure security, they may have a more significant, longer future. After reviewing data collected from 19 African countries, Logan (2013) found: "African traditional authorities have proved to be highly resilient, remaining just as much a part of the 'modern' political landscape as any legislature or local council." She concludes (p. 353) that the data:

> reveal an intensity of support for traditional authorities that challenges those who argue that these leaders are unwanted and undemocratic. While Africans find these leaders to be flawed, they enjoy widespread popular legitimacy, and most believe that traditional authorities have an important role to play in local governance. The public values the role traditional authorities play in managing and resolving conflict, and their leadership qualities and accessibility to ordinary people. Evidence also suggests that traditional leaders play an important symbolic role as representatives of community identity, unity, continuity, and stability.

The relationship between national elites and traditional authorities is that of two groups whose power bases are grounded in their ability to meet needs the other cannot effectively meet. This means they need to coexist and pursue common concerns of their members while competing, sometimes overtly and sometimes covertly, sometimes on the part of their groups, sometimes for themselves, for access to and control of land resources under customary land tenure. An important potential for collaboration on decentralization of land management exists, but in many countries distrust is high. Any attempt to decentralize decision-making regarding land access to traditional authorities, even if it only recognizes a *de facto* state of affairs, must involve clear, negotiated allocations of decision-making authority. The increased role of ethnicity in party politics threatens to make such collaboration even more difficult.

## Notes

1 IIED and FAO, long more aware of the positive aspects of customary land tenure than other development organizations (e.g., FAO, 1954), joined IIED in 2007 to jointly publish a remarkable short volume which highlighted change in customary land tenure in a way that had not been done before and drew heavily on the experience in French West Africa (Cotula, 2007).

2 "Anteriority" seems in this context to suggest that customary systems come to us out of the past, or perhaps look back in time for legitimating origins of rights. I was not familiar with the term and my efforts to understand it by checking several sources have only clarified that people of different disciplines and political persuasions use it to mean different things.

3 Customary tenure systems may emphasize the age of a rule to engender respect for it, but customary land tenure systems do not have anything like English law's "time out of mind" requirement for legal recognition of custom.

4 I associate the inappropriate extension of the term from the urban squatter situation to cases where customary claims exist with the work of Hernando de Soto (1989, 2003), though there may be earlier examples of which I am unaware. Whatever the case, de Soto is largely responsible for its popularization.

5 In Kipling's "Recessional," penned for the Diamond Jubilee of Queen Victoria, he asks the "Lord of our far-flung battle line" to preserve the empire's servants from falling into the "brash and boastful" ways of "lesser tribes without the law" who peopled the empire. "Recessional" was sung as a hymn to the tune "Melita" ("Eternal Father, Strong to Save") and at appropriate public gatherings of the time.
6 As an example, see the photos of African people in Bernatzik (1930). The photos from his journeys in Africa feature Africans in various stages of undress, with anatomical oddities, with lip-plates and scarification, or engaging in behavior such as blowing air into the anus of a cow in order to get her to release her milk, a practice that not only existed in Africa but was once practiced in China, India, and the Alps (see "Cow Blowing," Wikipedia).
7 The "law, equity and good conscience" provision of reception statutes is discussed in Chapter 2 of this book.
8 I owe this observation to my friend and former colleague at the University of Wisconsin (UW), Jim Riddell, then a doctoral researcher and later a UW faculty member with whom I taught the African Land Tenure course for some years. He later became director of FAO's Land Tenure Unit.
9 Kwame Opoku cites discussions of the point in the literature and comments: "I must confess immediately that I am unhappy to have to deal with this question for, to even pose it, it seems to me, is to question the very nature of African society as a human organization" (Opoku, 1976, p. 2). His irritation seems to me entirely understandable.
10 I also observed this in Ethiopia.
11 The term "communal" is itself imprecise and is used in at least five different senses in the land tenure literature. This is discussed in more detail later in this chapter.
12 It also differentiates them from tenure in the sense as it existed in medieval Europe. Commentary on the traditional land governance systems of northern Ethiopia, often characterized as feudal or semi-feudal, misses this point. Local "lords" receive obligations from those in areas they have been assigned, but do not confer land rights. The land rights are lineage rights, independent of the governance system and utterly unlike feudal systems.

## References


Allott, A.N. (1952). The judicial ascertainment of customary law in British Africa. *Modern Law Review*, *20*, 244–263.

Aluma, J., Drennon, C., Emmanuel, K., Kigula, J., Lawry, S., Muwanga-Zake, E.S.K., & Pete, N. (1989). *A study of social, economic, and tenure factors affecting land use and deforestation in Mabira forest reserve, Kibale forest reserve, and Kibale game/reserve corridor*. Markerere Institute of Social Research and University of Madison-Wisconsin Land Tenure Center.

Bennett, T.W. (1985). *The application of customary law in southern Africa: The conflict of personal laws*. Juta & Co.

Bennett, T.W. & Vermeulen, T. (1980). Codification of customary law. *Journal of African Law*, *24*(2), 206–219.

Bernatzik, H.A. (1930). *Der dunkle Erdteil: Afrika, Landschaft / Volksleben* [*The dark continent: Africa, the landscape and the people*]. Atlantis.

Berry, S. (2017). Struggles over land and authority in Africa. *African Studies Review*, *60*(3), 105–125.

Bruce, J.W. (1993). Do indigenous tenure systems constrain agricultural development? In D. Crummey & T. Bassett (Eds.), *Land in African agrarian systems* (pp 35–56). University of Wisconsin Press.

Bruce, J.W. & Knox, A. (2009). Structures and stratagems: Making decentralization of authority over land in Africa cost-effective. *World Development, 37*(8), 1360–1369.

Chauveau, J.P. (1998). La logique des systèmes coutumiers. In P. Lavigne Delville (Ed.), *Quelles politiques foncières pour l'Afrique rurale? Réconcilier pratiques, légitimité et légalité* (pp. 66–67). Coopération française.

Chitonge, H. (2018). The micropolitics of customary-land conversions in Zambia: Emerging trends and practices. In H. Chitonge and B.B. Umar (Eds.), *Contemporary customary land issues in Africa: Navigating the contours of change* (pp. 22–49). Cambridge Scholars Publishing.

Colson, E. (1975). *Tradition and contract: The problem of order.* Heinemann Educational.

Comaroff, J. & Roberts, S. (1986). *Rules and processes: The cultural logic of dispute in an African context.* University of Chicago Press.

Cotula, L. (2007). Introduction. In L. Cotula (Ed.), *Changes in "customary" land tenure systems in Africa* (pp. 5–14). IIED & FAO.

Cousins, B. (2007). More than socially embedded: The distinctive character of "communal tenure" regimes in South Africa and its implications for land policy. *Journal of Agrarian Change, 7*(3), 281–315.

Davidson, B. (1992). *The Black man's burden: Africa and the curse of the nation-state.* James Currey.

Delville, P.L. (2007). Changes in "customary" land management institutions: Evidence from West Africa. In L. Cotula (Ed.), *Changes in "customary" land tenure systems in Africa* (pp. 35–50). IIED.

Delville, P.L., Diongue, M., & Diouf, I.F. (2023). The practical norms of land governance in Senegalese communes: Institutional incompleteness, politicisation, semi-formality and bricolage. *Land Use Policy, 132*, 106828.

de Soto, H. (1989). *The other path: The invisible revolution in the third world.* HarperCollins.

de Soto, H. (2003). *The mystery of capital: Why capitalism triumphs in the west and fails everywhere else.* Basic Books.

FAO (1954). *Customary land tenure*. FAO.

Golan, E.H. (1990). *Land tenure reform in Senegal: An economic study from the peanut basin* (Land Tenure Center Research Paper No. 101). University of Wisconsin-Madison Land Tenure Center.

Golan, E.H. (1994). Land tenure reform in the peanut basin of Senegal. In J.W. Bruce & S. Migot-Adholla (Eds.), *Searching for land tenure security in Africa* (pp. 231–249). The World Bank.

Hoben, A. (1973). *Land tenure among the Amhara of Ethiopia: The dynamics of cognatic descent*. University of Chicago Press.

Honig, L. (2017). Selecting the state or choosing the chief? The political determinants of smallholder land titling. *World Development, 100*, 94–107.

Knight, R. (2010). *Statutory recognition of customary land rights in Africa: An investigation into best practices for lawmaking and implementation*. FAO.

Lavigne Delville, P. (2007). *Changes in "customary" land tenure systems in Africa*. IIED.

Logan, C. (2013). The roots of resilience: Exploring popular support for African traditional authorities. *African Affairs, 112*(448), 353–376.

MacGaffey, W. (2013). *Chiefs, priests, and praise-singers: History, politics, and land ownership in northern Ghana*. University of Virginia Press.

Meyers, G.W. (1991). *Land and power: The impact of the land use act in Southwestern Nigeria* (LTC Research Paper 108). University of Wisconsin-Madison Land Tenure Center.

Moore, S.F. (1972). Law and social change: The semi-autonomous social field as an appropriate subject of study. *Law & Society Review*, 7, 719–746.

Moore, S.F. (1986). *Social facts and fabrications: "Customary" law on Kilimanjaro, 1880–1980*. Cambridge University Press.

Opoku, K. (1976). *The law of marriage in Ghana: A study of legal pluralism*. A. Metzner.

Place, F. & Migot-Adholla, S. (1998). The economic effects of land registration on smallholder farms in Kenya: Evidence from Nyeri and Kakamega districts. *Land Economics*, *74*(3), 360–373.

Platteau, J.P. (2000). Does Africa need land reform? In *Evolving land rights, policy and tenure in Africa* (pp. 51–74). IIED.

White, C.M.N. (1958). Terminological confusion in African land tenure. *Journal of African Administration*, *10*, 128–129.

Wily, L.A. (2005, October 31–November 3). *The commons and customary law in modern times: rethinking the orthodoxies* [unpublished draft]. UNDP-ILC Workshop: Land rights for African development: from knowledge to action, Nairobi, Kenya.

Wily, L.A. (2008). Custom and commonage in Africa: Rethinking the orthodoxies. *Land Use Policy*, *25*(1), 43–52.

# 4 Legal and Economic Dualism

## Legal Dualism

Legal dualism is the coexistence of two systems of law within a single nation or polity (or other social space). In Africa the most striking instance of this is the coexistence within almost every African nation of (a) statutory law of the state and (b) customary law of indigenous peoples. In the case of land, the location of the land usually determines which of those two systems of law is applicable. If the land is within the territory of a tribe or community, it is the customary land law of that group—with the exception of parts of the territory taken from those groups by the state. Post-independence, states often allocated land that had been taken for use by colonists, to western forms of tenure such as ownership or leasehold, while retaining other land claimed by the colonial administration in government ownership. This meant that colonists from Europe who remained post-independence could continue to hold their land under European land tenures, while Africans continued to practice their local customary land law on land they held, even as it became statutorily owned by the state.

## Tenure Dualism and Economic Dualism

Legal dualism of land tenure systems has its roots in colonial land policy. It facilitated the gradual displacement of African peoples and taking their land. It helped create another dualism: economic dualism. Colonial policy created two "economies" or economic sectors based on land areas under the two different tenure systems.

One was the more 'modern' sector, land taken and provided to colonists, an economy that was integrated with that of the colonial power. It produced the food and other goods the colonial power required. Land in this sector was held by colonists and merchants who held land in western forms of land tenure introduced by colonial governments. This sector received virtually all public and private investment in development. Agriculture and other businesses of settlers and merchants were subsidized through a variety of discriminatory mechanisms. Discrimination consistently advantaged the more modern sector and its colonial population and disadvantaged the other, less-developed sector occupied by Africans.

DOI: 10.4324/9781003476429-5

The other economy was a larger, relatively undeveloped sector whose land and labor were not yet needed by the colonization process and in which traditional authorities were used to govern customary landowners. Land continued under customary land tenure systems. Rights in those systems were diminished by colonial courts to make it easier for the colonial administration to administratively appropriate it and place it under western tenure forms as needed. Often it has been declared state-owned land, with customary land tenure reduced to legally fragile systems of use rights on top of the state title. This sector receives little public or private investment and is systematically disadvantaged in relation to cash crop production and other economic opportunities through regulations that were explicitly or in their effect discriminatory.

The dual system developed under colonialism systematically advantaged one sector, that of the colonizers, over the other, that of the customary owners. *The two tenure systems, while presenting major contrasts, in fact functioned as one larger system. Anyone who wishes to understand dualism must focus not on the fact of their existence, but on the interaction between them.* The areas under customary land tenure and traditional authorities served the colonists' commercial farming operations as a labor reserve, a land reserve and an area from which valuable goods such as ivory, gold and jewels could be acquired through trade or extraction. When the advantaged "settler" sector needed additional land, it expanded at the cost of the disadvantaged "native" sector, through resettlement of the occupants and appropriation of their land at little or no cost. Once land is tenured in a western, marketable tenure, its value suddenly increases and can appreciate further as time passes, depending on market conditions. It also has the potential, in the cases of large farms or especially valuable land, to serve as security for a loan. That may depend on other factors more than the tenure in which the land is held.

## Implementing Tenure Dualism

How was the system of tenure dualism created? Colonizers identified the areas of land best suited to production of export crops. Negotiations with customary occupants led to their resettlement and surveying the land for large farms for colonists. The land was acquired in blocks around the country. The tenure geography of a colony would be islands of land under western tenures in a sea of customary land tenure. The particular western land rights in which land was provided to the colonists differed over time even within one colony. For example, the Kenya Colony over several decades provided land to colonists in 999-year leases, 99-year leases and freehold ownership. The colonial state's desire to maintain tight control over land and to generate rental revenue were factors in tenure choice. Political shifts to the left or right in the colonizing country also influenced land policy in its colonies.

In some British colonies, some African land was placed in a "trust" status, which established the authority of the colonial government, as trustee for the African occupants, to alienate land for colonist occupation. Most were classified as Native Reserves. These were administrative categories. It became clear with the passage of time that colonial governments could do whatever they wished with these lands. In Kenya substantial African lands were initially classified as Native Reserve Areas. The infamous "Barth Judgement" of 1921 (Court of Appeal for East Africa et al., 2017, p. 102) held that such areas were ultimately Crown Lands and "natives" in occupation of land there under custom were simply "tenants-at-will" of the state. They could be resettled and their land taken from them without compensation. While compensation had been paid for some land taken from the African peoples early in the colonial period, it was considered unnecessary after 1921, since the Crown was considered to own the land (Meek, 1949, esp. pp. 76–99; Okoth-Ogendo, 1991).

The colonial government had no incentive to recognize that African landholdings constituted a form of property, especially a form of ownership. That would mean that compensation was required. Colonial land policies tended to minimize the legal significance of customary land rights. Customary rights were mischaracterized as "communal" in nature, an indigenous form of public property. Terms of recognition differed from colony to colony, but in the majority of colonies a claim under a western property law, usually documented, prevailed over a claim under customary law (Meek, 1949; Okoth-Ogendo, 1991).

Discriminatory policies involved in economic dualism were designed for differential impacts on farmers in the two land tenure sectors. Laws and regulations and a variety of discretionary measures discriminated against those in the customary land tenure sector. African farmers there were denied many of the opportunities of their colonist counterparts holding land under imported tenures. While these patterns were most pronounced in the settler colonies of eastern and southern Africa, even in non-settler colonies, including almost all of France's colonies in sub-Saharan Africa, customary land tenure systems were not recognized as ownership. Opportunities for profitable interactions with the colonial country were directed toward settler farmers. A variety of legal barriers were erected to prevent African farmers, however efficient, from accessing those opportunities. Barring African farmers from selling their crops to colonial marketing boards was justified with the fiction that African farmers could not produce the quality required by the boards. Products needed disproportionately by white farmers with mechanized operations, such as petrol for mechanized agriculture, were subsidized. African farmers in the vast majority of cases continued to practice traditional farming and had access to only local markets for agricultural products. Governments also used tools such as hut taxes and school fees to induce Africans to offer their labor to the colonist sector, especially in southern Africa. Land left in the possession of indigenous people was so limited in productive capacity that such areas soon were regarded as essentially "labor reserves" for employers in the colonial agricultural sector and in towns and cities (Magubane, 1975; Dugard, 1980).

The colonial state, having been inserted at a larger scale than traditional polities (and thus higher in terms of the administrative hierarchy), assumed control over traditional institutions of public administration. Those institutions often had some role in land administration or allocation. Where they did not, the colonial administration gave them new legal authority over land and where they did not fit nicely into a western system of public administration, assigned control of land to local institutions that did. Control of land under custom through traditional authorities was at the heart of the system of indirect rule adopted by the British and to a lesser extent the French colonial authorities (Chanock, 1991, pp. 64–65).

## Islamic Land Law

Dualism is best understood as a way law was used to structure relations between colonists and indigenous people, one that emphasizes the law's role in control and domination of the African population. *But every country in Africa has many more than two distinct legal systems operating within its territory.* Another system is likewise influential and extensive, crossing legal, physical and ethnic boundaries all over Africa: Islamic law, or *Shari'a*. There are around 80,000,000 Muslims in Africa and 20 or so African nations whose inhabitants are mostly Muslims (i.e. in the Sahelian region and in coastal east and southern Africa). There is a significant Muslim community in many more countries in Africa. Islamic land law has melded with custom in interesting ways and in different contexts. Where *Shari'a* is not in force as the law of the state, it may still be in force for specific lands or legal contexts. It may be applied to Muslims as their personal law. Regardless of these limitations, the customary land tenure systems of many African peoples have been influenced by Islamic law.

Islamic law is a law of a different kind than either customary or statutory law. The difference lies in its different source of legitimacy. It is the revealed law of a religious faith. Its rules can ultimately be determined only by religious authorities, though when codified in national statute law, they come before the civil courts of the country concerned.

The legal framework within which *Shari'a* is applied varies from country to country. In countries where most citizens are Muslim, such as Sudan and Mauritania, *Shari'a* applies generally and to land specifically. In other parts of Africa with Muslim minorities, for instance Kenya or South Africa, there are specific statutes from the colonial period which provide for the application to Muslims of the *Shari'a* regimes of marital property and inheritance, including land property, as their "personal law." Where no specific provision is made in national law for application of *Shari'a*, but customary law is recognized, *Shari'a* was and is still often applied to Muslims as their custom. Even where national law does not provide for *Shari'a* to be applied at all, it can be found operative in Muslim communities. It is in the areas of inheritance and marital property that *Shari'a* is most strictly applied. It spread into most of Africa gradually, and its local *kadis* (judges) have historically accommodated customary land tenure under *Shari'a* systems (Anderson, 1960).

Islamic law has interesting affinities with western systems of law. It is a written law and was developed in the market economies of medieval Arabian cities. It has a right of ownership (*melk*) that is readily marketable. Often it clashes with African custom in ways similar to western law. It has a record of melding with African customary tenure systems quite well in some cases, including those of the Sudan and Gambia. These countries provided me with most of my opportunities to observe the interactions between customary and Islamic law.

Islamic law spread into sub-Saharan Africa initially through Muslim merchants from other countries who settled in the African towns where they traded and married local women. We have long had some fascinating accounts of how Islam spread in that period. From the 8th to the 18th century, Islam spread southward across the Sahara into the Sahel. In the 19th century holy wars played a more important role. In this early stage the process was relatively peaceful (Skinner, 1964; Willis, 2018). Because often the rulers were not initially Muslim, Muslims could not legislate their religious law. Local *kadis*, often from the same culture, were not too stringent. Even in northern Sudan, a long-Muslim area in which the ability to trace a line of descent to an Arab forebear was very important, hard liquor (*araki*) was a regular feature of village life when I visited those villages in the late 1970s.

During the colonial period some governments legislated to recognize Islamic law as "the personal law" of Muslims, applicable in cases of family matters, including inheritance. This created a potential for conflict. Islamic law provided for division of property among both male and female heirs, with a daughter receiving only half the share of a son. Customary law usually provided for either patrilineal or matrilineal inheritance. In my experience, in patrilineal communities influenced by Islamic and customary law, those in charge of distributing the property of the deceased will allocate personal property to daughters and real property to sons, achieving compliance with both systems of law. Such compromises tend to be mistrusted by zealots coming back to their home country after religious education in ancient and relatively conservative institutions of Islamic learning in Arab countries. Some are determined to cleanse Muslims from practicing normative materials from outside the Quran (considered by Muslims to have been dictated to the Prophet Muhammad by the Angel Gabriel) and the Hadith (the stories of Muhammad and his teachings, as recorded by his companions) (Tier, 1992).

Miles (2006, p. 100) suggests that the future of customary law must be considered in relation to its increasingly competitive relationship with Islamic law. He writes:

> Whilst both customary law and *Shari'a* have an influence beyond their more narrowly defined area of personal status law, their respective futures are quite different. *Shari'a*, as a reflection of the Islamic faith, will continue to grow and develop its position on the continent with few countries untouched by its impact. On the other hand, save in South Africa, where there has been a considerable body of diligent research, writing and codification, customary law faces an uncertain future.[1]

**Box 4.1 Islamic Law and Custom in Sudan**

I did a course on the spread of Islam in West Africa at the University of Ibadan many years ago, but most of what I know of the interactions between *Shari'a* and African custom comes largely from my five years in northern Sudan, a predominantly Muslim society, where I supervised studies by new graduates of the Law Faculty, appointed to local courts in rural areas (a tradition in the Sudan judiciary). They prepared papers and monographs based on their experience in dispute resolution.[2] We found it was difficult to consider any normative situation in northern and central Sudan and even parts of what has today become South Sudan without considering three bodies of law: the statutory law and common law of state, customary land law and Islamic land law. But for land matters, custom and Islamic law dominated (Abu Rannat, 1960; Mustafa, 1971).

As custom evolved, change in response to Islamic cultural values and law was a gradual process (as I also observed in Gambia), and the two bodies of law became one in the minds of most rural people. They think of their laws as both customary and Islamic, and indeed the notion that it could be otherwise is strange to them.

Examining Islamic law and its interaction with other legal systems in Africa is a good way to introduce a related, important concept: "legal pluralism." Merry (1988, p. 870) defines legal pluralism as the coexistence within a social space of several legal systems. There is nothing exclusively African or colonial about the coexistence of bodies of law with different original sources of authority within a country. It is the dominant structural feature of most legal orders worldwide (de Lemos, 2020). There is a fairly obvious question that arises at this point. What exactly is the relationship between the concepts of "legal dualism" and "legal pluralism"? The terms alone suggest that "legal dualism" might be a smaller, binary version of "legal pluralism," which is not at all the case.

Figure 4.1 illustrates "legal pluralism."

The state's law, the law in its statutes and the jurisprudence of its courts, is the smaller yellow sphere. International law reaches across international boundaries and so is shown overlapping the state sphere. Religious laws do that as well, and in fact have a much more concrete presence in many African countries than does international law. For example, Islamic law applies directly to land in some predominantly Muslim countries or is applied to certain land matters where the parties are Muslim or may govern those matters even absent any recognition by national law. Finally, the diagram shows a small "project land tenure" sphere, the case where a project in effect imposes norms other than those of state law in a project area.[3]

The customary sphere is smaller than that of the state. This is misleading to the extent that it shows customary land tenure as a kind of tenure rather than

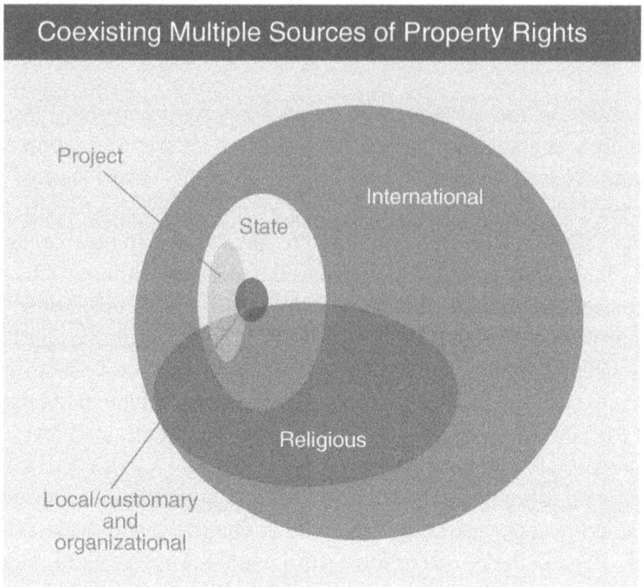


*Figure 4.1* Coexisting Multiple Sources of Property Rights

Source: Meinzen-Dick and Pradhan (2002).

showing all the scores of such systems that exist in most African countries. It seems that this reflects the fact that the polities under customary land tenure are individually smaller than the state and perhaps the legal dominance of state law in relation to custom. If total amounts of land covered by the systems were instead the criterion for the scale of the spheres, the sphere for customary land tenure would be larger than the state's sphere. In fact, a "tenure in practice" map of that nature would show some islands of state and individual ownership floating in a sea of custom.

The authority for alternative systems of law may come from their incorporation by recognition into the law of the state. More often, it comes from their social legitimation by the communities which apply them. Legally, these systems and their tenures may not exist, but they are nonetheless the reality on the ground. If the state may be tempted to ignore them legally, it cannot do so politically. And programs of development, to have any chance of success, must deal with the normative gap between the reality and the normal legal position.

Having so many land tenure systems in play in a country can be complex. When a household lives at the geographical confluence of multiple systems, it can result in a farmed holding of land not just under several tenures (depending on the land use) but under more than one tenure system. In the many African countries where Islamic law, customary law and the law of the state coexist, a successful farmer may hold a house in a suburban neighborhood under a registered title from the state, while farming a parcel of land held under custom and another, larger parcel he rents in from the local mosque's trust land (*waqf*) and grazing stock on a customary pasture in the village where he was born. It can also be messy: in situations where multiple land tenure systems coexist, it is common for those disputing over land to "forum-shop," that is, to try to find an institution (the forum, such as the courts or traditional mediators) which will apply the law which favors them in the dispute. Moreover, disputants unhappy with a dispute resolution in one forum will often seek redress in another forum, under different land tenure rules. Many observers see this as the major disadvantage of legal pluralism.

What does legal pluralism imply? Some may see it as a weakness on the part of national governments. "All states feature legal pluralism," writes de Lemos (2020, p. 191), "and only a limited number of high-capacity states have non-state justice actors firmly under their control. Even in these states, legal pluralism thrives through alternative dispute resolution mechanisms, arbitration agreements and international treaty obligations." In post-conflict settings, state institutions are weak and other actors (traditional leaders or bands of young armed men) may challenge the authority over land of state institutions. De Lemos (2020, p. 191) continues, "In states with lower levels of capacity, legitimacy, or both, seeking support from non state actors can serve as a conflict avoidance tactic or even a broader governance strategy that attempts to secure buy-in from powerful groups that may be skeptical of the state."

Messy or not, this land tenure "pluralism" has value in a political environment that discounts local culture and disempowers local communities. The acceptance of legal pluralism allows the communities concerned to maintain an important element of their culture and self-manage that system. Legal pluralism should not be seen as just a failure of nation-building, but with an appreciation of its positive potentials in terms of identity, autonomy and decentralization.

## Legal Dualism and Legal Pluralism

How are these two concepts related to each other? Legal pluralism describes several laws operating in the same social space. It does not carry with it the baggage of "legal dualism," which has become shorthand for a legal arrangement that allows one group to dominate another, as colonial law did African peoples. It is best to think of "legal dualism" as a negative potential in legal pluralism. It is not necessary that the law of the state recognizes the other legal system. It is sufficient that they exist and be in operation in the same state, policy or other social space. The use of "dualism" and "pluralism" in the land tenure literature is not clear or consistent. There is an ongoing debate on terminology focused on "pluralism" (see Moore, 2014; de Lemos, 2020). My own concern is that seeing the development of Africa's land tenure through the binary perspective of dualism may obscure the role of other forces, such as Islamic law, on the evolution of customary law. I suspect we need to begin with the concept of legal pluralism, using it unmodified to indicate the coexistence of multiple legal systems, and refer to the dualism of colonialism as "colonial dualism" (since other dualisms are possible). We might then use the term "legal dualism" for cases where only two systems are involved, implying nothing further if the term is unmodified. Through research we would want to study more closely the interactions between the different legal and land tenure systems in all cases of legal pluralism. Are there winners and losers, and who are they? How should we evaluate pluralism generally or a particular instance of pluralism in relation to achievement of development objectives?

## The Changing Nature of Colonial Dualism

McAuslan's (2005) influential position paper reminds us that dualism in the colonial context is not just two legal systems in the same social space. It is not just a benign indication that two systems are involved. It is a legal strategy for domination of one group within that social space by another, with winners and losers. Colonialism by conquest inserted a land tenure system that relied to a significant extent on land markets to determine allocation of land into an environment of many small polities with customary allocation-based systems. It allowed the two major system types to continue to function, but it created and enforced a boundary between them that it adjusted to meet its growing needs for land and labor. The land it took from customary systems it gave to colonists in western, marketable tenures while, for the time being, most rural land was left with the "natives" to be used under customary land tenure and the authority of traditional leaders.

Agriculture in the market-mechanism areas was privileged over that of African farmers under custom by (a) the colonial state's statutory protection of marketable rights; (b) its facilitation of their transfer through survey, titling and registration; (c) superior access to credit made available in part through their holding registered rights; (d) a network of regulatory measures that in effect reserved certain key cash crops to European farmers; (e) tax-free import and other subsidies to mechanized agriculture (effectively subsidies to scale); (f) proximity to infrastructure and government services constructed for their use; and (g) preferential access to linkages to European exporters, suppliers and technologies.

By comparison, the land held under custom by Africans was fenced off as much as possible from the developing export/import economy, the holders largely pursuing food security. Their land was not marketable under either customary or statutory law. As a result, this land acquired little or no market value, even in areas where some modernization of farming occurred, and could be taken by the state for the expansion of colonial agriculture without compensation for the value of the land. This created something like a value vacuum in the customary sector. Purchases there were very attractive to colonists and others desiring land, but legal prohibition of cross-system dealings in land under dualism, enforced both by the colonial government and traditional authorities, usually prevented development of a market for land held under custom.

## Why Dualism Still Matters

Tenurial dualism is not merely of historical interest. In most African countries it has survived the transition to independence. The two land tenure systems still coexist uneasily and sometimes clash destructively. Dualism is still the momentous structural reality of African land tenure. At the same time, and as always, it is the interactions between the systems to which we must pay attention because it is those interactions that will determine access to land and security of tenure for those who live on the land. What has changed in those interactions since the colonial dispensation?

Players have changed, as have interests. New national elites have gradually settled into the roles (and lands) occupied by the settlers in the dual tenure system. Economic dualism is gone as a policy, though remnants of agricultural policy that privilege large farms remain, as does the easier access to foreign markets for large operators. The policy issues of agricultural development are now framed in terms of a large farm/small farm dichotomy, each with its advocates, rather than racial privilege. Indirect rule is gone as a means of social control, and central governments pursue decentralization of government functions, including decentralization of land administration and natural resource management programs that challenge the role of traditional authorities under customary land tenure. Dependence on customary authorities by the state has been replaced by competition and tensions.

Most visibly, the new states have launched land tenure reform programs, programs that seek to change the terms on which people access and hold land. These have taken divergent political paths. Some affirm and seek to systematize new forms of community- or state-managed land tenure, while others pursue individualization, both with mixed results. Actual implementation has ranged from thorough to nominal. Other countries have sought solutions to immediate problems, without a long-term strategy related to a vision of economic development.

After independence, the legislative basis for dualism began to crumble. Most African countries decided that all land belonged to the state, but allowed customary tenure to continue, with many countries attempting to gradually shift authority over land away from traditional authorities to new civil authorities. This did not seem to affect the attitudes of the chiefs' subjects, who continued to take land matters to them, but chiefs found it harder to deal with outsiders seeking land in their areas. Intensified by the imbalances created under dualism, customary systems have been hit by demands for land from outsiders, which persist as a cause of rural land dispossession.

The direction of economic change, while fluctuating, has clearly been toward market-driven economics. The reception given by African nations to demands for land by foreign investors is very different from what might have been expected in the immediate post-independence period. African governments have not just permitted, but actively engaged in extensive takings of land from rural communities for investors. These are generating growing resentments and resistance.

This concludes Part I. Part II looks more closely at change processes in land tenure, asking why and how they change and evolve over time and assessing the relationship between land use and land tenure in different land use contexts: farms, pastures, trees/forests and rangelands.

## Notes

1 Miles (2006) is correct in that *Shari'a* is in some ways better positioned for the future than local custom, but he underestimates the potential of customary law and the significance of work on customary law elsewhere in Africa.

2 My teaching and research at the University of Khartoum, funded by the Ford Foundation's Sudan Customary Law Project, was designed and initiated by two other American instructors, Cliff Thompson and Jes Salacuse, who preceded me at the Faculty under Ford Foundation funding.

3 This case is that of a project for which the funder and the government agree on legal rules concerning land for the project area that are different from those generally in force. For example, the USAID project with the Ethiopian Ministry of Agriculture in the early 1970s, in which government in effect created a legal context for landlord–tenant arrangements in the project area that sought to increase modestly the security of tenure of tenants in the project area (Getahun, 2001, pp. 40, 46–47).

## References

Abu Rannat, S.M. (1960). The relationship between Islamic and customary law in the Sudan. *Journal of African Law*, *4*(1), 9–16.

Anderson, J.N.D. (1960). Relationship between Islamic and customary law in Africa. *Journal of African Administration*, *12*, 228–234.

Chanock, M. (1991). A peculiar sharpness: An essay on property in the history of customary law in colonial Africa. *The Journal of African History*, *32*(1), 65–88. https://doi.org/10.1017/S0021853700025342.

Court of Appeal for East Africa, Kenya High Court, Tanzania High Court, Common Market for Eastern and Southern Africa, & Court of Justice (2017). *The East Africa law reports*. Kabale University Library.

de Lemos, M. (2020). Legal pluralism and international development: Introductory notes on a dialogue between the two concepts. *Humanities and Rights Global Network Journal*, *2*(1), 190–233. https://doi.org/10.24861/2675-1038.v2i1.31

Dugard, J. (1980). South Africa's "independent" homelands: An exercise in denationalization. *Denver Journal of International Law & Policy*, *10*, 11–36.

Getahun, H. (2001). *Assault on rural poverty: The case of Ethiopia*. University Press of America.

Magubane, B. (1975). The "native reserves" (Bantustans) and the role of the migrant labor system in the political economy of South Africa. In H.I. Safa & B.M. DuToit (Eds.), *Migration and development* (pp. 225–268). De Gruyter Mouton.

McAuslan, P. (2005, October 31–November 3). Legal pluralism as a policy option: Is it desirable, is it doable? In *UNDP–International Land Coalition conference. Land rights for African development: From knowledge to action*, Nairobi, Kenya. www.undp/drylands

Meek, C.K. (1949). *Land law and custom in the colonies*. Frank Cass & Co.

Meinzen-Dick, R.S. & Pradhan, R. (2002). *Legal pluralism and dynamic property rights* (IFPRI CAPRI Working Paper No. 22). CGIAR Systemwide Program on Collective Action and Property Rights. https://cgspace.cgiar.org/items/06ca69e5-a766-4b1d-a5f0-5581296b076c

Merry, S.E. (1988). Legal pluralism. *Law & Society Review*, *22*(5), 869–896. https://doi.org/10.2307/3053638

Miles, J. (2006). Customary and Islamic law and its development in Africa. *African Development Bank Law for Development Review*, *1*, 99–154.

Moore, S.F. (2014). Legal pluralism as omnium gatherum. *Florida International University Law Review*, *10*(5), 5–18.

Mustafa, Z. (1971). *The common law in the Sudan: An account of the "justice, equity, and good conscience" provision*. Oxford University Press.

Okoth-Ogendo, H.W.O. (1991). *Tenants of the crown: Evolution of agrarian law and institutions in Kenya*. ACTS Press.

Skinner, E.P. (1964). *The Massi of Burkina Faso: Chiefs, politicians and soldiers*. Waveland Press.

Tier, A.M. (1992). Islamization of the Sudan laws and constitution: Its allure and its impracticability. *Recht in* Übersee/*Law and Politics in Africa, Asia, and Latin America*, *25*(2), 199–219.

Willis, J.R. (2018). Introduction: Reflections on the diffusion of Islam in West Africa. In *Studies in west African Islamic history* (pp. 17–55). Routledge.

# Part II

# Change in Land Use and Land Tenure

# 5 Farmland

## African Farms

Farming in Africa has been carried out largely by families on their smallholdings, supplemented by animal husbandry on the commons, both categories of land under customary land tenure.[1] These two categories of land raise different land tenure issues. This chapter focuses on farmland, while the next chapter deals with pasture. From pre-colonial times to well into the 20th century, these households produced food primarily for themselves. If production exceeded those needs, selling what they did not consume or store in local markets, often weekly open-air markets featuring foodstuffs, clothing and livestock. Large-scale commercial production came to Africa with colonialism and mechanization. Where land has been available and they have had access to technology and credit, African farmers have developed small and medium commercial operations. But in most countries, due to lack of access to technology and credit, they remained subsistence farmers. Especially during the colonial period, discrimination and regulatory impediments affecting African farmers meant that commercial farming remained largely limited to lands held by colonists. An exception was the extensive uptake of cash crops by African farmers in the non-settler colonies of west Africa. Stretching back to the colonial period, west African farmers have produced cocoa, tobacco, tea and, more recently, flowers that are exported by air to be sold from flower stands on the streets of European cities. Since independence, a class of African commercial farmers has emerged in the former settler colonies as well, usually by acquiring access to land in western tenures. As customary restrictions on land transactions weakened, they are increasingly accessing larger amounts of land for commercial farming that were held under customary tenure.

Traditionally, a male head of household managed the farm activities, though a wife might autonomously manage a small garden near the family home. She would be assigned fields of her husband's land, but farm them under his instruction, at least when he was present. Hoe cultivation was most common. In areas less plagued by animal diseases, the land was first ploughed using animal traction. Plowing was generally a man's work. His wife or wives and children provided most of the farm labour. Households worked together on community projects such as terracing, hillside afforestation, road repair, protecting crops against wild animals, or

DOI: 10.4324/9781003476429-7

construction of a village school or clinic. On the farm, neighboring households or groups of relatives might assist one another in times of intensive or urgent work, for harvests or when the arrival of locust swarms was anticipated. Most of these households lived in villages, of widely varying size, from ten or 15 households to thousands of households with their fields located outside the settlement area. Many of these very large villages have today developed into towns. There were also communities who lived in scattered hamlets, and some cases of peoples who did not rely primarily on farming, such as hunter-gatherers, migratory pastoralists, nomads and forest dwellers. Many African farms and villages continue to operate in a similar modality today, depending on their degree of exposure to current mainstream economic and social forces.

The management of family farming in Africa has changed over time. Farms managed by male heads of household are described above. Gradually, as opportunities for work on commercial farming operations or in non-farm employment grew, men sought work, which was more lucrative and provided cash needed to participate in a monetizing economy. By the 1970s and the 1980s, men had begun leaving farming to their wives and children and shifting their own labor to off-farm activities. That often required them to travel far and work there through the growing season in the case of commercial farm labor, or even for most of the year as was the case for mining in South Africa. Women took on new tasks on the farm. When the husband was out of communication for long periods, his wife took over its management. In South Africa, African populations were gradually forced off their own land and into so-called "homelands"—arid areas with poor soils on which farming could not support their populations. Here, these patterns of extended absence developed earlier. Both men and women were forced to work far from their homes for extended periods to earn money for remittances to support their families back in the "homelands."

Despite the cultural dominance of the household farming model in Africa, some post-independence governments enacted policies to promote group farming, challenging the family farming model. Such experiments have been implemented in countries with robust socialist orientations (e.g. Tanzania in connection with Nyerere's villagization program, Ethiopia under Mengistu Haile-Mariam, and Mozambique and Guinea-Bissau in their early years after independence). They hoped to achieve economies of scale and a more mechanized commercial agriculture. Instead they suffered from free-rider problems and weak management that can characterize group cultivation. Such programs were generally not well received by the supposed beneficiaries, who were used to family farming on family land. These experiments did not last long. With the de-collectivization programs in China and then in Russia and the other post-Soviet states, the family or other private farming of land has been widely accepted as a best practice for farms, in part because it maximizes labor rather than capital inputs and is comparatively efficient in terms of agricultural production per hectare. This may explain why the family farm remains the predominant form of farming in Africa, even after the major expansion in concession agriculture after 2000 (FAO, 2014).

It is useful to discuss tenure in farmland in terms of two fundamental needs of farmers: getting access to land to farm and securing one's tenure to that land. The first, while more fundamental, has received considerably less attention than it deserves in the writing on land tenure. For African smallholders, who usually have an initial holding as a member of a landholding community, their access issue is how to access additional land to expand production beyond the needs of their household. They have done so through contractual arrangements with other households, but the amount of land available to them on this basis is likely limited and other households are usually not interested in committing their land for more than a year or two. The second, security of tenure, concerns how securely one holds their land, which is a function of the tenure in which one holds the land, but other factors as well. Security of tenure is the subject of hundreds of thoughtful and rigorous research papers. But focusing on the situation in which the farmer already has land is not how the farmer sees the matter. The farmer's whole life is a struggle to get and hold onto land to support one's family, to feed them and to provide other essentials, such as school fees and medical costs.

## Access to Farmland

Most rural landholders in Africa gain access to their first farmland, the core of a viable holding, through their membership in a group defined by common descent or residence or some combination of the two principles. People in customary land tenure systems thus access land as either a lineage member, or by a more general notion of descent (as in a clan), or as a resident of a community (a member of a territorially defined community such as a village or a small town). The descent groups with well-articulated (if not necessarily accurate) lines of descent are referred to as lineage systems. In such systems members establish their membership and a right to lineage land by tracing their ancestry back to an ancestor who earned the rights to the land by first settlement or first cultivation. There are patrilineal, matrilineal and ambilineal systems, and all exist in Africa.

Patrilineal lineage systems trace ancestry in the male line, matrilineal systems in the female line, ambilineal systems through both male and female ancestors. In Africa, patrilineal systems are by far the most common and exist across the continent. There is a "matrilineal belt" that runs from west Africa across the continent into central and southern Africa. Ghana, Nigeria, Zambia, Malawi and Tanzania have matrilineal systems, though these are a decided minority (e.g. 20% in Tanzania). These matrilineal systems often differ as to whether land is passed from uncles to nephews through the female line or from mothers to daughters, the latter being more uncommon. As the value of land and improvements on land have increased, differences between families with respect to the amount of land held and its value have also grown. A nuclear family with more or better land becomes reluctant to see it pass to a nephew and wants it instead to go directly to their own children, in most cases, sons. Daughters inheriting land face increasing pressure to cede their inheritances to their brothers. Matrilineal systems are tending to break down and transition to the patrilineal model. Ambilineal systems, such as that of the Tigray of northern Ethiopia and Eritrea, are uncommon (Hilhorst, 2000; Douglas, 2013). Customary systems provide access to their members as a right, but the access is neither universal nor equal. In lineage systems, how much land one has depends on how many claims to lineage land one has and how many of those can be realized. Heirs in such a system acquire not only land held by one's parent but also any claims that the parent had but was unable to realize during his or her lifetime. Members of a lineage group also realize more or less of their claims depending upon skills and status in the community. The size of household landholdings (all the parcels of land held by the household) can differ substantially between households. In systems where land is allocated to households by community land authorities, some systems call for equal distribution, but others call for shares based on size of household or capacity to cultivate, or some other basis.

In a patrilineal system, all sons may inherit, or priorities may be prescribed, usually showing preference for the eldest or youngest son. A downside of inheritance for the heir in some patrilineal systems is that he must often wait until middle age to inherit the land. Even if he is given land earlier by the father, it may still be held by the father until the father dies. The frustration created by this explains the popularity among younger men of tenure systems that allocate them their own land upon marriage.[2] Additional land may be leased within the customary system or, if there is privately owned land or state-owned land available under leasehold nearby, the farmer can expand his holding in these tenure categories.

In matrilineal systems, land passes in the female line. These systems are often not the mirror-image of patrilineal systems. In many matrilineal systems, even though inherited land moves in female lines, the land goes from one male relative of the woman on whom the claim is based to another man, typically his sister's son. Because in the matrilineal case there can be more than one potential heir, some degree of discretion exists in choosing the heir, and the women of the family often play a significant role in choice of heir. As in patrilineal systems, the household's land is usually managed by a male head of household.

In communities by descent where claims are not based on well-articulated lineages, as in the case of a clan, descent from those considered members of the community is sufficient to establish a putative ancestry from a founding father or mother. Membership does not produce a claim to farmland beyond the land held by the member's parents, though the member can and often does apply to community land authorities for additional land. The group may have adoption or other mechanisms that allow membership to be established by an outsider.

In addition to inherited land, a farmer may borrow or exchange land with others temporarily and may in some cases lease land. If land is relatively plentiful, he may find land on the edge of a cluster of cultivated parcels or in the nearby bush or forest and simply clear and begin to cultivate it. This establishes a customary claim that he hopes will be recognized by the community, whether for a single season when shifting cultivation is practiced, or for longer, even permanently. Different communities exercise different levels of control in this respect.

In most customary contexts a member will not be able to buy land. Sales of land to non-members of the community are traditionally prohibited by most customary land tenure systems, and especially lineage systems. Access to land for members is the core reason for the existence and main function of the lineage system. Any transfer of land taking land out of the lineage group's control undermines the significance and authority of the lineage. If sales take place, they are often disguised as another more acceptable transaction such as a possessory mortgage. The growing acceptance of sales of customary land is discussed later in this chapter. Households may also be able to purchase land if the community's land or other land nearby has been subjected to a tenure reform that makes it marketable or is available on large commercial estates which are being subdivided for sale under individual tenure. Where such a diversity of tenures exists, it is possible for a farmer to hold land under both tenure systems, for example one parcel in a customary land tenure and another in statutory private ownership. This situation is unusual, however, because smallholders in customary communities typically have difficulty affording higher-priced registered land.

## Exclusion from Farmland

While access to land is normally the most important of the rights of membership in the landholding group under customary tenure systems, those systems often discriminate against certain persons or groups, denying them community land. In many societies in west Africa, some artisan classes, particularly ironworkers, are feared for the evil eye or other dark practices and denied land. In other cases, land is denied to devotees of a minority religion, such as Ethiopia's Beta Israel (an Amharic and Tigrinya-speaking indigenous African population in north-west Ethiopia who have followed the Jewish faith since the 14th century or earlier) or Muslims in Orthodox Christian communities. Such discrimination by local communities remains permissible under the constitutions of most African nations.

Gender is the most significant determinant of lack of land access. Most women live in patriarchal societies, and male control of land is a fundamental underpinning of patriarchal dominance. Under these systems women must depend on their husband or other male relatives for access to land. With a few exceptions, women cannot inherit or own land. Until marriage they depend upon their father, during marriage on their husband and after marriage (as widows or divorcees) on their sons or brothers. If a woman holds any right under custom in a patriarchal system, it is usually a right to farm the land of her husband, with varying levels of control over how that land is managed. It is a right contingent on her relationship with the male lineage members and can be lost if the relationship dissolves. In most regions of Africa, agricultural census data shows that female ownership of land is generally around 10%, and otherwise in the 10–20% range.[3]

Even where law and custom allow daughters to inherit land, it does not happen often. For example, under the Islamic law observed in inheritance matters in substantial areas of Africa, a daughter is entitled to inherit a share half the size of her brothers' shares in their father's property which includes his land. In practice the daughter's portion may be cash, gold/jewels, household goods or livestock, while land will go to her brothers. This reconciles the demands of customary law in patriarchal societies that land be kept within the lineage with the requirements of Islamic religious law (Abu Rannat, 1960; Anderson, 1960).

The denial of rights to land for women in patriarchal societies is reinforced by the close relationship between land inheritance and marital residence customs. Because men acquire their land by inheritance from their fathers or allocation from their village, a young man's land tends to be located in or near his home village, though he may lease or borrow land elsewhere. Custom's exogamy requirement for marriage in most patrimonial systems means that young men most often marry wives from villages other than their own. (This is not the position under Islamic law, which encourages cross-cousin marriage.) The new wife, who usually has no right to land in her home village, goes to reside with her husband and helps farm his family land.

**Box 5.1 Rural Women as Land Buyers**

In the Kenya highlands near Nakuru in 1988, I met four women who had decades earlier formed a farming group and were seeking land. Although land in the area was registered in private ownership, they found themselves unable to buy land. The community, they explained, still regarded the land as lineage land which should not be sold, especially to a woman. Instead, they persuaded a chief to lend them a piece of land to farm together.

Once their farm was underway, the women saved enough money from sale of their farm's produce to buy a plot of land with a small house, titled and registered in ownership in a nearby town. They were already renting it out. The rent would provide some support when they were too old to farm. Where available and affordable, land purchase can be an important option for women to have land of their own.

Women are major contributors to the farming economy in Africa but usually have no ownership rights to land they farm while the use rights they hold tend to be tied to a male owner and so are often insecure. This is discriminatory and contrary to the Convention on the Elimination of All Forms of Discrimination against Women. It is also increasingly counterproductive, since women are playing an ever-larger role in decision-making concerning family farming. Whereas several African governments have at least partially addressed this unfortunate situation through legal reforms, their enforcement in practice remains weak at best.

Any assessment of access under customary tenure must recognize that it both provides households with extraordinarily broad access to farmland and provides it as a *right* to men and their families. At the same time, it must recognize that the nature of the access provided to women leaves them with no land of their own, little ability to influence decision-making in the household and little say in community matters. It also renders them radically insecure in the event of divorce or widowhood. It is, ultimately, the most unacceptable feature of customary land tenure.

It bears reiteration that access is a dimension of land tenure that has been relatively neglected compared to security of land tenure. Current trends in land policy will reinforce or threaten that relatively broad access.

## Security of Land Tenure

As early as the 19th century, classical economists debated which tenures provided the greatest incentives to farmers to invest and produce. The element of tenure which most concerned them was the duration of the tenure (how long the land could be held). If a landholder is not going to hold land for long enough to cover the costs of an investment, he or she is unlikely to make them. Today, those seeking to understand whether a farmer holds his land securely enough to incentivize investments looks at a wider range of issues. If there is a consensus on any issue regarding land tenure, it is that "security of land tenure" is a good thing. The term is invoked solemnly at every development conference. Researchers assemble vast samples of farmers and their activities to determine whether it exists in a particular context.

If you listen carefully, however, the phrase is being used in quite different ways by different specialists. At its most general, "security of land tenure" means that a landholder is not in danger of losing his or her land, while insecurity of tenure means that the danger of loss does exist. But what of the case where the risk of loss is high, but the landholder is unaware of the risk? Then the matter gets more complicated.

Security of tenure is about an attitude and expectation. When an economist asks, "Is there security of tenure in this case?" the question being asked is "Does the tenure in which the land is held provide the landholder with confidence that he or she will hold the land long enough to benefit from an investment, sufficiently to want to make the investment?" This is about the effect of tenure on farmer incentives to invest. Economists specify the needed attributes of the tenure (the bundle of rights in the tenure) and use their presence or absence to decide if security of tenure exists. Those attributes are considered by most economists to be (a) tenure of a duration sufficiently long for him or her to recover costs and profit from an investment in the land and (b) a tenure with a bundle of rights sufficiently robust to protect the landholder for that period of time.

Usually, the rights treated as essential are the right to exclude others and the right to manage and use the land and take its product. These are tenure issues and those assessing security of tenure will usually know under what set of rights that farmer holds. Many economists also include a right to sell the land, but others—including this author—argue that a right to sell exposes the landholder to risk of loss of the land through forced or fraudulent land dealings and thus reduces tenure security.

Both tenure security and marketability are important to agricultural development, but it is clearly preferable to deal with each in its own right. As to duration, "sufficiently long" is going to differ for the crop being grown and other inputs. A smallholder planting a food crop and deciding to apply a chemical fertilizer will likely have the benefit of the fertilizer for one to two years and so will need to expect to recover the cost of the fertilizer in that time frame. In the case where trees are planted as a crop, it may take ten or 20 years to recover the investment. But there are also risks of land loss that have little to do with tenure, such as the seizing of one's land by a powerful official, a conflict that results in displacement or the inability to use one's land, its expropriation for a highway, or a lava flow from a nearby volcano.

Finally, any investment in farming is subject to a variety of risks that might not result in land loss but could result in the loss of one's crops: drought or flooding, locusts, diseases of plow animals, an epidemic of a human disease, or a crop disease. The result is that many smallholders farm under a cloud of risk so considerable that land tenure-related risk may be a relatively small part of it. Still, land tenure is a factor over which governments have some control and so, if it is clear that it is creating serious insecurity of tenure, discouraging investment and preventing increased productivity, governments need to know about it and, if they are able, address it through tenure reform. But it should be appreciated that it's very challenging to measure the extent of objective insecurity of tenure. Doing so would require reaching conclusions about the probabilities of a whole host of risks to losing one's land.

There is an alternative approach to assessing security of tenure, simpler and straightforward: ask the farmer if he or she thinks their tenure is secure. The farmer's perception of his or her security is at least as important as the actual risk of loss of land, because *it is one's perception of security or insecurity* that determines one's inclination to invest. But framing questions effectively to get at that perception is not simple. For example, a question might be framed: "Do you feel confident that you will still hold this land ten years from now?" A landholder may be reluctant to admit to a vulnerability to loss. If others knew of it, they might be able to take advantage of it in some fashion. It may be more productive for the researcher to explore perceptions of security of tenure and possible causes of any insecurity in relation to other, similarly situated farmers in the community first and only gradually bring the discussion back to the situation of the landholder being interviewed.

This attitudinal approach to measuring tenure security has another problem. The answers it gets tend to reflect not just insecurity due to the tenure in which the land is held, but also insecurity due to other factors that might cause loss of land. The farmer answering the question of whether they perceive they might lose rights or access to their land in the next ten years may also give an answer based in part on other non-tenure factors. If some insecurity is acknowledged, it's necessary to follow up and explore how far tenure is the cause of the insecurity acknowledged.

An alternative is for the researcher to work from the other direction to determine if security of tenure exists. The questions posed to the informants would concern what investments have been made and the duration needed to recover the costs. The presence of investments suggests some degree of tenure security and the choice of investments may give some sense of its extent. Tenure security, though sometimes discussed as if it were a yes or no question, is a matter of context and degree. For example, is tenure secure enough to encourage tree planting or terracing a hillside parcel? Does this farmer (or most similarly situated farmers) feel sufficiently secure to invest in hedgerows to prevent wind erosion? While investments beyond the labor of the family and their animals may indicate a degree of security tenure, their absence should not be taken as evidence of insecurity, as this may be caused by other factors.

If the researcher is familiar with the community being researched, he or she should be able to come up with a set of very useful questions to assess land tenure security. It may be helpful to use two or more of these approaches together and triangulate for a reasonable estimate of security of tenure. Where the results appear inconsistent, working out the reasons for the inconsistency can yield valuable understandings of tenure security. In a large farm survey, one may only have a single question for tenure security, which could generate findings that are seriously misleading.

While land tenure and its security can be very important in some circumstances, in other circumstances it may not matter much. A poor smallholder couple, who must plant a crop to feed their family, is unlikely to behave differently because they feel tenure insecure. It is the only land they have, and they have no other options to feed their family. The household, even where it is risky, will invest all the family's labor in their farm.

Finally, farmers' responses to increases of security of land tenure are highly contextual. Working in China on consultancies for the World Bank in the 1980s, I was puzzled by how strongly farmers had responded to the very modest incentives offered by the simple production contracts they received under the new Household Responsibility System of land tenure. That was the system that was hurriedly devised when China's farmers, in desperation, abandoned collective farming in the face of widespread famine after 1984 and returned to household farming. What I gradually appreciated was that farmers were not reacting to those specific incentives but to the promise of a return to family farming. This political aspect of responses to tenure security needs to be borne in mind when assessing a positive reaction to a tenure security improvement in other countries that have experienced extensive land conflict and tenure insecurity, including radical disruption to or abolition of their customary land tenure systems, such as in Rwanda and Ethiopia. The same improvement in land tenure in another African country with a reasonably stable customary land tenure system might get little or no investment response from farmers.

## Security of Customary Tenure

Until now, this section has dealt with land tenures generally. Until relatively recently, policy makers and project planners in mainline development institutions tended to assume that customary land tenure does not provide secure land tenure. This was primarily rooted in misleading colonial characterizations of them as "communal," "traditional" and "backward." In 1988, the Kenyan sociologist Shem Migot-Adholla and I launched a series of studies in several African countries which examined security of tenure under customary land tenure systems as compared with the experience of land titling and registration programs that sought to replace customary land tenure in the hope of delivering land tenure security. The studies, co-funded by the United States Agency for International Development and the World Bank, led to the conclusions that security of tenure was satisfactory under most customary land tenure systems at that time and that, where pressures on land were high and commercialization proceeding, customary tenure systems evolved to provide stronger transfer rights and, in some cases, full alienability (Bruce & Migot-Adholla, 1994). This provides support for Shipton's (1989) position that given the potential of African land tenure to evolve, there was no need for heavy-handed "reforms" of African customary land tenure. Other researchers have reached the same or similar conclusions (e.g. Toulmin & Quan, 2000; Cotula, 2007).

If holdings under customary tenures are reasonably secure in many cases, and may be relied upon to evolve, it is important to add that there are some cases in which they are decidedly insecure. In Eritrea, under the customary tenure *diessa* all the farmland was redivided and redistributed among the households of the community by lottery every seven years (Nadel, 1946). In his book on Amhara land tenure in Ethiopia, Hoben (1973) describes a "communal" tenure system in which competing and incompatible claims to land under custom drive relatives apart rather than providing any sense of solidarity.

Whether land rights will be insecure under a customary land tenure system will depend on both the rules and the context. Any insecurity created by the internal dynamics of these systems has been modest compared to that created by external actors. The most significant of those actors are governments and their agents, who take land for public or personal purposes using the power of the state. In some countries the state has from colonial times asserted its ownership of land held under customary land tenure. Alternatively, if customary rights are recognized by national law, agents of government may abuse the state's constitutional power of eminent domain, which allows the state to take land from owners in the public interest. This is abused by officials when they take land from customary communities to create huge "concessions" for outside investors.

These land grabs often target areas of land used less intensively, such as seasonal pastures, land with water sources used sporadically by nomads or land reserved by communities as expansion areas. This is land appropriation on a larger scale than in the past, and as populations have grown and land become scarcer, the problem of displacement or incorporation into production for the commercial farming operations of concessionaires has become far more serious. Chapter 8 provides a full discussion of the "The Great Land Grab" that developed in Africa after 2007 in response to forecasts of world food shortages. Beyond the harm directly caused to households whose land is taken, a pervasive insecurity of tenure is created, a sense that no land is safe. A sudden and unexpected land taking can generate real shock and insecurity over a substantial area, even if the land taken is small. I was made acutely aware of this later in my research in Tigray when I stumbled into the charged aftermath of a taking that had occurred seven years prior to my research there. That experience is described in Box 5.2.

**Box 5.2 Fear of Government Land Takings in Tigray, Ethiopia**

In the late 1960s the Ethiopian government took a parcel of land on a mountaintop in its northern province of Tigray. The land was taken to build a microwave communication station, a link in a chain of stations between Asmara and Addis Ababa. The community within which the parcel was located was 15 kilometers off any road, and the villagers pretty much managed their own affairs. I found them suspicious of outsiders, including their own government.

The land expropriated was a poor but cultivable field, ancestral (*risti*) land that had been farmed for centuries by the descendants of a first settler. The local farmers, in this community and those nearby, were stunned when the parcel was taken. Customary land tenure was recognized under the Ethiopian Civil Code, but neither customary law nor the country's statutes offered standards for valuing for compensation purposes land which was not marketable. The farmer who owned the land was given a job guarding the station as compensation. He and the community considered this inadequate compensation. The farmer complained to me that he had four sons, asking how could one divide a job among four sons?

The microwave station was a small concrete building full of electronics. Beside it on the mountaintop was mounted a large white cinema-sized screen which received the signal and bounced it onward to another screen on another mountain, and so on. It was built and operated by Nippon Electric under a contract with the central government. Once a month, a microbus with three or four Japanese technicians would drive up the winding dirt access road to the station to check the state of the equipment. A crowd of locals would gather and listen as the technicians called up and down the line, asking "ok?" and being told "ok!" After many such exchanges, they climbed back into their microbus. It wound down the mountain to go to the next station.

I arrived on the scene seven years after the land was taken, intent on doing my dissertation research on land tenure in a neighboring community, which had an interesting tenure history. Within days of my arrival, a rumor circulated that the foreigner asking about land was scouting the area for the Japanese and the government to identify more land for another microwave station. I spent weeks carefully explaining my purpose in doing the research, buying scores of beers at a roadside bar, and showing my respect for the local officials by driving them to weddings in neighboring towns in my research vehicle, a diminutive Fiat 600. I was successful in allaying fears and got started on my research.

A couple of months later, I was blindsided. I had spent a very pleasant afternoon in the hut of the elderly *chikashum* (chief) of the community bordering the community that was the principal focus of my study, the community in which the land had been taken for the microwave relay station. He was happy to talk with me over the coffee his wife brewed in a small black clay coffee pot over a few live coals. It was smokey, but bearable. He ranged widely over land matters in the neighboring community, including their land scandals, disputes and factions, but never mentioning names. My research assistant had come with me and the chief's *nechilebas*, a grizzled farmer who served as the *chickashum*'s part-time community policeman, was with us as well. He crouched in the shadows of the hut, leaning on his vintage rifle, possibly from the guerrilla war waged by Ethiopian patriots against Mussolini's troops during the brief Italian occupation in the 1930s.

As the afternoon wound down, my assistant reminded me that it was growing dark and asked if it was time for us to begin our return journey to the small town on the main road where we were staying. I responded "ok." At that, the local policeman jumped to his feet and pointed his rifle at me. "He's speaking Japanese!" he shouted. Confusion ensued. Now it was all too clear. My real purpose in being there was revealed. I was clearly connected to the technicians from the microwave station. After my attempts to explain failed to pierce the cloud of suspicion created, we thanked the *chickashum* for his hospitality and hastened back to our borrowed mules. It was a dreary ride.

I thought my research, at least in this area, might be over, but after two weeks I was able to resume my fieldwork. The local elementary school teachers in the roadside town, with whom I had shared my story, had sent their students home to their communities with the message that "ok" was indeed an English rather than Japanese word.

## Insecurity of Tenure

There are groups that are subject to discrimination and hold land only on a relatively insecure basis. Women do much of the hard work of farming in African societies but own little land of their own, principally because of the prevalence of patrilineal inheritance and patrilocal residence, reviewed in the discussion of access earlier in this chapter. In that situation, a woman cannot inherit land and is dependent on her husband for access to land during marriage. Lack of her own land seriously disadvantages women throughout the marriage, becoming acute when women are widowed or divorced. In the case of divorce, the divorcee will usually be sent back to her home village where she may or may not be accommodated by her birth family. If the husband dies, the widow may be driven from the village by her late husband's relatives, or she may be allowed to remain in the village, especially if there are children, particularly male children, to care for them and their land until they reach majority. After that, her access to land depends on her sons. In some societies, a widow who wants to stay in her husband's village may be required to marry (as a second or third wife) a brother of her deceased husband. Where a man dies of AIDs, his wife is usually driven from the community and even in cases of COVID-19, widows and children of men who died of the disease have been increasingly stripped of the deceased's land by his father or brothers (Doss et al., 2015).

Knowing these outcomes may occur at some point imposes a high degree of tenure insecurity on women, even during their marriages. This insecurity is compounded by dramatic power differentials in the marriage where men often are the ones to exert primary control over family land and its produce, even if she is the one to farm it. Despite African women's major role in agricultural production, even as decision-makers, their interests and perspective have usually been treated as irrelevant in assessing security of tenure on a household basis. How does a husband's life-long tenure affect land investment decisions of his wife, whose access to land depends upon a marital relationship which itself offers little security? Traditionally, men in most African societies control income from field crops and large livestock. Women control certain production areas, such as a home garden or trees in the family compound and may even be allowed to keep money earned when they sell produce grown on these plots. Women often have a customary use—as opposed to ownership—right to land from their husbands, but it is not so much a right bestowed by the community as a right which is part of the marital contract. It is not a right to a particular parcel of land but to "some land," an entitlement subject to manipulation by the husband. Even during marriage, a woman's lack of a right to land of her own results in her being treated as a lesser member of the community, with a lesser voice in community affairs and little role in community decision-making (Massay, 2020).

The failure of customary land tenure to provide rights to women is stark and unacceptable. In earlier times, when divorce was unknown, women were more likely to be more secure in their marriages and thus in their access to land, though it perhaps also came at a cost to their agency and self-determination. This is changing rapidly. I was amazed at how common divorce was in the villages I visited in the 1970s in Ethiopia. In the wake of the land reforms after 1974, when men and women were given equal entitlements of land, there was a dramatic increase in divorces. Attempts to legislate reforms in customary inheritance and family property law have generally been vigorously resisted by men. Some tenure reforms have made things decidedly worse for women. In tenure reform programs that have provided a right to sell land, that right has been given to the male head of household, empowering a husband to sell the family land out from under his family, something that would have been unacceptable under custom. This issue goes to the heart of the lineage system, and relying on evolution to work the needed reform will likely not succeed based on the experiences in more developed countries. The necessary statutory reforms also do not come easily, and again are not enough. They will only be enforced when women manage to draw upon other sources of power and mobilize on a broad base. Experiences with reforms of women's land rights are discussed in Chapter 17.

Are there other groups that are similarly disadvantaged with respect to land access? In the global land tenure literature, tenants (those who lease the land they farm from others) are a group seen as systematically disadvantaged, especially where they have little or no land of their own. Extensive tenancy based on radically skewed distribution of land is not common in Africa. Those who are members of landholding communities will have some land of their own. Generalization concerning tenancy is risky. Tenancy is a very flexible tenure, with several key terms left to the parties to specify. In most smallholder systems in Africa, tenancy performs benign functions, such as providing needed labor and draft power in the case of landholding households who, because of illness of the farmer or a plow animal, cannot cultivate their own land. There are also cases of "big men," such as chiefs or officials, who hold more land than they can farm and lease it out. Most leases in these customary contexts are annual leases, often involving sharecropping arrangements in which the rent is stated as a fraction (one-third is common) of the production of the rented land. The fraction depends upon a variety of factors, including who provides inputs such as seed or farm implements. Such leases are relatively insecure, if only for their brevity. For the landless, the terms to access are usually unattractive, but usually they lack other options.

This discussion of tenure in farmland has so far focused heavily on cases and situations of customary rights. Much smaller but significant amounts of land in Africa are held on leasehold or usufruct from the state, principally where land reforms have redistributed land and in countries that have legislated replacement of custom with statutory tenure. That statutory tenure is usually a lease or usufruct (use right), with the right vesting in an applicant who will usually be the male head of household, but in some cases may be a female household head, perhaps a widow. There are usually no provisions regarding the rights of wives of those who have been granted leasehold/usufruct rights, though in a few countries (e.g. Zimbabwe), there are some limited protections for wives. (Mutopo, 2014, discusses the Zimbabwe experience.)

Forest fallow, because it is exercised over a large area and the land under cultivation changes after a few years, does not comport well with permanent rights. There may or may not be significant customary controls over where a household moves next. The importance of security of tenure at household level will depend on the likelihood of returning to land they have used in the past. Irrigated farming is another mode of farming that may require a different approach to security of tenure. On irrigation schemes, other factors condition land rights. On large schemes where the state has incurred major costs in the development of dams and irrigation, the state is inclined to consider access to the irrigated land a privilege, conditional on satisfactory performance, rather than a right. On the large state-managed irrigation schemes such as the Gezira and the Rahad in Sudan, cultivation is carried out by households on plots allocated to them by scheme administrators on relatively weak tenure. These administrators directly assume functions such as crop selection, seed and input provision, canal maintenance, aerial spraying and marketing. A portion of the costs incurred by the state are deducted from the share of the revenues paid to the cultivator (Fruzzetti & Östör, 2019).

## Sales of Farmland

Many economists and other development specialists consider the ability to sell land a critical resource requirement for development. De Soto (2000) and others argue that the market will move land into the hands of more efficient producers, since those who have the greatest capacity to produce will purchase land from those who have lesser capacity, resulting in improved efficiency and higher production. In addition, while land is valuable whether it can be sold or not, land which can be sold has new and different potentials and so is more valuable. Many also contend the ability to transact in land will give rural producers access to formal credit for the first time, since they now have a marketable, and thus mortgageable, asset. Some economists argue that tenure reform to introduce marketability of rural land will empower African smallholders, primarily because it will allow them to use it as collateral (security) for loans to invest in their land. If an asset is not marketable, a formal sector lender will not take it as collateral. If the borrower were to default on repaying the loan, it will want to recover its losses by taking legal action to sell the land provided as collateral. A bank is not in the business of becoming a landlord or a real estate developer. It has no interest in land as security for a loan unless that parcel can be sold.

Unfortunately, experience has shown that commercial banks will generally not extend credit to smallholders, even if they have marketable land. This is because they cannot meet other loan criteria, including a banking credit history. Moreover, banks argue the administrative costs involved in the exercise of due diligence for the small amounts of loans sought by smallholders and the relative legal costs of foreclosure makes such loans entirely unprofitable for the banks. Improved credit access is thus not a convincing argument for a need to make land under customary land tenure marketable. De Soto (2000) is clearly misleading on this point (Bruce, 2012).

There are, however, other ways in which customary land holders are disadvantaged by lack of marketability. Under the law of the state, lack of a market value for land often means that the value of the land is not recognized or badly understated. If the land is taken by the state, the customary holder usually receives little or no compensation for the land itself. De Soto (2000) is right in his argument that the appreciation of land values that would come with marketability in the long term would lead to the development of domestic capital. In that long run, consideration would need to be given to how to divide the benefit of that appreciation between owners, who have invested in the land, and the state whose public investments have also contributed to the appreciation of value. Capturing that value has been an important element in land policy in some economies in Asia.

Registration of land rights in a marketable tenure such as private individual ownership immediately increases the value of the parcel registered. This is a phenomenon most often noted in urban and peri-urban contexts. In urban areas the jump in value can be dramatic. This usually does not happen except on a very modest scale in rural areas under custom, especially where there is not already a market for land.

**Box 5.3 A Conundrum: Small Farms, Efficiency and Land Markets**

The promotion, and especially forcing, of legal change to allow sales of land under custom does not produce the efficiency gains expected. There is a good deal of evidence that small farmers are more efficient land users than larger landholders. They use family labor, which is easy to manage and cheap compared to hired labor. Farm households often work so hard that economists write of their "self-exploitation" (Carter & Michuda, 2019). Mechanization, which requires larger farms, saves on labor, which families have, but makes less efficient use of land than family farms cultivated by more traditional means that allow more discriminating use of different soils on the holding and their location in different microclimates (Feder & Feeny, 1991). While economies of scale may exist in primary processing and marketing, there is little to suggest that they exist in production itself, at least where hired labor is not very expensive as in many developing countries. The appearance of efficiency in large farming operations is often due to state subsidies, one of the more important of which is the waiving of the import taxes on fuel and farm machinery. That impression of efficiency also arises from a confusion of efficiency with the appearance of modernity: surely that shiny tractor must make for greater efficiency than the African smallholder's plow and hoe? Not necessarily, if its actual costs in terms of access, maintenance and fuel are considered, subtracting subsidies from the government.

*The conundrum is this: while development specialists were confident that new markets in land formerly under custom would move land into the hands of the most efficient of these small farmers, this is not what has in fact happened.* Instead, in most studies of the development of a market in land held under custom, efficient small farmers are not acquiring, but rather selling land and selling it to larger and often less efficient producers. These are usually outsiders to the seller's community. Binswanger et al. (1993) concluded that differential credit access explains the conundrum. "Credit market imperfections" prevent small efficient farmers from gaining access to the credit that would allow them to participate as buyers in the land market. Commercial lenders tend to be leery of agricultural lending in the first place because of the inherent risks involved in farming, principally due to dependence upon the weather as well as vulnerability to pests, diseases and often volatile markets. They are even more reluctant to deal with smallholders whose demands are for small loans in often remote locations where there is limited data on land values and uncertain prospects for resale of the land in the event of foreclosure. Often too it can be difficult to foreclose on such a holding because of community resistance and customary claims from within the community. Finally, the banks are much happier with a loan applicant with a savings account and a steady record of salary deposits or who has borrowed money for other purposes and repaid his or her loan. Lack of a marketable title to land is only one obstacle to smallholders in obtaining commercial credit and giving them a marketable title does little to solve that problem.[4]

Because the majority of smallholders farming land under custom are unable to borrow from formal credit institutions, the land market that develops is a one-way street. Smallholders holding under custom sell their land cheaply because the transactions are not legally protected. They sell but rarely can buy land, resulting in the concentration of land rights in fewer, wealthier and often less efficient operators. The poor, if they can buy, must buy in extra-legal land markets, where land is less expensive and tenure less secure. Over time, this increases concentration of land in the hands of wealthier outsiders, the development of increasing landlessness in the rural sector and migration into towns and cities. This was a serious concern of the independence era generation of African leaders and remains a serious issue, not only due to equity concerns, but because governments are frightened by the rapid development of a politically volatile unemployed class.

The effectiveness of projects and programs that promote titling and registration of land under custom along with greater freedom to sell and mortgage it has been placed in question by their failure to improve access to credit and foster greater agricultural efficiency. Still, such projects have much to offer. Especially in those cases where broad insecurity of tenure exists, they can positively affect farmer investment in land even without improving credit access, through their assurance effects.

## Transactions and Sales of Land under Custom

Land sales are problematic under most customary land tenure systems. This is not a simple cultural preference on the part of those communities, but a reflection of the disinterest of farmers in selling their land, its loss being something they fear rather than desire, and the fact that permanent alienation of land to outsiders undermines the social and political basis for community-based governance of land.

Some customary systems over time come to accept sales of land, but most resist it resolutely. Sales are rare and often surreptitious, in part because customary tenure systems allow a range of other transactions that meet some of the same needs: gifts, loans, leases and exchanges. Shipton (1989, p. 58) writes that customary landholders under African tenure systems can often transfer land:

> for instance, by loan, swap, inheritance, devolution inter vivos, gifts, barter, pledge, share contract, encroachment, rental, or sale. These English terms do not reflect the variety, the flexibility and inventiveness, and the possible re-negotiability inherent in land dealings in many parts of rural Africa. Terms

> like “market” can become cognitive straightjackets for the analyst. Across the continent, local people do engage in land deals, whether by sale or not; and frequently these fail to show up in survey results because researchers are not asking the questions in the right way, or in enough different ways.

These can fulfill some of the needs of farmers for flexibility and additional land where sales are not possible and in cases where a sale would not meet the need because the need is or may be transitory. Deininger (2003) argues that leasehold markets have potential in this regard.

When land sales are illegal (i.e. without registered title), an extra-legal land market (sometimes called “black” or “grey” markets) may develop if there is sufficient frustrated demand for land. Such transfers are sometimes referred to as “informal” sales, the term signifying that the transaction was done outside the parameters of national law. I find the term “extra-legal” preferable to “informal.” Informal suggests something casual, less developed, of lesser dignity, even less enforced.

There is a need for care in generalizing about land sales, especially extra-legal sales. Because of a desire to see customary land tenure as evolving toward a land market that includes sales, some of those assessing the extent of sales have unwittingly elevated temporary or partial transactions to mean sales transactions (Chimhowu & Woodhouse, 2006; Colin & Woodhouse, 2010). It is also important to be aware, especially in thinking about whether a land market is functioning, that a few sales do not a land market make, at least a market with the virtues we associate with markets (e.g. one with competitive pricing). Nor can it be assumed that that change is unidirectional. Marketization of land can stall and even roll back. In Côte d’Ivoire, development of a land market was fueled by locals returning home after displacement by war. When the demand was satisfied, the market quieted, only to flare again when the earlier buyers reached old age and wished to convert some land to cash rather than leave it to their heirs. In other cases, plots acquired on the market, which are the individual property of the purchaser, have sometimes been transformed into family property when the purchaser died and returned to governance by customary land tenure (Colin & Ayouz, 2006).

It is not uncommon for parties to differ over the nature of a transaction. This is especially true when the parties come from different ethnic groups with different cultural assumptions about property. What one party describes as a sale may not be seen as a sale by the other. It may be that the transaction is not a land sale in the full western sense of a complete and permanent transfer of the right concerned. This often happened in private transactions between colonists and local Africans, and it happens among Africans as well. For example, even in the case of a transaction involving monetary payment, the transaction may still be sufficiently embedded within the culture that traditional land authorities see themselves “allocating,” rather than selling, land.

A well-documented example of this in west Africa is the *tutorat* institution, which involves the relationship between a land-providing and land-receiving group. It originated prior to the introduction of cash crops and has evolved over generations. Land was provided by communities in areas with plentiful land with the aim of attracting new farmers to sparsely populated areas. Those invited were an important asset; land had little value without people to farm it. The *tutorat* institution provided land to the in-comers and involved a commitment on their part to support the social order of the community. The institution was formalized through periodic gifts expressing gratitude from in-comers to land providers. As population densities rose and land became scarcer, the periodic gifts became monetized. Phased planting of perennial crops such as cocoa gave rise to permanent farms. The process has become more individualized over time and now young men access land in this manner without involvement of their family. This individualization is in very different stages in different countries in west Africa. The *tutorat* remains embedded in custom. Such land cannot be sold under custom, and the institution retains its character as a relationship rather than a simple transaction at a moment in time.

How long have sales of land under custom been going on? There are historical records of extra-legal sales of land under custom in many African countries, including Togo, Sierra Leone, Nigeria, Ghana, Madagascar, Ethiopia, Senegal and Zambia, from surprisingly early dates.[5]

My own observation was that by the 1970s, sales of land did occur from time to time in some, but not many, of the communities I visited in Africa that held their land under custom. In some exceptional cases they were relatively open. In most cases they were surreptitious or not mentioned to strangers, and sometimes disguised as another sort of transaction, such as a long-term lease or a possessory mortgage. They were, I was reasonably sure, sales in fact if not in form. I have on three occasions been told, in the village context, that sales are contrary to custom, only to be offered land for sale in a later private conversation, in all cases by a chief. In one case, in Tigray Province, Ethiopia, the offer was particularly clear. I wondered about the genuineness of the offer. This was a very traditional community. If I had pursued the matter, would the chief have found a piece of land for me? Or was it a scam, an offer to sell something that could not possibly be sold, a parallel to the story of the con man who sold the Brooklyn Bridge to a naïve visitor to New York? Or would the chief have used my expression of interest to denounce me as having lied about my intentions for studying land tenure in his village? I dropped the matter. The last possibility seemed a little too likely.

Several months later, in another district further north in Tigray, I stumbled on a record of land sales. At a parish church, a priest offered to show me the principal treasure of the church, a Bible he called the Golden Gospel (*wengele zework*). It was old, leather-bound and hand-written in Ge'ez, the liturgical language of the Ethiopian Orthodox Church. Having paged through, admiring the calligraphy, I noticed there were several notes in a much rougher hand on the end pages. They proved to be records of a half-dozen dealings in land, rudimentary, very brief (a sentence or two) and somewhat cryptic: the nature of the transaction not specified, just the names of parties, land location and a cash figure. Some were signed, and some dated. Several were from the 1940s, and there were others from the next 50 years, but none had been registered in the ten years before I saw them. That period of most frequent activity roughly paralleled the years of the brief Italian occupation of Ethiopia. In traditional communities in northern Ethiopia, disguised sales often took the form of a possessory mortgage, a situation where a creditor of a land owner takes possession of the latter's land until the loan is repaid, though sometimes the intent is to not repay and thereby transfer the land to the creditor.

It is also possible for sales of customary land to emerge and become common with remarkable rapidity. An instance from Mozambique in Box 5.4 provides an example.

**Box 5.4 The Development of a Market in Customary Land in Nampula, Mozambique**

In Mogovolas District in Nampula Province, Mozambique, a market in land under custom has developed. Its relatively rapid emergence is striking because at independence customary systems did not accept customary land sales and, since independence, the state in Mozambique has consistently sought to prevent policy that would legalize transactions in rural land. By way of historical background, the ruling party at independence in 1975 was FRELIMO, a Marxist party with a dim view of private land ownership and a deep suspicion of markets in land rights. FRELIMO warned that land markets would concentrate the land in fewer hands and increase landlessness. The country's independence constitution abolished customary land tenure, declared all land owned by the state and specifically prohibited sales of land. The government embarked on a program of land takeovers for large state farms and launched attempts to collectivize agriculture on both colonial-era Portuguese commercial farms and in the customary land tenure sector. The FRELIMO government's attempts to assume control of land angered traditional authorities and contributed to the emergence of RENAMO, an insurgent movement. A bloody civil war lasted from 1977 to 1992 and ended in mutual exhaustion, without a decisive victory for either party. While FRELIMO was still in power, RENAMO controlled large parts of the country. Vast numbers of citizens had been displaced from their homes and fields. In the first years after the war, land policy was something one could not discuss publicly. The unenforceability of the old land policy was clear. RENAMO demanded recognition of customary land tenure.

A national land conference led to the 1997 Land Law (Law no. 14/97) which retained state ownership of land but recognized customary land tenure systems as legally protected systems of use rights on that land. It limited transfers of rural land, including customary land, to four cases: (i) through direct state allocation as a consequence of an explicit request and following the approval of a required land use plan; (ii) by allocation in the context of customary land right systems ("allocation" interpreted as an administrative act by community land authorities); (iii) by simple occupation, individually or collectively, without the blessing of community or state, provided that it is in good faith (that is, without intent to violate the rights of others); and (iv) indirectly, through the authorized transfer of improvements located on the plot resulting in the effective transfer of the land itself. It does not provide for sale of customary land, but evasions of the law occur where demand for land is strong.

A 2008 study of the development of markets in land rights (Manicane, 2008) found that sales of customary land had become increasingly common in Mogovolas District, 90 miles from the coast in densely populated Nampula Province. The main ethnic group in Mogovolas are the Macuas, a matrilineal people, most of whom are Muslim. Virtually all land in Mogovolas is held under customary land tenure and formalization of land rights through government programs is quite limited. Only 7% of the respondents hold state-issued land certificates, and they are all larger farmers (above four hectares), private sector investors and/or absentee landowners. There are some concessions and non-farm employment in the area, but family farming predominates. Less than 10% of those interviewed for the study had any knowledge about the 1997 land law and their rights under it. Those who knew of the prohibition of rural land sales tended to ignore it, and the government had no capacity to enforce the prohibition.

Mogovolas has a well-developed extra-legal land market. The study survey showed that plots allocated by the state represented less than 7% of plots, those allocated under the customary systems 27%, and those simply occupied without customary allocation 41%. The remaining quarter of the surveyed households (25%) in the area had acquired land through the extra-legal market in the last five years in comparison to 11% of households nationally. Extra-legal land sales had existed for a long time but began to rapidly grow 15 years before the study when displaced people settled in the area after the civil war. Trading land once involved gifts as tokens acknowledging the customary authority but "with time the payments have become more closely related to exchange value of the parcels" (Manicane, 2008, p. 49). Access to land has become more costly, and people who need land increasingly turn to less densely populated areas.

Buyers in Mogovolas included a few investors with full-time jobs and income who wanted to acquire land but avoid dealing with officials. They were also landless immigrants and households who had some customary land but needed more. The household respondents who reported having bought customary land extra-legally said that they had done so to increase agricultural production. Those who sold land said that they had done so to pay for special events such as marriages. The sellers are, however, not primarily individual holders but rather traditional authorities, especially the heads of lineages, who sell land they consider their own.

There are also individual sales, but these are fewer and tend to create problems. For example, in 2002 plans by the local government to take customary land for mining forced private sales of land by lineage heads to avoid the lower levels of compensation provided under the expropriation law. Lending and renting also occur, and those who rent out land are usually those who have more than they can farm or cannot operate it themselves. Rentals are most often to relatives, friends or newcomers.

The study concludes that sales of land under custom are today accepted as part of custom. Traditional authorities both provide community consent to transactions and engage in transactions on their own behalf. Chiefs continue to exercise social control of land. The land market is seen as a healthy development. Officials are for the most part negative toward them, considering the transactions a source of conflict between communities and outsiders. The acceptance of land sales and the development of a land market as part of the customary land tenure system is remarkable in that it has overcome, within a very modest period, the obstacles posed by traditional customary prohibition of such sales and the ongoing opposition of government and state law to such sales.

The study discussed in Box 5.4 raises interesting questions about how we should see customary land sales and what they say about the relationship between custom and law. Have the parcels sold become owned land in the western sense, ripped out of the customary land tenure system by the act of sale? It seems from the study that they are instead seen by the communities as part of an evolved customary land tenure system, in which the member's tenure in farmland includes a right to sell his land. This leaves a legally ambiguous situation in which such transactions are contrary to national law while also arguably protected by the state law's acceptance of customary law as the law governing land for which no formal title has been issued.

What is less clear from the study is what impact this is having upon the concept of membership in the community and the concept of community itself, and how this is affecting perceptions of authority over land within the communities. Can the buyer, especially if he or she is from the ethnic group, become the equivalent of a first settler who establishes a lineage? In a non-lineage system, could the buyer, by marriage or a fictive adoption or simply by showing respect and allegiance to the local customary authority (or some combination of these), establish himself or herself as a member of the community? Not all buyers may want to do so, and a buyer may be able to find a way to affirm that he or she does not hold land governed by the community, instead establishing the parcel as private, individually held land, independent of the customary land tenure system. In most countries this could be done by getting the parcel of land registered in whatever tenure the state offers to land users under the national land law. The land would then become a part of the statutory system of land tenure.

Does marketability of their land enrich smallholders? While a legally marketable title will usually increase the value of the land held, most smallholders cannot afford the required formalities and processes. More often, their land is taken from them by someone with greater wealth and power, after which it is registered in the name of the grabber, who needs to register it primarily because he has no right to it under custom. Where publicly subsidized titling programs are announced, the owners may not be enriched by their land becoming marketable, because in anticipation of implementation of that policy, officials or private actors may strip them of their land before the transition. During the transition, they are vulnerable to corruption and manipulation of registration processes in order to reduce or reject their claims. For those that acquire a marketable title, they live with risks of corruption in the registration system and of emergencies which may force them to sell their land. Because some land has been privatized, even land under custom will typically increase in value on the black market, just by virtue of its potential sale value once titled. In the end, if the smallholder still has his land when full marketability is achieved, the member's *right* and that of his descendants to land of the community may be diluted and eventually destroyed. On the other hand, some customary systems seem to survive the transition, though changed by it, as in Mogovolas.

In many cases land is becoming marketable through collusion of local, traditional authorities with national level authorities to sell unallocated or even allocated customary land to outsiders. In some instances, under custom or the official "customary law" of the state's courts, they may have a right to do so, even in the case of land already allocated to locals (see Chapter 15 in relation to Ghana). Most often those sales will contravene custom and, in some cases, national statutory law as well. As we will see in the following chapter, it is becoming clear that most national land authorities in Africa are not seriously committed to providing security of tenure for Africa's smallholders. They are quite prepared to repeat earlier experiences of expulsion from land, impoverishment, social disintegration and urbanization as occurred during the highland clearances in Scotland and the closing of the open field system in England in the 17th and 18th centuries.

## Notes

1 It is not possible to provide a full description of African land use systems in this book, but Bassett and Crummey (1993) is a good resource that takes into account the relationship between land use and land tenure.

2 In interviewing those who had been through the land reforms of the 1970s and 1980s in the northern highlands of Ethiopia, I found that an earlier right of access to land for young men was often seen as the only advantage of the village allocation systems that replaced customary land tenure in those reforms. It played a key role in creating a constituency for those reforms and the governments carrying them out (Rahmato, 1984).

3 FAO and the CGIAR (2018). Agricultural census data shows that globally, less than 20% of holders of land rights are women. In western and Central Africa as well as North Africa, less than 10% of land right-holders are women. The numbers are only slightly higher in Asia, mostly in the 10–20% range. Some global examples: women are holders of these percentages of land rights: > 40% Latvia and Lithuania, > 30% Malawi, Chile, Thailand, < 10% Senegal, Mali, Lebanon, Saudi Arabia, United States. Note that these data concern landholding, defined as "defined as the person who makes major decisions regarding resource use, and exercises management control over the operation of an agricultural holding," as opposed to land ownership, which includes rights to alienate land. In Africa, most of the women shown as holding land in agricultural censuses are likely

female heads of households. Agricultural censuses do not often include nuanced questions as regards women's landholding or land ownership. See Cooper and Bird (2012) and Doss et al. (2015).

4 Most credit experts have concluded that savings institutions, which have a rich history in Africa, are a better credit option for smallholders. This depends on the amounts available from a particular savings institution and rules on repayment (Blavy et al., 2004).

5 Land sales under custom are found widely in Africa. For Ghana, see Migot-Adholla et al. (1994, p. 100). For Burkina Faso, Côte d'Ivoire, Nigeria, and Rwanda, see Lund (2000, pp. 5–9).

## References


Abu Rannat, S.M. (1960). The relationship between Islamic and customary law in the Sudan. *Journal of African Law*, *4*(1), 9–16. https://doi.org/10.1017/S0021855300000498

Anderson, J.N.D. (1960). Relationship between Islamic and customary law in Africa. *Journal of African Administration*, *12*, 228–234.

Bassett, T.J. & Crummey, D.E. (Eds.) (1993). *Land in African agrarian systems*. University of Wisconsin Press. https://doi.org/10.2458/v2i1.20171

Binswanger, H.P., Deininger, K., & Feder, G. (1993). *Power, distortions, revolt, and reform in agricultural land relations* (Policy Research Working Paper No. WPS1164). World Bank Group. https://documents.worldbank.org/pt/publication/documents-reports/documentdetail/304261468764712147

Blavy, R., Yulek, M.Â., & Basu, M.A. (2004). *Microfinance in Africa: Experience and lessons from selected African countries* (Working Paper No. 2004/174). International Monetary Fund. www.imf.org/en/Publications/WP/Issues/2016/12/31/Microfinance-in-Africa-Experience-and-Lessons-From-Selected-African-Countries-17710

Bruce, J.W. (2012). Simple solutions to complex problems: Land formalization as a "silver bullet." In J.M. Otto & A. Hoekema (Eds.), *Fair land governance: How to legalise land rights for rural development* (pp. 31–56). Leiden University Press. https://doi.org/10.26530/OAPEN_595092

Bruce, J.W. & Migot-Adholla, S. (Eds.) (1994). *Searching for land tenure security in Africa*. World Bank/USAID.

Carter, M.R. & Michuda, A. (2019). The distribution of productive assets and the economics of rural development and poverty reduction. In M. Nissanke & J.A. Ocampo (Eds.), *The Palgrave handbook of development economics: Critical reflections on globalisation and development* (pp. 377–408). Palgrave Macmillan. https://doi.org/10.1007/978-3-030-14000-7

Chimhowu, A. & Woodhouse, P. (2006). Customary vs private property rights? Dynamics and trajectories of vernacular land markets in sub-Saharan Africa. *Journal of Agrarian Change*, *6*(3), 346–371. https://doi.org/10.1111/j.1471-0366.2006.00125.x

Colin, J.P. & Ayouz, M. (2006). The development of a land market? Insights from Côte d'Ivoire. *Land Economics*, *82*(3), 404–423. https://doi.org/10.3368/le.82.3.404

Colin, J.P. & Woodhouse, P. (2010). Interpreting land markets in Africa. *Africa*, *80*(1), 1–13. https://doi.org/10.3366/E0001972009001235

Cooper, E. & Bird, K. (2012). Inheritance: A gendered and intergenerational dimension of poverty. *Development Policy Review*, *30*(5), 527–541. https://doi.org/10.1111/j.1467-7679.2012.00587.x

Cotula, L. (Ed.) (2007). *Changes in "customary" land tenure systems in Africa*. IIED.

Deininger, K. (2003). *Land policies for growth and poverty reduction* (Policy Research Report No. 26384). World Bank Publications. https://hdl.handle.net/10986/15125

De Soto, H. (2000). *The mystery of capital: Why capitalism triumphs in the West and fails everywhere else*. Black Swan.

Doss, C., Kovarik, C., Peterman, A., Quisumbing, A., & Van Den Bold, M. (2015). Gender inequalities in ownership and control of land in Africa: Myth and reality. *Agricultural Economics*, *46*(3), 403–434. https://doi.org/10.1111/agec.12171

Douglas, M. (2013). Is matriliny doomed in Africa? In M. Douglas & P.M. Kaberry (Eds.), *Man in Africa* (pp. 121–135). Routledge.

FAO (2014). *Towards stronger family farms: Voices in the international year of family farming*. Food and Agricultural Organization of the United Nations. www.fao.org/3/a-i4171e.pdf

FAO and the CGIAR Research Program on Policies, Institutions and Markets (2018). *The gender gap in land rights*. Food and Agricultural Organization of the United Nations. www.fao.org/3/i8796en/I8796EN.pdf

Feder, K. & Feeny, D. (1991). Land tenure and property rights: Theory and implications for development policy. *The World Bank Economic Review*, *5*(1), 135–153. https://doi.org/10.1093/wber/5.1.135

Fruzzetti, L. & Östör, Á. (2019). Agricultural schemes: Tenants and institutions. In *Culture and change along the blue Nile* (pp. 153–170). Routledge.

Hilhorst, T. (2000). Women's land rights: Current developments in sub-Saharan Africa. In C. Toulmin & J. Quan (Eds.), *Evolving land rights, policy and tenure in Africa* (pp. 181–196). IIED. www.iied.org/7416iied

Hoben, A. (1973). *Land tenure among the Amhara of Ethiopia: The dynamics of cognatic descent*. University of Chicago Press.

Lund, C. (2000). *African land tenure: Questioning basic assumptions* (Drylands issue paper). IIED. www.iied.org/9023iied

Manicane, T.J. (2008). *Informal land markets in rural Mozambique: The case of Mogovolas district in Nampula province* [Masters of philosophy dissertation, University of the Western Cape]. UWCScholar. https://uwcscholar.uwc.ac.za/items/af008ecd-6b12-4aa0-b044-b10e7c580a03

Massay, G. (2020). The struggles for land rights by rural women in sub-Saharan Africa: The case of Tanzania. *African Journal of Economic and Management Studies*, *11*(2), 271–283. https://doi.org/10.1108/AJEMS-03-2019-0120

Migot-Adholla, S.E., Benneh, G., Place, F., & Atsu, S. (1994). Land, security of tenure, and productivity in Ghana. In J.W. Bruce & S.E. Migot-Adholla (Eds.), *Searching for land tenure security in Africa* (pp. 97–118). The World Bank.

Mutopo, P. (2014). In L. Cliffe, J. Alexander, B. Cousins, & R. Gaidzanwa (Eds.), *Outcomes of post-2000 fast track land reform in Zimbabwe* (pp. 115–140). Routledge.

Nadel, S.F. (1946). Land tenure on the Eritrean plateau. *Africa*, *16*(1), 1–22. https://doi.org/10.2307/1156534

Rahmato, D. (1984). *Agrarian reform in Ethiopia*. Scandinavian Institute of African Studies.

Shipton, P. (1989). *How private property emerges in Africa: Directed and undirected land tenure reforms in densely settled areas south of the Sahara*. Harvard University (HIID & Dept. of Anthropology).

Toulmin, C. & Quan, J. (Eds.) (2000). *Evolving land rights, policy and tenure in Africa*. IIED.

# 6 Pastures and Rangeland, a Conundrum

## Small Farms, Efficiency and Land Markets

### Grazing Patterns in Sub-Saharan Africa

Livestock play major roles in most African farming systems. Communities of sedentary farmers often use oxen to plow, needing pastures nearby for their cattle, on which they rely for milk and other products. Others rely on herds of small livestock such as sheep and goats. Both require grazing near residences for care of animals about to birth and for plow animals in the plowing season. In drier regions, agropastoralists may rely on some farming. They rely more heavily on livestock for trade, moving herds seasonally to graze different ecological zones. Many graze their livestock on lightly controlled open range. If there are villages in the area, locals will probably assert a right to control grazing on their land. They may extract fees or compensation in kind, such as allowing livestock to graze stubble in harvested fields in return for the animals' manure. In the most arid regions, nomadic peoples migrate to maintain access to water and grazing throughout the year, relying more on camels than other stock, and on access points to resources such as wells and waterholes to eke out a precarious existence.

Most farming and agropastoralist communities have pastures they consider to belong to the community, and on which members of the community have rights to graze their livestock. Community members manage pastures collectively as "commons." Pasture land is claimed by a group whose members determine that it should be used for pasture and are entitled to the use of the commons simultaneously. This land use is truly "communal." Management of a commons may be effective or ineffective, typically involving enforcing the community's use rules including closing portions to allow recovery or to provide preferred access for especially needy stock, such as cows with calves or oxen in plowing season.

Those undertaking long migrations in search of seasonal grazing land do not rely on local community-held pastures. They have to find needed resources in response to variable weather and rainfall patterns. Security of land tenure plays a more limited role in these situations since migratory routes differ from year to year. Land grazed one year may not be visited again for years after. A flexible framework that protects the secondary rights of pastoralists and allows them to adjust to changing conditions is needed (Moritz et al., 2014; Butt, 2010).

DOI: 10.4324/9781003476429-8

Promoting, especially forcing, legal change to allow sales of land under custom does not produce the efficiency gains expected. There is evidence that small farmers are more efficient land users than larger landholders. They use cheap, easily managed family labor rather than hired labor. Economists describe their hard work as "self-exploitation" (Carter & Michuda, 2019). Mechanization, requiring larger farms, saves on labor, which families have, but makes less efficient use of land than family farms cultivated by more traditional means, allowing more discriminating use of different soils on the holding and their location in different microclimates (Feder & Feeny, 1991). While economies of scale may exist in primary processing and marketing, there is little to suggest that they exist in production itself, at least where hired labor is not very expensive as in the global south. The appearance of efficiency in large farming operations is often due to state subsidies. One of the more important is waiving import taxes on fuel and farm machinery. The impression of efficiency also arises from a confusion of efficiency with the appearance of modernity: surely that shiny tractor must make for greater efficiency than the African smallholder's plow and hoe? Not necessarily, if its actual costs in terms of access, maintenance and fuel are considered, subtracting subsidies from the government.

*The conundrum is this: while development specialists were confident that new markets in land formerly under custom would move land into the hands of the most efficient of these small farmers, this is not what has in fact happened.* In most studies of the development of a market in land held under custom, efficient small farmers are not acquiring, but rather selling land and selling it to larger and often less efficient producers. These are usually outsiders to the seller's community. Binswanger et al. (1993) concluded that differential credit access explains the conundrum. "Credit market imperfections" prevent small efficient farmers from gaining access to the credit that would allow them to participate as buyers in the land market. Commercial lenders tend to be leery of agricultural lending in the first place because of the inherent risks involved in farming, principally due to dependence upon the weather as well as vulnerability to pests, diseases and volatile markets. They are even more reluctant to deal with smallholders who demand small loans in often remote locations where there is limited data on land values and uncertain prospects for resale of the land in the event of foreclosure. Often it can be difficult to foreclose on such a holding because of community resistance and customary claims from within the community. The banks are much happier with a loan applicant with a savings account and a steady record of salary deposits or who has borrowed money for other purposes and repaid the loan. Lack of a marketable title to land is only one obstacle to smallholders in obtaining commercial credit and giving them a marketable title does little to solve that problem.[1]

Because the majority of smallholders farming land under custom are unable to borrow from formal credit institutions, the land market that develops is a one-way street. Smallholders holding under custom sell their land cheaply because the transactions are not legally protected. They sell but rarely can buy land, resulting in the concentration of land rights in fewer, wealthier and often less efficient operators.

The poor, if they can buy, must buy in extra-legal land markets, where land is less expensive and tenure less secure. Over time, this increases concentration of land in the hands of wealthier outsiders, the development of increasing landlessness in the rural sector and migration into towns and cities. This was a serious concern of the independence era generation of African leaders and remains a serious issue, not only due to equity concerns, but because governments are frightened by the rapid development of a politically volatile unemployed class.

The effectiveness of projects and programs promoting land titling and registration under custom along with greater freedom to sell and mortgage has been placed in question by their failure to improve access to credit and foster greater agricultural efficiency. Still, such projects have much to offer. Especially in cases where broad insecurity of tenure exists, they can positively affect farmer investment in land even without improving credit access, through their assurance effects.

As noted above, nomadic pastoralists instead need a flexible framework that protects the secondary rights of pastoralists and allows them to adjust to changing conditions (Moritz et al., 2014; Butt, 2010).

## The Tragedy of the Commons

Communal land use was long criticized by economists as leading to land degradation. It is still often considered less sound than individual management of livestock on owned land. An influential article (Hardin, 1968) restated the argument against collective use and management of pastures that had prevailed since the destruction of customary commons in England and Scotland two centuries earlier (McCay & Acheson, 1987). Pasturing individually owned livestock on a common, Hardin asserted, led inevitably to degradation of the resource through overgrazing. Each individual would seek to maximize his benefit by introducing more of his animals onto the pasture. While it might occur to a rational user to withhold the additional animals in the interest of long-term sustainable use of the resource, that would achieve nothing because that user cannot compel others to do the same. Instead, all users would add additional stock to the pasture, ensuring that it would be overgrazed and degraded. This sad inevitability was termed "the tragedy of the commons" (Hardin, 1968). Individual ownership of pasture was seen to be the only solution.[2]

## The Real Tragedy: Botswana Partitions Its Rangeland

The concept of the tragedy of the commons informed Botswana's reform of its customary pasture land tenure arrangements in 1975, a reform which became the best studied and most publicized example of an unfortunate application of a theory from western economics in an African context. The Tribal Grazing Land Policy (TGLP) was proposed on the basis of a 1972 report by a Ford Foundation-funded consulting team. It was approved by the government and implemented with the approval of Botswana's new Tribal Land Boards.

At the time, Botswana was one of a handful of countries in Africa in which the interests of livestock owners were dominant in national politics. Its population consists largely of Tswana livestock owners, including many who are now city and town dwellers but were raised in the pastoralist culture. A large part of the population still keeps some cattle. In most African countries pasture tenure barely gets a nod in land policy documents. In Botswana it is the principal land tenure issue and received far more careful attention. Customary land tenure was fully recognized by law during the British Protectorate. Independent Botswana continued on this path. Tribal land (land under custom) comprises 71% of the country's land area, freehold about 4% and state land 25% (Clover & Eriksen, 2009).

The cattle of the Tswana traditionally grazed extensive common pastures exclusive to the community concerned. Historically, management of the land and herds was dictated by the highly dynamic arid and semi-arid ecosystem and regulated by communities at ward, village and tribe levels (Taylor, 2007). Tswana villages had areas of historic use in the communal range where cattle were kept seasonally by most families (but year-round by large stock owners) and from which herds moved across the pasture as its conditions changed seasonally or to avoid localized drought and contagion. There had not been in recent times an institution with effective control of the range and management plans were not in place. Individual herd managers had quite a lot of discretion as to where they grazed their animals. During the colonial period, livestock numbers on the commons increased substantially and colonial authorities responded to the need for more water by promoting the drilling of boreholes on the commons, typically by syndicates of livestock holders created to raise the funding for this major investment.

Boreholes are deep narrow wells, bored rather than dug. A machine hammers a steel liner deep into the earth, providing access to the aquifer where water is available even in times of severe drought. Those who invested in the boreholes were rewarded with private property rights to the borehole, de facto control of the surrounding land and the opportunity for year-round pastoral production. By independence in 1966, the percentage of land with access to permanent water sources had risen from 20% to 45%, and the national herd increased three-fold. Borehole development reduced the need for seasonal migration for water, and both cattle and herding communities became more sedentary. This increased pressure on the pasture around the boreholes. By 1970 a national herd of 3,000,000 cattle was considered on the horizon and range degradation was a national concern (Arntzen, 1998; Peters, 1994; Frimpong, 1995). In 1972, in response to a 1970 conference in Gaborone on Sustained Production from Semi-arid Areas, the government invited Robert Chambers and Michael Feldman to do a consultancy on rural development in Botswana. Their report (Chambers & Feldman, 1973) was the basis of the 1975 national policy on tribal grazing land (Government of Botswana, 1975; Sechele, 2018).

The government accepted the theory of the tragedy of the commons: that individually owned herds on common pastures inevitably overgrazed and destroyed the pastures. The TGLP, adopted by government in 1975 (Government of Botswana,

1975), called for a zoning of rangeland into commercial, communal and reserve areas and then, based on that zoning: (a) granting large cattle owners exclusive rights to rangeland for commercial ranches; (b) retaining village ownership and management of rangelands sufficient for communal grazing for small and medium owners of cattle; and (c) protecting reserves for future expansion of communal grazing. Under the policy, district-level Land Boards allocated eight-square-kilometer tracts of land identified as suitable for commercial ranches to large cattle ranchers, who obtained exclusive rights to the land under 50-year renewable leases (Frimpong, 1995). The policy required fenced ranches of a uniform size and shape, without regard for differences in soil, vegetation and topography. Most often the ranches went to existing large cattle ranchers with boreholes (Peters, 1994). Implementation of the policy prioritized establishment of commercial ranches. Contrary to assumptions, almost all land identified as suitable for commercial ranching was already used by people, and no land was demarcated as reserve (Malope & Batisani, 2008). An unanticipated negative impact also materialized: the creation of the ranches with their fencing interfered with movement of people and livestock. The nomadic San, masters of living on arid land resources, found the migratory patterns they had once relied upon blocked by fences and guards (Frimpong, 1995).

Other problems ensued. Contrary to the assumptions of policy makers, many commercial ranchers overstocked their land and did not erect fencing, asserting their right as tribesmen to graze their cattle on communal land, enlarging their grazing land at the expense of the villagers' herds confined to communal land (Cullis & Watson, 2005). In 1991, the National Policy on Agricultural Development recognized that some of the assumptions underlying the TGLP were erroneous (among others, the availability of unused land for commercial ranches) and that the anticipated benefits of the TGLP had been slow to emerge. In response, the National Policy on Agricultural Development (Government of Botswana, 1991) expanded areas for commercial ranches to include the land surrounding private boreholes. That land had been under the *de facto* control of the borehole owners, but now the borehole owners could exclude others from those pastures.

As of 2005, a total of 342 ranches (intended to be commercial) had been allocated under the TGLP, amounting to about 4% of Botswana's land. An additional 602 ranches had been demarcated, representing an additional 4% of land. Botswana's cattle population stood at between 2,500,000 and 3,000,000 in 2011 (Taylor, 2007). Grazing in communal rangelands accounted for 86% of the cattle and 71% of farmers in Botswana, while private grazing in ranches accounted for 14% of the national cattle herd and 5% of the land area (Government of Botswana, 2013; cited in Mosalagae & Mogotsi, 2013).

Statistics relevant to the productivity of the commercial herd show a mixed picture. Communal ranches have higher livestock birth rates, but also higher mortality rates. Commercial ranches report increasing off-take rates while the rates for traditional ranches decreased. Large producers provided more than half of the cattle delivered to government abattoirs in 2009, compared with 12% delivered by 4,893 small producers (Government of Botswana Meat Commission, 2009). A review of commercial ranches conducted for the Ministry of Agriculture reported that only 30% of them were economically successful (Burgess, 2002). One critic suggested, tongue in cheek, that the real value in the commercial ranches may be in their transfer, land speculation being far more profitable than commercial ranching (Taylor, 2007).

In 2009 24.3% of the rural population lived below the poverty line and Botswana had one of the world's highest rates of income inequality (UNECA, 2015). The overall contribution of agriculture to GDP continued to fall, reported at 1.9% in 2008 compared to 43% in 1966 (Government of Botswana Ministry of Finance and Development Planning, 2010). Beef accounted for 80% of the sector's contribution. Botswana had preferential terms for export to EU markets but produced only an average of 63% of its quota in the 2000–2010 period, citing continued challenges of drought, pests and disease, low use of new technology and the high cost of key inputs. Disease outbreaks caused Botswana Meat Commission abattoirs to be ineligible to export cattle products to the EU (Government of Botswana Ministry of Finance and Development Planning, 2013).

Most smallholders (those with fewer than 40 head of cattle) rely on village grazing areas (VGA) (land within a 10–20km radius of the village) for grazing their cattle. One-third of the cattle using VGAs are owned by an estimated 60,000 smallholders. Two-thirds of the cattle using VGAs belong to large farmers, including those with commercial ranches who use communal land to avoid the cost of development and maintenance of infrastructure (e.g. fencing) that would have ensured them exclusive use if developed. Shifting cattle to communal areas allows their commercial ranch land to regenerate for use in times of drought or other environmental stress (Centre for Applied Research, 2007b; Malope & Batisani, 2008). There has been a steady increase in the number of farmers (traditional and commercial) using VGA (from 41% in 1980 to 60% in 2002), and VGAs are considered among the most irretrievably degraded land. In contrast, grazing pressure on commercial ranches has declined due to stagnation in the sector. Fenced rangeland was reported as understocked and underutilized, as compared with communal areas (Centre for Applied Research, 2007b; Government of Botswana Ministry of Finance and Development Planning, 2013). The degradation of the VGAs has impacted smallholder and poorer communal households most dramatically because they are unlikely to qualify for loans to establish commercial cattle ranches, and they rely more heavily on the natural resources of communal lands for a diversity of livelihood sources. Women are more likely to have restrictions on their mobility and are thus more dependent on local livelihood sources (Malope & Batisani, 2008; Centre for Applied Research, 2007a, 2007b).

Cattle post areas (CPAs) are the alternative system for cattle raising on communal land. The CPAs are established around boreholes, most of which are owned by syndicates. The land is less degraded than in VGAs, but access to CPAs by communal households is increasingly restricted as the land is converted into ranches and used for expansion of settlements (Centre for Applied Research, 2007b). An increasing number of rural households own no livestock (63% in 2002/2003 from 50% in 1984/1985), a trend some attribute to the reduction in grazing land. Most rural households continue to rely on agriculture for at least a portion of their livelihoods. Those without livestock must purchase livestock products (milk) and rent livestock services (such as plowing) (Malope & Batisani, 2008; Centre for Applied Research, 2007a, 2007b). Women's percentage of cattle ownership is declining (as of 2011, only 25.5% of cattle are owned by women (Government of Botswana, 2013, p. 3), and they have declining access to the economic, social and cultural benefits of cattle ownership (Government of Botswana Ministry of Finance and Development Planning, 2013). Employment opportunities on commercial farms have been estimated to be fewer than those created by cattle posts. As rural livestock ownership has declined, so too has the informal employment associated with cattle ownership (Government of Botswana Ministry of Finance and Development Planning, 2013).

The government's commitment to the TGLP continues. Between 2010 and 2013, Land Boards allocated 62 additional commercial ranches. The mid-term review of National Development Plan 10 identified the need for extension programs to assist traditional farmers and demarcation of community grazing land "to facilitate good range management and adoption of good husbandry practices" (Government of Botswana Ministry of Finance and Development Planning, 2013, p. 33).

In the over 40 years since the adoption of the TGLP, it has largely failed to achieve its stated objectives, in part because the assumptions about the impact of private rights on range conditions were largely erroneous. Meanwhile, less desirable economic, social and environmental consequences have stacked up. Available data suggest that the policy has failed to improve rangeland quality and herd management, and the benefits of the privatization of communal land are concentrated in the hands of a few elites (Peters, 1994; Cullis & Watson, 2005; Taylor, 2007).

What can we learn from the TGLP experience? A technological innovation, the borehole well, contributed to a perceived crisis in livestock production, a dramatic land policy decision and implementation of a major program of tenure reform. Individualization has not had the anticipated impact on range condition, which has not improved. The TGLP led to a substantial redistribution of pasture access due to the boreholes. Tenure individualization of a common resulted in elite capture of pasture resources, while smallholder benefits were dwarfed by their loss of access to grazing, sparking a trend of widening economic inequality.

## Rethinking the Tragedy of the Commons

The Nobel-Prize-winning research by Professor Elinor Ostrom and her colleagues at Indiana University has prompted major shifts in thinking on the commons, offering perhaps the most important advance of the 20th century on land tenure theory (Ostrom, 1990). In western economic thought, the commons were long treated as a free-for-all, chaotic and inefficient, and the conventional wisdom has seen this as reason for calling for individualization. Ostrom noted that contrary to expectations, many commons work well, including some in developed countries such as Switzerland. She identified key factors affecting their success when it comes to management of natural resources. Drawing on her work, those dealing with land tenure in the commons began to use the term "common property" to refer to a commons that is legally well-grounded and well managed. They then used the term "open access resource" to describe the situation where land used as a commons is not being protected against outsiders and not managed effectively overall.

The "tragedy of the commons" was flawed. Why assume just one rational user? Why could a group of rational users in the form of a community not set ground rules for managing the commons and enforce those and, in the case of pastures, control the number of animals grazing on rangelands? Hardin was challenged by those who were aware of relatively positive experiences with community management of shared pasture resources in the global south. Hardin's model assumed communities would or could not establish such controls, but they clearly did establish them and, in many cases, enforced them (Ostrom, 1990).[3] Individual ownership of pasture was not the only workable option (Ciriacy-Wantrup & Bishop, 1975).

## Common Property Management

The successful management of collectively owned resources requires security of tenure. The community needs to be able to control livestock numbers, so it must have the right to exclude livestock. The community must own the pasture (or other commons resource) or hold it in some other robust collective tenure, such as a long-term leasehold. The make-or-break question, does a community require an institutional structure with competence, skills and will for commons management to be effective? Ostrom (1990) researched the determinants of effective common property management and found that groups are more successful in common property management if: (a) group boundaries and property boundaries are clearly defined; (b) rules on use of collective goods are appropriate to local conditions; (c) individuals affected can participate in modifying the rules; (d) the rules of commons management are respected by higher authorities from outside the community; (e) a system exists for monitoring members' behavior; (f) a graduated system of sanctions is employed; (g) members have access to low-cost conflict resolution; and (h) commons management is nested in a wider regional network of management systems.

In other words, effective management is an essential attribute of a "common property resource" that distinguishes it from an "open access resource." While secure collective rights to the commons may be necessary for effective commons management (even if these are not exclusive rights), they are not sufficient (Ostrom, 1990). If a collectively held resource is not well-managed by the community and is open to all users without constraint, it is still an open access resource.

Would a common property solution have worked better in Botswana? As suggested earlier, it is not easy or simple to create institutions that deliver effective management of common property in cases where they have not developed. Attempts were made to establish common property management on VGAs in Botswana, but these initiatives have not performed well. This may be due to the dominance of the sector by commercial ranches and their practice of grazing their stock on the commons when the grass there is at its best (Peters, 1994).

In a study that flags the centrality of institutional arrangements, Lawry (1988) examined the successes and failures of a donor-sponsored range management scheme in Lesotho, and as Ostrom posited, finds institutions—in this case choice of management institutions—are the largest challenge. Box 16.1 presents an excerpt from a subsequent paper relaying the study results.

**Box 6.1 Community Management of a Range Commons in Lesotho**

In a pilot range management project in Lesotho, the Government of Lesotho and the United States Agency for International Development established a grazing association at Sehlabathebe in the Drakensberg Mountains and gave it management control over a badly degraded watershed. A popularly elected executive committee was responsible for administering a grazing management plan which provided for the seasonal rotation of livestock among winter grazing areas near villages and summer grazing areas in the surrounding mountains. Livestock found grazing in violation of the plan were subject to impoundment by range riders, local enforcement agents paid by the association. Range conditions improved, but rule violations were common.

Subsequent research identified two principal reasons for low acceptance of the plan. The original plan did not take sufficient account of traditional grazing patterns, or of constraints faced by individuals in adopting new patterns. Large numbers of livestock already rotated seasonally between winter pastures in the villages and summer pastures in the mountains, but the grazing plan sought to impose universal adoption of a more complex grazing rotation. Individual grazing strategies were dictated by a variety of factors, such as availability of herding labor, herd size and species composition. These factors were themselves related to such household characteristics as age, sex and residential status of the household head, and the relative importance of livestock and remittances as income sources. Only about 16% of households cited livestock production as their principal source of cash income, though 84% of households owned livestock. About half of the working-age males were absent, most working in the mining sector in South Africa. Fifty percent of household cash income was in the form of remittances from mine workers.

> A second and more intractable factor hindering plan adoption (including adoption of the amended plan) was that many villagers did not recognize the authority of the executive committee to regulate range use. Traditionally, village chiefs had been responsible for grazing regulation, but attentiveness to their regulatory functions had waned. The executive committee was dominated by large holders, principally mohair and wool producers, who despaired over poor grazing conditions and who saw in the association an opportunity to take matters into

their own hands. Many villagers (including some large holders willing to observe the grazing plan) gained the impression that the association existed principally to serve the interests of executive committee members.

Democratically constituted user groups must rely on the sanction of their membership to enforce rules. Where interests are heterogeneous and views toward appropriate resource use standards vary, sufficiently strong support for enforcement of many kinds of rules will not emerge. Reliance upon existing structures of elite authority, such as chiefs, may be appropriate in some situations. However, local authority generally is losing ground to state authority. Traditional authorities especially have lost or are losing their legitimacy, and patron-client relationships are weakening. Some integration of the traditional and democratic authority might have been more effective.[4]

## Migratory Pastoralism and Disequilibrium

What of migratory pastoralists? Their livestock do not graze a nicely bounded community pasture near the village. In arid or other sparsely endowed regions, herds travel long distances each year, taking advantage of the seasonal change in ranges to meet their needs. Migratory pastoralism ranges from true nomadism to agropastoralism, where the community has a home base, usually occupied year-round by some members of the community who farm there. In such a case there may be "near pastures," commons exclusive to the community; "far pastures" that may or may not be shared with other communities, and migratory routes which go through the land of other communities. We also find pastures in some African countries that are controlled directly by the government (e.g. reserves). But what of the right to cross the land of others and feed on browse along their routes, routes that may change over time? And, how about pastures which may have no clear user boundaries and whose use may be shared among several groups? Those pastures are not exclusive but may in some cases be subject to customary rules on access and coordination among user groups. If not, they are open-access situations, with great potential for conflict.

From a policy perspective, migratory pastoralism is often seen as an anachronism, which will not survive the challenge of externally driven, competing land uses (e.g. "land-grabbing" for farming, mining or other uses). Climate change may also render some areas of migratory pastoralism unviable. Although adaptability is a key characteristic of migratory pastoralism, the rapid pace of climate impacts on landscapes may stress their capacity to adapt. Finally, and probably the most important, the aspirations and demands of the pastoralists themselves are changing. Migration has often come at a high price in terms of access to schools, village clinics and other public services (Krätli & Dyer, 2009; Gammino et al., 2020).

Sustainability of these systems matters. Migratory pastoralism tends to be economically sound because it efficiently uses large areas of land according to the seasonal availability of forage and water resources (Young et al., 2016). It is environmentally sound because it has a very light footprint and pastoral cultures are typically highly sensitive to sustainability issues (Scoones & Graham, 1994.) If it came to an end, indigenous cultures and ways of life would die with it. The collapse of pastoralist systems likewise has the potential to result in social disintegration and desperate poverty.

Until relatively recently, accepted wisdom was that the only way to save pastoral systems was to change them fundamentally. Tenure reforms have sought to convert migratory pastoralism to a more sedentary pastoralism, replacing migration with individual or group ranches, each with a water source and clear boundaries. As a general approach, these individual and exclusive common property solutions seem sound enough. Yet while these programs succeeded in ending migration, they have failed to deliver the anticipated improvements in range conditions on the new ranches. Ranch owners struggle to recover the high cost of well drilling and fencing and to do so tend to overstock the ranches. In some cases, ranch owners have eased pressure on their ranches by releasing their livestock onto remaining communal grazing, as has happened in Botswana. In addition, the disturbance of the local ecosystems involved in the creation of the ranches has sometimes produced serious negative impacts on range condition.[5] Finally, the exclusive common property approaches have, as in the case in Lesotho and Kenya, suffered from insufficient attention to group cohesion and the ranch management institution. In Kenya, as part of a major land tenure reform, group ranches were created for pastoralists, but have tended to break up, the land partitioned among their members (Ng'ethe, 1992).

Tenure reform programs for the most part have not been able to provide sustainable livelihoods for the broad membership of migratory pastoralist communities. A geographically broader exclusive common property approach, titling to the pastoralist group an entire region through which their migrations moved, runs into objections by other groups of livestock holders and farmers who have customary rights in those areas. This creates a need for some form of shared rights and co-management by different groups of land users with a regulatory framework for land use within the common property. Challenging as that may sound, such customary arrangements do exist, notably in Mali's Inner Niger Delta (Cotula & Cissé, 2006).

Behnke (1992) argued that reform not preserving the mobility and flexibility inherent to migratory pastoralism will not work. Because of unpredictable rainfall and other weather conditions, arid lands are disequilibrium situations in which sustainability is possible *only* by constant adjustments in response to change. The genius of migratory pastoralism is its wide-ranging, flexible and opportunistic land use, which makes viable use of a land resource with little other economic value. They recommend:

1. A land use planning approach rather than a land tenure reform approach to migratory pastoralism. Governments seeking to sustain the environmental and economic advantages of migratory pastoralism should thus consider providing participatory, multi-stakeholder and iterative (periodically reconsidered and revised) land use planning on a large scale.

2. Legal recognition of the authority of community institutions over their grazing lands, and a lead role for them in land use planning.
3. Fair and effective procedures for negotiation with pastoral communities regarding new activities on their land to avoid those activities undermining pastoralism.
4. Mechanisms to resolve land use disputes between migratory groups and sedentary users.
5. Demarcation and registration of individual rights in residences and group rights over pastures already under common property.

The challenge is the political will to protect migratory pastoralists' land use patterns. Pressure from competing uses may come from commercial farming or higher value activities such as mining. Activities which interfere with migrations and are clearly destructive may be allowed by governments to continue if advantageous to a powerful few. In arid central Sudan, pastoralist migrations have since the 1980s been disrupted by mechanized shifting cultivation of extensive areas for rainfed sorghum, which delivers a crop only in years of exceptionally good rainfall. The land is state-owned and allocated to commercial farmers on leases that tend not to be altered when the farmers move on to different areas every few years because of the unsustainability of cultivation on arid, low fertility soils (Shazali & Ghaffar, 1999).

## Women and Pastoralism

To what degree do women have rights to livestock and the pasture needed to feed them? In the case of pasture commons, rights of grazing may be seen as belonging collectively to households. In that case, a female-headed-household might be seen as having a direct access right, but whether she independently grazes the stock may depend upon the size and composition of her livestock. If she only has goats, which are generally grazed on less fertile private land, she may not use the commons. If she has only one to two cows, she may as a matter of practical necessity need to "loan" them to a larger stockholder who will receive some compensation for herding them with his own cattle on the commons. If she is married, her husband will likely graze or arrange to pasture her animals with the other household stock. She might herself arrange for her stock to be grazed if she has a large herd. Women generally do not participate in decision-making with respect to management of the pasture commons, but this may again depend on whether the woman is a household head and the extent of her livestock holdings.

Pastoralist women usually find opportunities to acquire and accumulate wealth through livestock rather than land. In almost all pastoralist societies, women have the right to acquire and own livestock independent of their husbands. As a result, women are actively involved in management of livestock and in the processing and sale of livestock products. Women in fact become major livestock owners in some pastoralist societies. It is hard to overstate the importance of this because livestock, unlike land in traditional contexts, is a marketable good, a source of cash. In communities where women become substantial holders of livestock, their entry into community decision-making is facilitated.

## Land Tenure and the Future of Pastoralism

Livestock husbandry can be a profitable line of business and, with good management institutions, an efficient and sustainable use of the land resources on which livestock rely. From a tenurial standpoint, it raises special issues, largely because grazing is, even in sedentary communities, an activity which demands flexibility to adjust use of pasture to the needs of different animals. Those who make adjustments, the herders, must have the flexibility to do so. So long as animals rely upon browse rather than on purchased feed, there will be a need for institutions to manage their movement. Those institutions require particular attention in organizing and coordinating use of pasture. There are a wide range of options for managing pasture use. Pastures can be managed by the state (e.g. grazing leases on federal land in the United States), by corporations or by community institutions, and, in the exceptional case of a ranch with sufficient water resources, by an individual rancher. Security of tenure is an issue in all of these cases, but the institutions and their capacity to manage will be the principal challenge in most circumstances.

## Notes

1 Most credit experts have concluded that mutual savings institutions, which have a rich history in Africa, are a better credit option for smallholders. This depends on the amounts available from a particular savings institution and rules on repayment (Blavy et al., 2004).
2 But see Netting (1976) for analysis of long-standing pastoralism in Switzerland.
3 If one had looked carefully, one could have found similar cases of successful commons in the European experience, such as Netting (1976). Swiss communities had been managing grazing commons effectively for centuries in the middle of Europe.
4 Lawry (1990, pp. 410, 413–415).
5 See, for example, the widespread infestations by mice and rats in reformed areas of western China's rangelands (Z. Li, personal communication, March 19, 2015).

## References

Arntzen, J. (1998). *Economic valuation of communal rangelands in Botswana: A case study* (CREED Working Paper No. 17). Environmental Economics Programme, IIED. www.iied.org/8096iied

Behnke, R. (1992, January 13–17). *New directions in African range management policy* [Conference proceedings]. Workshop sponsored by the Commonwealth Secretariat and held at Matopos, Zimbabwe. www.researchgate.net/profile/Roy-Behnke/publication/265398405_New_Directions_in_African_Range_Management_Policy/links/55f437b908ae6a34f6608a8e/New-Directions-in-African-Range-Management-Policy.pdf

Binswanger, H.P., Deininger, K., & Feder, G. (1993). Agricultural land relations in the developing world. *American Journal of Agricultural Economics*, *75*(5), 1242–1248. https://doi.org/10.2307/1243465

Blavy, R., Yulek, M.Â., & Basu, M.A. (2004). *Microfinance in Africa: Experience and lessons from selected African countries* (Working Paper No. 2004/174). International Monetary Fund. www.imf.org/en/Publications/WP/Issues/2016/12/31/Microfinance-in-Africa-Experience-and-Lessons-From-Selected-African-Countries-17710

Burgess, J. (2002). *FAO country pasture/forest resources profile*. FAO. www.scribd.com/document/346398134/FAO-Forage-Profile-Botswana

Butt, B. (2010). Pastoral resource access and utilization: Quantifying the spatial and temporal relationships between livestock mobility, density and biomass availability in southern Kenya. *Land Degradation & Development, 21*(6), 520–539. https://doi.org/10.1002/ldr.989

Carter, M.R. & Michuda, A. (2019). The distribution of productive assets and the economics of rural development and poverty reduction. In M. Nissanke & J.A. Ocampo (Eds.), *The Palgrave handbook of development economics* (pp. 377–408). Palgrave Macmillan. https://doi.org/10.1007/978-3-030-14000-7_11

Centre for Applied Research (2007a). *Draft country assessment report: Botswana*. Prepared for SADC MAPP.

Centre for Applied Research (2007b). *Natural resource accounting of Botswana's livestock sector*. Botswana Department of Environmental Affairs.

Chambers, R. & Feldman, M. (1973). *Report on rural development in Botswana* (Government Paper No. 1). The Institute of Development Studies and Partner Organisations. https://hdl.handle.net/20.500.12413/190

Ciriacy-Wantrup, S.V. & Bishop, R.C. (1975). "Common property" as a concept in natural resources policy. *Natural Resources Journal, 15*(4), 713–727. www.jstor.org/stable/24880906

Clover, J. & Eriksen, S. (2009). The effects of land tenure on sustainability: Human security and environmental change in southern African savannas. *Environmental Science & Policy, 12*(1), 53–70. https://doi.org/10.1016/j.envsci.2008.10.012

Cotula, L. & Cissé, S. (2006). Changes in "customary" resource tenure systems in the inner Niger delta, Mali. *The Journal of Legal Pluralism and Unofficial Law, 38*(52), 1–29. https://doi.org/10.1080/07329113.2006.10756689

Cousins, B. (2000). Tenure and common property resources in Africa. In C. Toulmin & J Quan (Eds.), *Evolving land rights, policy and tenure in Africa* (pp. 151–180). DFID/IIED/NRI. www.iied.org/7416iied

Cullis, A. & Watson, C. (2005, March). *Winners and losers: Privatising the commons in Botswana* (Securing the Commons No. 9). IIED. www.iied.org/9529iied

Feder, G. & Feeny, D. (1991). Land tenure and property rights: Theory and implications for development policy. *The World Bank Economic Review, 5*(1), 135–153. doi.org/10.1093/wber/5.1.135

Frimpong, K. (1995). A review of the tribal grazing land policy in Botswana. *Pula: Botswana Journal of African Studies, 9*(1), 1–16.

Gammino, V.M., Dias, M.R., Pallas, S.W., Greenleaf, A.R., & Kurnit, M.R. (2020). Health services uptake among nomadic pastoralist populations in Africa: A systematic review of the literature. *PLoS Neglected Tropical Diseases, 14*(7), e0008474. https://doi.org/10.1371/journal.pntd.0008474

Government of Botswana (1975). *National policy on tribal grazing land* (Government Paper No. 2 of 1975). Government Printer.

Government of Botswana (1991). *National policy on agricultural development* (Government Paper No. 1 of 1991). Government Printer.

Government of Botswana (2013). *Annual agricultural surveys preliminary results for 2011*. Government Printer.

Government of Botswana Meat Commission (2009). *BMC annual report*. Government Printer.

Government of Botswana Ministry of Finance and Development Planning (2010). *National development plan 10*. Government Printer.

Government of Botswana Ministry of Finance and Development Planning (2013). *Mid-term review of NDP 10*. Government Printer.

Hardin, G. (1968). The tragedy of the commons: The population problem has no technical solution; it requires a fundamental extension on morality. *Science, 162*(3859), 1243–1248. https://doi.org/10.1126/science.162.3859.1243

Krätli, S. & Dyer, C. (2009). *Mobile pastoralists and education: Strategic options* (Education for Nomads Working Paper No. 1). IIED. www.iied.org/10021iied

Lawry, S.W. (1988). Private herds and common land: Issues in the management of communal grazing land in Lesotho, southern Africa [Doctoral dissertation, University of Wisconsin-Madison].

Lawry, S.W. (1990). Tenure policy toward common property natural resources in sub-Saharan Africa. *Natural Resources Journal, 30*(2), 403–422.

Malope, P. & Batisani, N. (2008). Land reforms that exclude the poor: The case of Botswana. *Development Southern Africa, 25*(4), 383–397. https://doi.org/10.1080/03768350802316179.

McCay, B.J. & Acheson, J.M. (Eds.) (1987). *The question of the commons: The culture and ecology of communal resources*. University of Arizona Press.

Moritz, M., Hamilton, I.M., Scholte, P., & Chen, Y.J. (2014). Ideal free distributions of mobile pastoralists in multiple seasonal grazing areas. *Rangeland Ecology & Management, 67*(6), 641–649. https://doi.org/10.2111/REM-D-14-00051.1

Mosalagae, D. & Mogotsi, K. (2013). Caught in a sandstorm: An assessment of pressures on communal pastoral livelihoods in the Kalahari Desert of Botswana. *Pastoralism: Research, Policy and Practice, 3*(18), 1–20. https://doi.org/10.1186/2041-7136-3-18

Netting, R.M. (1976). What alpine peasants have in common: Observations on communal tenure in a Swiss village. *Human Ecology, 4*(2), 135–146. https://doi.org/10.1007/BF01531217

Ng'ethe, J.C. (1992). Group ranch concept and practice in Kenya with special emphasis on Kajiado District. In J.A. Kategile & S. Mubi (Eds.), *Proceedings of the workshop held at Kadoma Ranch Hotel, Zimbabwe, 20–23 July 1992*. International Livestock Centre for Africa.

Ostrom, E. (1990). *Governing the commons: The evolution of institutions for collective action*. Cambridge University Press.

Peters, P.E. (1994). *Dividing the commons: Politics, policy, and culture in Botswana*. University of Virginia Press.

Scoones, I. & Graham, O. (1994). New directions for pastoral development in Africa. *Development in Practice, 4*(3), 188–198. https://doi.org/10.1080/0961452491000077821

Sechele, L. (2018). Urban, elite and professional bias in public policy formulation in Botswana: The case of tribal grazing land policy. *International Journal of Social Science Research, 6*(2), 33–43. https://doi.org/10.5296/ijssr.v6i2.12347

Shazali, S. & Ghaffar, A. (1999). *Pastoral land tenure and agricultural expansion: Sudan and the horn of Africa* [Paper presentation]. DFID workshop on Land Rights and Sustainable Development in sub-Saharan Africa, Berkshire, UK.

Taylor, M. (2007). *Tenure reform and the future of communal rangelands in Botswana*. Commons Southern Africa 16, CASS/PLAAS Occasional Paper. Programme for Land and Agrarian Studies, University of the Western Cape.

UNECA (United Nations Economic Commission for Africa) (2015). *Botswana—country profile*. UNData. https://data.un.org/en/iso/bw.html

Young, H., Behnke, R., Suleiman, H., Robinson, S., & Mohamed, A. (2016, August). *Risk, resilience, and pastoralist mobility*. Feinstein International Center, Tufts University.

# 7 Forests and Trees

## Trees on the Farm

Household tree-planting on owned land is legally straightforward in western tenure systems, both regarding the right to plant and tree ownership. Trees are considered "fixtures" (more or less permanently attached to the land) owned by the land owner unless there is a contractual provision to the contrary. Consider a landholder who is deciding whether to intercrop trees with the crops on his fields, an agroforestry technique. Between the food crop rows, the farmer plants tree seedlings in rows. Trees enrich the soil. We might imagine that this farmer will be unlikely to invest in seedlings if he is not secure in his tenure for a substantial period. This reasoning is not reliable in many African contexts. Tree-planting may be a strategy for securing access and long-term rights to land, rather than an activity requiring tenure security to that land at the outset. The existence of trees owned under custom by the person who planted them also establishes the planter's right to the land (Fortmann & Bruce, 1988).

Under many customary systems, trees can be owned independently of land. In early America, colonists thought that Native Americans had so much land that they didn't care much about rights in land, but might care very much about rights in a stand of sugar maples. In west Africa, labor supplied in planting commercial tree crops typically earns an interest in the farm, including the land (Berry, 1988). Ownership can also be mixed. Along the Nile in northern Sudan, date-palms are co-owned by three parties: the owner of the plot of land, the planter of the seedling and the owner of the irrigation pump that irrigates the land. At harvest, the co-owners will spread blankets on the ground and, on them, divide their dates into shares.[1] Trees sometimes have gender dimensions. Tree species may be identified with men or women, and some trees cannot be planted or cared for by women, for whom they are taboo (Fortmann, 1985).

Ignoring these rules can have serious consequences. Fortmann (1985) warns that a government-sponsored attempt to introduce alley-cropping on farmland can fail because the landholders fear that seedlings provided by the government will affect their land rights. She describes cases where intended beneficiaries of tree-planting projects resisted planting government-supplied seedlings on their land for fear that

DOI: 10.4324/9781003476429-9

these trees would enable the government to later claim ownership of their land (Fortmann, 1985).

## Cocoa in West Africa

The introduction of cocoa, a new cash crop, in Ghana created demand for land for production on a commercial scale, causing migration into areas where forests could be cleared for cocoa production. Demand for land by farmers migrating across ethnic boundaries in search of land caused tenure in Ghana to evolve toward greater individualization and marketability. This drove land use changes generally accommodated through the evolution of customary land tenure.

Cocoa, a crop of Central American origin, was brought into west Africa around in the middle of the 19th century and had become a significant export crop by 1880, joining coffee and oil palm. Demand for cocoa exploded in Europe. The strong market for cocoa in time led to plantings being established in Africa, initially in coastal areas, first in Ghana and soon afterward in Nigeria and Côte d'Ivoire. Adoption of cocoa was not the result of government promotion, simply a market response by farmers and small merchants to a cash crop opportunity. Its implications for land tenure were far from the minds of the emerging capitalists who migrated to find the land they needed for their cocoa farms (Hill, 1963).

Beginning in the 1890s and through the 1920s, cocoa farmers from near the coast were moving inland seeking larger areas of land for cocoa cultivation. Migrant cocoa farmers from ethnic groups such as the Akwapim and Krobo, among the first to plant cocoa, moved north into the sparsely populated forest zone where they bought land from local chiefs. The Akwapim were familiar with land sales. In the Akwapim Ridge area, purchases of land were common even before the arrival of cocoa. Undeveloped land was sold not by their principal chief, the Omanhene, but by sub-chiefs from the villages who represented local lineages. Sale of undeveloped land by ordinary individuals was prohibited, but they could sell their developed land. Land sales and mortgages were long-standing elements in Akwapim customary land tenure, and sales to strangers (members of other ethnic groups) originated at least a century earlier.[2]

To obtain land for cocoa farms, patrilineal groups organized themselves into "companies" of men from the same town and bought a large block of land. The block would be divided among the members into individually owned strips, an approach consistent with existing tenures in the area. Matrilineal communities also bought land in large blocks, but in collective ownership (Hill, 1963).

Extension of cocoa into other tribal areas where the custom of sale was not so well-established stimulated changes in the relationship between ownership of trees and ownership of land. Rights in trees distinct from land pre-dated the introduction of cocoa. Economic trees generally belonged to those who planted them. Since cocoa was developed for its commercial value, increased planting led to the growth of a market in trees themselves. Planters could alienate the trees by lease, gift, mortgage or sale. In some communities, rights in trees traditionally implied rights in the land where they were planted. In others this was not the case. In practice, the value of these trees gradually led to a general acceptance that a sale of the trees of a cocoa farm carried with it the rights to the land (Gastellu, 1980; Hill, 1963; Lloyd, 1962; Chauveau & Colin, 2007)

There were tenure developments in the trees themselves. The principle that trees belong to the individual who plants them suggests that tree crops will be individual property. Instead, circumstances resulted in complex and qualified patterns of tree and farm ownership. Most farmers hired labor at various times in the production cycle. By "investing" their labor in a farm, those workers might build up an interest in it over time. Since cocoa trees live for many years, tree farms were often inherited, creating new interests in the trees and the farm. The result was multiple, overlapping rights in the trees (Hill, 1963; Berry, 1975, 1988).

Twenty years after the first cocoa plantings in the Akwapim Ridge area, the Ashanti to the north took up cocoa cultivation and sought land in forests. Land sales were unknown there. Ashanti planters got land from local chiefs on often ambiguous terms. The nature of the rights has been actively contested in the courts for decades as land has grown scarcer and the land-providing lineages have sought to reassert their ownership of the land. Migrants argue their transaction was a virtual sale, not a legal relationship that can be terminated. They assert that periodic payments to the local chiefs by the migrants, originally in kind (e.g. kola nuts), are symbolic gestures intended to remind the community of the transfer of ownership. The land-granting communities contend that the transactions were loans of the land, analogous to a rental, and assert that recurrent payments, which have in recent times often been monetarized, confirm it as a rental. Different versions of tension between "early-arriving lineages" and "late-arriving lineages" exist in most west African countries and have become increasingly contentious with growing population pressure on land (Quan, 2007, pp. 59–60).

There is not a singular impact of cocoa on "customary land tenure." How cocoa was received and the adjustments made to custom depended on both the land tenure rules of the tree-planters (who came from several ethnic groups) and the rules of the land tenure system where they found land to plant their trees. Results vary from place to place, shaped by population densities, tenure arrangements and the market environment at the time of initial plantings and consequent events. Those results are not a predictable result of tenure system interactions. Each instance must be understood in its cultural and economic context, its history and the power relationship among the parties involved. Social status and relative power often determined outcomes with respect to trees and tree farms. At custom (as in all systems, in reality) all people are not equal before the law (Seidman & Seidman, 1994; Hill, 1963).

## Community Forests

Trees are found on community-owned land. Firewood is typically scarce in the vicinity of villages. If a woodland or forest exists near the village, there will usually be rules governing its use, possibly differing from case to case. Community members may be allowed to gather fallen branches for fuel, make charcoal to sell to passing trucks, graze cattle in the forest, hunt or gather high-value non-timber forest products (NTFPs) such as mushrooms and medicinal herbs. There may be locations within the forest with valuable species such as groves of economic trees in which some members of the community may have individual rights. There may be a site within the forest, such as a "spirit forest" or a spring regarded as sacred, that is respected and protected by the community. Such locations are sometimes used for coming of age and other ceremonies.

Other rules may have to do with rights to and management of specific resources in the forest. Indigenous forest management tools include taboos on damaging uses of forest resources, limitations of forest use by community members and agro-forestry practices. Communities may seek to conserve their forest resources, but pressure to find land for young families means the forest is also a resource the community may need to use for expanding cultivation.

Customary land tenure systems usually provide for exclusion of outsiders from community forests. Where the power to exclude is claimed by the community, there may be customary exceptions. The community may permit a migrating pastoralist group to pass through with their animals each year to graze on a remote wooded area.

The status of the forest as belonging to a particular community may be debatable. Where a community has access to a forested area, it commonly lies at the edge of the community, on its boundary with another community. Its use may be shared by the community on the other side of the boundary.

Information on traditional community forest management or on shared forests is limited. My own experience is the shared forest on the boundary between the parishes of Mahago and Elibat in southern Tigray, Ethiopia, in the early 1970s. There was no comprehensive plan for coordinated use or abstention from use, but rather simple rules such as "People from Mahago may collect firewood east as far as the ruins of the monastery but may not take more than they can carry themselves." When attempts have been made to establish boundaries for the communities in forested areas, claims show substantial overlap (Berry, 2001). Land tenure policy and law reform issues in relation to community forestry are discussed further in Chapter 8 on other natural resources.

## State Forests

Most large forests are owned by the state, not by individuals or communities. In many African countries, there is a national law or constitutional provision declaring that all forests belong to the state. The scope of such provisions depends on the definition of "forest," which depends upon the extent of tree cover in the country concerned. A "forest" in some parts of the Sahel would hardly be recognized as such by a forester from the Democratic Republic of the Congo. In any country, it is hard to say where the forest begins and ends. This contributes to contestation over control of land between ministries responsible for forests, agriculture and land. Much of what is shown as "forest" on old maps or referred to as such in legislation may have been under cultivation by farmers for generations. In Liberia, the definition of forest land under the Forestry Agency is expansive: "all land capable of forestry" (Bruce, 2013).

Land in state forests is a valuable resource, not only to locals for traditional uses, but also to the nation for timber, NTFPs, fauna and other biodiversity and their role as a carbon sink. Simultaneously there are customary rights holders living in or around the forest who gather food and fuel, pasture their cattle and sometimes farm in it. Colonial foresters and forestry agencies insisted that forests must be state property so that they could defend them against local people, many of whom depend upon forest products to meet household needs. Efforts to close forests to locals are often counterproductive. When denied a right to use the forest and its resources, locals have less interest in its sustainable use. Protection against unauthorized cutting, whether for timber or for charcoal making, has been a challenge for governments. Many state forestry management institutions lack the capacity and budget. Protection programs are often undermined by staff corruption. Where efforts at exclusion from state forests are effective, they can impoverish nearby communities and destroy entire ways of life.[3] In response to sustained and vigorous criticism from the larger conservation and development communities, forestry agency attitudes toward local participation in forest use and management have gradually shifted. Forest agencies sought to create incentives for local communities' forest preservation, providing forest guard jobs to locals while simultaneously allowing locals limited access for traditional uses, such as gathering fallen limbs for firewood or hunting for home consumption. More recently, some forestry agencies have contracted with local communities for forest protection, a more effective strategy. Greater access and control provided to communities has heightened their interest in forest sustainability (Lawry et al., 2012).

## Communities in the State's Forests

Some forest management agencies have organized local users to enhance opportunities to derive income from forest products. The forest agency contracts specific areas of forest to local families for collection of NTFPs. In these projects, commonly characterized as community-based natural resource management projects, benefits are shared. Most of these projects provide user groups with little security of access or tenure.

Realizing that lack of local economic opportunities is a driver of damaging incursions into the forest, forest agencies are embracing an integrated approach to forestry and, increasingly, devolution of areas of forest land to local communities for income-earning enterprises. These forestry initiatives in Africa typically involve local people through contractual arrangements, providing for community control and benefit-sharing. The community may operate the project directly or contract with commercial partners to carry out timber extraction or eco-tourism. Activities must comply with a management plan developed by the partners and approved by the forest agency. The duration of the arrangement is conditional upon compliance with the plan and achievement of the stipulated purposes. The most recent generation of these programs provide for increasingly strong tenure for communities to forest land, but they almost never devolve full ownership of the forest land from the state to the communities.[4]

## Climate Change and REDD+

Since 2008, alarm over climate change drove the United Nations and other agencies to launch programs to compensate developing country governments for the preservation and enhancement of forest carbon stocks under the rubrics REDD and REDD+.[5] These programs compensate governments for the costs of conservation and the opportunities that are foregone by maintaining forests instead of converting them to other uses. Forests in areas not currently under protection regimes, such as recreational state forests and forest reserves, are preserved and rehabilitated.

Early REDD projects, funded by international and bilateral donors, were conceived as conservation projects naïvely overestimating the capacity of most African governments to deliver on protection commitments for these forests. Outside state forests and reserves, protection arrangements were minimal to non-existent, while community use and demand for forest resources were substantial. Little or no funding went to the communities that were disadvantaged by more rigorous forest protection. REDD projects tended to require formation of associations of user groups based on state-prescribed criteria rather than existing community institutions, creating issues of authority over land in some communities.

In most of Africa, the state claims ultimate ownership of forests and argues that it should both receive forest carbon benefits and determine their allocation to others. Initially, this meant allocation of budgetary resources. Often, those benefits have gone to local government, failing to reach the households that have suffered loss of income due to increased protection of the forest (Lawry et al., 2012). Customary rights were not recognized. Customary use patterns were threatened and compensatory benefits were misdirected. With little incentive to cooperate in such circumstances, tensions between national governments and local communities over control of forest land emerged frequently in the first generation of REDD projects (Alusiola et al., 2021).

Only gradually was it recognized that, for these projects to succeed, local communities who actually used the forest areas had to be incentivized to cooperate. REDD's failure to address the land tenure situation realistically was recognized as a threat to its sustainability (Knox et al., 2011). The REDD+ Strategic Program adopted by the United Nations in 2016 emphasized sustainable forest management and development, opening possibilities for community forestry as a strategy for sustainable use also achieving the forest protection objective. By this time, advocates of customary land users saw REDD+ as a means of obtaining state recognition of customary land rights. Secure land tenure is an incentive for community delivery of environmental services. Increasing production of environmental services could be rewarded with providing communities stronger forms of forest tenure. Security of tenure benefits usually take time to deliver. They are not a substitute for more immediate, highly tangible benefits, but rather a supplement critical for sustainability.[6] The most expedient way to provide security of tenure for customary rights within forests is for the government to quickly devolve a use right over the land to the community. Contractual arrangements, such as long-term leases from governments to local entities responsible for sustainable development, are an alternative.

In the context of state forest, classification and control of the forest by the forest agency has turned the state's *de jure* tenure into *de facto* tenure. For older state forests, any customary claims are far in the past and no longer seem relevant. The forestry agency's presence allows it to dominate negotiations and exercise supervision. The culture of most forestry agencies limits the extent to which tenure is used as a benefit and incentive. Contractual arrangements with communities allowing them to use state forest land tend to provide limited and conditional security of tenure for the community organizations holding the contracts. This land is virtually never devolved in full ownership to the user groups or communities. In the case of ungazetted forests on state-owned land that are used by local people who feel they have customary rights in the forest, and if forest projects there interact with local government as much or more than with the forestry agency, the potential for robust tenure benefits for communities should be greater. It will also depend on options under national legislation for devolution and transfer of state-owned land.

How economically effective are community-based natural resource management efforts? They clearly provide income and other opportunities to communities, but are they also capable of generating the investment needed for sustained development and how important are tenure arrangements to that success? A United States Agency for International Development-funded review of forest devolution in 16 countries (Lawry et al., 2012)[7] found that tenuous use rights and weak benefit-sharing did not provide the incentives to motivate users to invest substantially in forest improvements and protection. While forest laws had been revised to provide stronger tenure and autonomy, forest agency officials usually provided less than the laws allow. Despite these challenges, the authors conclude that there is growing evidence that "forests under community ownership have better ecological outcomes, when measured by forest cover, than state-managed forests. Livelihood outcomes are generally better under community ownership" (Lawry et al., 2012).

While states have a mixed record of providing protection for forests, their role is essential. Where state authority collapses, large areas of state-owned forest may be destroyed. There is wealth there, enough to attract powerful interests if there is an opportunity to appropriate it. In 2008, I was travelling from Monrovia to the capital of Bong County, Gbarnga. On a major road, we drove through a mile of forest. The forest seemed largely intact, surprising me. Only a few years earlier Liberia had come out of decades of civil war and conflict. Protection for forests and other public resources had collapsed. I remarked on this to the driver. "Wait," he said. He turned into an access road that ran into the forest. After 100 meters, we emerged into a vast open area, stretching as far as the eye could see, clear-cut and turning into brush. The trees along the road had been left to screen the deforestation.

## Notes

1 Heirs of a deceased tree-planter often inherit the ownership share of the deceased as joint property with the other owners, so the co-owners are often numerous, many of them holding very small fractional interests in the tree and claiming their share of the dates. Under the Anglo-Egyptian Condominium Law in Sudan, land registration instituted by the government along the Nile included registration of tree ownership with the

government legislating maximum denominators for shares, below which a share could not be registered (Thompson, 1965).

2 Hill remarked that writers on cocoa-farming, discovering land sales and discomfited to find something that seemed to them "decidedly uncustomary," always assumed that land sales were something new. "Whether the date is 1910 or 1960, land sales are always supposed to be increasing … and to be a new factor in the situation" (Hill, 1963, p. 138).

3 In the late 1990s, in connection with a World Bank consultancy in Albania, I had an opportunity to visit the great state forests in the north of the country, many of which are in commercial production. Driving up and down through mountains covered with great trees, passing trucks piled high with massive tree trunks headed to the mills, we pulled into a small town for something to drink. I was struck by how poor the housing seemed and how ragged their clothes were. My host noticed and remarked that this was a poor region and that the people here required subsidies from the government to survive. It struck me that those in the small town were poor because the state had appropriated the wealth of the region: its forests. They lived in poverty in the shade of that great wealth.

4 Some of these forest areas are quite large, as in the case of the forests of the indigenous territories in Latin America. These indigenous communities generally have broad authority to manage their territory, though they cannot sell it. While in most cases the ultimate ownership of an indigenous territory remains with the state, the indigenous group holds the land by right conferred by legislative or other official designation, not by contract nor by permission. See Ortega (2004).

5 REDD+ refers to "reducing emissions from deforestation or forest degradation, and the role of conservation, sustainable management of forests, and enhancement of forest carbon stocks in developing countries."

6 Wily (2001) provides an insightful review of Tanzania's community development experience and the African experience of tenure in community forestry, reflecting on how community forestry has developed under a range of tenure regimes—on owned land, on community land and on devolved state land—and the implications of this for future community forestry development.

7 Most of them in Asia; in Africa, only Cameroon and Sudan are covered.

## References

Alusiola, R.A., Schilling, J., & Klär, P. (2021). REDD+ Conflict: Understanding the pathways between forest projects and social conflict. *Forests*, *12*(6), Article 748. https://doi.org/10.3390/f12060748.

Berry, S. (1975). *Cocoa, custom and socio-economic change in rural western Nigeria.* Clarendon Press.

Berry, S. (1988). Property rights and rural resource management: The case of tree crops in West Africa. *Cahier des Sciences Humaines*, *24*(1), 3–18.

Berry, S. (2001). *Chiefs know their boundaries: Essays on property, power and the past, Asante, 1896–1996.* Heinemann and James Currey.

Bruce, J.W. (2013, February 2). Options for Liberia: Organizing for better land governance, a report to the Land Commission.

Chauveau, J.P. & Colin, J.P. (2007). Changes in land transfer mechanisms: Evidence from West Africa. In L. Cotula (Ed.), *Changes in "customary" land tenure systems in Africa* (pp. 65–80). IIED.

Fortmann, L. (1985). The tree tenure factor in agroforestry with particular reference to Africa. *Agroforestry Systems*, *2*(4), 229–251. https://doi.org/10.1007/BF00147036

Fortmann, L. & Bruce, J.W. (1988). *Whose trees? Proprietary dimensions of forestry*. Westview Press.

Gastellu, J.M. (1980). L'arbre ne cache pas la forêt, ou: usus, fructus et abusus. *Cahiers ORSTOM, Série Sciences Humaines*, *17*(3–4), 279–282.

Hill, P. (1963). *The migrant cocoa-farmers of Southern Ghana: A study in rural capitalism*. Cambridge University Press.

Knox, A., Caron, C., Miner, J., & Goldstein, A. (2011). Land tenure and payment for environmental services: Challenges and opportunities for REDD+. *Land Tenure Journal*, *2*, 1–39.

Lawry, S., McLain, R., Swallow, B., & Biedenweg, K. (2012). *Devolution of forest rights and sustainable forest management: A review of policies and programs in 16 developing countries* [Conference presentation]. Tetra Tech ARD for USAID.

Lloyd, P.C. (1962). *Yoruba land law.* Oxford University Press.

Ortega, R.R. (2004). *Models for recognizing indigenous land rights in Latin America* (Biodiversity Series, Paper No. 99.) World Bank Environment Department.

Quan, J. (2007). Changes in intra-family land relations. In L. Cotula (Ed.), *Changes in "customary" land tenure systems in Africa* (pp. 51–62). IIED.

Seidman, A.W. & Seidman, R.B. (1994). *State and law in the development process: Problem solving and institutional change in the third world.* Palgrave Macmillan.

Thompson, C.F. (1965). *The land law of the Sudan: Cases and materials*. Faculty of Law, University of Khartoum.

Wily, L.A. (2001). Forest management and democracy in East and Southern Africa: Lessons from Tanzania. *IIED Gatekeeper Series* (95th ed., pp. 2–20). w.iied.org/sites/default/files/pdfs/migrate/6350IIED.pdf

# 8 Other Land and Natural Resources "Beyond the Village"

To a casual observer the landscape beyond the farms seems largely unpopulated, unused and unmanaged.[1] There was until quite recently in Africa a persistent notion of vast areas of vacant land, unused and virtual *terra nullius* land belonging to no one and hence available to takers. It is a myth. It was rarely the case even in the colonial period, and it is certainly not true today.[2] Few areas in Africa are unused by rural communities and their members. Nearly all rural land is claimed by those communities, though many boundaries are vague or contested and may be subject to negotiation (Berry, 2001). This is the most actively contested land in Africa, with locals and outsiders struggling to establish legal claims to it or retain control.

The land may be grassland, too remote for effective control by the community, perhaps up on an escarpment, with different rainfall or flooding patterns, or valued for seasonal grazing of the community's livestock. It may be forested land with all the riches the forest has to offer. It may be "wasteland," dry land sparsely covered with scrub plants and used, if used at all, for casual grazing by less discriminating feeders, typically goats. Within this "land beyond the farms" one may find grazing commons much better managed by the community. In some places, the land has potential for cultivation and is expansion land for new farms, in others it does not. One may even find an occasional parcel, cultivated by a community member with little good farmland, taking advantage of an exceptionally good rainy period to snatch a crop from land normally not worth planting.

These lands are often along one or more of a community's boundaries with other communities and may be subject to competing claims. Lacking a clear boundary, the community's land may transition into land which the community does not claim as its own but to which the community considers it has use rights. These, often seasonal, rights of use may be shared with other communities, even other ethnic groups. The vast flooded pastures of the White Nile's Sudd in South Sudan are one such example, though these days the area is increasingly reduced by the river's lessening flow.

How to characterize the tenure in this community-held "land beyond the farm?" It is certainly not open access because outsiders are excluded, but it also does not conform to the principles of effective common property management as described by Ostrom (1990), including the existence of clear boundaries. I have heard it referred to as property of the landholding community, but also as territory often

DOI: 10.4324/9781003476429-10

lacking clear definition and distinction of the two terms. It is clear that there are rights and rules that govern these commons, even if they are shared and at times ambiguous.

## Community Forest Use

In many parts of Africa, it is not unusual for a community to have access to a forest. These are usually smaller forests, ranging from substantial forests that one might not be able to walk across in a day to tattered remnants of a forest. There may be legal ambiguity over whether they fall within the territory of a community or under some state forestry agency. There may be conflicting claims to the land. Colonial and post-independence states have taken the great forests of Africa and turned them into reserves and state forests, the intention being to protect them from degradation by local users. Often there are villages at the edge of those state forests whose members depend heavily upon them for their livelihood, notwithstanding that their use by the villagers is illegal. In some countries where funds are not available or there is civil disorder or war, the state's policing of forest borders waxes and wanes, permitting major incursions.

Where communities have no rights to use the forest, they have limited interest in its conservation. Where villagers have access to the forest, by right or opportunity, they go to the forest to graze their livestock, "for the pot" (own consumption), gather firewood, fell trees to build their homes and sometimes engage in lucrative (if illegal) charcoal-making. They gather a wide range of readily marketable non-timber forest products: animal skins, edible forest products (e.g. fruits, mushrooms, grubs) and plants and body parts of animals important to traditional medicine.

Outsiders often see the forest as a wild and ungoverned space. Those who use it are aware of rules and practices expected to be observed. Those rules are most often prohibitions and limitations on use, including taboos; for example, this fruit cannot be gathered before this flower blooms; fish cannot be taken from this stream by men of the village before completion of an annual ceremony; women can only take from the forest as much firewood as they can carry themselves; this lake is a spirit lake; those who use it must perform certain ceremonies before they can do more than pass through the area in daylight hours; no one from this village may hunt in the forest beyond the abandoned, rusty engine block of a truck.

These small rules create a loose web of norms and recognized good practices. They serve sustainable use and, where communities share the use of a forest on their border, limit conflict between different communities who access the forest. The sanctions for these rules are often supernatural. They can be forms, such as fines or other type of compensation.

The communities who use forested land and other "land beyond the farm" look to benefit if valuable resources are discovered there, and at the same time seek opportunities to derive new value from existing resources. Such opportunities often bring with them new regulations of the state and new government agencies which seek to guide or control the activity. Below two cases are considered: the discovery of gemstones and the sport hunting of large animals.

## Artisanal Mining

Artisanal mining is mining by individuals, families or groups that is largely carried out in the informal sector using little or no mechanization. It has been practiced since before the colonial period. It has progressively grown both in economic importance and as a policy problem for African states. The minerals involved are mostly gemstones (diamonds and sapphires) and gold. Artisanal mining requires only modest capital and modest areas of land, usually the site where the minerals have been discovered. While villagers do mine on their own lands, much of the mining is done by migrant miners, moving from site to site when discoveries are made (Hentschel et al., 2002). In Africa, women make up 45–50% of those engaged in artisanal mining (UNECA, 2002). Women are usually involved in ore processing, and selling and providing food to the miners, rather than digging and other heavy mining activities (IGF, 2018).

Almost all African constitutions declare sub-surface minerals as belonging to the state, with South Africa being a major exception (Wily, 2001; Knight, 2010). Sourcing minerals from artisanal mining operations is usually illegal. In most African countries, artisanal mining is governed by local custom, rather than the legal framework governing mining. The mining operation may be on land held by a community member or held by the community collectively, claims often not recognized by state law. The lack of effective government regulation and control have had negative local impacts, including significant environmental degradation in surrounding areas through secondary activities generated by artisanal mining (e.g. woodcutting), lack of implementation of labor and health standards, and insecurity stemming from the continuing struggle for control between the state, local communities and the miners themselves.

Where small-scale mining is under government control, there will usually be a small concession given by the government to a management company, which gives the company an exclusive right to mine in an area. The company is obligated to turn over the product to a government agency holding a legal monopoly to market such minerals. The firm managing the concession and the miners from whom the minerals were obtained receive a contractually specified amount from the sale of the mineral. Minerals are valuable resources often coming to public attention suddenly, when "discovered," at which point their extent and value is typically not clear to nearby communities, paving the way for future disputes over ownership of such resources. Conflicts also arise where exploration and operations are conducted by large commercial mining companies in areas with artisanal mining. These conflicts sometimes assume national and even international significance, as when artisanal mining finances insurgencies (e.g. "blood diamonds") (Hentschel et al., 2002).

Governments often wish to bring uncontrolled artisanal mining practices into line with statutory law, which may have special provisions on artisanal mining. Governments are advised by industry experts to create objective, consistent, transparent and non-discriminatory regulatory mechanisms, which offer easy access to mining titles and legal production. Decentralization of related government services is also recommended. Mining authorities are urged to coordinate activities with local administrations and communities (Hentschel et al., 2002).

This version of formalization has been challenged by an alternative vision that calls for reform and the legalization of customary practices, a policy issue that coincides with a larger debate concerning formalization of customary land tenure (Bruce & Roth, 2005).

Artisanal miners generally attempt to avoid formalization. The reasons given for this are: (a) their desire to avoid taxes or other burdens coming with formalization; (b) their desire to avoid the bureaucratic requirements of formalization; (c) their skepticism concerning benefits of formalization; and (d) corruption on the part of officials (Hentschel et al., 2002).[3] Lack of governmental capacity to enforce rules and provide the services and benefits anticipated in legislation or regulations acts as a further disincentive to miners to be legalized (Hentschel et al., 2002). Artisanal miners will be reluctant to be legalized where there are no obvious incentives for them to do so.

While formalization programs tend to begin on the assumption that the activity concerned is unregulated, artisanal mining is rarely uncontrolled. The communities where it occurs often have their own rules regarding artisanal mining. This should not be surprising, as gemstones and gold in small amounts have flowed out of Africa and into Europe and Arabia for centuries. Across sub-Saharan Africa, governments are finding it extremely difficult to replace customary rules, which show considerable vitality and are often the most important determinant of miner behavior (Hentschel et al., 2002). In Guinea, the government has attempted to formalize procedures for artisanal mining, but has not been able to replace customary practice, which still controls access and procedures (Huntington & Marple-Cantrell, 2021). Similar situations have been reported in Ghana and other African countries.[4] Understanding these customary systems is critical to building arrangements that satisfy communities as well as the responsible government agencies (Huntington & Marple-Cantrell, 2021).[5]

**Box 8.1 Customary Governance of Artisanal Mining in Guinea**

Small-scale diamond mining in Guinea is organized and regulated by local customary land owners and village headpersons according to a set of customary rules and behavioral prescriptions that are well-known by indigenes and national and transnational migrants (Muriaas, 2009). In areas where mining occurs, customary land owners assert their ownership to land through the location of their ancestral graves, which confers upon them the legitimacy and authority to manage relationships between miners and local communities (Chanakira et al., 2019). Land transfers for artisanal mining occur within long-standing informal land markets regulated by customary authorities. Customary land owners negotiate short-term use and access rights on mining sites for a fee under a framework similar to a short-term parcel rental (Chimhowu and Woodhouse, 2006).

Source: Huntington and Marple-Cantrell (2021).

The presence of artisanal mining in community territory classified as "community reserves" presents additional governance challenges. Reserves have too often been Trojan horses bearing central government and extractive industries. It is not unusual to see references to "conservation land-grabbing" or "green-grabbing" (Holmes, 2014; IIED, 2013).

In Madagascar, artisanal mining sometimes occurs in local reserves intended for conservation and community-based natural resource management initiatives. Attitudes toward illegal mining in local communities are influenced by the way in which the land for the reserve was obtained from the community and the extent to which the reserve is controlled by and serving the needs of the local community. While the communities have traditions regarding protection of natural resources from overuse and damage from economic activities, influxes of migrant miners often ignore traditional limits on incursions, not only into the reserve but into sacred forests or other taboo areas. Defense of conservation reserves from mining is the responsibility of the Government of Madagascar, which takes its roles in their protection seriously. In cases of major invasions, it calls in the army to seal the boundaries and shoot violators (Baker-Médard, 2012).[6]

If these problems are to be confronted successfully and a fair system of benefit sharing devised, a starting point is rethinking the meaning of "informality." "Informality" has in the case of artisanal mining been used to characterize customary arrangements by reference to what they are not (legitimated by the state), rather than what they are: an alternative, socially legitimated set of rules governed by sub-state polities (Siegal & Viega, 2009).[7] The discussion should be about two different systems, their objectives, the benefits they confer and on whom they confer them, how they affect behavior, the enforcement mechanisms in each and what would need to be done to link them effectively. Those taking this approach must consider how they propose to handle diversity in local systems and address problems noted in customary practices: inequality in the distribution of benefits and resources, corruption, elite capture and greater exclusivity of land use and access rights on the basis of local versus "stranger" distinctions (Huntington & Marple-Cantrell, 2021, citing Berry, 2009; Hirons, 2011, 2014; Muriaas, 2009; Putzel et al., 2015).

Linking customary and state systems requires understanding the customary setup and the particular rural context.[8] It is unlikely to be successful if it means replacing customary practices with those dictated by the state. Under the current model, formalization will vest power and rights of control in government and officials, not artisanal miners or mining communities. Addressing this would require reforms in the law concerning rights in the product and distribution of the funds generated by their sale. Is the state ready to recognize the customary rights of artisanal miners and mining communities in the product and in the revenues provided by sale of the product? Will it be willing to strike compromises necessary to incentivize miners to observe the rules in a system that links customary norms and practices with laws of the state in a complementary fashion?

In the absence of such solutions (or governments more capable of simple enforcement), tensions and conflicts seem likely to continue among government agencies, rural communities and migrant mining populations. These tensions are not just about processes and practices, or even formalization, but about power and the distribution of the wealth created by artisanal mining. What miners and their communities say by their behavior is that they think they should have a right to far greater benefits from wealth found within their boundaries.

## Community Wildlife Management

In the mid-1980s, a radically different approach to wildlife management was developed and piloted in Africa, styled "community-based wildlife management" (CBWM). A new approach was needed because large wildlife populations were declining under the "fences and fines" approach where the state is responsible for protecting wildlife by fencing them in reserves and fining poachers. The land for the reserves had been taken from local communities' commons, their "land beyond the farm." Denied access to the reserves, the communities bordering them (or within which the reserves were located) did not have sufficient incentives to refrain from poaching wildlife when opportunities arose.

Some working on wildlife management issues concluded that state enforcement alone would not suffice but should be accompanied by providing incentives for local communities to conserve wildlife. Pioneering work was done in Zimbabwe by the CAMPFIRE program of the Centre for Applied Social Sciences of the University of Zimbabwe.[9] CAMPFIRE sought to incentivize sustainable community wildlife management by allowing communities to license sport hunting of large mammals on their lands, including on reserve lands within their territories, a lucrative line of business (Murphree, 1994).

Given loss of confidence in the old approaches, it seemed that governments and communities should be able to see the mutual advantage in the new approach. Communities had long complained of exclusion from reserves and economic opportunities connected with the reserves. They knew the animals well and should be able to manage them. In practice, some of these assumptions proved problematic. Governments' embrace of the new approach proved lukewarm. Many officials saw wildlife as a national resource and considered that they should be managed for the benefit of the nation as a whole, rather than benefiting local communities. They were reluctant to give up their control of wildlife and any benefits that they derived from it. In 1994, the International Institute for Environment and Development (IIED), after reviewing the progress and impacts of 15 Community Conservation Services and CBWM programs and projects in Africa, found that some national governments were reluctant to support the approach because it was perceived to threaten central authority (IIED, 1994). In Zimbabwe and other countries in southern Africa, where governments had only recently been elected by majority rule, the model was politically sensitive. Emphasis on public consultation and community empowerment felt to them like lack of control (Songorwa et al., 2000).

However attractive the theory of CBWM, opinions on it remain divided. It has vocal critics. An Africa-wide review in 2005 concluded that it is "less effective than it is said to be" and works only in some places under certain conditions (Songorwa et al., 2000, p. 621). There were implementation difficulties. It was not unusual for opposition to the approach to develop in communities who had undertaken to implement it. Those who lived and farmed in these communities complained that wildlife had become a serious threat to their lives and crops. Large mammals, including elephants, are very dangerous. Fatalities sometimes occurred. This was the main source of local opposition to CBWM programming (Songorwa et al., 2000).

Much of the difficulty appears to have stemmed from lack of an adequate legal framework for program activities. The CAMPFIRE program in Zimbabwe functioned for a decade on the basis of memos. Legal ambiguities also troubled the implementation of CBWM in Tanzania. Under Tanzania's 1999 land laws, the Land Act No. 4 and the Village Land Act No. 5, all land in the country is divided into reserved, village and general land. Reserved lands include Game Reserves and Game Controlled Areas. The Village Land Act defines village lands as areas which are customarily used and occupied by local people living in registered villages and which may have been demarcated during any previous administrative procedure or where neighboring communities have agreed to their boundaries. Many areas were simultaneously village land and reserved land, without rules that defined the relationship between them or those who administered them. From the villagers' standpoint, this was major interference with their control of village land (Stolla, 2005).

Cases discussed here suggest the limits of protections provided by conservation laws, which tend to leave the state and its agencies in a controlling position with respect to land. This allows the state to reassert itself as owner when other valuable land uses arise and to subsequently disempower the community. This is often framed in the literature as a failure to protect a community interest. This is so in Tanzania, where reserve land belonged to (i.e., was owned by) the community, independent of its status as a reserve. Asserting state ownership in some countries appears to enable the state to alter the tenure and management of land held by communities for reserve purposes, such that the community can no longer use or benefit from the reserve.

It is difficult to form a balanced view of the CBWM experience because conservationists remain divided as to the relative merits of the "fines and fences" and the CBWM conservation models. Two decades after the last broad reviews of CBWM, it is important that more recent experiences be reviewed. There is clearly value in the approach, and it would be worthwhile establishing what set of conditions are required for the model to function effectively. Perhaps CBWM is best seen not as a substitute for "fences and fines," but as a complementary approach, especially appropriate for smaller land management units within or bordering rural communities.

## The Great Land Grab

"The Great Land Grab" is a pejorative term often used for the extensive contracting by developing country governments of state-owned land to foreign investors for export agriculture, expelling in the process those who held and farmed the land by customary right.[10] Foreign investment in agriculture was nothing new to Africa, and there had long been hopes that it would grow. When I taught at the University of Khartoum from 1975 to 1980, features in local papers and magazines touted Sudan as the future "breadbasket of the world." At that time, there was little investment beyond the massive public irrigation projects supported by international donors. External private sector investment grew gradually in Sudan and elsewhere in Africa, and then exploded from 2007 as the result of an anticipated world shortage of foods, edible oils, biofuels and industrial agricultural products. African governments had extensive state-owned lands and needed hard currency, investment capital and access to new technologies and management skills that would come with large-scale export agriculture.

## Land Grab or Give-Away?

"Land Grab" suggests a forcible taking, and if you ask, "by whom?" you're likely to be told "foreign investors." Given that governments transferred these lands to investors willingly, the "grab" has been by governments, which have taken land from its customary owners to contract to those investors. The concession process reaffirms the state's ownership of the land, ignoring customary claims of ownership and depriving communities of land use. Concessions typically provide investors long-term (usually several decades) land use rights, while the state remains the owner. Private customary rights of local inhabitants are lost in the process, since these had never been recognized by the government, their extinction and loss of possession leave the state secure in its ownership claim to the land.

Granting concessions does not privatize the land. Before there were concessions, land was government land *de jure*; *de facto*, it was land held privately under custom. In assigning land to a concessionaire, the government's ownership of the land is affirmed. When it replaced customary users with concessionaires, customary users lost *de facto* control of the land under custom. The concessionaire became the *de jure* holder of the right to use the land, conferred by the state by virtue of its *de jure* ownership of the land. The *de facto* has been aligned with the *de jure*. The distinction between *de jure* and *de facto* is irrelevant to the new status quo.

The result is not surprising. Customary rights in Africa are protected poorly, if at all, by national land laws. Customary land is cheap to acquire where both traditional customary policies and national policies have kept it from entering the formal land market. Investors seeking to acquire land often decline to purchase land even when it is available to own, and instead target land under customary land tenure because it can be acquired at little or no cost, either through abuse of the state's power of compulsory acquisition or through black-market purchases of land from a chief or other traditional ruler (Amanor & Ubink, 2008). Often the customary lands targeted were commons areas, rangeland or forests (Anseeuw et al., 2012). The relative ease and low cost of large land acquisitions made Africa the continent most affected by the Land Grab.[11]

## Dealing in Land

In a land deal, the investor is negotiating with the government agency with responsibility for management of state-owned land, most frequently a Ministry of Lands. Often several government agencies have the power to grant concessions. These may include a concessions bureau and/or a line ministry managing state land for a particular purpose, such as the Ministry of Agriculture or the Forestry Authority. In the case of an agricultural concession, the investor might need to negotiate with the Ministry of Lands for land, the Ministry of Agriculture on the development plan for the farm, the Ministry of Natural Resources for water rights, the Treasury for repatriation of profits, and so on. This can mean anything from hopping between the offices of the different agencies in different parts of town to undertaking needed procedures within a single office building based on a well-integrated process. A streamlined process usually requires legislation to establish and enforce.

In addition to government authorities, a foreign investor often needs access to investment funds from its own government. There might be a bilateral investment protection agreement between the two countries. Some embassies are very proactive in identifying investment opportunities for their nationals and provide substantial advisory and logistical support (Cotula & Vermeulen, 2009). It is not unusual these days for the investor's side of the negotiations to consist entirely of public institutions. To use a Chinese investor as an example, the negotiations may involve a provincial investment corporation from China, supported by funding and an economist from China's Belt and Road Initiative and receiving substantial logistical and other support from its embassy.

Close examination of investment contracts reveals major differences in the legality, structure and outcomes of land deals and diverse roles of domestic elites and governments as partners, intermediaries and beneficiaries (Hall, 2011). One group of participants rarely mentioned in the literature plays an important role. The investor may identify retired officials from the Ministry of Lands, often surveyors with useful knowledge of landholdings and contacts with local authorities, and hire them as consultants. Consultants identify land for the investor and assist in negotiations. Lack of transparency and disparities in power and knowledge in negotiations between investors and local communities should lead governments to guide and protect the communities involved. Both retired and current ministry staff often act like agents of the investor. This has encouraged corruption and capture of project benefits by these staff.

## Leases and Concessions

Tenure instruments by which investor deals are memorialized can be deeds for purchases of privately owned land or, more often, leases or concessions on state-owned land. A lease is a contract under which the state receives rent from the investor for use of the land for a specified period of time, after which the land reverts to the owner, the state. It will specify, in varying degrees of detail, the nature of the intended use (commercial real estate, agricultural, etc.), but usually in general terms.

A concession resembles a lease in some key respects. Both leases and concessions typically have initial terms of 20–40 years, but some are as long as 99 years. Like a lease, a concession is a long-term contract by which the state provides the investor with use of its land. It is more akin to a joint venture in that it is typically characterized by shared profits and interest in the outcome.

A concession is best thought of as a hybrid between a grant of a long-term land use right and public/private collaboration in a joint venture. The state provides the land and various incentives (tax holiday or deferred customs charges for exports or other similar privileges). The investor provides the capital and technical and management expertise. The concession sets out, often in considerable detail, a plan of development with projections of land development and output. The common purpose in most cases would be developing export-oriented agriculture, associated improvements in public infrastructure and services and profits. The government does not charge rent or charges only a nominal rent. It receives a share in the profits from the concession. Unlike renting land where investors are careful not to take more land than they need due to the cost of renting. Without rent, a concessionaire will almost invariably take more land than they can fully develop if it is on offer.

In practice, the distinction between leases and concessions can blur. Some contracts which call themselves "leases" are written like concessions and vice versa. The concessions vary widely in content and style. Some are short and unspecific, granting extensive areas of land for long terms in exchange for little public revenue and vague promises of jobs or investment. Transparency has increased substantially in recent years. Many concessions can be accessed on government internet sites.[12] Increasingly, one finds mention of social and environmental protections and greater specificity regarding community benefits. The fundamental issues of land takings and compensation are not addressed in the concessions but are instead treated as unrelated matters (Cotula et al., 2011; Cotula, 2011).

In 2016, GRAIN assessed the first ten years of the land grab in Africa. GRAIN is a small non-governmental organization (NGO) which has assembled one of the two major data sets on land deals, relying on data provided by its network of local NGOs. GRAIN's findings remain representative of the situation today. They found that some of the more outrageous land deals had collapsed. In 2009, in perhaps the most widely publicized example, public outrage over the 1,300,000-hectare Daewoo project in Madagascar helped bring down the government, leading to the suspension of the deal. GRAIN's 2016 database documents 491 large-scale land grabs taking place over the past decade. Of these, 126 deals failed. GRAIN concluded that their collapse helped to explain why the growth in farmland deals had slowed since 2012 and why the overall number of hectares had declined (GRAIN, 2016).

As time has passed, the environment for concessions has changed. New categories of investors, such as pension funds and trade conglomerates, seek land for an increasing variety of purposes. Instead of a "wild land rush" environment, investors are confronted with multiple guidelines for responsible land investment.[13] Guidelines are voluntary and focused primarily on the need for more consultative and transparent processes. Unable to obtain more fundamental reform, such as recognition of and compensation for customary rights, advocates for affected communities have focused on creating procedural fairness in planning land acquisitions and development, using consultation as a medium that allows an affected community to make a claim for benefits from the project. Such benefits may include jobs, improvements in local infrastructure, schools and health facilities. Another approach is providing a fund for local development managed by the local government. Questions have arisen as to whether such funds end up benefiting those most adversely affected by the concession. The consultation approach will usually be effective only if government has clear policies requiring tangible benefits for communities and reliable advice for communities is available from government or NGOs.

Any assessment on the overall impact of a land grab on national land tenure systems must begin with an effort to establish how large a portion of a nation's available farmland is already covered by concessions and how much land remains. A study by Schoneveld (2014) includes data on this point. Table 8.1, taken from that study, is revealing.

*Table 8.1* Farmland Investments and Land Availability in Key Investment Destinations

| *Country* | *Total area potentially available (ha)* | *Land acquired, as % of total available land (%)* | |
|---|---|---|---|
| | | *Category 1 data* | *All data categories* |
| Sierra Leone | 389,450 | 305.48 | 332.47 |
| Liberia | 700,650 | 153.56 | 153.56 |
| Nigeria | 769,850 | 86.74 | 101.81 |
| Ghana | 2,076,400 | 93.35 | 99.53 |
| Ethiopia | 7,750,050 | 28.54 | 28.54 |
| Senegal | 3,209,150 | 14.72 | 19.24 |
| Mozambique | 12,456,300 | 14.82 | 16.88 |
| Gabon | 2,456,600 | 16.28 | 16.28 |
| Republic of the Congo | 6,816,200 | 12.23 | 13.11 |
| Zambia | 15,699,950 | 11.70 | 12.39 |
| Tanzania | 7,144,900 | 8.33 | 12.07 |
| South Sudan | 22,860,000 | 6.36 | 8.38 |
| Mali | 10,630,850 | 6.77 | 6.90 |
| Cameroon | 5,510,050 | 5.47 | 6.74 |
| Madagascar | 28,216,300 | 5.39 | 6.26 |
| DR Congo | 17,810,350 | 1.61 | 2.00 |
| Kenya | 17,302,100 | 1.81 | 1.85 |
| Sub-Saharan Africa | 361,284,550 | 5.33 | 6.29 |

Source: Schoneveld (2014).

The first four countries in the table are in an alarming situation. In Liberia and Sierra Leone—the smallest countries of the four—it is hard to imagine how more than 100% of potentially available land has been allocated by the government to investors. The percentage taken for concessions is less daunting in Mozambique, which is much larger, but still has a land acquisition ratio so high that it calls for urgent attention. Where concessions are not a high percentage of national land, judgment on impacts would need more information on the concessions' location. The concentration of land acquisitions in a limited portion of a country is common, typically in the underdeveloped interior of a coastal state, or in a remote frontier province. In such circumstances, as in Ethiopia's south-west frontier with Sudan, the level of takings and the consequent loss of land rights by customary land users will affect prospects of ethnic minorities who hold land in these regions. In more arid environments, concessions will likely be clustered along rivers, where they appropriate water and depend on water rights as well as land.

Schoneveld (2014) concludes that governments are ill-equipped or unwilling to effectively regulate these investments, resulting in the progressive concentration of land in the hands of foreign corporate interests. Governments' mechanisms to capture potential gains are also typically lacking. Land acquisition occurs at prices not reflecting the land's true value. Civil society organizations (CSOs) have emerged in countries such as Cameroon, Liberia, Mozambique, Tanzania and Senegal, showing that important domestic processes of collective action are emerging around these issues. The author recommends that CSO activities focus on enhancing community capacity to claim their legal rights in the context of rights infringement and campaign for the adoption of simple and enforceable safeguards: increasing land rental rates; allocation of (parts of) land rental revenues to host communities; reducing the duration of leaseholds; return of the land to host communities upon expiration of concessions or leaseholds; and allocating returns from foreclosure to host communities (Schoneveld, 2014).

It can be helpful to examine closely the case of one nation, to better understand the forces at play and the issues involved. Consider Liberia, which has been particularly affected as compared to other African countries.

## Concessions and Tenure Change in Liberia

In 2007, when the Land Grab began, Liberia was a post-conflict country, its fledgling government only then beginning to assume government functions that had previously been handled by United Nations (UN) civil authorities. The newly elected government was desperate for domestic investment and welcomed investors wanting land. Access to land was to be had through the land tenure system established by the Americo-Liberians, who in 1847 established a colony of freed slaves from the United States on the Liberian coast. The Colony of Liberia had developed a dualistic land tenure system largely resembling those European powers had established in their colonies in Africa. Colonists received land in private ownership, at first purchased from locals, but later from the state. After Liberia became a republic, the state claimed all the land of the interior as state-owned land by right of conquest. The customary rights of the locals were not recognized, leaving them as "tenants at will" of government, liable to expulsion without compensation. This gradual dispossession of customary landholders was resented. In 1980, junior officers led by Sergeant Samuel Doe enacted a coup. He called for land reform but did not in the end pursue reform. The country spiraled into civil war after Doe was murdered in 1990. After decades of maladministration and atrocities, UN Peacekeepers restored order. A UN Civil Administration assumed many government functions. The large-scale land acquisition by Firestone in Liberia, described in Box 8.2, is one of the first major corporate Land Grabs in Africa.

**Box 8.2 Firestone in Liberia**

As the Land Grab began, Liberia was no stranger to foreign companies seeking land for concessions. The Firestone Rubber Plantation, the largest business in Liberia and the largest rubber plantation in the world, had been established in 1926. The Liberian government granted Firestone a 99-year lease for 1,000,000 acres (to be chosen by the company anywhere in Liberia) at an annual rent of six cents per acre. Firestone provided a US$5,000,000 loan at a 7% interest rate to the government to pay its foreign debt and build a harbor needed by Firestone. The loan was given in exchange for Firestone exercising complete authority over the government's revenues until the loan was paid. In 2005, the Firestone Company and the Liberian government signed a new 37-year deal raising the rent to 50 cents per acre. The Liberian government has been heavily indebted to the Company since 1928 for most of the concession's existence. The Company played roles in politics, labor management and the civil wars that ended in 2003 with the arrival of UN Peacekeeping Forces. Today, the plantation can be visited easily. Located an hour outside the capital, near Monrovia airport, it hosts some of the best schools and the best hospital in the country, the first choice of Monrovia's elite. When the Land Grab began in 2007, Firestone was still expanding production into land granted to it in 1926, but which had remained undeveloped.

The Grab was not about one plantation, but hundreds. Refer to the figures for Liberia in Table 8.1. How can over 300% of available land have been taken for concessions? Two facts explain this. From the outset there has been real ambiguity about what land should be considered available. The legal status of land under custom as owned by government was not clear. There were persuasive legal arguments that it did not all belong to government or, if it did, that government had no right to abrogate those rights (Stevens, 2014).

Most cocoa plantations in the interior of Liberia have been acquired by local farmers through a document called a tribal certificate, signed by a chief, stating that he is allocating land to the applicant. Most applicants will have earlier applied to purchase this land from the Office of the President and been required by that Office to obtain the tribal certificate as proof that the land was available and allocated by a chief to the individual. Once confirmed, the applicant is required to pay the purchase price to the government, after which the title would be issued. Most applicants felt they had no need of a title as long as they had the commitment of the chief in writing,and skipped the payment and title portion of the deal. The tribal certificate was treated as a grant of customary land from the chief, though it was an administrative step in a larger process. It was not legally effective in transferring land rights. Later, a Land Commission established under the administration of President Ellen Johnson Sirleaf concluded that tribal certificates should be recognized as land titles, subject to certain conditions.

Many concessions overlap. This happens in other countries to some extent, but more commonly in Liberia where several agencies have the authority to grant concessions. Some concession overlaps are compatible because they are for different activities that can be carried out on the same land, e.g. mining exploration and agriculture. In other instances, there is a clear potential for conflict, now or later, as development proceeds. Risks will only increase due to the tendency of concessionaires whose concessions do not promise exclusive land use (e.g. mineral exploration concessions) to appropriate as much land as they can for exclusive use within the area covered by the concession (Corriveau-Bourque, 2010).

For rural Liberians, the loss of access and possession of land represented by the concessions are alarming. Dispossession by concessions effectively extinguishes their customary rights. Contracts provide that if concessions should fail or the concession expires, the land reverts to the government, not customary rights holders. Limited smallholder access to land increases pressure for new stable, rotational systems of agriculture to replace forest-fallow farming. This, in combination with cocoa and other tree crop production, constitutes most of Liberian agriculture. It is not clear whether they will be able to get land elsewhere and whether they will have access to the training, tools, inputs and marketing chains needed to succeed. Officials at the national level watch the stream of refugees from the rural sector flowing into Liberia's cities, growing unemployment and crime and potential for political instability (personal conversation with the Chairman of Liberia's Land Commission, Dr. Othello Brandy). Land rights loss creates objection and reaction. Researchers and advocates have urged radical revision of national laws to provide recognition to customary rights that, with other reforms, would prevent customary land being taken without community consent and only with reasonable compensation (Cotula, 2011; Schoneveld, 2014).

## Land Tenure Reform and Concessions

Tenure reform is essential to positive change in the concession process. If government claims ownership of land used under custom and local communities lack land rights recognized under national law, they are at the mercy of government and investors. Without a statutory property right, they have no firm ground on which to take a stand, no right to say "no" to a concession they think will not succeed or may not treat them fairly. Both land policy experts and advocates of these communities have long recommended land rights reform through legal recognition of both community-level and family-level customary land rights (Wily, 2021; Larson et al., 2022; Gilbert, 2017). Liberia launched a tenure reform process almost immediately upon resuming control of governance in 2006. Unfortunately, reforms were not achieved until well after the Land Grab was underway.

When the Sirleaf administration took office in 2006, key officials associated with Sirleaf recognized that the Americo-Liberian monopoly of political power was ending and remembered earlier demands for reform of the country's land tenure system. They concluded that a fairer land tenure system was urgent for a peaceful future for Liberia. Principal among them were former President Amos Sawyer, the Chair of the Sirleaf-appointed Governance Commission, and a former Minister of Agriculture Dr. Othello Brandy. Sawyer and Brandy discussed the need with Sirleaf, who agreed to create a team to assess the situation regarding land access and property rights, based in the Governance Commission.[14] Brandy developed a legislative proposal to create a Land Commission, which was enacted in 2009 and chaired by Dr. Brandy. With funding from several foreign and international donors, the Land Commission began a program of research, public consultation and policy discussions that included government agencies in collaboration with representatives of a new, but vital, civil society with land concerns. The Commission paved the way to the National Land Rights Policy in 2017 and the Land Rights Act in 2018.

## The Land Rights Act and Concessions

The 2018 Land Rights Act recognizes customary land tenure rights, provides communities with protection of their customary land equivalent to private ownership rights and requires free, prior and informed consent by communities to concessions affecting their customary land. The Act did not revise most terms of existing concessions, but gave communities an interest in the concession. It provides that at the end of the concession, the land returns to the community's customary land rather than reverting to the state. Lacking is: (a) regulations requiring identification of customary groups from which land is taken and the creation of entities representing those groups to facilitate reversion to former holders and the ability to share in the revenue from concession operations; (b) an adequate system of monitoring and financial supervision to ensure that concessions do not defraud government of anticipated income; (c) a program of systematic review to "right-size" concessions through excision of land beyond the concessionaire's capacity to develop that is returned to communities as customary land; and (d) developing an agricultural policy and programs including an initiative to assist and support small farmers. The new Land Authority, bestowed with comprehensive authority over land, was charged with implementation of the reform program.

## A Contradiction?

The period during which Liberia's land tenure reform was planned and enacted—roughly 2007–2015—coincided with the busiest years of the Land Grab. That government began considering reforms to address the legal vulnerability of customary landholders so early reflects unusual foresight on the part of the officials. Political struggle for reform gained much of its urgency from Liberia's history of concession-granting. By 2015 vast areas of customary land were allocated to concessions, though little actual displacement had occurred then. How could a government pursue a concessions policy that stripped small farmers of their customary access to land and at the same time be struggling to reform its land rights system to make it much more difficult and costly for government to appropriate their land for concessions?

The government's hurried acceptance of concessions and land law reform were not at the outset seen as in direct conflict. In the late 2000s, no one imagined how vast the extent of concessions would become. No one was confident that the government could enact a major tenure reform program. Governments are not monolithic. Different agencies represented different constituencies. The Land Commission's ties were to the Ministry of Lands, Mines and Energy; to the Governance Commission; and to constituencies including rural and environmental NGOs and CSOs, progressives with equity concerns and leaders of ethnic communities reliant upon customary land. The Concessions Commission and the concession-granting ministries such as the Ministry of Agriculture and the Forestry Agency were linked to constituencies that included commercial farmers, agribusiness interests and government agencies involved in public finance. Surveyors from the Ministry of Lands, Mines and Energy played on both teams, balancing interests on one side with opportunities on the other. The Land Commission group was most concerned with ending centuries of land injustice dividing the Americo-Liberian and indigenous communities and averting communal conflict over land. The Concessions Commission's primary objective was revenue generation and agricultural development and modernization. The former was intentional, the latter more a response to opportunities.

There was no official acknowledgement of dissonance between the two programs, though participants gradually became aware of it. In the Office of the President, it seemed that officials did not see this as a management problem requiring integration of objectives into a set of clearer, internally consistent priorities, but as a political problem of balancing demands of advocates of two sets of objectives, pending the enactment or failure to enact the tenure reforms. There were significant interactions between institutions and agencies that might have been expected to be aligned against each other. A number of Land Commissioners were called frequently by the President to go to the field to calm tensions and mediate disputes flaring between local residents and concessionaires. The government officials concerned seemed reasonably comfortable with ambiguity as the concession and reform development processes moved forward in parallel.

Concessions have been signed and are being implemented while implementation of the reform agenda has moved very slowly. The Lands Department staff has been shifted to the new Land Authority. The Presidency failed to limit the concession process in anticipation of the projected reform and rather than relying heavily on concessions. The Ministry of Agriculture should have developed an agricultural development strategy prioritizing smallholder development. With greater foresight, schemes could have been designed to allow smallholders to enjoy the benefit of scale that came with their new community ownership of land and encourage smallholder collaboration with concessions, such as out-grower schemes. Far too much land had gone into concessions before reforms were accepted. This complicated implementation of the land tenure reform law. Much land that was to be owned by local communities and their members instead remained property of the state due to pre-existing concession agreements.

### The Balance

The rapidity of Liberia's embrace of concessions has disoriented international observers and alarmed those most affected, the country's customary landholders. Because of slow expansion of concessionaire operations on existing concessions, customary landholders have yet to feel its full impact. They appreciate the long-term implications. The performance of and government revenue from concessions have fallen far short of expectations. Most of the land involved remains unused by the concessionaires (Bruce, 2013).

## The Future of the Land Beyond the Village

Land beyond the village, on the borders of the community, is not just a resource for meeting today's needs. It is often the future expansion land of the community, encroached on gradually to provide farmland for new households. These areas may seem lightly or infrequently used, giving the impression that they are unowned. This has serious consequences when governments decide that land rights must be titled and registered. Failure to meet criteria in the registration law—which usually requires "occupation" or "possession"—leaves that land as ownerless and, thus, under national law, the property of the state. Communities and institutions holding land under custom often do not have the "legal personality" needed by national law to be registered as an owner of land (Bruce, 2003).

Without specific legal provision to protect them, a community's pasture, soccer fields and sacred groves can be acquired by its legal owner, the state, and responsibility for its management shifted to national institutions having no local presence. A legal framework is often lacking that provides legal recognition to traditional authorities and structures their relationship with national land administration. Many traditional institutions, including clans and lineages, straddle the fence between private and public, working in ways national law does not easily accommodate.

Competition for land and resources in these areas will only grow more intense. Two cases examined in this chapter, artisanal mining and wildlife management, have been localized. Concurrently other developments have been underway on a much larger scale and shed a light on the vulnerability of customary land rights across the continent.

## Notes

1 Most studies of rural land tenure up until the 1960s tended to focus on land under relatively intensive, stable farming systems that rely heavily on crop rotation and fertilizers. This is usually the most fertile, better watered land, located in areas where competition for land is most significant and security of tenure becomes an issue. My own experience is more with those systems, including farmland under irrigation and agroforestry, and

less with swidden cultivation, forest fallow and migratory pastoralism, though I have some first-hand experience with all of these systems.

2 You can test the myth. Drive your four-wheeled drive deep into what seems a deserted and inhospitable region belonging to no one, say in the western Sudan. You have a flat tire or get stuck in the sand. You sense deep isolation as you tackle the task of getting your vehicle moving again. One by one, people begin to appear. They don't so much arrive as materialize: a woman with a child and a water-can, a herder leaning on his spear, two boys who might be students. They stand quietly, watching as you work, curious.

3 Hentschel et al. (2002, p. 33) observes, "In certain cases, the lack of political will to create an adequate enabling framework for legalization can be explained by personal interests related to the possibilities for corruption, money laundering, and similar illegal practices, enabled by the informal status of the sector. It is also sometimes the case that the government is attempting to attract international mining companies to invest in the country and ASM artisanal mining may be seen as a disincentive."

4 Mensah (2021) uses a legal dualism model to urge rethinking of important assumptions regarding artisanal mining in Ghana. She uses the approach to challenge the dominance of the sector by the state and to assert the legitimacy of informality. She argues that such a "decolonizing socio-legal lens" is best suited for developing more relevant understandings of legality, legitimacy and access to property rights in legally plural contexts such as Africa.

5 The Huntington and Marple-Cantrell (2021) study by Cloudburst under a contract with the United States Agency for International Development included development of a large data set on customary practices in two regions of Guinea and represents a rare quantitative study of customary practices in Africa.

6 Baker-Médard (2012) is a strong comparative study. By focusing on just two communities in Madagascar, the author provides a depth that clarifies the impact of local situations, including local histories, on how patterns of behavior regarding artisanal mining develop.

7 Siegal and Viega (2009) focus their article, dealing with the position of artisanal mining in Uganda, on this issue of definition of informality, in light of the work of de Soto (2000).

8 Research that explores customary systems and institutions in sufficient depth to inform strategic and implementation approaches is still quite limited, and quantitative studies even more rare. Huntington and Marple-Cantrell (2020) is the only African study of which I am aware that developed a large body of survey data on these issues.

9 See: https://landportal.org/organization/centre-applied-social-sciences#:~:text=Research%20interest%20in%20environmental%20and,Zoonsis.

10 The World Bank rejects the term and prefers "large-scale agricultural investment."

11 This link between the pre-existing land tenure system and land grabbing is based on the findings of World Bank research by Arezki et al. (2010) and Deininger (2011) that suggest investors specifically target countries with weak tenure regimes. Schoneveld (2014) challenges the linkage and concludes from its data that no inverse relationship could be observed between investment intensity and, for example, quality of natural resource governance, labor rights and land tenure security. It asserts that countries that afford some of the most far-reaching protection to customary land rights (e.g. Ghana, Mozambique, Tanzania and Zambia), have the most investment. This author believes that Schoneveld may have relied too heavily on statements of policy rather than experience with protections of customary land, and is confident of the linkage established by the Bank studies.

12 See, for example, Government of Liberia (2025).

13 See, for example, FAO (2012).

14 My first contact with the Liberian tenure reform effort came in 2007, when I visited Liberia in connection with a World Bank study of Liberia as an instance of post-conflict land issues and policy making. I met with the staff of the Governance Commission,

and at their request returned in 2008 to work with them on planning for and drafting the Act to establish the Land Commission. After retiring from the Bank in 2009, I went to Liberia on consultancies for the Governance Commission and then the Land Commission, annually or semi-annually through 2015. The work included development of a report on security of land tenure and needed reforms in land tenure in Liberia (Bruce, 2008), involvement in planning for its initial public consultation on felt needs for tenure reform, training for the Land Commissioners and Staff, development of a strategy for legal reforms (Bruce & Kanneh, 2011). I also held consultations with the Commission and its working groups on matters such as its program of studies on customary land tenure in Liberia, the Land Rights Reform Policy Paper authored for the Commission by Dr. Mark Marquardt, an initial draft of the Liberian Land Authority Act, development of a drafting and public awareness strategy for the Land Rights Act, discussions of drafts of the Land Rights Act with the Liberian Drafting Team, and implementation planning for the Land Rights Act, concluding with a report to the Commission in 2015 on tasks remaining to facilitate realization of the policy directions charted by the Commission. It was an extraordinary opportunity for extended involvement in a significant reform, all too rare for consultants, and the most satisfying involvement in my policy and law reform work through the Bank. I am grateful to Dr. Brandy, Chair of the Commission, and the several World Bank colleagues who entrusted me with the work and made it possible.

## References

Amanor, K.S. & Ubink, J.M. (2008). *Contesting the land and custom in Ghana: State, chief and the citizen*. Leiden University Press.

Anseeuw, W., Wily, L., Cotula, L., & Taylor, M. (2012). *Land rights and the rush for land: Findings of the global commercial pressures on land research project*. International Land Coalition.

Arezki, R., Deininger, K., & Selod, H. (2010). *Interest in large-scale land acquisition for agribusiness investment: Extent and determinants of the global land grab* (Policy Research Working Paper). The World Bank.

Baker-Médard, M.S. (2012). Conflicting treasures: Contrasting resource use governance in two artisanal gemstone mining sites in Madagascar. *Journal of Political Ecology, 19*(1), 221–237. https://doi.org/10.2458/v19i1.21728

Berry, S. (2001). *Chiefs know their boundaries: Essays on property, power and the past, Asante, 1896–1996*. James Currey.

Berry, S. (2009). Building for the future? Investment, land reform and the contingencies of ownership in contemporary Ghana. *World Development, 37*(8), 1370–1378. https://doi.org/10.1016/j.worlddev.2008.08.017

Bruce, J.W. (2003). Property rights issues in common property regimes for forestry. *The World Bank Legal Review, 1*, 257–305. https://doi.org/10.1163/9789004503014_007

Bruce, J.W. (2008). *Insecurity of land tenure, land law and land registration in Liberia* (Report No. 46134-LR). Environmental and Natural Resources (AFTEN), Africa Region, for the World Bank. https://documents1.worldbank.org/curated/en/158491468050694915/pdf/461340ESW0P10310Box334099B01PUBLIC1.pdf

Bruce, J.W. (2013). *Options for Liberia: Organizing for better land governance* [Report]. The Land Commission.

Bruce, J.W. & Kanneh, B.N. (2011). *Reform of Liberia's civil law concerning land: A proposed strategy* [Report]. The Land Commission. www.lla.gov.lr/index.php/downloadable-resources/consultants-reports?download=120:civil-law-on-land-report

Bruce, J. W. & Roth, M. (2005). *Formalization, legal reform and legal empowerment of the poor* (Overview and Issues Paper). ARD for USAID.

Chanakira, D.K., Mujere, J., & Spiegel, S. (2019). Traditional leaders and the politics of labour recruitment in Zimbabwe's platinum mining industry. *The Extractive Industries and Society*, *6*(4), 1274–1281.

Chimhowu, A. & Woodhouse, P. (2006). Customary vs private property rights? Dynamics and trajectories of vernacular land markets in sub-Saharan Africa. *Journal of Agrarian Change*, *6*(3), 346–371. https://doi.org/10.1111/j.1471-0366.2006.00125.x

Corriveau-Bourque, A. (2010). Confusions and palava: The logic of land encroachment in Lofa County, Liberia. *Canadian Journal of Development Studies/Revue canadienne d'études du développement*, *31*(1–2), 27–48. https://doi.org/10.1080/02255189.2010.9669329

Cotula, L. (2011). *Land deals in Africa: What is in the contracts?* IIED. www.iied.org/sites/default/files/pdfs/migrate/12568IIED.pdf

Cotula, L. & Vermeulen, S. (2009). Deal or no deal: The outlook for agricultural land investment in Africa. *International Affairs*, *85*(6), 1233–1247. https://doi.org/10.1111/j.1468-2346.2009.00859.x

Cotula, L., Vermeulen, S., Mathieu, P., & Toulmin, C. (2011). Agricultural investment and international land deals: Evidence from a multi-country study in Africa. *Food Security*, *3*, 99–113. https://doi.org/10.1007/s12571-010-0096-x

Deininger, K. (2011). Challenges posed by the new wave of farmland investment. *The Journal of Peasant Studies*, *38*(2), 217–247. https://doi.org/10.1080/03066150.2011.559007

de Soto, H. (2000). *The mystery of capital: Why capitalism triumphs in the west and fails everywhere else*. Basic Books.

FAO (2012). *Voluntary guidelines on the responsible governance of tenure of land, fisheries, and forests in the context of national food security*. www.fao.org/4/i2801e/i2801e.pdf

Gilbert, J. (2017). *Land grabbing, investments & indigenous peoples' rights to land and natural resources: Case studies and legal analysis* (Report No. 26). IWGIA. https://iwgia.org/images/publications/new-publications/land-grabbing-indigenous-peoples-rights.compressed.pdf#:~:text=International%20law%20on%20indigenous%20peoples'%20land%20and,indig%2D%20enous%20peoples'%20land%20and%20resource%20rights

Government of Liberia (2025). *Concession cadastre portal*. https://portals.landfolio.com/liberia/

GRAIN (2016, June 14). *The global farmland grab in 2016: How big, how bad?* https://grain.org/e/5492

Hall, R. (2011). Land grabbing in Southern Africa: The many faces of the investor rush. *Review of African Political Economy*, *38*(128), 193–214. https://doi.org/10.1080/03056244.2011.582753

Hentschel, T., Hruschka, F., & Priester, M. (2002). Global report on artisanal & small-scale mining. *Mining, Minerals and Sustainable* Development, *70*(1). www.iied.org/sites/default/files/pdfs/migrate/G00723.pdf

Hirons, M. (2011). Managing artisanal and small-scale mining in forest areas: Perspectives from a poststructural political ecology. *The Geographical Journal*, *177*(4), 347–356. https://doi.org/10.1111/j.1475-4959.2011.00405.x

Hirons, M. (2014). Decentralising natural resource governance in Ghana: Critical reflections on the artisanal and small-scale mining sector. *Futures*, *62*, 21–31. https://doi.org/10.1016/j.futures.2013.11.005

Holmes, G. (2014). What is a land grab? Exploring green grabs, conservation, and private protected areas in southern Chile. *Journal of Peasant Studies*, *41*(4), 547–567. https://doi.org/10.1080/03066150.2014.919266

Huntington, H. & Marple-Cantrell, K. (2021). Customary governance of artisanal and small-scale mining in Guinea: Social and environmental practices and outcomes. *Land Use Policy*, *102*, 105229. www.sciencedirect.com/science/article/abs/pii/S0264837720325679

IGF (2018). *Women in artisanal and small-scale mining: Challenges and opportunities for greater participation*. IISD. www.iisd.org/system/files/publications/igf-women-asm-challenges-opportunities-participation.pdf

IIED (1994). *Whose Eden? An overview of community approaches to wildlife management*. https://www.iied.org/8260iied

IIED (2013, September). *"Land grabbing": Is conservation part of the problem or the solution?* (Issue Briefing). http://pubs.iied.org/17166IIED

Knight, R.S. (2010). *Statutory recognition of customary land rights in Africa: An investigation into best practices for lawmaking and implementation* (Legislative Study No. 105). FAO.

Larson, A., Frechette, A., Ojha, H., Lund, J.F., Monterroso, I., Riamit, K., & Baa, O.E. (2022). Land rights of indigenous peoples and local communities. In C. Pedrick (Ed.), *The land gap report 2022*. www.landgap.org/.

Mensah, L. (2021). Legal pluralism in practice: Critical reflections on the formalisation of artisanal and small-scale mining (ASM) and customary land tenure in Ghana. *The Extractive Industries and Society*, *8*(4), 100973. www.sciencedirect.com/science/article/abs/pii/S2214790X21001386

Muriaas, R.L. (2009). Local perspectives on the "neutrality" of traditional authorities in Malawi, South Africa and Uganda. *Commonwealth &* Comparative *Politics*, *47*(1), 28–51. https://doi.org/10.1080/14662040802659389

Murphree, M.W. (1994). The role of institutions in community-based conservation. In D. Western (Ed.), *Natural connections:* Perspectives *in community-based wildlife conservation* (pp. 403–427). Island Press.

Ostrom, E. (1990). *Governing the commons: The evolution of institutions for collective action*. Cambridge University Press.

Putzel, L., Kelly, A.B., Cerutti, P.O., & Artati, Y. (2015). Formalization as development in land and natural resource policy. *Society & Natural Resources*, *28*(5), 453–472. https://doi.org/10.1080/08941920.2015.1014608

Schoneveld, G.C. (2014). The geographic and sectoral patterns of large-scale farmland investments in sub-Saharan Africa. *Food Policy*, *48*, 34–50. https://doi.org/10.1016/j.foodpol.2014.03.007

Siegal, S. & Viega, M.M. (2009). Artisanal and small-scale mining as an extralegal economy: De Soto and the redefinition of "formalization." *Resources Policy*, *34*(1–2), 51–56. https://doi.org/10.1016/j.resourpol.2008.02.001

Songorwa, A.N., Bührs, T., & Hughey, K.F. (2000). Community-based wildlife management in Africa: A critical assessment of the literature. *Natural Resources Journal*, *40*(3), 603–643. www.jstor.org/stable/24888539

Stevens, C. (2014). The legal history of public land in Liberia. *Journal of African Law*, *58*(2), 250–265. https://doi.org/10.1017/S0021855314000059

Stolla, F. (2005). *Wildlife management areas: A legal analysis* (Occasional Paper No. 5). Tanzania Natural Resources Forum.

UNECA (United Nations Economic Commission for Africa) (2002). *Compendium on best practices in small-scale mining in Africa.* United Nations Economic Commission for Africa. http://repository.uneca.org/handle/10855/5447

Wily, L.A. (2001). Reconstructing the African commons. *Africa Today*, 77–99. www.jstor.org/stable/4187390

Wily, L.A. (2021). Challenging the state: Devolutionary tenure transitions for saving and expanding forests. *Human Ecology*, *49*(3), 285–295. https://doi.org/10.1007/s10745-021-00231-2

# 9 Change, Evolution and Reform

## Evolutionary Theories for Land

If land use change requires change in land tenure, are those changes just unconnected events, or do they add up to more than that? Students of development have suggested that there is a progression in agricultural development that can usefully be seen as stages, with different stages of change having their characteristic land use practices and associated land tenure arrangements.

Evolutionism is defined as "[a] theory which proposes that long-term social change happens in stages, that it is linear, gradual and irreversible, and that it is progressive" (Graaff & Le Roux, 2001). In 1965, the development economist Ester Boserup put forward her Evolutionary Theory of Land Tenure (Boserup, 1965).[1] She concluded from her research that increased population pressure on land is the principal cause of changes in land use and thus the cause of an evolution of land tenure systems. As population and demand for land grows, land is used more intensively, causing land tenure to adjust and provide stronger, longer-term individual rights in land to protect more substantial investments needed for intensification. We can recognize some of the linkages she points out in the experience of the global south, but influences other than population growth appeared to be in play.

An influential article on land use change by Lambin et al. (2001, p. 261) suggests an approach that is less exclusively focused on population growth as the cause of change:

> Common understanding of the causes of land-use and land-cover change is dominated by simplifications which, in turn, underlie many environment-development policies … Cases reviewed support the conclusion that neither population nor poverty alone constitute the sole and major underlying causes of land-cover change worldwide. Rather, peoples' responses to economic opportunities, as mediated by institutional factors, drive land-cover changes. Opportunities and constraints for new land uses are created by local as well as national markets and policies. Global forces become the main determinants of land-use change, as they amplify or attenuate local factors.[2]

This approach identifies opportunities presented and the choice to seize or ignore those opportunities as central to processes of change. In the short term, land use

DOI: 10.4324/9781003476429-11

change can be altered by a new crop, a new market for an old crop or a technology for crop production. In the long term, major forces such as population growth or contraction or climate change may play more significant roles, but these too are matters affected by policies and programs. This approach more clearly recognizes the role of agency. Communities and nations make decisions that affect change-paths over time, and some of the most important concern land.

This chapter raises in a preliminary way an awkward question: given that evolution seems a relatively friendly and flexible process, and given that African institutions are less rigid and have a greater than average capacity to change and self-reform, the prospects appear open-ended and sunny. So, why is Africa experiencing an unprecedented growth of conflict, even violent conflict, related to land? It is a question to which I return in the process of reviewing the continent's history of reform of customary land tenure in Part III.

## Why Does Customary Land Tenure Change?

In Part II, we have examined examples of several land use changes occasioning changes in customary land tenure. The factors driving change were opportunities to be seized. In Botswana, introduction of a new well-digging technology allowed those who invested in it to establish *de facto* control over large areas of communal rangeland, positioning them to obtain rights over that land when the government decided that more intensive, individualized management of the land resource was needed. This transformed a collective resource to an individual resource. In Ghana, a new and valuable tree crop initially relied on a customary recognition of rights in trees as distinct from ownership of land to provide tree-planters security of tenure in the trees, making possible the conversion of vast areas of forest land to tree crop plantations. Under custom, a valuable tree could be owned separately from the land. Later, when whole plantations of economic trees were being bought and sold, the land on which they stood was necessarily going with the trees, establishing an early precedent for sale of land. This is the story of how a collective right became an individual right (by the tree planting) and then how that resource came to be marketable. The idea of selling land did not come to Africa with colonialism. Well before that, sales of land were a possibility recognized by African communities. They were resisted because they threatened to take land out of the community's stock of land and transfer it to an outsider. Community members rarely had any interest in selling their land. It was the main, usually the only, source of their livelihoods and the food they ate. Their other options were few and far between. Losing their land was something to be feared.

In the case of Mozambique, something different is happening, different because the socio-economic context is very different. It happened after colonialism and the advent of independence. The vast majority of the country is still under customary land tenure. In many areas of the country, custom has not yet accepted sales of land, but custom is changing. Government has recognized customary land rights and, in addition to community land rights, is offering all citizens the conversion of that right into an individual use right, perpetual and inheritable, from the state. At the same time the state prohibits selling both the customary right and the state-granted use right. In one coastal area, a hot development area, the author finds that sales have been accepted by custom and become common in spite of their legal prohibition. The forces driving these changes are not a single discrete opportunity but the many modern needs that can be satisfied only with cash. Men and women now have some livelihood options other than farming.

These three cases are not unique to the countries from which the examples here were chosen. The tendency for land tenure to become more individualized and monetized is at play in burgeoning market economies across Africa. The opportunity to buy land is eventually extended to buyers who have no connection to the community. Absent clear policies to the contrary, these transfers gradually become full sales of land (complete, not partial; unconditional, not revocable; and permanent, not temporary).

## How Does Custom Change?

Because customary law is unwritten, there is no book of rules to be revised when it changes. Custom can change relatively easily, without many formalities. Because of this, it is often hard to identify the exact point in time when custom changes. At its most simple, the process of change can seem automatic. It can begin when a member or members of a community begin to behave in a manner contrary to the current set of rules in place. An opportunity arises and they take advantage of it, notwithstanding that their behavior is contrary to custom in some way. If no one complains and authorities do not react badly, the number of community members ignoring the custom grows.[3] The basis of customary law is community consensus. As that consensus shifts and the change becomes general, so has the custom. Custom can change without an official public enunciation of the reform.

If someone complains about the violation of a customary norm, say to the chief or to others with some responsibility for this area in the life of the community, it is then a public matter. This is more likely to happen if the violation harms or inconveniences others, or infringes on the interests of some community authority, or involves an area of shared interest. There are then discussions and consultations with people advocating different courses of action. There might even be a meeting, then a decision, not necessarily broadcast but not secret either. Word gets around, and remarkably quickly.

In the case of "customary land tenure" moving toward permitting sales of land, the matter is one of shared interest and great import. There will inevitably be extended discussions in the community if time allows. Communities under custom typically allow a range of transactions in land that do not result in permanently alienating land belonging to the community. Examples are loans of land, leases and other temporary arrangements. The first real sales may be transfers among members disguised as transactions acceptable at custom, for instance a possessory mortgage accompanied by a commitment that the loan will never be repaid. When outsiders begin to offer significant payments for land under custom (significant locally), this practice may be extended to them. Such developments often take place where a number of other relationships and obligations are being monetized. If a chief has historically received a token gift when allocating land to a community member, that gift may become a cash payment. Over time, the amounts and frequency may grow until it begins to feel like chiefs are engaging in sales of unallocated land to community members. After a few decades of this, a visitor inquiring whether sales of land can be practiced under the custom of the community will be told that a sale of land is possible and accepted as part of custom. Other times, there are intentional changes in customary land tenure; such instances are provided in Chapter 16.

Some customary systems have evolved their own inexpensive, but effective, ways of keeping records of transactions involving land. An example from Tigray, Ethiopia was the copying of critical details of a land transaction into the blank pages at the end of a parish church's large ornamental Gospel. Customary systems have sometimes taken the initiative to codify their customary land laws, though this has most often been done at the initiative of outsiders, including missionaries, colonial officials and judges in search of simple rules to apply.[4] Codification, while convenient, has a downside. It freezes custom in the printed text as it is at the time of publication and so deprives it of its flexibility, a valuable attribute. Even given this drawback, the approach still has advocates who argue for benefits outweighing the drawback and add that in the age of word processing, updating a text is not so difficult.

The processes involved in these cases are never simple and can reverse themselves as demand for new land waxes and wanes over time. We need to be careful in how we think about the growing number of monetized transfers of land. They are often not land sales in the full sense. Different participants view monetized transfers differently (Chauveau & Colin, 2007). Remember that when we read about customary land tenure evolving to accept sales, it is not happening in all land use or tenure niches. The author is likely writing about a house plot or farmland, two niches in which tenure is traditionally more individual. The anthropological literature is full of cases of customary systems adapting, in some cases through the transformation of a customary right into a similar right under western law. In an anthropological classic, Sally Falk Moore describes two transitions in customary tenure: one in which a right to reclaim lands left behind by its owner is replaced with a concept of abandonment, thereby allowing them to be reassigned to others, and another where a right of relatives to object to a land transaction is transmuted into a right of first refusal (Moore, 1991).

Customary land tenure is changing without anyone setting out to change it, but as a result of other changes, which may be endogenous or have external origins. They seem to be evolving along the lines that Boserup predicted, becoming more individualized (Migot-Adholla et al., 1991). The ability to do so is remarkable, as in the case from Mozambique, where evolution toward sales of land has prevailed in spite of the fact that both the country's statutory law and its customary land tenure prohibited the sale of rural land (Júnior, 2009).

## Evolution and Reform

The possibility of evolution in land tenure poses an interesting problem for land policy. If land tenure systems have adjusted themselves to meet new needs, can they not evolve to meet the needs that Boserup posits? Prior to independence there were clear indications, especially in the parts of the country where Africans had been most exposed to western tenures and the market economy, of the evolution of customary land tenure systems toward stronger individual rights and marketability of land. The decision-makers involved were not impressed by the rate of change. They were convinced that these systems were stagnant, unchanging, dictated by inflexible custom, namely a bottleneck. It seems ironic that customary tenure has been faulted and taken off the development agenda for not having evolved in imitation of western land tenure, when colonial policy had been to keep these two land tenure systems as separate from one another as possible, to prevent sales of customary land, to increase chiefly authority and to emphasize the communal aspects of customary land tenure (Feder et al., 1988).

There had been a long-running debate on whether "customary land tenure" has acted as a constraint to increasing agricultural production. Some authors, such as Dorner (1972) and the World Bank (1974), had been inclined to believe that it has and called for instituting reforms, while other scholars urged restraint and allowing local communities to work out the needed reforms through custom (Noronha, 1985). They urged that customary institutions should be valued for their capacity to adjust to meet new needs. That debate emerged when, immediately after Kenya's independence in 1964, the World Bank confidently put its considerable financial and professional weight behind a national program of systematic titling and registration (STR) for Kenya. The model for the program came largely from a World Bank-funded program of STR that converted much of the best farmland in the Kingdom of Thailand to private individual ownership from 1984 to 2004. Gershon Feder at the Bank and his Thai colleagues had carried out studies that showed solid benefits of the tenure reforms so the Bank had both an economic model and processes it considered tested (Feder & Feeny, 1991). Kenya, with its infant STR program now embraced by the post-independence government, seemed a natural.

The program in Kenya was ongoing, initiated by the colonial government in the 1950s. World Bank funding with British participation enabled a gradual expansion of the program. The program initially generated mostly positive commentary, but by the second half of the 1970s, empirical studies by independent researchers from localities around the country where implementation had begun were published. They suggested that implementation was moving forward, but there were early indications that at least one theoretical assumption of the Bank's model was proving unreliable. Title did not appear to be improving registered smallholders' access to credit. The researchers found that the STR approach was having significant and unanticipated (or unacknowledged) negative social impacts. Some authors began to express serious reservations about the land registration program.[5] These initial indications of problems with the program fuelled an expansion of the debate and second thoughts with regard to the viability of an evolutionary solution.

## Evolution as a Policy Option

Advocates of STR have always seen evolution as part of the picture, but as inadequate by itself and requiring more dramatic state intervention to ensure its satisfactory conclusion. By the mid-1980s, influenced by the reported problems with the STR program in Kenya, some researchers and commentators began to see state-*guided* evolution as an independent option, an alternative to the more invasive, state-*led* STR approach. The question they asked was: will it be more beneficial to rely on rural communities making decisions to address their perceived needs as they arise, including the needed changes to "customary land tenure," or is there instead a need for the state to intervene decisively and largely in advance of any broad demand for reform of "customary land tenure"?

Early supporters of an evolution option cited the capacity of African traditional communities to adjust their custom to facilitate seizing new opportunities. They questioned whether the STR program was really necessary? Or was it a case of wasteful overkill where, with a bit more patience, the desired outcome would have eventuated?[6] They concluded that broad, state-driven land tenure reform was not needed in most "customary land tenure" situations because the problems with "customary land tenure" in Africa had been overstated, and policy should focus instead on guided evolution in community contexts (Bruce, 1993). Empirical studies, most of them from Kenya, continued to show negative social impacts of STR and weak economic gains,[7] and that whatever the problems or successes of the STR program in Kenya, agriculture was doing well there—better than in most other countries in the region. In the absence of empirical evidence of substantial positive impacts by STR on investments and yields, proponents of formalization sought to associate the program with the general success of smallholder agriculture in Kenya. Could it instead have been lifting many regulatory restrictions on Africans processing or exporting key cash crops that deserved most of the credit for the impressive performance by African smallholders in the years after independence?

The debate waxed and waned. Around 1990, the World Bank and the United States Agency for International Development (USAID) launched a set of coordinated studies in several African countries that dealt with both the impacts of STR (managed by John Bruce and Michael Roth at the Land Tenure Center and supervised by Joan Atherton of USAID) and the evolution of customary land tenure (managed and implemented by Shem Migot-Adholla of the World Bank). The studies' results, published in 1993, were mixed but the editors concluded that: (a) African customary land tenure was evolving and was doing so in a manner generally consistent with expectations under the Boserup model; and (b) that STR was often, at best, premature in relation to those evolutionary processes and had had disproportionately large, negative social impacts relative to economic impacts provided (Bruce et al., 1994).

In 2003 Hernando de Soto published his blockbuster account of community-driven formalization of urban land in Lima, Peru (de Soto, 2000). He asserted that land formalization was a pro-poor program that would place capital in the hands of the rural poor and create a stock of domestic capital badly needed by governments.

De Soto's case for formalization came under attack as an inappropriate intercontinental transplant from an urban Latin American context to a rural African context,[8] but his books are an effective popularization of formalization issues and have been remarkably influential (Bruce, 2012). They largely account for US foreign assistance becoming available for formalization programs after 2010.[9]

Most researchers' general opinion of STR programs, informed by independent empirical studies, remains highly critical. Date analysis collected from farm surveys in 1987–1988 in a total of ten regions in Ghana, Kenya and Rwanda by Migot-Adholla et al. (1991) concludes that:

> The evidence supports the hypothesis suggested by historical studies, that African indigenous land rights systems have spontaneously evolved from systems of communal control towards individualized rights in response to increases in commercialization and population pressure. Cross-sectional data on the incidence of land improvements and on land yields provide little support for the view that limitations under indigenous law on the right to transfer land are a constraint on productivity.

A review by Lawry et al. (2017, pp. 80–81) concludes that persistence in the erroneous belief that indigenous land rights systems obstruct agricultural development has promoted "ill-starred investments … and reforms," reducing the security of tenure of Africans holding land under customary land tenure. There is a clear research-based consensus against STR in the social science communities. Economists and lawyers remain divided on its merits. Notwithstanding the negative consensus in the social science research community, aid agencies seem immune to their findings. While aware that the programs have been attacked as badly conceived and wasteful, donors ignore serious negative social impacts. They may have accepted them long ago as unavoidable collateral damage. The de Soto take on formalization continues to attract capable defenders.[10] One would anticipate objections from African countries experiencing the STR programs. Researchers contributed extensively to what is known about the effects of these programs, but an African response was long in coming.

Events in Kenya, home of Bank's flagship STR program in Africa, may indicate that the response may still be coming. During the late 1990s, a popular movement led by Kenyan non-governmental organizations and civil society organizations helped give rise to the formation of the Njonjo Commission in 1999, which was appointed to review the country's land policy and laws and recommend a broad set of reforms, including the incorporation of customary tenure into statutory law. Shortly thereafter, a national land conference rejected a key land policy that underlay Kenya's titling and registration program, and several land laws were amended that had allowed registration to be used to appropriate the lands of customary users. Reforms to the Constitution and creation of new land laws resulted in full recognition of customary land rights for the first time. Those events in Kenya are addressed in Chapter 12 where they are used to illustrate evolution and reform as policy options through examining the Kenya program in depth.

**What of Evolution?**

What remains to be said of evolutionary change? As a policy option, it is on the shelf in all but a few African countries. Those who favor STR are not opposed to evolution, which they are confident is tending toward individualization and privatization. There are a number of possible positions on this. One is that evolution is so messy and slow as to be irrelevant. Alternatively, one can argue that STR is speeding up evolutionary processes that are inevitable, but lagging badly. Those few countries that have embraced evolution are more comfortable playing the long game, trusting evolution's ability to find the best direction in the long term. That list is impressive, but not very long: Ghana, Liberia, Mozambique, Uganda, Botswana, Swaziland, South Africa and, since the early 2000s, Kenya. They all see, to various degrees, a future for customary land tenure in Africa. Most have explicitly provided for its protection in their constitutions.

If evolution is seen as the "road not taken" in today's land policy discussions, and attention focused on STR, it is what is happening in Africa, all over the continent, on vast lands that dwarf the STR efforts. Most of the land tenure reform programs launched by African nations in the 1970s and 1980s, including STR programs, were spottily implemented and directly affected a small fraction (under 5%) of land used under "customary land tenure." Evolution has continued in areas where reform programs have not been implemented. Policy messages sent by STR programs regarding acceptability of land sales are presumably having some impact on popular perceptions of tenure issues, but no attempt has been made to measure them.

In a 2019 article, Chimhowu argued that a new customary land tenure had evolved and that acceptance of sales of land has become so general that it was time to confirm it though legal action, either through a STR process that registers private tenure holding by holding, or by national statutory enactments recognizing the legality of sales of "customary land tenure," nationwide (Chimhowu, 2019). Even if more actual land sales are taking place, are they broadly distributed? Generalization of the process, not a very precise standard, is difficult to establish on the basis of available data. The position can vary greatly, even locally. One finds at a rural crossroads where the core of what will be a town has been constructed and a cluster of small villages in its vicinity is where some people have come to accept sales of land. Or, it is a line of communities along well-travelled roads where sales have gained acceptance. Beyond those few villages, one finds there are broad swathes of country where sales of land are still viewed with great suspicion and, if they occur, are surreptitious. Unfortunately, there is no large, longitudinal data set that provides the needed information on land sales and attitudes toward them. A well planned and culturally sensitive sample survey to assess these measures for all land under "customary land tenure" in even one country in Africa would be helpful.

STR has not placed a great deal of new land on the registers in the years since independence, with the exception of Kenya, but neither have evolutionary processes. Rural Africans are still not interested enough to pay to have their land surveyed, titled and registered. The few who do so are not planning to farm the land concerned. The various European colonies in Africa had for a century been denying both Europeans and Africans not resident in the communal tenure areas access to land there. Those who slipped through the legal barriers were primarily well-connected Europeans. At independence, the legal basis for dualism began to crumble. New constitutions, invariably containing human rights provisions, were enacted. That brought an end to any explicitly race-based barrier, and gradually many of the regulatory provisions that had in effect denied Africans the opportunity to become commercial producers were repealed. Those Africans who had experience with Western tenure forms took the lead and were greatly advantaged in acquiring land from customary holders or, in the case of unallocated land, chiefs with authority over the land. One ethnic group in Kenya, the Kikuyu, were able to parlay a limited experience with registration of their customary holdings into domination of the emerging real estate market around Nairobi and the Rift Valley. There were similar cases elsewhere in Kenya.

During colonialism, customary and state authorities had previously collaborated to prevent sales transactions. As central governments made such transactions possible, it fell to chiefs and other authority figures to discourage these purchases. Fearing their powers, most independence governments acted to limit traditional authority with respect to land. While this did not mean that chiefs suddenly lost the respect and cooperation of members of their communities, it did mean that outsiders who came looking to buy customary land found chiefs less able to oppose them. Where such transactions were entered into by a local community member and an outsider, the parties to the transactions could use sporadic titling and registration to protect their land, as had European land-grabbers before them. This occurred in some cases, but such sales were often kept quiet, not exactly secret, but also not registered. In that case, it is not easy to generalize about how such land is being managed.

Resistance to the sale of land under custom relied on members of communities understanding that by taking land out from under community control, such sales undermined the ability of the system to meet their and their heirs' land needs. In my experience, most Africans understand this clearly. I have heard it voiced many times, not only in relation to land sales but in discussions of land rights for widows. Widows, it is feared, if allowed to retain and actually assume the land rights of their deceased husbands, might marry outsiders who would take the land out from under the control of the community. Such subtractions from the land of the community can be sustained and even reabsorbed through processes for affiliation in some circumstances, but if they reach a certain frequency, and if buyers are not willing to be absorbed and abide by the community governance system, the community institutions that have controlled land will no longer be able to sustain the system.

## "It's Inevitable, Really"

A very British voice, predicting the demise of customary law, overheard in conversation with a University of Khartoum colleague in 1976 after a lecture about the Faculty of Law's Customary Law Project. If evolution continues on its present track, his prediction may turn out to have been right. But should it be inevitable? Was legal dualism, which has shaped the evolution of customary land tenure, inevitable? Was colonialism itself inevitable? The inevitability that many western donors and development practitioners seem to feel may not be so much a matter of what *must* happen, but what they hope will happen. They would like the end result they favor to be seen as destiny. The sense that something is meant to happen seems to confer a moral authority on the process leading to it. We surrender what agency we do have if we think that way. When the welfare of millions of vulnerable people is at stake, it is perfectly reasonable to try to push evolution off one track and onto another. This will not be easy. There may be real and significant costs of maintaining the needed deviation.

In the end, the evolution toward an environment permissive to sales of land under "customary land tenure" is only going one place: private, individual property. Under either of the scenarios laid out here, at least in the dualism situation, the transition will not take very long. It has been gradual but is accelerating. Whatever was of value in the systems of customary land tenure will likely be largely lost. Many Africans will lose their land in the process and migrate into cities. This approach is not the only one taken. A number of African countries have sought to move away from this path in alternative directions. Part III examines these reform options.

## Notes

1 Boserup's book has been tremendously influential and attracted extensive commentary, both positive and negative. A good starting point would be Hunt (2000).
2 Today, such an assessment might give more weight to climate change than we did in 2007.
3 Someone once told me I could think of this as "snowball deviance," an analogy to a small snowball rolling down a snowy hill, gathering more snow, growing larger and larger, gaining weight and speed and momentum. It's an entirely unhelpful analogy for Africa; perhaps someone can come up with a more appropriate analogy.
4 Well known examples are the Code of Lerotholi (1903) in Lesotho (Juma, 2011). Others probably exist but have not received much attention, for example *tigrinnya* codifications of "customary land tenure" for each of the highland provinces of Italian Eritrea, compiled at the initiative of the Italian colonial government in the early 1940s.
5 See, for example, Harbeson (1971), Cohen (1980), Migot-Adholla et al. (1994), Bruce et al. (1994) and Okoth-Ogendo (1986).
6 Cohen (1980), Boserup (1981), Noronha (1985) and Bruce (1988) have countered that the indigenous tenure arrangements are dynamic in nature and evolve in response to changes in factor prices. In particular, it is argued that there is a spontaneous individualization of land rights over time, whereby farm households acquire a broader and more powerful set of transfer and exclusion rights over their land (Atwood, 1990; Platteau, 1996).
7 Chapter 12 on Kenya's experience references these studies.
8 See, for example, Kingwill et al. (2006).
9 In spite of enthusiasm for de Soto's reasoning among members of the George W. Bush administration, some senior USAID staff remained unconvinced. USAID was seen by the Bush administration as not having been sufficiently responsive to their priorities in a wide range of issues. In January 2004, the US Congress established a second bilateral US foreign assistance agency, the Millennium Challenge Corporation (MCC), designed

to funnel large tranches of US foreign assistance to support policy and project initiatives it considered strategic. The MCC shortly thereafter developed a land and property rights program which began funding STR programming. The World Bank's STR programming likewise continued to grow and from 2000 saw a significant expansion into several countries in French-speaking Africa. Britain returned to funding STR in its Rwanda program. The African Union's Declaration on Land Issues and Challenges (2009) confirmed the impact of the STR programming and the formalization reasoning behind it in the minds of many African planners, including those looking at the land tenure sector.

10 While a large and impressive critique of STR has built up over the years, it continues to have effective advocates. Frank Byamugisha, a retired Bank land administration expert, has written positively in a variety of publications for the vision behind the Bank's program. See Byamugisha (2013) and Chimhowu (2019), writing of the evolution of customary land tenure, argues for recognition of "a 'new' customary land tenure," more individualistic, more monetized, and more transactable. Chimhowu notes that sales of land under customary tenure have spread widely in recent decades. He admires that evolutionary process but considers that it has become so generalized that it is now time to confirm it with formalization, including STR. He argues that customary land tenure has, as evidenced by widespread illegal sales, lost its ability to protect customary users, and he is critical of the costs of informal networking and social capital creation, together with the loss of money farmers spend on traditional social occasions, money which might otherwise be invested in more productive ways. Like Chimhowu, Joireman and Tchatchoua-Djomo (2023) support formalization. After years of emphasizing economic benefits of formalization, advocates of formalization are increasingly asserting social rationales for formalization.

## References

African Union (2009). Declaration on land issues and challenges. www.refworld.org/legal/resolution/au/2009/en/69177

Atwood, D.A. (1990). Land registration in Africa: The impact on agricultural production. *World Development, 18*(5), 659–671. https://doi.org/10.1016/0305-750X(90)90016-Q

Boserup, E. (1965). *The conditions of agricultural growth: The economics of agrarian change under population pressure*. Routledge.

Boserup, E. (1981). *Population & technological change: A study of long-term trends*. University of Chicago Press.

Bruce, J.W. (1988). A perspective on indigenous land tenure systems and land concentration. In R.E. Downs & S.P. Reyna (Eds.), *Land and society in contemporary Africa* (pp. 23–52). University Press of New England.

Bruce, J.W. (1993). Do indigenous tenure systems constrain agricultural development? In D. Crummey & T. Bassett (Eds), *Land in African agrarian systems* (pp. 35–56). University of Wisconsin Press.

Bruce, J.W. (2012). Simple solutions to complex problems: Land formalization as a "silver bullet". In J.M. Otto & A. Hoekema (Eds.), *Fair land governance: How to legalize land rights for rural development* (pp. 31–56). Leiden University Press.

Bruce, J.W., Migot-Adholla, S.E., & Atherton, J. (1994). The findings and their policy implications: Institutional adaptation or replacement? In J.W. Bruce & S.E. Migot-Adholla (Eds.), *Searching for land tenure security in Africa* (pp. 251–265). Kendall/Hunt.

Byamugisha, F.F. (2013). *Securing Africa's land for shared prosperity: A program to scale up reforms and investments*. World Bank Publications.

Chauveau, J.P. & Colin, J.P. (2007). Changes in land transfer mechanisms: Evidence from West Africa. In L. Cotula (Ed.), *Changes in "customary" land tenure systems in Africa* (pp. 65–80). IIED.

Chimhowu, A. (2019). The "new" African customary land tenure: Characteristics, features and policy implications of a new paradigm. *Land Use Policy*, *81*, 897–903. https://doi.org/10.1016/j.landusepol.2018.04.014

Cohen, J.M. (1980). Land tenure and rural development in Africa. In R.H. Bates & M.F. Lofchie (Eds.), *Agricultural development in Africa: Issues of public policy* (pp. 349–400). Praeger.

De Soto, H. (2000). *The mystery of capital: Why capitalism triumphs in the west and fails everywhere else*. Basic Books.

Dorner, P. (1972). *Land reform and economic development*. Penguin Books.

Feder, G. & Feeny, D. (1991). Land tenure and property rights: Theory and implications for development policy. *The World Bank Economic Review*, *5*(1), 135–153. https://doi.org/10.1093/wber/5.1.135

Feder, G., Onchan, T., Chalamwong, Y., & Hongladaron, C. (1988). *Land policies and farm productivity in Thailand.* Johns Hopkins University Press.

Graaff, J. & Le Roux, P. (2001). Evolutionist thinking. In J.K. Coetzee et al. (Eds.), *Development: Theory, policy and practice* (pp. 45–61). Oxford University Press. https://studyabroad.marquette.edu/_customtags/ct_FileRetrieve.cfm?File_ID=30351

Harbeson, J.W. (1971). Land reforms and politics in Kenya, 1954–70. *The Journal of Modern African Studies*, *9*(2), 231–251. https://doi.org/10.1017/S0022278X00024915

Hunt, R.C. (2000). Labor productivity and agricultural development: Boserup revisited. *Human Ecology*, *28*, 251–277. https://doi.org/10.1023/A:1007072120891

Joireman, S.F. & Tchatchoua-Djomo, R. (2023). Post-conflict restitution of customary land: Guidelines and trajectories of change. *World Development*, 168, 106272. https://doi.org/10.1016/j.worlddev.2023.106272

Juma, L. (2011). The laws of Lerotholi: Role and status of codified rules of custom in the Kingdom of Lesotho. *Pace International Law Review*, *23*, 92–145. https://heinonline.org/HOL/LandingPage?handle=hein.journals/pacinlwr23&div=7&id=&page=

Júnior, T.M. (2009). *Informal land markets in Rural Mozambique: The case of Mogovolas District in Nampula Province* [Doctoral dissertation, University of the Western Cape]. UWCScholar. https://uwcscholar.uwc.ac.za/items/af008ecd-6b12-4aa0-b044-b10e7c580a03

Kingwill, R., Cousins, B., Cousins, T., Hornby, D., & Royston, L. (2006). *Mysteries and myths: De Soto, property and poverty in South Africa* (Gatekeeper series No. 124). IIED. www.iied.org/sites/default/files/pdfs/migrate/14517IIED.pdf

Lambin, E.F., Turner, B.L., Geist, H.J., Agbola, S.B., Angelsen, A., Bruce, J.W., Coomes, O.T., Dirzo, R., Fischer, G., Folke, C., George, P.S., Homewood, K., Imbernon, J., Leemans, R., Li, X., Moran, E.F., Mortimore, M., Ramakrishnan, P.S., Richards, J.F., . . . Xu, J. (2001). The causes of land-use and land-cover change: Moving beyond the myths. *Global Environmental Change*, *11*(4), 261–269. https://doi.org/10.1016/S0959-3780(01)00007-3

Lawry, S., Samii, C. Hall, R., Leopold, A., Hornby, D., & Mtero, F. (2017). The impact of land property rights interventions on investment and agricultural productivity in developing countries: A systematic review. *Journal of Development Effectiveness*, *9*(1), 61–81. https://doi.org/10.1080/19439342.2016.1160947

Migot-Adholla, S.E., Hazell, P., Blarel, B., & Place, F. (1991). Indigenous land rights systems in sub-Saharan Africa: A constraint on productivity? *The World Bank Economic Review*, *5*(1), 155–175. https://doi.org/10.1093/wber/5.1.155

Migot-Adholla, S.E., Place, F., & Oluoch-Kosura, W. (1994). Security of tenure and land productivity in Kenya. In J.W. Bruce & S. Migot-Adholla (Eds.), *Searching for land tenure security in Africa* (pp. 119–140). Kendall/Hunt.

Moore, S.F. (1991). From getting and lending to selling: Property transactions reflecting historical changes on Kilimanjaro. In K. Mann & R. Roberts (Eds.), *Law in colonial Africa* (pp. 108–127). James Currey.

Noronha, R. (1985). *A review of the literature on land tenure systems in sub-Saharan Africa* (Report No. ARU43). World Bank Press.

Okoth-Ogendo, W.H.O. (1986). *The perils of land tenure reform: The case of Kenya*. University of Nairobi digital repository. https://erepository.uonbi.ac.ke/bitstream/handle/11295/35689/059_The%20perils%20of%20land%20tenure%20reform-%20the%20case%20of%20Kenya.pdf?sequence=1&isAllowed=y

Platteau, J.P. (1996). The evolutionary theory of land rights as applied to sub-Saharan Africa: A critical assessment. *Development and Change*, *27*(1), 29–86. https://doi.org/10.1111/j.1467-7660.1996.tb00578.x

World Bank (1974). *Land reform sector policy paper*. World Bank.

# Part III

# Land Tenure Reform

# 10 Indigenous Land Tenure Reform

## Mahago-Elibat c. 1898

### The Need for "Whips"

Mahago-Elibat lies 15 kilometers off the motor road between the national capital of Addis Ababa and Makelle, the capital of the province.[1] There were several hundred families living there, and each family farmed its own land using ox-drawn plows and produced a variety of grains and vegetables. The village chief, known as a *chicka-shum*, was both responsible for ensuring that the residents paid their taxes to government and represented the community to government. In most of Ethiopia, the occupant of this position was appointed by government. In Tigray it was hereditary.

I went to Mahago-Elibat because I had been told on a previous visit to the area that in desperate circumstances two generations earlier, the community had dramatically reformed its customary land tenure system. As I talked with villagers later, they explained that it was a reform their grandfathers did themselves, without help from government (and, I feel compelled to add, without the benefit of foreign advisors or models of land tenure from "more advanced" countries). Their original land tenure system was called *risti*. The reformed tenure was known as *chiguraf-gwoses*, which means "attracts whips." "Whips" in this context symbolized men with plow oxen who could contribute substantially to production in the community and thus the ability of the community to pay its annual tax debt to the imperial government.

Why did the people of Mahago-Elibat need "whips?" The peasants who farmed the land of Mahago-Elibat had for centuries held land as *risti*, by right of inheritance from an ancestor who had established a property right in the land by settling there, clearing the land and bringing it under cultivation. These estate-founders were known in *Tigrigna* as *kegni*, or sometimes *nai kidim abo* (first father). In the case of Mahago-Elibat, the ancestors were warriors, many of them from noble families, who resettled the area with their families in around 1543 AD, after their participation in a long but ultimately successful war to drive from Tigray an invading Somali army under the Imam Ahmad ibn Ibrahim al-Ghazi, known in Tigray as "Ahmed Gragn" ("Ahmed the Left-Handed"). There were 12 *kegnis*, 11 men and one woman, mostly from Tigray but including one Amhara "captain" from the Wello region. They settled estates of quite different sizes. The largest was several

DOI: 10.4324/9781003476429-13

times the size of the smaller estates. Some had better land (flatter, less rocky, better watered, terraced) than others.

### Evolution of a New Tenure

*Risti* land was by custom inherited in both male and female lines, but male-male inheritance was far more common. Women do appear in genealogies provided as a basis for land claims, but over nine out of ten *ristegnas* telling me about their claim to a parcel identified a man as the person who had held the land immediately before them and through whom they claimed *risti*. To hold or claim *risti*, one did not need to reside in the community where the land was located, so long as one could establish an acceptable line of descent. The vast majority of those who held *risti* in Mahago-Elibat were residents or claimed through parents who had once resided in the area. Living farther away was clearly a practical disadvantage. You can only go so far to plow with your team of oxen. Parcels under *risti* were very small and the holding of each family was fragmented into several such parcels, often in the states of several different *aknis*. Those far parcels were often leased out to farmers living nearer to them, usually on an annual, share rent basis and always with care to ensure that the lessee did not have a potential competing *risti* claim to the parcel.

In addition to *risti*, a second tenure existed for agricultural land in Mahago-Elibat, the result of an indigenous land tenure reform in the 19th century. That tenure was called *chiguraf-gwoses*. It was adopted to help rebuild the community after it was devastated and depopulated by the disastrous Great Famine (1888 to 1892), caused by loss of most plow animals to an epidemic of rinderpest and a consequent drop in local food production compounded by a two-year drought. The community decided the reform was needed to attract new farmers with oxen, i.e. "whips," and increase the capacity of the community to bear its assigned tax liability to the empire.

The people of the village did not know much about how the reform decision had been made. It had happened in their grandparents' time, though they had all been told the story of what happened. They were clear on one point: it was a change at the initiative of the community, not the government, and it made it possible for their taxes to be paid. The reform was not made in isolation. While Mahago-Elibat was the only *addi* in south-eastern Tigray that had land under this reformed tenure, they told me it was more common in northern Tigray and still further north in the large Tigrayan-inhabited areas of the province of Eritrea. There the tenure is referred to as *diessa* or *shihena*. It is not clear where or when the tenure originated, but it seems there has long been a body of shared knowledge about it as a tenurial option among communities in northern Ethiopia.

### Integration and Further Adaptation

The community—and other hard-hit communities in Tigray—decided to offer some of their land to anyone who had plow oxen, would come to reside in and farm in the community and would help share the tax responsibilities of the community. A newcomer who met those requirements would be given land, regardless of whether he had a descent-based claim to land. This land was not given to them temporarily but as a permanent right that their sons could inherit. They were not given the land as *risti*, but under a communal tenure managed very differently than *risti*. *Chiguraf-gwoses* land was allocated to newcomers according to the amount of land that the household had the ability to cultivate. Households with more workers, and especially more plow oxen, got more land. The expectation was that anyone should have enough land for their family to survive. When after several generations the *chiguraf-gwoses* became crowded, the elders who administered the *chiguraf-gwoses* would take land from larger holdings to create parcels for families in the community who did not have enough land. By the time I was doing my research, most households in the community had land in both *chiguraf-gwoses* and *risti*. Only around 10% of households held land in only one or the other tenure. How could this happen? Ambilineal inheritance under *risti* had made it possible to integrate the families that had come to Mahago-Elibat for the *chiguraf-gwoses* and the original inhabitants. Sons of migrants had married local women, with descent lines from the *kegnis*. The migrants' sons had pursued claims to *risti* land using those descent lines. At the same time, men from the community who lacked enough *risti* land had gradually been accepted as applicants for land in *chiguraf-gwoses*.

Those who farmed the land under those tenures could articulate their relative advantages. *Risti* remained the fundamental, base tenure. It linked a person to the original rights of the community's ancestors to the community's land, including *chiguraf-gwoses* land. *Chiguraf-gwoses* was no longer thought of as an expedient solution for raising tax revenues, but rather as a valued option, representing different priorities and values and having its own advantages and disadvantages. They explained that "*chiguraf-gwoses* is good for the poor and weak." *Risti* suffered from complex descent claim litigation that roiled the life of the community. There was no equivalence between the two tenures. *Risti* was the root of the right of the people of Mahago-Elibat to their land. It was broadly accepted that a community could decide to change its *chiguraf-gwoses* back to *risti* if desired, but that it would require a strong consensus to realize such a change.[2] I was assured that if this were to happen, people knew the exact location of the old boundaries that defined the estates of their ancestors and their descendants. While it seemed unlikely that such a change would take place in Mahago-Elibat, another researcher engaged in research in the nearby Enderta region of north-eastern Tigray suggests that such cases are common there and that most of the *risti* communities he studied there reported having been under *chiguraf-gwoses* at some point in their history (Bauer, 1985).

Today, both *risti* and *chiguraf-gwoses* are gone, replaced by statutory land use rights under the "Derg" regime following the overthrow of the last emperor and the 1975 Land Reform Proclamation. Further reforms have followed as governments have changed. Today farmers no longer own their land as they did under *risti* tenure, but instead hold a right of use from the regional government of Tigray, which now owns the land. The current system is sometime said to resemble *chiguraf-gwoses*, in that descent is no longer important and residence is required. But there is an important difference: the autonomous region of Tigray now owns the land.

The community no longer has the autonomy to manage its land and its tenure system as it did at the end of the 19th century.

### Flexibility and Resiliency

If all that has changed, what is the relevance of this land tenure reform story in one community in Tigray to African land policy today?

1. It substantiates assertions in the literature and elsewhere concerning the capacity of African communities to institute and manage reform of their customary land tenure themselves. It shows how quickly this can happen and that reform in rural communities is not limited to gradual adjustments to changing circumstances. It can be quick and dramatic, based on genuine community autonomy.
2. It demonstrates a small peasant community's capacity to diagnose problems and implement changes radically altering a tenure system deeply embedded in local culture and find solutions based in their culture.
3. It shows how a community was able to open itself outsiders and integrate them into the community, using their customary acceptance of *risti* claims based on lines of descent that included women to give them the same *ristegna* identity in the community as its earlier members.
4. It demonstrates how carefully the people of that community distinguished between the virtues of *chiguraf-gwoses* as an expedient measure for hard times and its value as another option alongside *risti*.
5. It demonstrates one way in which a community built flexibility and resiliency into its tenure system to help their descendants and others cope with disaster.

The last point is of great relevance as we move into an age of global warming and changes in human land use that will be required. Years after I finished my study, I learned from another researcher farther north in Tigray, where *chiguraf-gwoses* is far more common, of instances where communities toggled between the two customary land tenures more than once (Bauer, 1985).[3] I found this surprising and impressive.

Locally driven reforms have many advantages. They take the particularity of each community into account and are likely to be a better "fit" than one-size-fits-all, top-down land tenure reforms. They are more difficult today because national governments now assert more direct control over land and land rights. Local reforms are harder to accomplish without support from some quarter in national government. National governments usually see locally initiated reforms as diluting their authority.

Their potential still exists, nonetheless. Under a laissez-faire policy on customary land tenure on the part of national government, communities could be encouraged, rather than required, by government to revise their land tenure rules. Assistance could be provided to them, for instance by land non-governmental organizations (NGOs). While not done in such laissez-faire policy contexts, the international land NGO Namati developed a valuable body of experience in Liberia, Mozambique and Uganda with a process managed by local NGOs working with selected villages to establish local reform priorities and processes. Under this model, the government's role is to encourage and fund the process and provide formal legal recognition to the custom as reformed. The study tested the relative effectiveness of three assistance approaches: provision of educational activities alone; assistance through training and engagement with community facilitators; and a more robust program of information and advice. Action research with local communities has been employed with some success by Namati though registration of the reforms to ensure their durability was not always possible. Such a process can provide broad participation in identifying felt needs and opportunities for reform and avoiding capture of the process by local elites (Knight et al., 2012).

## Notes

1 The material for this chapter is drawn from my unpublished doctoral dissertation (Bruce, 1976).
2 During my study in Tigray, the communities there asserted a clear right to change their own custom without reference to national or local government. The line of demarcation of social control of land and its production between government and the community is nicely encapsulated in a local saying, "To the nobleman his *gulti* (taxes), to the farmer his *risti*." One section of the property provisions of the Ethiopian Civil Code (1960) was drafted explicitly with the customary land tenures of northern Ethiopia in mind. I found the courts in Tigray were entirely unaware of those provisions or their relevance to land rights in Tigray. Indeed, the judges seemed to have had training only on the Civil Procedure Code. On the origins and intent behind the provisions on communal land tenure in the Civil Code, see Mandefro (1969).
3 For more recent research on these tenures, see Weldu Hailemariam (2020).

## References

Bauer, D.F. (1985). *Household and society in Ethiopia: An economic and social analysis of Tigray social principles and household organization* (Monograph No. 6). African Studies Center, Michigan State University.

Bruce, J.W. (1976). *Land tenure reform planning and indigenous communal land tenures: A case study of the tenure of Chiguraf-Gwoses in Tigray, Ethiopia* [SJD Dissertation, School of Law, University of Wisconsin-Madison]. Berkeley Law Catalog.

Knight, R., Adoko, J., Aduma, T., Kaba, A., Salenmao, A., Siakor, S., & Tankar, I. (2012). *Protecting community lands and resources: Evidence from Liberia, Mozambique, and Uganda*. Namati and IDLO.

Mandefro, B. (1969). Agricultural communities and the civil code. *Journal of Ethiopian Law*, *6*(1), 145–199.

Weldu Hailemariam, A. (2020). From rəsti to čəguraf-gosäs and vice-versa: Revisiting the dynamics of land tenure systems and security in Enderta, Tigray. *Annales d'Éthiopie*, *33*(1), 303–316.

# 11 Land Reform in Africa

## Two Types of Land Reform

Land tenure reform is one of two principal types of reforms concerning land. The other is redistributive land reform dealt with tangentially in this book. It requires discussion since both reforms are common and important in Africa. These two basic types of reform can be lumped together as "land reform," a comprehensive term for reforms related to land. Until roughly 30 years ago, the term "land reform" was used only for redistributive land reform. Today, its usage has been broadened to include both types of reform and virtually any reform affecting land (e.g. land administration reform). In discussing either redistributive land reform or land tenure reform, it is best to be specific rather than risk confusion by referring to them as "land reform."

## Redistributive Land Reform

Redistributive land reform is intervention by the state or other public entity to shift the land of some landholders to others, typically those who lack land and/or those from whom it was taken illegally or unfairly. In redistributive reforms, the state uses its constitutional power of eminent domain (power to expropriate land for public purposes) to take land, paying compensation as required by national law. In some cases, the land is purchased from willing sellers on the market, using public funds, then distributed to the reform beneficiaries. Redistributive land reform is important in many parts of Africa, especially in the former settler colonies. Since independence, redistributive land reforms have been initiated in countries across Africa to take land from European settlers and redistribute it to indigenous citizens, especially in eastern and southern Africa. Redistributive land reforms have been carried out since independence in Ethiopia, Kenya, Tanzania, Mozambique, Malawi, Zimbabwe, South Africa and Namibia.

A redistributive land reform may take land because there are people who hold a great deal more land than others, and many who own no land at all or too little land to provide a livelihood. Once land is taken, it is broken up into smaller holdings and given to the landless and land-poor to achieve greater equality and/or to achieve another land policy objective, such as the efficiency associated with small

DOI: 10.4324/9781003476429-14

family farms. Sometimes the large lands targeted for land reform are owned as large units by their owners but managed and farmed in small units by tenant farmers who have leased them from the owners (their landlord). In those cases, it is possible to redistribute the land to the tenants simply by transferring the ownership of the parcels they already farm as tenants. This is known as a land-to-the-tiller reform since the tenant cultivating the land is given the land as his or her own. In other cases, the landless are resettled from elsewhere on lands that government has taken from large landowners and subdivided for redistribution to the landless.

Another category of redistributive reform is collectivization reform, typically carried out in communist countries. Land is taken from both large and small private owners and consolidated into large collective farms. These reforms are justified by the governments carrying them out as providing greater equity and economies of scale. Another form of redistributive land reform is de-collectivization, a reform in which large collectively owned and operated units are broken up into smaller units and distributed in private tenures to households and other private actors. Collectivization and de-collectivization reforms have been rare in Africa, affecting little land and abandoned by governments relatively quickly.

Redistribution to the land poor and those displaced by colonialism has been a major element in African land policy since independence and an important consideration in the struggle for independence. African agriculture before colonization was smallholder agriculture. Large accumulations of land owned and managed by individuals or institutions were rare. Colonial land usurpation created the need for redistributive land reform in Africa. New governments after independence have taken land given to Europeans by colonial governments and returned it to those from whom it was taken or their successors in interest. "Successor in interest" may mean the communities or ethnic groups from whom the land was taken or their members (e.g. Ethiopia and Kenya). In other countries (e.g. Zimbabwe), land reform beneficiaries have been any black citizen who meets the reform beneficiary requirements regarding landlessness or production potential. Some redistributive reforms provide compensation to those from whom the land was taken in the reform, but most African reforms have not done so. In restitution situations, governments seek to avoid paying compensation, except in some cases for the value of improvements on the land. The terms of a particular reform typically reflect the strength of the bargaining positions of the groups and institutions negotiating them more than principles in the matter.

Redistributive and tenure-based land reforms are sometimes combined in a single reform program. It is common for a redistributive land reform to distribute land to reform beneficiaries in a tenure different from that held by the one from whom the land was taken. Land taken from settlers who owned the land has often been redistributed to reform beneficiaries in a different tenure, for instance leasehold tenure. The usual practice is to refer to these reforms as redistributive reforms with a land tenure reform element. These reforms can be unfair on a personal basis. International law provides little support to those losing land in such reform as when the person from whom the land is taken has paid market value for the land rather than inheriting it from a colonist forebear given the land by the colonial government.

This was the case in South Africa's post-Apartheid redistributive land reform, although initially, land was purchased from white farmers on a willing-seller basis (Deininger, 1999).

## Reform of African Land Tenure

The notion that customary land tenure needs reforming comes from the colonial era and reflects colonial-era critiques of customary land tenure. They remain relevant because they recur in more sophisticated forms in modern critiques of customary land tenure in the economic development literature. A number of land tenure reforms were underway at the time of independence, the major being the reform in Kenya. Historians of colonialism and land tenure scholars have tried to determine the extent to which colonial policies and practices have influenced post-colonial programs. Part of that literature has focused on differences between French and British colonial administrative practices. There has been ample discussion of the extent to which such differences reflected different ideologies or simply what available funds would allow. Such comparisons are not easy. British and French empires in Africa each had some colonies in which a good deal of land was used to resettle European colonists to farm, and other colonies in which there was little prospect of resettling European populations because of climate and disease. In the latter, both colonial powers were more interested in taxation, trade and controlling labor than in large-scale land takings. Land tenure dualism existed in all the colonies but affected more land in settler colonies.

Those comparing British and French colonialism have tended to see the two as having different attitudes toward customary land tenure and traditional authorities. In West Africa, colonists were fewer. The French encouraged Africans in their colonies to see themselves as an extension of France, loyal to the French empire. A transformative approach of this nature required greater direct control for suppression of practices inconsistent with their vision and creation of new local government institutions to replace traditional institutions, The French appear to have seen this process in social and political terms. The British approach was to reinforce traditional authority and customary land tenure in the areas not immediately needed for colonists, that is, most of the colony. The British took advantage of traditional rulers, strengthened their roles in governing customary land tenure and extended the dominance of traditional authorities into the era of independence.[1]

How did this change in the first years after independence? In Francophone Africa in the 1960s and 1970s, there were high-level discussions of appropriate models for administrative decentralization, including control over land. Most preferred to limit devolution of decision-making and retain centralized control over land. France's attitudes toward customary land tenure had always been negative. Since these discussions were about decentralization to new civil authorities, not traditional authorities, this was consistent with colonial policy. The new national leaderships in Anglophone countries were likely even more aware than their Francophone counterparts of the strong roots of traditional authorities in their local communities. Both sets of new political elites argued that ethnic pluralism was a threat to national unity and sought to assert control over land, undermining traditional authorities' most important source of power. In some countries, ownership of all land was already vested in the state at independence. Others took the same step by nationalizing all land. In some countries, such as the Sudan in 1970, this was accompanied by specific abolition of customary land rights. More often, customary land tenure, which had had only weak recognition previously, became a legally very tentative and temporary phenomenon on top of, but clearly legally subsidiary to, statutory ownership of land by the state.

One Anglophone country embarked on a different path. Kenya embraced colonial reform intended to replace customary ownership with private land ownership. By destroying customary land tenure, it attacked the role of land as a source of authority and power more directly than the nationalization law in other countries. In the 1950s, Kenya initiated implementation of a national land tenure reform program to replace landholders' customary rights with private individual ownership of land, backed by registered title. The Kenyan experience with that program has provided both a test of critical assertions concerning customary land tenure and the extent to which replacing them with private individual ownership can increase agricultural production. These theories and outcomes are examined after a fuller introduction of this reform model and its objectives in Chapter 12, which presents the concrete situation of Kenya. It's a good starting place because it is the precursor of most tenure reforms being implemented in Africa today.

## Major Land Tenure Reform Models

The varied tenure reforms carried out in Africa are most usefully grouped and discussed, at least for policy purposes, in terms of their tenure objectives, that is, the new tenure(s) that the reform seeks to deliver to the landholder.

There are four broad types of land tenure reforms that have been or are being carried out in customary land tenure areas of Africa:

1. Reforms converting rural landholders' customary rights to private ownership based on the western model or another statutory tenure which is, like ownership, inheritable, alienable and may be mortgaged.
2. Reforms that nationalize land, seeking to replace customary land tenure with individual, long-term use rights from the state in tenures that are inheritable but not alienable nor mortgageable.
3. Reforms that seek to replace customary land tenure with a statutory form of community-based control of access to and use of land that is held as under custom by virtue of membership in that community and in a tenure which can be inherited, but not sold nor mortgaged.
4. Reforms that provide full legal recognition to customary land tenure and seek to provide customary rights the same protection and status as private ownership and state ownership.

Before getting into the differences between these reform types, it is worth noting some characteristics they have in common. All are reforms of customary land tenure and have been or are being carried out in rural areas. Land in urban areas under a statutory tenure before independence has been retained in that tenure or converted to another statutory tenure, most frequently involving change from private ownership to a long-term use right. Ghana is exceptional as the one country in Africa with substantial urban land under customary land tenure. In all cases of reforms in which land was nationalized, urban land continuing under statutory land tenure seems to have been assumed from the outset. The reform debates in the years leading to independence concerned rural land.

These reforms were almost all intended not to "reform" customary land tenure but to replace it. They were reforms of statutory law that removed or limited in major ways whatever provisions in national law that provided state legal recognition to customary land tenure. Those "reforms" expressed ideological discomfort on the part of the new elites with customary land tenure and their concern about the considerable power of traditional authorities. Unlike many nationalizations of land in Asia and Latin America, nationalization reforms in Africa were rarely driven by a desire to institute collective or state agricultural production. With a few exceptions, these reforms retained household farming systems and household rights to land in one form or another. Proponents of collective production sometimes saw traditional communal management of some land (usually pastures) as evidence of an African culture leaning toward collective production. In the few cases where government instituted collective farming (Ethiopia, Guinea Bissau, Mozambique and Tanzania), these experiments were not extensive and did not last long or enjoy much success. Since these attempts at collective production, most African governments that adopted socialist orientations in the immediate post-independence period have shifted away from them. Since the de-collectivization and privatization of land in China and Russia, collective and state farming options have largely ceased to be considered appropriate tenure models for Africa.

What happened to statutory land tenures affected by nationalizations? In the case of rural land, if the European holdings were extensive nationally, the solution would normally be redistributive land reform. The land would be taken and redistributed to the landless in a statutory tenure consistent with state ownership. Where the amounts of privately owned rural land were relatively modest, the customary land holder was either allowed to continue to hold the land in ownership, as in Kenya, or the tenure was converted into a tenure more consistent with state ownership of the land, such as a long-term use right from the state, as in Tanzania.

Since governments which nationalized all land wished to continue reliance on household cultivation of land, they needed to prescribe a new use rights system for rural land to replace customary land tenure. With the exception of Botswana,[2] governments did not turn ownership or control over to the customary communities that had governed it prior to colonization. They instead enacted reform laws that provided for the new statutory systems to replace customary land tenure entirely. At the same time, legislators understood that the administrative reach of the new governments was quite limited, realizing that they would need to tolerate (continued) coexistence of customary and western tenure systems in the short term. Most reform laws provided for continued operation of customary land tenure in parts of the country where the new system of land tenure had not been implemented. While tenurial dualism that had characterized these colonies was altered dramatically in these laws, customary land tenure largely continued as the reality on the ground, gnawed at the edges by reform implementation. Today, customary land tenure remains by far the predominant form of land tenure on the continent.

The following chapters discuss in some detail country experiences with the four basic models of land tenure reform noted above. The first category examines Kenya's and Rwanda's experiences with replacement of customary land tenure with a freely marketable tenure backed by statutory law. In the Rwandan case the tenure is a long-term leasehold, providing landholders with a registered title that is freely marketable and mortgageable and thus the effective equivalent of private ownership.

## Notes

1 On British colonial land policy, see Berry (1992). For French colonial land policy, see Delville (1999). There is in fact an ongoing debate on a variety of related issues including the extent to which any differences between land tenure paths in French and English colonies reflected policy or financial constraints. A great deal depends on the local context. Firmin-Sellers (2000) involves a carefully drawn contrast between two situations, one in Ghana and one in Côte d'Ivoire, which are reasonably comparable, but in which easy generalizations about impact of colonial policy are overwhelmed by the many less generalizable factors influencing unpredictable outcomes.

2 Botswana is an important exception, in that very substantial amounts of state-owned land was "retribalized" after independence in 1966. In 1966, freehold land comprised about 6% of the total land area of the country. Estimates just before 1996 placed freehold land at 5%, state land at 25%, and tribal land at about 70% (see Ng'ong'ola, 1996).

## References

Berry, S. (1992). Hegemony on a shoestring: Indirect rule and access to agricultural land. *Africa*, *62*(3), 327–355. https://doi.org/10.2307/1159747

Deininger, K. (1999). Making negotiated land reform work: Initial experience from Colombia, Brazil and South Africa. *World Development*, *27*(4), 651–672. https://doi.org/10.1016/S0305-750X(99)00023-6

Delville, P.L. (1999). *Harmonising formal law and customary land rights in French-speaking West Africa*. International Institute for Environment and Development.

Firmin-Sellers, K. (2000). Institutions, context, and outcomes: Explaining French and British rule in West Africa. *Comparative Politics*, *32*(3), 253–272. https://doi.org/10.2307/422366

Ng'ong'ola, C. (1996). Land tenure reform in Botswana: Post-colonial developments and future prospects. *South Africa Public Law*, *11*(1), 1–29.

# 12 Ownership and Alienability Reforms in Kenya

## Land Titling in Africa

The basic concept of Kenya's post-independence land tenure reforms is simple: confirm existing boundaries of parcels held by individual landholders under custom, but rather than assigning customary land tenure, providing a marketable title that assigns the holder statutory private individual ownership. In Rwanda, the concept is largely the same, only the marketable "titles" are 99-year, renewable leaseholds issued by the state. This model has for some time been an option in most countries in Anglophone Africa, but only recently has been replicated for rural land reform in Francophone countries, which initially chose to emphasize decentralization of land administration and supervision of agricultural land use rather than altering tenure.

The process by which this reform model is implemented is both controversial and important. It is called land titling, featuring demarcation of the parcel and registration of its title while cancelling all unregistered customary rights in the land. It also promised an exaggerated security of tenure protecting future purchasers of the land from any other claims. In Kenya and Rwanda, it has been implemented nationwide, in striking contrast to implementation failures with similar models across the continent. Before discussing the case of Kenya, we need to look closely at this process.

From their earliest days in Africa, colonial governments surveyed and registered landholdings they appropriated from Africans for colonists in individual tenure. Registration of African rights was rare. Where it did occur, it was usually to meet special needs of colonizers, usually a political need. Following the Anglo-Egyptian reconquest of the Sudan in 1888–1889, after the *mahdiyya*, the British dealt with endemic land disputes stemming from a nearly a decade of war through the survey and registration of individual properties.[1] Dispute resolution also relied on the existence of date palms that under custom linked owners to their land. A decade later, in what would become Uganda, the surveying and titling of land to their customary holders was mandated by the Buganda Agreement of 1900, a peace settlement between Britain and the Kingdom of Buganda leading to Britain's declaration of a British Protectorate in 1897.[2] In both post-conflict contexts, land titling and registration established what proved to be relatively stable land tenure regimes.

DOI: 10.4324/9781003476429-15

Uganda's purportedly drew on local custom but, in fact, seriously distorted it. Sudan's purported to create and register land in private ownership but actually aligned it with custom under Islamic law, that already allowed land sales. In both cases, titling and registration of rights as instituted deviated from the law and practice of land titling and registration in England and the previous practice in the colonies, which was "sporadic" land registration. Sporadic land registration was a service provided by government *at the request of* a land titleholder to make a public record of that title. In Sudan and Uganda, what was implemented was quite different: "systematic titling and registration," a comprehensive and compulsory process carried out by government. The next section spells out the difference between these approaches in detail to explain how systematic registration has become a remarkable tool for the implementation of tenure reform.

## Deed Registration, Title Registration, Systematic Titling and Registration

Deeds registration began as a service provided by government to those involved in a sale of land. A person who buys land can take the resultant deed evidencing the sale to a government office where the deed is entered into the register and a record maintained so the buyer can prove the purchase in the future. It can be consulted by those considering a subsequent land purchase. There is no legal requirement that one register one's transaction. If the transaction is fraudulent or legally inadequate in some respect, registration of the deed does nothing to its registration. If an owner sells the same property to two buyers, the buyer who is the first to register the sale is allowed to retain the property, while the other buyer must sue the seller for damages. The purpose of registration is to make existing owners more secure in their property and to facilitate land transactions by providing prospective buyers with better information than they would otherwise have as to whether the person offering to sell it is in fact the owner of the property.

How does it work? A clerk in a government registry copies deeds presented to him in chronological order in a large register book. If one wants to find the record of a sale, an index is usually available that allows a search for the record by the names of the parties. The early registrations provided only crude descriptions of the location of the land concerned, but this improved when modern surveys became available. Many national land administration systems including almost all countries in Africa still rely on deeds registration. Modern versions are more helpful because their information has been computerized.

A better system, called title registration (or sometimes "land registration") was developed in the late 19th century in New South Wales, Australia.[3] It was also called the Torrens system after the Australian who invented it. Title registration is a parcel-based system. There is a register—like a folder—for each parcel of land. The register bears a unique parcel identifier, an ID also used on the survey documents and to identify the parcel on any official map on which it is shown. Upon application from the holder, the registration agency takes responsibility to examine the documentation presented and determine the title's validity. If validity is confirmed, the state registers the title and guarantees it with a few exceptions. It is this guarantee that distinguishes title registration from deeds registration. It increases confidence in land sales.

When first adopted in Australia in 1858, title registration was as sporadic and voluntary as deeds registration, a process that could only be initiated by individual application by the landholder. This was the form in which it was introduced before the turn of the century into some countries in Africa, often primarily for urban titling. The shift to a parcel-by-parcel systematic approach led by the state was gradual. Governments gradually began to comprehensively locate all titled and registered parcels on a map of a region, an import from countries in the French tradition, which had long been developing "cadastral maps" of parcels linked to their owners for land tax administration. Later governments sought to make sure that the new system eventually covered all land. They made registration compulsory for any owner who wished to transfer their land ownership. Registration was compulsory only if the owners sought to transact in their land. Parcels still come onto the register only when their owners are seeking to transact. In Kenya and other countries modeling their law on the Kenyan statute, colonial governments added a provision that the government could systematically survey, adjudicate and register every landholding in that area, even over the objection of the owners.

Title registration on a systematic basis created a tool for "tenure reform" in the colonies. Colonial governments could now order registration in private individual ownership or some other statutory tenure of all holdings under customary land tenure in a specified area. The process cancelled legal recognition of existing customary rights, replacing it with new registered private land rights guaranteed by the state, affecting mostly Africans. It was piloted in Uganda and Sudan around the turn of the century, and in Kenya in the final decade of British rule. Typically, sporadic registration in a deeds registry continued to exist in parallel with the new system. In former British colonies it is not unusual to find both a deeds registry and a Torrens-style title registry.

In tenure reform programs implemented through systematic land registration, as in Kenya, government makes an order declaring a described area to be an adjudication district. Following consultations with the community, teams of mediators and/or adjudicators and surveyors move systematically through the area ascertaining who holds land and whether their right to the land is unchallenged.[4] Under virtually all title registration laws, recognition is based on the fact of occupation, rather than the customary right. Because land registration laws require no such inquiry but rely instead on observable facts such as occupation, there is little discussion of the fine points of customary land tenure. Reforms do not reform existing customary rights in the land but proceed on the assumption that such rights as may have existed at custom mean little or nothing under the law of the state. In effect, the state is creating a property system *de novo*. The holdings are surveyed and registered with the registration recorded in the file for the parcel and referenced to a map of holdings in a designated area. Customary landholders keep their existing parcels but receive new, legally conclusive rights in those parcels, often guaranteed by the state. In some countries, those holding registered parcels are given a title certificate, but in others no such document is provided on the grounds that doing so would encourage attempted "off-the-register" transfers of titles. Land registration has gone from being only a public service to being a major property rights management tool for government (Larsson, 1991).

While systematic registration of private land ownership seeks to provide farmers with greater security of tenure, it changes tenure rights and lines of authority with respect to land. Before the process, the landholder owes his rights to the community; after it, he owes them to the state. It is disruptive to the existing social order, breaking the connections between community and land, breaking land out of lineage and other family systems and placing decisions to sell land entirely in the hands of the registered owner, furthering the emergence of an impersonal land market. Projects implementing this model have been generously funded by bilateral and multinational donors. For both donors and governments, systematic registration has many advantages. The process has been worked out in detail, field tested and repeatedly revised. Consultation and flexibility in implementation have increased. Land registration laws and regulations spell out detailed, on-the-ground procedures involving interaction with local landholders to define and survey holdings, making legal changes in tenure status potentially more impactful than simply writing a law in the city capital. In spite of the close historical association of individualization with systematic title registration, a similar field-based process could be utilized for systematically registering land to communities or other groups or for implementing land tenure reforms with different objectives.

These projects are not "technical" fixes. "Survey," "registration" and "titling" sound like matters of information, recording what already exists, but "adjudication" concerns a function usually constitutionally reserved for judges. In recent laws, "adjudication" has tended to disappear and be replaced by vague wordings implying such matters are resolved by local consensus. This may or may not be a good thing, depending on how communities in the case at hand achieved consensus. Disputes arise and are resolved, with winners and losers. Someone is making those calls without the protections of property rights normally available to litigants. A systematic survey and registration process is a dramatic intervention by central governments in rural communities. By omitting community-managed land from registration, it impliedly confirms the state's ownership of all land other than residential and cultivated land. By negating the intimate connection under custom of property in land, of descent, identity and belonging, it destroys a critical basis of community cohesion and personal identity provided by the customary land tenure system. It replaces it with an imported tenure model already existing in other, colonized parts of the country. Those affected have little to say in the change. The systematic nature of the process makes it effectively involuntary, even in those cases where the compulsion is not explicit or where "consultation" is required. This is the case even though it affects the livelihoods, family dynamics and values of every household in the affected communities, constituting an exercise in social engineering.

The affected rural communities have responded with unease and suspicion of the process, and sometimes resistance. I observed this in the early 1970s as a Peace

Corps Volunteer legal advisor in the Ministry of Lands. A systematic land titling and registration endeavor was being proposed by the Food and Agriculture Organization of the United Nations. A team from the Ministry, convinced that they might be able to implement a pilot program in the absence of legislation, attempted a small-scale pilot exercise in Hararghe Province. At first, it went well enough in spite of some local resistance. It had to be abandoned when the area's university students returned home on a break and told their parents that the government had no authority to carry out the land registration process.

Where an adequate legal basis has been laid, affected communities must accept the process. If their land is not registered in their names, they risk having no legal rights to it. Kenya's land registration law and others modeled on it specifically nullify any customary rights not reflected in the registration. Very few want the new system. When the process is completed and government people have gone back to the capital, most rural communities don't use it. Transactions and inheritances continue to go unregistered. In areas where the habits of engaging with a formal registration system are not already established, registered right-holders continue to behave much as they did before registration, dealing with traditional authorities concerning land matters. Twenty years later, the register reflects many deceased persons as right-holders. It is no longer an accurate record of rights in land, and so is quite useless.

The Achilles' heel of these programs has proved to be the difficulty of sustaining them. Their sustainability was based on the expectation that the beneficiaries would value their new rights over their land enough to update them in the system. Most beneficiaries have no interest in selling their land. It is the primary asset supporting their families. Selling it is about the last thing they would consider doing. If the advantage of this approach has been its broad application in a number of countries, its actual implementation has often proven superficial and fragile in the face of the persistence of customary land tenure norms.

## The Impetus for Titling Reforms

In the 1950s, with the prospect of independence looming, colonial governments in Africa considered what might best be done about the state of African agriculture. Modest attempts by colonial governments to improve African agriculture had not been successful. Colonial agriculturalists and administrators insisted that customary land tenure could not provide a basis for developing modern agriculture. This viewpoint was common in much of colonial Africa. It was particularly strong in British colonies and was most clearly articulated in British eastern and southern Africa. If Africans held their land in private individual ownership, they further suggested, Africa might be able to develop a class of larger, more successful farmers, freeholders who would embrace property rights and related conservative values in a manner similar to British landed families (Swynnerton, 1955). There was a political motivation. Where a colonial government expected its colonists to retain the land they had been given during the colonial period, it wanted it retained in western tenures the colony had introduced. The case for this would have been more difficult to make if Africans had continued not to have access to the land under those western tenures. Tenurial futures were a key part of negotiations between Britain, its colonial governments and independence movements in the run-up to independence.

By the end of the colonial era, the Gambia, Sierra Leone, Ghana, Malawi, South Africa and Zimbabwe had deed registration systems and Nigeria, Tanzania, Sudan, Uganda and Kenya also had the legislative basis for land title registration (Simpson, 1976; Meek, 1946). The former settler colonies had well-established legal, technical and administrative infrastructures for managing land survey and registration. Conversion of all customary land to statutory tenure forms was a huge task. While governments had been able to cover a significant part of the costs of sporadic registration (done only at the request of owners) through fees charged for those services, customary landholders were reluctant to pay even modest fees for this new "service," especially given its compulsory nature. Wherever in Africa systematic titling and registration has been implemented, government must absorb all or a large part of the costs. To avoid this, they have turned to development assistance funding as a source of the needed funds (Burns et al., 2007).

The model for systematic titling and registration, developed in Kenya, rapidly became the tenure intervention preferred by most major international development agencies, including the World Bank, which provided part of the funding for the registration work in Kenya in the 1960s and remains the largest funder of such programs (Burns et al., 2007). Reforms adopting this model are almost always implemented in an investment project mode, with international or bilateral donor funding of millions of dollars annually for a multi-tranche national program of land titling and registration that may run for 8–12 years. No African country has been able or willing to fund such a program without such assistance, except for a recent relatively simple and inexpensive process in Ethiopia, discussed in Chapter 14. Dependence on donor funding to implement these programs is grounded in the fact that Africans, distrustful of government interventions affecting their lands and having under custom felt relatively secure in their holdings, had little incentive to pay for a state-issued title. It is not surprising that they have also frequently failed to make the effort required of them to maintain these systems, failing to register their transfers.

This chapter now turns to the tenure reform experience of Kenya. Kenya's program was the first truly national program of land titling and registration in Africa. Under implementation by the late 1950s, it is the model for most land registration programs in Africa. Kenya is the best documented tenure reform in Africa, the model for reform favored by the World Bank and most other mainstream donor agencies. While it accounts for the bulk of foreign assistance on land matters to African countries, it remains highly controversial.

## Background to Kenya's Reform

Colonial Kenya was a settler colony and a clear case of a dual land tenure system. There was one system of land tenure for colonists and one for Africans. Land taken from Africans to be given to colonists was designated Crown land and was given to colonists in either freehold ownership or, in the case of those who would farm, Crown leaseholds that ranged from 99 to 999 years. Leaseholds were renewable. Rights and responsibilities were comparable to those of owners. Allocations of Crown land were registered, at first under sporadic land registration at the behest of the beneficiary landholder. Kenyans held their land under custom in so-called Native Reserves, where they were permitted to continue relying on their traditional leaders and custom to govern access to and use of land. Their landholdings were given little legal protection. In the early colonial period, land held by "natives" were characterized as Trust Lands, held by government in trust for their inhabitants. Over time, Africans' land rights were further diminished. In the Barth Judgement of 1921, England's Privy Council held that customary users were no more than tenants-at-will of the Crown, whose tenancies could be terminated at will by the government (Meek, 1946; Okoth-Ogendo & Winston, 1991).

Customary land tenure systems generally prohibited the sale of lands. Colonial governments, including Kenya's, felt no need to prohibit such sales, at least within rural communities (Meek, 1946). Africans from outside the reserves could not purchase land in the reserves and needed the permission of the provincial governor even to lease land there, usually for trading goods and services with the population of the reserves. Africans from towns and Crown lands were barred by custom from acquiring land in the reserves. Africans were also barred from acquiring Crown land in western tenures. These dualistic legal provisions sought to prevent markets from blurring the sharp boundary between land under custom and land under western law.

At a policy level, the notion that African populations should eventually hold their land in western tenure forms had long been a subject of debate. As early as 1933 the Land Commissioners in their annual report urged that development of private individual ownership should be the policy objective. Meek (1946) notes that in some parts of Kenya lands were already being bought and sold contrary to custom. He cites Kiambu District as an example. The rationale and objectives of the reform of customary land tenure, an individualization and privatization reform, are set out in the "Swynnerton Plan" of 1954. It predicted that if its recommendations for individual ownership for Africans were followed, "the able and energetic or rich Africans would be able to acquire more land and bad or poor farmers less, creating a landed and a landless class. This is a normal step in the evolution of a country" (Swynnerton, 1955, p. 10). Small-scale registration pilots in Kenya were expanded rapidly in strategic villages as a part of a counter-terrorist program created in response to the so-called "Mau Mau" rebellion, a violent opposition to continued colonial rule referred to by the colonial government as "the Emergency." In its closing years, the colonial government expanded titling and registration programs in Kikuyu areas in the central highlands and in Luo areas near Lake Victoria. Areas selected for these first programs were where land had already begun to be transacted under customary tenure. Kenyan political parties campaigning for independence condemned the program as an attack on African culture. The independence government under the leadership of President Jomo Kenyatta did an abrupt reversal of policy and embraced the tenure reform program.

**Reform Rationale**

Kenya under Kenyatta largely accepted the colonial critique of customary land tenure and the colonial prescription for dealing with the problems it raised. Three critiques of customary land tenure were especially important in the Kenyan case as rationales for the individualization reform: (a) the "communal" nature of African land tenure and its impact on farmers' incentives to invest in their land; (b) farmers' inability to sell or mortgage land under custom and its negative impact on farmer access to capital for investment; and (c) the substantial fragmentation of farmers' landholdings into many separate parcels of land (believed to be due to land inheritance rules under custom) resulting in inefficient use of labor and failure to adopt productivity-enhancing capital items such as plow oxen or tractors. The Kenyan reform, with its individualization of rights, increased security of tenure, plus a right to devise or sell or mortgage one's land without community oversight would seem to address these problems directly. In Kenya and later in other reform contexts, the reasoning behind the reform often proved faulty. That reasoning was either based on mistaken assumptions about customary land tenure or the impact of the proposed reforms.

Beginning in the 1960s, reforms in Kenya took off. In the areas under customary land tenure, the work of titling and registration went forward with the continued assistance of British experts and the World Bank group of donors, including the British government, supporting the Kenyan program. Urban and rural land in western tenures continued under those tenures, while land taken from "white farmers" for redistribution to Africans—as in Kenya's Million Acre Scheme—went to them in western land tenures, rather than reverting to customary land tenure (Leo, 1981).

**Legal Basis and Implementation**

The land registration system used in colonial Kenya, known as "deed registration," was an awkward and expensive process, requiring an application by the landholder and payment of substantial fees for the services. Under the reform, the conversion of many thousands of small parcels held by "native" Kenyans called for a more proactive and efficient approach. This approach was produced by a series of legal reforms using a model of land registration called the Torrens System, or "title registration." The necessary reform of the law governing titling and registration and "native" landholding involved three key pieces of legislation: (1) the Native Land Tenure Rules (1955), that emphasized that customary holdings were to be maintained, legitimized existing spontaneous tenure changes and laid down the process of systematic tenure reform; (2) the Native Lands Registration Ordinance (1959), that legalized individual freehold for Africans, made first registration unchallengeable, and complemented a corresponding act that established Land Control Boards; and (3) the Land Act (1968), that provided for group rights for pastoralists and areas where consolidation was inappropriate. Kenya was then in a position to implement, systematically, titling of all land in a region in private individual ownership, based on an order from the Ministry with or without the consent of landholders.

**Lessons from Kenya**

Much has been learned in the 50+ years of experience with implementation of the reform model in Kenya:

*1. Registered titles for farmland have arguably produced some measurable increases in farm productivity, but more modest than hoped.*

The early work in Kenya was not able to benefit from the methodologically and quantitatively stronger economic research carried out on areas brought under the system in more recent times. Kenyan smallholder agriculture has done relatively well. The tenure reform model has received a large part of the credit. Studies by social scientists were increasingly skeptical about the economic benefits, expressing alarm about some social impacts. Later, when better econometric studies were done, impacts on investment and growth in production were found to be less than earlier experiences with the model in Asia, particularly Thailand (Feder, 1987). Often, the impacts have been marginal. The relatively weak response in Kenya and in Africa generally may have been because systematic registration had been initiated too early, before market forces had developed very far and before the development of any broad demand for the titles the projects provide (Migot-Adholla et al., 1994a; Bruce et al., 1994). This reflected, those researchers thought, an underestimation of the security of tenure provided by customary land tenure systems. They concluded the potential for a tenure reform program to raise productivity has been over-estimated (Atwood, 1990; Migot-Adholla et al., 1991; Bruce, 1993).

Lack of robust impact on investment was due to the faulty assumption that freehold titles would make it possible for African smallholders to obtain loans from commercial lending institutions to invest in their land, on the basis of mortgaging their land as security (see Carter et al., 1994) and the general discussion of reasons for this failure in Chapter 5 of this book). While African land tenure systems have communal elements, most of the land being registered was farmland, the land in which the strongest individual rights existed under custom, often inherited over many generations and, in most cases, not managed by traditional authorities once placed under cultivation by a family.[5]

*2. Attempts to address communal and seasonal grazing patterns of pastoralist Masai through issuing private ownership titles to "group ranches" for grazing associations have resulted in a clear trend toward sub-division and individualization of pastoral commons.*

The potential for irrigation in these areas led to a transition from total dependence on livestock to agro-pastoralism. In the 1980s, a wave of subdivisions in the ranches took place, eventually tending toward individual holdings with an emphasis on irrigated agriculture, reflecting some dissatisfaction with the distribution of benefits within the grazing associations. It appears that the greater profitability of irrigated farming and the cost of investments in irrigation and fencing led participants to seek out individualization of tenure, possibly seeing it as more secure (Mwangi, 2007). A mistake of reform planners was the notion that group use of a common would result in the "tragedy of the commons," the inevitable degradation of range condition through over-use. Grazing land used as a commons might easily become degraded in the absence of adequate community management of stock numbers on the land. This was not inevitable. Africa presents many examples of commons managed effectively by the land-owning communities whose members use them, both in terms of prevention of outsider use and regulation of member use in the interest of sustainability. Cases of resources under shared use that have become degraded are also easy to find. Evidence of adequate resource management is uneven and cannot be generalized. Problems are more effectively addressed through support for improved land management than though individualization of land tenure. This issue is discussed in greater detail in Chapter 6 on pastures and rangeland.

*3. Consolidation of fragmented household landholdings, an important element in the Kenyan program, was found to be unpopular, complex and in some contexts ill-conceived.*

Kenyan smallholders often farmed land consisting of distinct parcels at different locations. Fragmentation was assumed to exist primarily as the result of land subdivision and inheritance by different children. The Kenyan government saw fragmentation as highly inefficient in terms of both labor and use of capital items, calling for consolidation into one or two parcels per owner before survey, titling and registration. Subdivision of landholdings by inheritance was a preoccupation of British agriculturalists observing Africa farming patterns from the beginning of the 1900s. The inheritance of land by all descendants (or even all male or female descendants) of a deceased owner and the subdivision of his or her parcels of land over time was a practice they considered bizarre. In England, all land in an estate went only to the eldest son, keeping the entire estate in the hands of one heir. The excessive subdivision of holdings, they argued, resulted in farmers often holding a dozen or more small parcels of land, sometimes distant from one another. They worried about the high cost incurred by the farmer from moving from one parcel to another to perform farm tasks, and the inefficient use of capital items, such as farm machinery or plow oxen.

The British attempted to limit fragmentation of holdings in their early land registration programs for African landholders in Sudan, Uganda and Kenya. Those programs included consolidation of the parcels of land held by a household into one or more larger parcels. The consolidation element of these programs proved unpopular and difficult to administer. Its role was reduced as the program was extended to less densely populated areas of Kenya and to other African countries where systematic titling was implemented. The practice never again attained the same high profile it had achieved in Kenya. Studies of land consolidation efforts in Kenya contributed to a growing body of evidence that much observed fragmentation could have been avoided through land lending or other kinds of transactions under custom. Fragmentation was often valued by cultivators for the access it provided to a variety of soils and micro-climates. Wilson (1971) and Haugerud (1983) questioned the reform's assumptions about fragmentation of holdings, suggesting strongly that fragmentation was better viewed as a positive land use strategy by smallholders rather than an efficiency problem created by rigid customary norms for inheritance. It is accepted today that fragmentation must be evaluated in terms of both positive and negative impacts on achievement of a variety of objectives, including productivity, food security and environmental sustainability (Atwood, 1990; Ntihinyurwa & de Vries, 2021).

### Other Lessons from Kenya

In addition to the lessons above, some negative impacts and their seriousness have become clear or been highlighted by Kenya's experience. These are often described as "unanticipated negative impacts." Many were clearly predictable.

*4. The exclusive focus on registration of individual rights leaves many community or other family rights unregistered. The state considered unregistered land to be state-owned.*

Failure to register land not farmed by households effectively stripped communities of large swathes of land they considered theirs and used, often as a commons or as generally available for future allocations to community members. Dispossession is not a publicly stated purpose of registration programs. Governments and donor agencies are intensely aware of it. It has been a motivating factor for governments to undertake these programs. Tenure reforms are presented as a means of securing Africans' rights to their customary land. But legislation redirects all customary rights of communities (as opposed to individuals and households) to the state and its organs of central government. From the state's perspective, this is a legal resolution of problematic *de facto* control of virtually all rural land by local communities, one which greatly advantages the state. This is criticized by many earlier researchers who studied the implementation of the program in Kenya (Sorenson, 1967; Brokensha & Glazier, 1973; Coldham, 1978, 1979; Shipton, 1988; Okoth-Ogendo, 1982, 1986; Mkangi, 1983). The failure to secure community rights to their broader land claims was a missed opportunity of historic proportions. Mkangi (1983) specifically accuses the Kenyan government of using land tenure reform and systematic registration to grab land for itself. The struggle for control of land between local communities and the state is the source of much of the land conflict seen in Africa today.

*5. Systematic land registration programs often extinguish not only community rights in the land registered (their declared intention), but also the individual rights of other private persons.*

Field studies found that the process not only ignored collective land rights but also individual rights that were not the rights of the primary right-holder (the household head who was registered as the owner of the land) (Coldham, 1978; Brokensha & Glazier, 1973; Njeru, 1978; Shipton, 1988; Pala Okeyo, 1980). For example, a customary right of way across land of a neighbor, or some other customary arrangement for a neighboring parcel resembling an easement or livestock holders' customary right—whether within the community, outside the community or migratory pastoralists—to seasonally graze their animals on crop residues on farmers' land.

*6. Individual land titling to household heads negatively affects women's access to land and security of tenure.*

Most customary land tenure systems in Africa are patrilineal in nature. Women do not inherit land and usually have access to land only through their husbands or male relatives. Although a woman may not hold land in her own right, in many societies she may have "secondary rights," a right to use land belonging to her husband to sustain herself and their children. Sometimes this is considered a part of the customary marriage contract, or sometimes as an independent right at custom. It is placed at grave risk when systematic registration provides the husband with a sole right to sell or mortgage the land. It is not unusual to find cases where a husband has sold land registered in his name "out from under his family," leaving them stripped of a vital resource. In Kenya, the field studies of Coldham (1979), Pala Okeyo (1980) and Shipton (1988) discuss the loss of rights by women in the land tenure reform. This problem was anticipated in Kenya. Land Committees were established to which women could apply to have a sale blocked if it would leave the family impoverished. These proved ineffective (Coldham, 1978; Migot-Adholla et al., 1991). In Asia and Latin America, the expanding practice of joint registration in the names of spouses or a statutory requirement of spousal consent has helped ameliorate these risks. African lawmakers have been reluctant to accept such innovations.

*7. In Kenya and later elsewhere in Africa, land title registration programs have struggled with persistent sustainability issues.*

To maintain a land registration system, landholders engaging in transfers and successions must come forward to register those transfers. Local inhabitants not convinced of the importance of an individual title fail to apply for those changes in the registry. Inheritance is handled according to custom. Registered owners seek the advice of traditional authorities on land matters rather than the appropriate government offices. The register becomes an historical document, a snapshot of rights at a moment in time and of limited probative value regarding the current status of rights. Custom remains the primary determinant of behavior with respect to land.

This was the case in the early 1980s in Sudan in areas where titles had been registered for decades. One of the experiences raising questions in my mind about the sustainability of first registration came on my visit to a land registry in a town a half-day drive north of Khartoum along the Nile. We asked for the registry records held by the courts under the Sudanese system, and were shown to a shed, full of badly deteriorated documents due to a roof that had clearly leaked, some half buried in dust and with a pigeon nest atop them. Migot-Adholla et al. (1994a, 1994b) mentions registries fallen into disuse in Kenya, though in less specific terms, in his recommendations for Ghana.

Where titles were issued but the recipients do not wish to sell or borrow against their land or see no prospect of doing so in future, systematic registration does not change the culture of landholding and how people deal with their land. Registered landholders continue to follow rules under customary land tenure, with land passing in unregistered successions and to engage in a variety of temporary or reversible transactions and sometimes in sales that they do not register to avoid fees. Thus, the register ceases after a decade or two to be a reliable record of landholdings, and a gap develops between rights as shown in the registry and the rights as recognized by the community (Wilson, 1971). Beyond the matter of sustainability, this contradiction has the potential to cause disputes and create new insecurity of land tenure.

*8. Predictions that land titling and registration would reduce the number of land disputes and conflict may be accurate so far as parcel boundary disputes are concerned, but there are studies that suggest it can cause or intensify other types of disputes and conflicts.*

After systematic titling and registration processes are complete, including appeals which may arise during or immediately following the process, research indicates a diversity of outcomes when it comes to disputes (Moreda, 2023; Lawry et al., 2017; Roth et al., 1994). Some studies suggest that registration itself may cause disputes (Tchatchoua-Djomo et al., 2020; Migot-Adholla et al., 1994a). A line of cases in the Sudan judiciary concerns the validity of a registration statute that provides that a registered transaction in land prevails over a prior, unregistered transaction (Mustafa, 1971). Other disputes provoked by these reforms concern transactions or inheritances under custom in communities where farms have been registered, but most residents continue to act as if they held their land under custom (Yamano & Deininger, 2005). Here both parties are members of the local community, these tend to be resolved in an adjudication or mediation by a local traditional authority rather than by a court, which would apply statutory law. The dispute may challenge an action by a registered owner who contravenes custom, a case that is mediated by customary authorities. The registration process can thus increase tensions and conflict between classes or factions within communities and create resentment on the part of those who consider they have lost rights, including those who lost valid secondary rights. Such conflicts may play out in families (sometimes on a generational basis), in local politics or in alternative dispute resolution fora, such as chiefs' adjudications or mediations. While registration may have clarified parcel boundaries and legal ownership, it usually has not erased expectations about land rights based on custom (Coldham, 1978; Brokensha & Glazier, 1973; Shipton, 1988).

*9. The conclusiveness of land registration provides exceptional protection, not only to the farmer, but also to those whose claim to land is questionable because it was obtained in an illegal or illegitimate manner.*

This includes groups resettled by governments on the ethnic territories of another group over the latter's objections; entrepreneurs who have purchased land under custom from customary holders who did not understand the transaction and did not grasp the potential value of their land, so that such deals are later regarded as fraudulent; officials who have illegally appropriated public or private land for themselves through abuse of their positions; and other citizens who, through corrupt practices, have acquired land illegally or in some other manner regarded as illegitimate (Southall, 2005; Nyangito, 2013).

While these outcomes of tenure replacement projects are generally seen by governments and donors as either positive or as necessary "collateral damage," some other outcomes have been genuinely unanticipated. At the turn of the century, after several decades of implementation, most of Kenya's best farmland had been titled and registered. By then land registration had become the most politically charged topic in public policy debates in Kenya and a widely recognized source of violent conflict. How did this happen?

## Kenya's "Reform of the Reform"

Several developments accounted for the groundswell of opinion against key elements in the land tenure reform program as pursued since independence.

First, rapid growth in demand for land under custom in the years since independence. Sales in land had been prohibited by most customary land tenure systems in Africa. The colonial state had supported them, wishing to preserve its monopoly of control over the movement of land from one side of the dual system of land tenure to the other. In the wake of independence, this began to change. The two tenure systems still existed, but the legal walls between them began to crumble. Regulatory provisions preventing Africans from acquiring ownership of land in areas of the country under customary land tenure were racially discriminatory on their face and unconstitutional. They were gradually repealed. Members of ethnic groups involved early on in systematic land registration projects, such as the Kikuyu, took advantage of their knowledge to acquire land cheaply in areas still held under custom. Land markets had not yet been operating in these areas, except for the occasional black-market transaction at rates well below those for land with registered ownership. Many purchases were in the Rift Valley, not far from Nairobi, from pastoralist peoples such as the Maasai. Modest levels occurred in other parts of the country, including the coastal areas. The money came from African businessmen and from families' savings. Demand for land found one important expression in the formation of "land companies," a mechanism whereby entrepreneurs encouraged small investors to pool funds to buy large tracts of land with a view to subdividing them later (Gravesen, 2020).

### Box 12.1 Land Companies, Nairobi 1977

I was in and out of Nairobi often during the late 1970s and the 1980s. Kenya probably had more land tenure experts who were Africans than any other nation. Even if I was just transiting in Nairobi, I would stay over a day to try to talk with some of them, especially serious researchers such as H.W.O. Okoth-Ogendo and Shem Migot-Adholla at the University of Nairobi. On those visits, I was struck by how often land concerns featured in the local newspapers, often in cautionary stories of land scandals and frauds. Growing numbers of Kenyans were increasingly aware that land was a limited good and was going to become more expensive. This awareness was heightened by the early land registration carried out in the highlands. As I visited Kenyan researchers, I talked with them about this. I also talked to people whom I met each day: taxi drivers, waiters, secretaries at the university and staff at the hotel where I stayed.

Land and housing in Nairobi were already costly. Renters on modest salaries worried about where they would live when they retired. Land in rural areas from which they originated had been titled and registered and, partly as a result, had become more expensive. Attitudes toward land and family had changed. They felt it would be difficult for them to return to their village of origin as people had a generation earlier when one could just go back and ask the family for a small plot of land for a simple house, just enough to grow a few "mealies" for food and keep a few goats. There was not enough land there anymore.

For many the only option for relatively inexpensive access to land was a "land company." Land companies, as the term was used in Kenya then, were companies formed by entrepreneurs and (less often) groups such as employee associations. Their purpose was to pool the funds of purchasers of modest means to buy land that was divided among investors. The company was usually organized for a single large purchase and managed by the company organizer. The land for purchase would still be under customary land tenure, much of it in the unregistered lowlands of the Rift Valley. Land was cheap there compared to areas closer to Nairobi. The organizer would set up the company, then publish an announcement describing in general terms the intended land purchase and inviting investments by those aspiring to own land. The organizer would use the invested funds to purchase the land and register the new title, after which the land would be divided among and titled to the investors. Land-buying companies were notoriously untrustworthy, and investors were often defrauded. Companies were in local newspapers almost daily. People's sense that they needed to have some land was strong, and they continued to invest in them. It felt frenzied. I have felt something of this in other countries in Africa over the years, but nothing as intense as in Nairobi in those years.

Chiefs of pastoralist tribes such as the Maasai sold land to these outsiders. Today these transactions are viewed by the sellers' descendants as illegitimate because buyers took advantage of their ancestors' lack of understanding of the implications of a "sale" of land and their ignorance of land values. The outsiders who purchased it and later settled there and others who settled there as part of government resettlement programs have long been resented. The protections provided to registered land ownership by Kenyan law has made the injustices involved difficult to remedy in the courts. Areas where large numbers of outsiders settled and became a political force have become flash points for conflict and on occasion communal violence (Boone, 2011). Kenya's national politics are substantially tribalized, and conflicts over land go national on occasion, especially in the run-up to national elections. In more difficult years, there have been dozens of deaths and burning of villages in attempts at ethnic cleansing.

Second, corruption flourished in the administration of public land and in the operation of land administration institutions dealing with privately held lands. Bribery grew more common, and land transactions that should not have made their way through the titling and registration process did so. Officials turned a blind eye or were themselves involved in questionable "land deals." The conclusiveness of land registration, intended to protect farmers and other landholders, in time came to be seen largely as a means by which corrupt officials protected the land they had illegally or otherwise illegitimately acquired. Appropriating and registering state-owned land in private hands has been a preferred form of illegal enrichment by officials in Kenya. The land registration law made title registration legally conclusive and not subject to challenge. This provision, a distinguishing characteristic of title registration intended to increase tenure security, had come to be seen by most Kenyans, quite accurately, as a shield for scoundrels. Attempts were made to stem growing corruption and to hold the powerful people involved responsible. Some of these were quite serious, but needed follow-through was never there.[6]

The third factor souring public opinion against reforms was increasing land use by politicians and political parties as a tool in political competition. Officials used unregistered land for manipulative political purposes in the customary tenure areas of the Rift Valley and some areas on the coast, abusing state allocation authority over such land. Officials used lands as currency to buy off local and national leaders and manipulated land issues and disputes to their own advantage and the advantage of their parties. This sometimes involved "straw man" arrangements to hide the identity of purchasers. The prominence of land issues in politics has been responsible for electoral violence and marred national elections.

The result of these three trends was increasing competition for and conflict over land, increasingly accompanied by violence. Some of the conflict has been in the courts, but violence on the ground has become common, filmed and disseminated. In the videos, one sees members of ethnic groups who had lived in these areas for generations being driven from their homes, their goods on their back as their homes are torched by men wielding machetes. I have seen these conflicts widely reported in the local press and their tribal element readily acknowledged.

These circumstances led to a "reform of the reform" of land tenure in Kenya that peaked in 2012 and continued sporadically (Boone, 2011; Harbeson, 2008), reworking the reform pursued by government since independence. The new reform was driven by a civil society campaign led by the Kenya Land Alliance and resulted in the amendment of Kenya's Constitution in 2010. The amended Constitution mandates creation of a National Land Commission to ensure effective land reform. Its roles, set out in Article 67(2) of the Constitution, are to manage public land on behalf of national and county governments, initiate investigations into present or historical land injustices and recommend appropriate redress, and monitor and have oversight responsibilities over land use planning throughout the country. The Constitution as amended provides for the restitution of land taken illegally or illegitimately, and a national conference on land created a groundswell for further change. Several new laws were passed in 2012: the Land Act 2012, the Land

Commission Act 2012 and the Land Registration Act 2012. The Land Act declared void the legal conclusiveness of title registration and gave full legal recognition to customary land rights. It removed the power of the president to grant land, vesting it in the National Land Commission. It made possible restitution of lands illegally appropriated by officials and land purchased for nominal prices from chiefs who did not understand the permanence of a sale or market value of the land.

The implementation of the 2012 reform program was delayed by political wrangling over membership on the Commission, which ended up in court and consumed most of 2013. By 2015, the Land Commission and the Ministry of Lands were in court in a dispute over the boundary between the operational responsibility of the Ministry of Lands and the supervisory responsibility of the Land Commission when it came to land registration activities. Implementation of the reform laws continues to lag. The reforms were enacted under pressure from civil society, but some staff and officials in the Ministry of Lands are less than fully committed to the reforms. The same is true of some politicians.

How to assess Kenya's "reform of the reform?" The biggest change in land policy is the reversal of the commitment to replacement of customary land tenure with statutory private ownership of land. This has required a substantial body of law on the framework for recognition of customary land tenure. This is contained in the Constitution, the Land Act 2012 and the Community Land Act 2016. The laws are promising in many ways, but have limitations that threaten achievement of their objectives. A thorough and thoughtful review of the provisions of the laws by Wily (2018), who is generally optimistic, warns that the powers of state agencies remain too open-ended and create risks of further malfeasance by officials and other problems in implementation of the reforms.[7]

Turning back to the reform as conceived in the 1960s, how successful should the program be considered after 60 years of implementation? In terms of speed and coverage of implementation, the model has been successful. Title registration in Kenya, if slow by standards of recent projects such as Rwanda, has been done with greater rigor and competence than in other African countries and has been impressive in the aggregate. Only in Rwanda and Ethiopia has higher coverage been achieved, in Rwanda because it is a much smaller country and in Ethiopia because it is a much simpler system which attempts much less.

Serious doubts remain as to the effectiveness of the program in promoting investment and economic growth. The promised increase in smallholder access to credit clearly did not materialize as anticipated. Some have questioned the reform's more general economic impact. Kenyan agriculture did well in the years after independence. It is unclear whether factors such as the removal of prohibitions against Africans producing high value commodities such as tea, coffee and dairy products coupled with substantial investment in communications and roads were more important than reforms in land tenure arrangements.

The model has performed badly by a real-world standard: continued political viability. It is no longer the policy of the Kenya government to replace all customary land tenure with private individual ownership of land. The latter continues to be an option for rural communities, but it should only happen when communities themselves initiate it. This depends on effective implementation of the "reform of the reform." This cannot be assumed. The national land administration bureaucracy built up over 60 years is extensive. These officials have continuing functions in the land administration system, and they are not going anywhere. Some among them favor rolling back the recent reforms (Boone et al., 2019).

Kenya has, in reaction to excessive protections of titles provided to right-holders under post-independence reforms, reduced security of tenure in relation to the state by approving restitution for transactions judged illegitimate, but not illegal, and by diluting excessive security of tenure provided to a registered owner under the law on registration. This reduction is appropriate in many cases but may invite abuses of the new provisions by those in government and interested persons outside government "reclaiming" land sold in legitimate transactions or land for which no previous right existed. It has the potential to become a tool for land-grabbing. These concerns may not materialize, but use of the law on registration to create insecurity for some even as it creates security for others has been a major fact in registration in Kenya, as have corruption in land administration and manipulation of the system for political purposes.

## Replacement Reforms Elsewhere in Africa

Kenyan reforms converted existing landholders under custom to holders of rights of private, alienable ownership. African countries coming to independence with a more socialist orientation also pursued individualization, but combined it with a nationalization objective. They converted customary land to state-owned land, leasing it to former customary holders on user rights less than full ownership. In both cases, the element cut out of the picture is the community and its customary land governance, leaving individuals holding land from the state under statutory tenures and governance.

In Chapter 13, we tackle this second type of individualization, considering the country reform experiences in Senegal and Nigeria. Both were pioneers that nationalized their land in the 1960s. Senegal is now making an effort to reach a consensus on a "reform of the reform." Chapter 14 deals with more recent reforms of a similar nature in Rwanda, Côte d'Ivoire and Ethiopia.

## Notes

1 al Madiyyah was an Islamist religious movement that in 1881 rose up against the Egyptian government and after four years of revolt, ruled for another four years until 1889. Registration of the many small peasant holdings along the Nile in full ownership was readily accepted in Sudan since full ownership (*ulf*) had long existed there under Islamic law. In the end, however, the government decided that while the process had been worthwhile for the valuable irrigated areas along the Nile in northern Sudan, it was not cost-effective to carry out such a process in rain-fed farm areas. See Simpson (1955).

2 In contrast to Sudan, land in Buganda was registered in large blocks to members of the traditional nobility, turning their subjects into tenants. The tenure in which the large estates were registered is a form of private ownership called *mailo*, an innovation which has become over the years a key element in Bugandan identity and played an important role in the land reform politics of the 1990s (Brushfield et al., 1956; Green, 2006).

3 S. Rowton Simpson was Advisor on Land Tenure to the colonial office, an enthusiastic supporter of tile registration on the Torrens model and very much involved in the development of the Kenya program of systematic land titling and registration. His 1976 book on land law and registration deals with the development of the system and its spread in the former British colonies in Africa (Simpson, 1976). See also Zevenbergen (2002).

4 The fact that titles are determined administratively rather than judicially is a major distinction from deed registration and one that has posed constitutional difficulties. This in part accounts for the failure of the new system to achieve general acceptance in the United States. Under the US federal system, responsibility for land law is constitutionally assigned to the states, and so land registration is on a state basis. Adoption of the Torrens title registration was as a successor to existing deed registration systems. In addition to the due process issues raised by administrative adjudication of land rights, there was a lack of evidence that the system provided significantly better security of tenure than the weaker deed registry system as supplemented by the relatively inexpensive system of title insurance, with its records, developed by the private insurance companies. The costs of converting the system from deeds to title registration also had substantial costs. Vested interests (the title insurance companies) also played a role in limiting its spread. Title registration on the Torrens model exists in all or parts of only a half dozen US states today (see https://en.wikipedia.org/wiki/Torrens_title).

5 As early as 1958, a colonial land tenure officer in what was then Northern Rhodesia noted the problem of "terminological confusion in African land tenure" and provides his concerns about use of the term "communal" for customary land tenures (White, 1958).

6 Njonjo (2002).

7 Wily commends the definition of a community that includes modern as well as traditional forms of community, *and the provisions recognizing that* communit*ies hold their land under* a *full-fledged property right*, and the fact that, not just the community's land, but individual parcels within the community holding will be formalized, providing two levels of legal protection. Both communal rights to land and secondary rights (rights derived from the rights of others) are explicitly recognized. The institutions for community land governance are considered sound as are the provision for access to land by investors. However, she concludes, the powers of the state are too open-ended, and there are risks that the Ministry of Lands or county governments will seek to exclude certain land areas from being registered to communities. Moreover, government has broad power to take community land for public purposes when this happens, and compensation is token. Wily notes that the political will for securing community titles waxes and wanes and that many officials see community title as a stepping stone to subdivision into individual titles. The fact that communities are given a choice of holding their land under custom or private ownership creates the possibility that the government agencies involved will find ways to provide funds and staff for communities establishing private statutory rights but not those pursuing customary ownership.

## References

Atwood, D.A. (1990). Land registration in Africa: The impact on agricultural production. *World Development*, *18*(5), 659–671. https://doi.org/10.1016/0305-750X(90)90016-Q

Boone, C. (2011). Politically allocated land rights and the geography of electoral violence: The case of Kenya in the 1990s. *Comparative Political Studies*, *44*(10), 1311–1342. https://doi.org/10.1177/0010414011407465

Boone, C., Dyzenhaus, A., Manji, A., Gateri, C.W., Ouma, S., Owino, J.K., Gargule, A., & Klopp, J.M. (2019). Land law reform in Kenya: Devolution, veto players, and the limits of an institutional fix. *African Affairs*, *118*(471), 215–237. https://doi.org/10.1093/afraf/ady053

Brokensha, D. & Glazier, J. (1973). Land reform among the Mbeere of Central Kenya. *Africa*, *43*(3), 182–206. https://doi.org/10.2307/1158522

Bruce, J.W. (1993). Do indigenous tenure systems constrain agricultural development? In D. Crummey & T.J. Bassett (Eds.), *Land in African agrarian systems* (pp. 35–56). University of Wisconsin Press.

Bruce, J.W. & Migot-Adholla, S.E. (Eds.) (1994). *Searching for land tenure security in Africa*. Kendall/Hunt.

Bruce, J.W., Migot-Adholla, S., & Atherton, J. (1994). The findings and their policy implications: Institutional adaptation or replacement? In J.W. Bruce & S. Migot-Adholla (Eds.), *Searching for land tenure security in Africa* (pp. 251–266). The World Bank.

Brushfield, T.N.N., Relton, A.J., & Mitchell, A.P. (1956). Land registration in Buganda. *Empire Eurvey Review*, *13*(99), 194–202. https://doi.org/10.1179/sre.1956.13.99.194

Burns, T., Grant, C., Nettle, K., Brits, A.M., & Dalrymple, K. (2007). *Land administration reform: Indicators of success and future challenges* (Agricultural and Rural Development Discussion Paper No. 37). Land Equity International.

Carter, M.R., Wiebe, K.D., & Blarel, B. (1994). Security of tenure for whom? differential effects of land policy in Kenya. In J.W. Bruce & S. Migot-Adholla (Eds.), *Searching for land tenure security in Africa* (pp. 141–167). The World Bank.

Coldham, S.F. (1978). The effect of registration of title upon customary land rights in Kenya. *Journal of African Law*, *22*(2), 91–111. https://doi.org/10.1017/S0021855300009591

Coldham, S.F. (1979). Land-tenure reform in Kenya: The limits of law. *The Journal of Modern African Studies*, *17*(4), 615–627. https://doi.org/10.1017/S0022278X00007473

Feder, G. (1987). Land ownership security and farm productivity: Evidence from Thailand. *The Journal of Development Studies*, *24*(1), 16–30. https://doi.org/10.1080/00220388708422052

Gravesen, M.L. (2020). Twilight institutions: Land-buying companies & their long-term implications in Laikipia, Kenya. In J. Lind, D. Okenwa, & I. Scoones (Eds.), *Land, investment and politics: Reconfiguring Eastern Africa's pastoral drylands* (pp. 144–154). James Currey.

Green, E.D. (2006). Ethnicity and the politics of land tenure reform in central Uganda. *Commonwealth & Comparative Poli*tics, *44*(3), 370–388. https://doi.org/10.1080/14662040600997148

Harbeson, J.W. (2008). Land reforms and politics in Kenya, 1954–70. *The Journal of Modern African Studies*, *9*(2), 231–251. https://doi.org/10.1017/S0022278X00024915

Haugerud, A. (1983). The consequences of land tenure reform among smallholders in the Kenya highlands. *Rural Africana*, *15/16*, 65–89. www.cabidigitallibrary.org/doi/full/10.5555/19841807312

Larsson, G. (1991). *Land registration and cadastral systems: Tools for land information and management*. Longman Scientific and Technical.

Lawry, S., Samii, C., Hall, R., Leopold, A., Hornby, D., & Mtero, F. (2017). The impact of land property rights interventions on investment and agricultural productivity in developing countries: A systematic review. *Journal of Development Effectiveness*, *9*(1), 61–81. https://doi.org/10.1080/19439342.2016.1160947

Leo, C. (1981). Who benefited from the million-acre scheme? Toward a class analysis of Kenya's transition to independence. *Canadian Journal of African Studies/La revue canadienne des études africaines*, *15*(2), 201–222. https://doi.org/10.1080/00083968.1981.10803973

Meek, C.K. (1946). *Land law and custom in the colonies*. Frank Cass & Co.

Migot-Adholla, S.E., Hazell, P., Blarel, B., & Place, F. (1991). Indigenous land rights systems in sub-Saharan Africa: A constraint on productivity? *The World Bank Economic Review*, *5*(1), 155–175. https://doi.org/10.1093/wber/5.1.155

Migot-Adholla, S.E., Place, F., & Oluoch-Kosura, W. (1994a). Security of tenure and land productivity in Kenya. In J.W. Bruce & S. Migot-Adholla (Eds.), *Searching for land tenure security in Africa* (pp. 119–140). The World Bank.

Migot-Adholla, S.E., Benneh, G., Place, F., & Attu, S. (1994b). Land, security of tenure, and productivity in Ghana. In J.W. Bruce & S. Migot-Adholla (Eds.), *Searching for land tenure security in Africa* (pp. 97–118). The World Bank.

Mkangi, G.C. (1983). *The social cost of small families & land reform: A case study of the Wataita of Kenya*. Elsevier Science.

Moreda, T. (2023). Beyond land rights registration: Understanding the mundane elements of land conflict in Ethiopia. *The Journal of Peasant Studies*, *50*(5), 1791–1819. https://doi.org/10.1080/03066150.2022.2120813

Mustafa, Z. (1971). *The common law in the Sudan: An account of the "justice, equity, and good conscience" provision*. Oxford University Press.

Mwangi, E. (2007). Subdividing the commons: Distributional conflict in the transition from collective to individual property rights in Kenya's Maasailand. *World Development*, *35*(5), 815–834. https://doi.org/10.1016/j.worlddev.2006.09.012

Njeru, E.H.N. (1978). *Land adjudication and its implications for the social organization of the Mbere*. Land Tenure Center, University of Wisconsin, Madison.

Njonjo, C.M. (2002). *Report of the commission of inquiry into the land law system of Kenya on principles of a national land policy framework, constitutional position of land and new institutional framework for land administration*. Republic of Kenya Digital Library.

Ntihinyurwa, P.D. & de Vries, W.T. (2021). Farmland fragmentation, farmland consolidation and food security: Relationships, research lapses and future perspectives. *Land*, *10*(2), 129. https://doi.org/10.3390/land10020129

Nyangito, W. (2013). *The principle of sanctity of title as a challenge in repossession of illegally acquired public land: A case for review* [LL.M project paper, University of Nairobi]. University of Nairobi eRepository.

Okoth-Ogendo, W.H.O. (1982). The perils of land tenure reform. In J.W. Arntzen, L.D. Ngcongco & S.D. Turner (Eds.), *Land policy and agriculture in eastern and southern Africa. Selected papers presented at a workshop held in Gaborone, Botswana.* The United Nations University.

Okoth-Ogendo, H.W.O. (1986). *The perils of land tenure reform: The case of Kenya*. Department of Public Law, Faculty of Law, University of Nairobi, Nairobi, Kenya. https://erepository.uonbi.ac.ke/bitstream/handle/11295/35689/059_The%20perils%20of%20land%20tenure%20reform-%20the%20case%20of%20Kenya.pdf?sequence=1

Okoth-Ogendo, W.H.O. & Winston, H. (1991). *Tenants of the crown: Evolution of agrarian law and institutions on Kenya*. ACTS Press.

Pala Okeyo, A. (1980). Daughters of the lakes and rivers: Colonization and the land rights of Luo women. In M. Etienne & E. Leacock (Eds.), *Women and colonization: Anthropological perspectives* (pp. 186–213). Praeger.

Roth, M., Cochrane, J., & Kisamba-Mugerwa, W. (1994). Tenure security, credit use, and farm investment in the Rujumbura pilot land registration scheme, Uganda. In J.W. & S. Migot-Adholla (Eds.) *Searching for land tenure security in Africa* (pp. 169–198). The World Bank.

Shipton, P. (1988). The Kenyan land tenure reform: Misunderstandings in the public creation of private property. In R.E. Downs & S.P. Reyna (Eds.), *Land and society in contemporary Africa* (pp. 91–135). Harvard Institute for International Development.
Simpson, S.R. (1955). Land law and registration in the Sudan. *Public Administration and Development*, *7*(1), 11–17.
Simpson, S.R. (1976). *Land law and registration*. Cambridge University Press.
Sorenson, M.P.K. (1967). *Land reform in the Kikuyu country: A study in government policy*. Oxford University Press.
Southall, R. (2005). The Ndungu report: Land & graft in Kenya. *Review of African Political Economy*, *32*(103), 142–151. www.jstor.org/stable/4006915
Swynnerton, R.J.M. (1955). *A plan to intensify the development of African agriculture in Kenya*. Government Printer.
Tchatchoua-Djomo, R., van Leeuwen, M., & van der Haar, G. (2020). Defusing land disputes? The politics of land certification and dispute resolution in Burundi. *Development and Change*, *51*(6), 1454–1480. https://doi.org/10.1111/dech.12621
White, C.M. (1958). Terminological confusion in African land tenure. *Journal of African Administration*, *10*, 124–130.
Wilson, R.J.A. (1971). *The economic implications of land registration in Kenya's smallholder areas* (Staff Paper No. 91). Institute of Development Studies, Nairobi University.
Wily, L.A. (2018) The community land act in Kenya opportunities and challenges for communities. *Land*, *7*(1), Article 12. https://doi.org/10.3390/land7010012
Yamano, T. & Deininger, K. (2005). *Land conflicts in Kenya: Causes, impacts, and resolutions*. The World Bank.
Zevenbergen, J. (2002). *Systems of land registration: Aspects and effects*. Netherlands Geodetic Commission.

# 13 Individualization to a State-Granted Use Right

## Senegal and Nigeria

### Sporadic Registration of State-owned Land

Most countries in Africa that carried out land tenure reforms in the years after independence declared or confirmed all land as owned by the state. Socialist ideologies and concern that land markets would create widespread landlessness convinced them that land needed to be publicly owned. Some reasoned that land, as essential as air, should be free as the air and argued for a right to land. Zambia's first president, Kenneth Kaunda, announced "land without value" as the basis of his country's land policy (Bae, 2023). These countries pursued individualization policies centered on use rights, usually leases or usufruct rights from the state, rather than marketable ownership rights. These reforms declare or confirm that all land is owned by the state, and either convert customary rights in land to statutory use rights at the stroke of a pen or provide a process by which this is to happen over time, at either government or landholder initiative. Often, the land concerned is already state land.

Under colonialism, extensive areas of land in African colonies were deemed as owned by the state or crown, including lands occupied and used by African peoples. Often these were 90% or more of the national territory, with only 10% or less having been granted to colonists and investors as statutory rights. At independence, most African countries retained this land, occupied by their customary users, in state ownership. Nigeria, Senegal and Mali, and later Sudan, Ethiopia and Uganda, also nationalized the land that had been in private ownership, converting the title of the owner to a long-term leasehold or use right. (Uganda has more recently instituted private ownership.)

Examples of this tenure reform model vary considerably. In Senegal, land was nationalized and provision made for issuing certificates of use rights. Conversion was sporadic, at the request of the landholder, and has been pursued by only a few landholders. Senegal took a broader land governance approach, seeking decentralization of authority over customary land more than any generalized replacement of customary land tenure. Nigeria has a mature land tenure system, going back to the 1960s. Notwithstanding critical assessments of that system, Nigerians seem insufficiently uncomfortable with its dated sporadic registration system to make a major

DOI: 10.4324/9781003476429-16

change. In contrast, Côte d'Ivoire has recently launched an ambitious program of systematic registration of long-term use rights.

**Senegal**

Chapter 2 has a brief description of the approach taken toward land tenure in France's African colonies. French colonial administrators had a broader transformative vision for African society than their British counterparts. They had, like British colonial administrators, depended upon chiefs and other traditional authorities as intermediaries in ruling African subjects. The French had from early days planned their eventual replacement. The French initially created a colonial bureaucracy with local government offices at municipality (urban) and commune (rural community) levels staffed by French colonial officials. Local African staff were gradually incorporated into those offices and the role of traditional authorities gradually reduced, with an expectation that local administration would become more decentralized and democratic over time. Land tenure reform would be a part of that transformation. Land rights were not seen as central or as urgent a matter as in British colonial thinking.

Senegal had long been seen by France as the most advanced of its African colonies. The first major land tenure reform in Francophone Africa was enacted in 1964 in post-independence Senegal. Under colonial rule, customary law jurisdictions were allowed to exist alongside a French-modeled legal code. Only 2–3% of land had been registered as freehold during the colonial era, primarily in or near urban areas. In 1964, the new government passed the National Domain Law (Law 64–46), seeking to remove access to land from the control of traditional authorities. The Law, still in effect, classified 97% of land in Senegal as National Land "held by the state." This is often stated as "owned by the state." This distinction could be important in the right political context. My own experience is that such legal distinctions rarely make a difference when dealing with state power. States getting possession of land act like they own it. While existing privately owned land remained under private ownership, the law did not allow creation of new private ownership.

With rural land placed entirely within the national domain, the National Domain Law gave communes the responsibility to allocate use rights to residents, including for use under customary principles so long as the land is used productively. All land transactions are prohibited. In 1976, a modification of the National Domain Law extended the state's public domain—land owned by and to be managed by the state—to include subsurface land, inland waters, ocean shores and offshore waters. The law also identified different types of land tenure: ownership, leasehold (granted for terms up to 30 years and renewable), occupancy rights and land-use allocations under customary practices.

The Rural Community Law, passed in 1972, provided the structure for the elected rural councils and the extent of their authority regarding land governance. The rural councils received the authority to allocate a variety of land use rights under certain conditions and to deal with land disputes in their jurisdictions. The

Decentralization Law of 1996 clarified the subnational governance structure at the regional and municipality levels in both urban and rural areas. In rural areas, it confirmed the responsibility of elected rural councils for allocation of land rights to members of the community for personal use and for establishment of agricultural production standards. The councils were authorized to reorganize common lands within their territories belonging to the state and administered by rural councils that can allocate and take back land. They are authorized to manage unallocated areas of national land, such as forests, pastures and livestock corridors. Councils have yet to take advantage of this authority (Bourgoin et al., 2020; cited in Delville et al., 2023).

Despite the land allocation authority granted to commune-level councils by the 1964 law, its implementation has been highly varied. In eastern Senegal, only 0.2% of land under family farming is allocated by the commune compared to more than 47% in the Senegal Delta (Bourgoin et al., 2020; cited in Delville et al., 2023). Most of the land in Senegal continues to be governed by customary law. According to one study, more than 30 years after the law's enactment, customary holders did not feel it useful to seek out state-issued certification of land rights (Delville et al., 2023).

In rural areas land is held by families and lineages. Loans, leases and gifts of land have been common under custom and are governed by local customary law. Customary rules have evolved over time. Traditional collective rights have become more individualized in many places. Rural communities often ignore national land legislation and manage their lands according to evolved custom. As in other African rural contexts, Senegal's courts developed a body of jurisprudence on customary land tenure that over time has diverged from the reality of customary practice (Snyder, 1981). While their land is legally owned by the state, rural communities see themselves as "owners." Custom has continued to evolve, with land rentals and even sales to immigrants, illegal under statutory law, becoming common. Rural councils sometimes legitimize them by reallocating land from the seller to the buyer after the fact (Faye, 2008).

Although Senegalese women play a key role in agriculture, only 6% of them own agricultural land (World Bank, 2024). The 2001 Constitution grants equal access to and ownership of land for women and men. The 1964 National Domain Law does not include specific articles on gender equality nor provide for the registration of use rights in the name of couples, families or other collective entities. These legal limitations, added to persistent traditional social norms, constitute permanent barriers to guaranteeing women equitable and secure land rights.

Women are hindered from acquiring land through allocations to them as individuals and through transactions. According to Delville et al. (2023, p. 9):

> Analyzing land governance "in action" in Senegal communes confirms that the political stakes of land tenure are crucial for understanding practices. While details in procedures and tools may vary from one commune to another, the practical norms of land governance largely overlap. Land allocations are handled in a highly personalised manner, giving priority to external requests and the regularisation of sales, largely excluding women. The most sensitive allocation requests do not go through official channels.

In 1996, new decentralization laws made it easier for the state to take over land under custom. Now it has authority to attract and negotiate with new investors and others seeking agricultural land. Control over state-owned lands under customary land tenure can be transferred to state use and control: (1) when it instigates a project on national land, which it can do after simply consulting the regional council and the rural community or communities concerned and informing them of the decision without needing to register the land in question; and (2) when lands classified as "pioneer lands" (*zones pionnières*) are earmarked for special developments. This means that the state can then allocate or transfer all or part of these areas to natural or legal persons without having to first incorporate them into state lands by registering them in its name. There have been abuses and surprisingly successful resistance (Delville et al., 2023).

Around 2006, international demand for land began to escalate rapidly. The Senegalese government in turn encouraged private investment in agriculture and biofuel production, generating several attempted or effective large-scale land acquisitions by domestic and international investors. Legally, the state had the powers it needed to take land for these investment projects. Resistance to appropriation of lands in Senegal has been strong and relatively effective, due in part to assistance from national and international non-governmental organizations and the expansion of technologies such as email and cellphones to facilitate organizing. Frustrated by bureaucracy and corruption and faced with continuing resistance, several investors had abandoned their projects by 2019 (Gagné, 2019). There are calls on all sides for more effective land governance, but the institutions created by the 1964 reform appear to be either incapable of or unwilling to push back against informal land processes, including extralegal transactions.

The wide gap between what the law requires and actual behavior as regards land means land tenure reform is considered a consensus policy priority. It has proven curiously difficult to pursue reform effectively. A variety of major policy planning initiatives since 1996 have foundered. The most recent, significant for the substantial funding and input of external expertise involved, began in 2012. The Food and Agriculture Organization of the UN (FAO) was keen for opportunities to implement the UN's recently approved Voluntary Guidelines on tenure in lands and other resources. Senegal seemed an excellent opportunity to make a difference. With FAO's support, the government moved forward on a well-conceived, open-ended program, allowing broad consultation and public education and offering opportunities for a consensus to emerge on what reforms were needed. A National Commission on Land Reform (CNRF) was created. Following public consultations and other inputs, it developed and published its land tenure policy proposals in October 2017. They were never officially approved by government, and the CNRF was eliminated at the end of 2017 (FAO, 2020).

In 2017, the World Bank entered the picture as the principal funder of research and policy development for the Senegalese government. The Bank produced a think-piece on modernizing the rural land sector in the Senegal River Basin (World Bank, 2017). The report urged that rather than attempting to quickly reach a broad consensus or comprehensive solution, the government and civil society should work gradually and consultatively toward solutions to specific issues and seek to identify shared interests and grounds for a broader consensus. The World Bank appeared to be guiding the Senegalese down the same path as its earlier land projects in Africa.

By 2019 the pursuit of land tenure reform was endorsed in the government's Emerging Senegal Plan, 2019–2023 (Boulanger et al., 2019) with the objective specified as "the gradual transformation of the current occupancy rights of rural inhabitants into real rights, which would lead to a degree of controlled land transferability" (Government of Senegal, 2019). By 2022, the Bank was providing US$80,000,000 for a project called the Senegal Cadastre and Land Tenure Improvement Project (P172422), the purpose of which is to "strengthen the Recipient's capacity for the implementation of its cadaster at a national level; and to increase the number of land rights registered in selected areas." It includes funds for strengthening land institutions and public sector capacity for improved land administration service delivery and "an innovative national cadaster that considers individual and collective land use rights" (Government of Senegal, 2019). The project's second component is to "formalize individual or collective use rights, as they exist." This seems to suggest that land rights *at custom* will be recorded, a novel approach for the Bank which has not been done in earlier projects of this nature because a policy decision for replacement of custom with private ownership had already been made.[1] It seems that the decision may await the development of policy consensus on whether collective use rights are to be recorded. The importance of these changes in approach will only become clear after some time. The Bank's project site provides no information on the state of implementation.[2]

Despite these encouraging developments, land reform attempts in the past two decades (reflected in multiple successive commissions established since 1996) have not yet been successful. This includes the work of the last Land Reform Commission, established in 2012 and dissolved in 2017 following extensive and inclusive consultations that led to a comprehensive policy document (cf. section 3 of FAO, 2020). Why has tenure reform proved so difficult in Senegal? It is not easy anywhere. Formalization of tenure is not simply a matter of bringing a legally disordered sector into general compliance with law. It often changes land law and property rights, creating winners and losers. Formalization shifts control of land from local communities to the state or other outsiders and, with it, income and power. The people affected by formalization may feel better off under informal arrangements or simply prefer to avoid the cost of paperwork, fees and imposition of standards and the time these require. This is especially true when they see no benefit accruing from formalization. Some officials who administer land may oppose reform because they are involved in illegal or otherwise inappropriate appropriation and transfer of land to outsiders. The information provided by systematic land registration can also render land more visible and thus vulnerable. But these considerations are not unique to Senegal.

Another disincentive to formalization can be interactions among powerful factions and interests over decades to benefit from land transactions. Members of central and local governments and traditional society often control access to land by outsiders and divide the rewards for that access. It appears to be a relatively stable system, probably because it is working effectively for a range of powerful interests. Largely unwritten, such arrangements sometimes acquire many of the characteristics of a formal system. Delville et al. (2023, p. 1) describe this situation in Senegal:

> this article reveals the administrative practices and routines, often far removed from the rule, that constitute communal land governance in action. Favoured by lasting legal loopholes, a set of semi-legal or even illegal practices have become widespread, through successive bricolage, on the part of elected officials and communal administrations as well as by the land administration. To varying degrees depending on the socio-economic and political contexts of the communes, they allow access to land for actors from outside the commune, and the legalization of illegal sales, while at the same time favoring the clientelist consolidation of the power of elected officials and their enrichment. This politicized governance of land is tolerated by the central government, which also uses the law to serve its political allies and promote its own projects.

Power holders resist reforms disrupting such systems until they lose power or reforms better accommodate their needs. This is a political problem. Any reform activity upsetting the current arrangement will require a political solution. Since formalization has been the central theme in reform dialogue and since formalization favors central governments who make law, it would not be surprising to find that the political tension obstructing reform is between central and local government. This seems to be the case (Delville et al., 2023).

Land governance reforms such as in Senegal may have land tenure reforms as an element in the program. They are more concerned with authority over land and decentralization efforts. In the case of Senegal, the land governance reform had key land tenure elements: the new availability to customary landholders of a land rights certification from the state. The tenure component was nested within a new legal framework for local land management by communes and municipalities.

**Box 13.1 State Ownership of Land and Leasehold Tenure for Agricultural Land**

In cases where the state owns land that can be allocated to farmers for agricultural production, what tenure should the state provide to the land users? There's a wide range of options. The choice depends heavily on the land use involved. It runs from seasonal permits to leases providing as much security of tenure as ownership, apart from perpetuity. Such an almost-ownership lease is uncommon. One is more likely to find them in countries with land under both state and private ownership, rather than in countries having all their land in state ownership.

Most countries embracing state ownership of all land are more likely to seek a relatively high degree of control over production and develop leases that are conditional on compliance with specific land use terms. They tend to see farmers as privileged to have been given land by the state and under a duty to use it well, as the state intended. This viewpoint can give rise to excessive supervision of agricultural production. Since the land is a benefit conferred by the state for a particular purpose, the responsible official will tend to resist requests to change crops or other aspects of land use from what is framed in the lease contracts. That translates into contractual provisions that:

1. Over-specify the farming process that must be followed, destroying the flexibility that farmers must have to contend with the uncertainty that affects farming.
2. Place excessive reliance on penalties for failing to meet standards rather than relying on incentives and farmer education to improve farming practices.
3. Include vague requirements regarding land use, such as "uses all best farming practices" or "compliance with all Department of Agriculture policies and instructions."
4. Make failure to achieve those standards a basis for the government to terminate the contract under which the farmer holds the land.

This creates a situation in which corrupt officials can obtain bribes for not reporting non-compliance with contracts, playing on farmers' fears of losing their land. This combination of vague conditions and termination as a possible sanction creates a risk of loss, and so insecurity of tenure. A bank would understandably hesitate to lend money on the security of the lease. The risk is amplified by the fact that state land is almost always made available to cultivators at a cost less than actual value, and much less than the actual value in some situations, such as frontier development programs and programs to establish land reform beneficiaries on their new holdings. The difference between value and price is the opportunity for a bribe in an allocation situation. When land is being allocated, officials who have some discretion in dispositions of state lands are able to favor one allottee or another and, in the case of sitting tenants, to leverage bribes or even cause termination of an existing lease on the grounds that the holder violated some vague condition. Such corruption undermines economic development. There are other characteristics of state land ownership systems that tend to affect economic growth negatively.

Box 13.2 provides an illustration of over-supervision of agricultural production in Nigeria's Ogun State. This practice is sometimes associated with Francophone Africa because so much productive land there is owned by the state. The Nigeria case makes clear that it can and often does happen wherever agriculture is practiced on land owned and allocated by the state.

The legal situation regarding land in Senegal is representative of that in most Francophone countries in Africa. The land is owned by the state. Farmland is managed and farmed by households and the grazing by traditional communities under their customary law. Provision is made for farmers to obtain statutory land rights based on a certificate from the government. This is handled through sporadic, rather than systematic, land registration. The strictures against selling land are still enforced by customary institutions in most areas but are eroding due to market forces. Certification of a customary right by the state does not make the right legally marketable.

How to assess this model in relation to Senegal? There is widespread feeling that the land governance system in Senegal is antiquated. Practice diverges from what is provided by law. This is unlikely to be a matter of ignorance of the law or simple carelessness regarding the law's requirements. The problem is likely to lie in factors such as unworkability of formal arrangements, their failure to respond to felt needs, unacceptability of costs in time and energy imposed by formality, corruption infecting the system and the interests of those who wield power.

The answer to such problems is unlikely to be simply formalization, in the sense of bringing practice into line with existing law. Formalization, if it is only about better enforcement of the law, is nothing new, except that a more forceful enforcement approach, systematic titling and registration, is deployed. It may be more realistic to "formalize the informal," accepting some of the redistributions of benefits provided by current informality and ensuring that formalization takes account of the interests of those resisting it (Bruce & Roth, 2005). There are vested interests in such cases. Compromises are often needed. If the opposition to reform proposals has come from local governments leery of the highly centralized nature of the land registry system and of the likelihood that in time that system will provide the central government with land information that has been largely the domain of local government, resistance from local interests would be entirely understandable. What accounts for the fact that opposition to tenure reforms in Senegal have been more substantial and successful than elsewhere? Might it have been something in the history of local governance reform that accounts for this? This is a line of research worth pursuing.

Given the many drawbacks of systematic land titling and registration projects, would Senegal be better off continuing to rely on sporadic land registration? Sporadic registration has problems of its own that systematic titling and registration were developed to avoid. When an individual applies for and is willing to pay the fees associated with cadastral survey and registration of his parcel, it is because that individual has a very clear notion of what he wants to do on the land, and it cannot be done without a registered title. In the case of a sporadic registration, there is almost always an investment impact, though it may or may not be in agriculture. The willingness to pay the fees for sporadic titling signals the holder's intent to invest in the land. Sporadic registration is where most corrupt practices linked to land registration occur. Dealing with a single plot in isolation can be done without neighbors noticing or understanding what is going on. Later they might find out that land they claim as their own has been registered to someone else. The public nature of systematic titling and registration makes this less likely to happen. Under sporadic titling, even when service fees for surveying and registration do not cover the full costs, they reduce the level of the government's subsidization of the process. Governments which support systematic work have little choice but to charge no fees or only nominal fees for the service since those receiving the "service" did not ask for it and would be extremely resistant to paying (Bruce & Knox, 2009; Burns et al., 2007).

## Nigeria

As the most populous country in Africa with major oil and gas resources and a quarter of its GDP from agriculture, Nigeria is a powerhouse. It is ethnically diverse and has a large Muslim population. Two of its states in the north have adopted Islamic law. It came to independence in 1974 and has a reputation for weak governance and a high level of corruption in both its private and public sectors (Hennings, 2021).

Nigeria, like most British colonies, tolerated customary land tenure under the doctrine of indirect rule. Prior to independence, virtually all land was held under customary land tenure, administered for the British by the chiefs. Colonial courts would take cases on appeal and deliver judgments on the nature of tribal custom, often with African assessors (interpreters) of customary rules. On paper this came to an end when the post-independence government enacted the Land Use Decree of 1978. It abolished customary land tenure and declared all land state-owned. As in many other African countries, the government sought to displace chiefs as the managers of land. The land nationalization came from a military regime of questionable validity and was not welcomed by the former colonial power.

Although Nigeria has a uniform statutory land tenure system, Nigeria's state governments, rather than the central government, hold the land in trust for the people of Nigeria. Any Nigerian can apply for a Certificate of Occupancy for land anywhere in the country, irrespective of the applicant's ethnic origin or sex. He or she applies to the state, not the nation. The Act limits interests in land to a single certificate holder, who has the sole right and absolute possession of the land and all improvements on the land. Those who wish to acquire a Statutory Certificate of Occupancy are required to have land allocated to them, which is then certified. Alternatively, those holding land under custom can apply for an allocation of land from the regional government, then apply for certificates for their land, converting it to statutory tenure. The local government may grant a Customary Right of Occupancy rent-free to any person or organization for agricultural purposes, subject to the limitation that no person may hold more than 5,000 hectares for grazing purposes or more than 500 hectares for cultivation. The process of acquiring land is long and complex and generally costs more than the annual income of a smallholder. Land subject to customary land tenure retains that status until a Certificate of Occupancy is applied for and granted. Because government does not accept sales of land under customary certificates and land under statutory certificates requires government consent, a busy informal land market has developed (Ghebru &

Kennedy, 2019), a market in customary rights involving both certified and uncertified customary holdings, technically illegal but accepted as a fact of life.

The governor of a region can grant a Statutory Right of Occupancy to any person for urban or rural land. The period of the award, i.e. the term of the lease, is determined by the region. The governor has power to set the rent for any land granted under a Statutory Right. He may revise the rent, with few restrictions, and can, at his discretion, waive the rent in circumstances where it would create hardship. The Customary Right of Occupancy involves rights of access, succession, duration and rental. It takes the legal form of a lease. Both Customary and Statutory Rights of Occupancy can be revoked for failure to comply with the terms of the lease as spelled out in the Certificate of Occupancy. A rights-holder may transfer, assign or mortgage any improvements on the land, but not the land itself, and may engage in such transactions only with the consent of the regional governor. Inheritance of rights of occupancy, whether statutory or customary, is according to the customary law of the community where the land is located or, in the case of Muslims, Islamic law. Rights of occupancy may be revoked in the public interest. Should that occur, compensation is payable only for unexhausted improvements on the land, not for the loss of use of the land itself.

As in other countries relying on state ownership of land, Nigeria has suffered from the paternalism and conditionality of land rights associated with state ownership. Box 13.2 on the requirements for making a successful application for farmland in Ogun State, eastern Nigeria, illustrates some problems of state use rights allocated by government.

**Box 13.2 Requirements for Agricultural Land Allocation in Ogun State, Nigeria Requirements**

1. Letter of intent to the Hon. Commissioner Ministry of Agriculture by the applicant.
2. Collection of an application form.

    a) Corporate Applicant (Greater than 20 hectares).
    b) Individual Applicant (Below 20 hectares).

3. Submission of Documents:

    - Current Ogun State Tax Clearance Certificate for three (3) consecutive years.
    - Ogun State Development Levy for three (3) consecutive years.
    - Current Bank Statement of Account
    - A detailed feasibility report on the proposed project.
    - Certificate of Incorporation.
    - Company's Article of Association.
    - Personnel Profile of the Directors of the Company.

After meeting the above stated conditions, the applicant will be interviewed by a panel, after which allocation of land will be granted after the following fees are paid:

- Premium fee.
- Annual Ground Rent.
- Crop Enumeration Service Charges.
- Cost of materials for crop enumeration exercise.
- Crop compensation.
- Cost of Survey (obtainable from Bureau of Lands & Survey).

Source: Obayelu et al. (2017), referencing Ministry of Agriculture Ogun State, Nigeria.

There are problems with state-issued leasing contracts characteristic in systems based on state land ownership:

1. Access to land is being used to collect a remarkable range of fees, many of them unconnected with the land. The transaction costs involved discourage prospective applicants, especially customary landholders, from applying for certificates of occupancy.
2. There is a reference to a "detailed feasibility report for the proposed project." It is not unreasonable to require a general statement of intention as to use, but a detailed plan is likely to cause problems. Unexpected issues often arise and plans easily change. When this happens, does the plan attached to the lease need to be changed? Might a change of plans be considered by the government as a failure to meet the terms of the lease and so a basis for termination of the certificate of occupancy? Such issues provide leverage that officials can use to extract bribes from certificate holders and create insecurity.
3. Broad discretion was granted by the Land Use Decree to regional officials involved in administration of the Act, especially with respect to fees and ground rent. An annual ground rent is charged, which in most cases is well below the market rental value of the land. In those circumstances the difference between the nominal cost charged and the actual value of the land is a recipe for corruption, enabling a dishonest administrator to pocket the difference. Unfortunately, such behavior is very common.

**Box 13.3 Leasehold Tenure for African Smallholders?**

What are the pros and cons of leasehold tenure as an alternative to ownership for Africa's small farmers? If all land is owned by the state and one needs a subsidiary tenure for land users, who in rural areas are mostly smallholders, what should that tenure provide? The most common form of user tenure in countries that have nationalized land is leasehold, the temporary transfer of land from the state to the user for a specified term and "consideration" (something in return for use of the land, usually rent). While the basic content of ownership is the same anywhere, leasehold is an extraordinarily flexible land tenure. The parties specify most of the terms. Leases can play different roles in different circumstances. One must know the terms of the lease before comparisons with ownership are possible. How flexible are leases? An agricultural lease may be as short as a day, or a growing season, or as long as 99 years. It can be longer in some common law jurisdictions that have legislated to extend the maximum period. The rent may be nominal or high and doesn't need to be aligned with market value. The degree of discretion in land use given to the tenant may be broad or narrow. The lease can be inheritable or terminate with the death of the lessee. It may be possible to transfer the remaining term of the lease to another tenant, or not, depending on what it says in the lease. A lease can be written to provide long duration, a low rent and full discretion to use the land in any fashion. It can be inheritable and marketable. If so, it will be worth as much or very nearly as much as the same land in full ownership. Is this approximate ownership not sufficient security of tenure and marketability?

Perhaps, but in Africa, countries that have nationalized land and relied on leasehold as their principal statutory tenure for landholders have done so precisely so that they could limit the rights of landholders, especially by preventing sales. Rwanda provides its smallholders with the lease that, of all those in Africa, most closely approximates ownership. Most African governments have preferred to have planning rather than the market handle distribution of land and its use. Their leases tend to provide weak rights, modest duration and limited freedom of management. There are careful provisions to protect the state's right to resume control of the land should the tenant violate some term of the lease. In such cases, modest or no compensation is paid for the loss of the use of the land, though there may be compensation for improvements.

Often local supervisors or agricultural agents see themselves as protectors of the state's land against its users. They lack confidence in farmers and do not trust them to exercise initiative. They believe farmers need supervision to ensure they use "best practices." This sort of paternalism, with roots in the colonial period, has carried through to agricultural and land administration agencies in Africa where the state owns the land and relies upon leasehold or other use rights as the principal user tenure for farmers.

Leases under Nigeria's Land Use Decree take advantage of the flexibility available in crafting leases. Statutory rights of occupancy are granted by the state governor for 99 years and may be renewed. Governors also determine the rent and other terms and conditions. Additional lease terms for Statutory Certificates of Occupancy are specified by state governors to fit the circumstances of their state.

Customary rights of occupancy are certified by a local Land Use Committee for 50 years and may be renewed for another 50 years. Customary Rights of Occupancy are inheritable but cannot be sold or mortgaged, nor may they be subleased without the consent of the governor or the local government. Both types of certificate holders must pay an annual fee as rent, which is set by each state. This fee discourages all but larger commercial producers from seeking statutory certificates, as does the prescribed process of application, which is long and costly. The number of occupancy certificates is low except in urban areas. Most smallholders continue to operate under customary land tenure and chiefs retain considerable authority in rural communities. Smallholders also avoid certification so they can participate in lively informal markets in land rights among customary landholders.

Nigeria's formal land tenure system resembles that of Senegal in important ways. Both are "mossbacks," of roughly the same age. Both took a gradualist approach to tenure reform, relying on survey and titling at the initiative of landholders. The result has been policy-driven legal change outpaced by evolutionary change that had custom accepting marketability before a statutory tenure regime could be implemented.

It is disturbing to realize that in our present situation, this is what tenure evolution looks like. It is not what proponents of "tenure evolution rather than reform" had in mind. The dynamic operating to produce change here has nothing to do with intensification leading to marketability, but rather with the dualism discussed throughout this book. Persons with money and demand for land find a hole in the fence between their territory where sales of land are legal and a territory where they are forbidden. They slip across the boundary to purchase land available informally and often illegally, but cheaply. They can protect the purchase by having the land surveyed, titled and registered, improving their security of tenure and opportunities to benefit from appreciation. These buyers are not landless or smallholders for the most part, but people with money and influence. This is not about empowerment of the poor, who are almost always the sellers. It is about developing processes of cooperation among officials and chiefs that prey on the disadvantaged and ill-informed. Those processes have the capacity to reshape custom over time. Acting on a larger scale, officials seeking to move land from under community control may use the expropriation power of the state to further private, rather than public, interests.

It is also about corruption made possible by undervaluing land under customary land tenure and providing too much discretion and opportunity for officials responsible for allocating and protecting that land. It is about the corrosive effect of corruption on the rule of law, creating networks of mutual interest running between officialdom, traditional authority and the wealthy. Those networks can be extraordinarily resistant to change and reform, and in these two countries have effectively stifled achievement of the socialist objectives of the governments that enacted the reforms.

What are the prospects for acceptance of reforms in these two countries? Of the two, Senegal has the benefit of a long-running dialogue on land tenure issues, and the encouragement of a major donor with strong expertise and experience in the implementation of similar projects. In Nigeria, proposals for reform have failed to get political traction and there has been no broad-based national dialogue on the issues raised. There is a further major obstacle to reform in Nigeria. Nigeria's 1984 Land Act has been re-enacted as part of the country's constitution. Change in the Act now requires the supermajority required for changes in the Constitution itself.

Now we turn to two countries, Côte d'Ivoire and Rwanda, that have recent and ongoing projects for systematic determination of the land rights of households. Unlike Senegal and Nigeria, these countries have chosen to impose fewer restrictions on marketability of those rights.

## Notes

1 One of the benefits of the new World Bank engagement in Francophone Africa has been its direct engagement in dialogue with French researchers and their less economic and more anthropological approaches to customary land tenure.

2 See: https://projects.worldbank.org/en/projects-operations/project-detail/P172422.

## References

Bae, Y.J. (2023). Analyzing the connection between customary land rights and land grabbing: A case study of Zambia. *Land*, *12*(1), Article 200. https://doi.org/10.3390/land12010200

Boulanger, P., Dudu, H., Ferrari, E., Mainar Causapé, A., Angelucci, F., Baborska, R., & Meilland, T. (2019). *Plan Sénégal emergent 2019–2023* [Dataset]. European Commission, Joint Research Centre. http://data.europa.eu/89h/d728da87-5575-42b8-924e-3da6928b94fd

Bourgoin, J., Diop, D., Dia, D., Sall, M., Zagré, R., Grislain, Q., & Anseeuw, W. (2020). Regard sur le modèle agricole sénégalais: pratiques foncières et particularités territoriales des moyennes et grandes exploitations agricoles. *Cah. Agric.*, *29*: 18. https://doi.org/10.1051/cagri/2020018

Bruce, J.W. & Knox, A. (2009). Structures and stratagems: Making decentralization of authority over land in Africa cost-effective. *World Development*, *37*(8), 1360–1369. https://doi.org/10.1016/j.worlddev.2008.08.011

Bruce, J.W. & Roth, M. (2005). *Formalization, legal reform and legal empowerment of the poor: Overview and issues paper*. ARD for USAID.

Burns, T., Grant, C., Nettle, K., Brits, A.M., & Dalrymple, K. (2007). *Land administration reform: Indicators of success and future challenges.* World Bank (Agriculture and Rural Development Discussion Paper No. 37).

Delville, P.L., Diongue, M., & Diouf, I.F. (2023). The practical norms of land governance in Senegalese communes: Institutional incompleteness, politicisation, semi-formality and bricolage. *Land Use Policy*, *132*, 106828. https://doi.org/10.1016/j.landusepol.2023.106828

FAO. (2020). *The voluntary guidelines: Securing our rights—Senegal.* FAO. https://openknowledge.fao.org/server/api/core/bitstreams/671aec08-24d0-4661-815a-12c3a3901d44/content#:~:text=These%20Voluntary%20Guidelines%20have%20been,achieve%20food%20security%20for%20all

Faye, J. (2008). *Land and decentralisation in Senegal* (Issue Paper No. 149). IIED. www.iied.org/12550iied

Gagné, M. (2019). Resistance against land grabs in Senegal: Factors of success and partial failure of an emergent social movement. In *The politics of land* (Vol. 26, pp. 173–203). Emerald Publishing Limited. https://doi.org/10.1108/S0895-993520190000026012

Ghebru, H. & Kennedy, A. (2019). *Nigeria land governance reform: What needs to be done to stimulate demand and support market growth?* (Policy Research Brief No. 97). Department of Agricultural, Food, and Resource Economics, Michigan State University.

Government of Senegal (2019). *Dakar: Emerging Senegal plan.* Government Printer.

Hennings, A. (2021). *Nigeria: Context and land governance.* Nigeria Federal University of Technology.

Obayelu, A.E., Arowolo, A.O., & Osinowo, O.H. (2017). Land tenure, governance and accountability in Nigeria: The implications on food production to feed the present and the future. *Journal for the Advancement of Developing Economies*, *6*(1), 1–35. https://doi.org/10.32873/unl.dc.jade6.1.1

Snyder, F.G. (1981). Colonialism and legal form: The creation of "customary law" in Senegal. *The Journal of Legal Pluralism and Unofficial Law*, *13*(9), 49–90. https://doi.org/10.1080/07329113.1981.10756258

World Bank (2017). *Senegal–Support to Senegal rural land policy ASA: Modernizing the rural land sector* (Report No. AUS0000690). World Bank.

World Bank (2024). *Land rights and gender inequality in Senegal: Gender gap analysis part I.* The World Bank. https://documents1.worldbank.org/curated/en/099157510302419205/pdf/IDU1b679a79b15c401496c1a228198aef2f6223c.pdf

# 14 More Recent Individualization to Use Rights

## Rwanda, Côte d'Ivoire and Ethiopia

### Rwanda

Advocates of systematic registration and titling projects have been encouraged by reports of their recent effective implementation in Rwanda, on a nationwide basis no less. Rwanda is a small country of rolling green hills with one of the highest population densities in Africa. A former colony of Belgium, it has since colonial times had a Civil Code that provides for formal legal titles to land. These were available only in towns and cities and required substantial investments in the land. Prior to 2008, only 1% of its land had been registered. The remainder was governed by custom (Bruce, 2007).

Rwanda experienced successive waves of ethnic violence between 1959 and 1994. The ethnic Tutsi people had long exercised political dominance over the numerous, poorer Hutu people. In 1959 the Hutu rose up against the Tutsi, massacring many of them. Thousands of Tutsi relocated to Uganda and other countries in eastern Africa. In 1994, an army of Tutsi assembled in Uganda entering Rwanda and sweeping across it and back into power. Many Hutu fled into the Democratic Republic of Congo and elsewhere, though many remained. Land was the cause of the fighting. In its aftermath, there were overlapping claims for the land by members of the two ethnicities. Simultaneously, the authority of traditional leaders and customary land tenure had been weakened. The Tutsi-led Rwandan Government introduced a land sharing policy in 1995/96 focusing on the eastern part of the country. Where there were disputed claims for land, the claimants were made to share the land between them. One element of the policy was the "*imidugudu*" (villagization) program (Bruce, 2007).

In the years after peace was restored, population growth and development increased land values. An active informal market in land developed. Citizens increasingly called for better access to formal titles. Because land in Rwanda is owned by the state, the titles had to be long-term leases from the state. In 2003, the government launched a national consultation on land tenure, leading to drafting the National Land Policy (2004) and the enactment of the Organic Land Law in 2005. The Organic Land Law provided that land "is the public land of all Rwandans" (effectively state ownership), but that land would continue in the hands of its present

DOI: 10.4324/9781003476429-17

holders and be farmed by them under a 99-year "emphyteutic" lease from the state. This is a tenure of Roman origin that is recognized by both common and civil law.

Emphyteutic leases are classified as a form of ownership because they are the functional equivalent of ownership. First, it is registrable as a "title." Second, it can be conveyed by the lessee to another person. It can also be conveyed to a bank as collateral for a mortgage. In both cases of lease conveyance, no government consent is required. Substantial fees are charged by the registry office for transfers. Under article 7, the law gave equal protection to customary land rights and transactions (purchase, gift, exchange and sharing) and to land rights under written law. It is an unusual choice because most governments that insist upon state ownership of the land have sought to replace, either immediately or gradually, customary tenure (Payne, 2011).

After further consultations and successful field trials, in 2011 the government launched its Land Tenure Regularization Program. Its aim was to issue a registered title to every landholder in Rwanda through a low-cost, systematic process, covering the entire country. Within three years, it was expected to register and allocate 7,900,000 land titles. Funding and technical assistance were provided by Britain's Department of Foreign and International Development. The target was considered bizarrely ambitious by many commentators, including this author, who over the years had watched project after project of this nature come up well short of much more modest output targets. Under LTRP, 10,300,000 parcels of land were demarcated and registered between 2009 and 2013 (Biraro et al., 2015). The success appears to have been due to a participatory process driven by a regime more authoritarian and effective than most (Republic of Rwanda, 2008).

Equally remarkable has been its success in registering women's land rights, something not prioritized in other projects in Africa, except for Ethiopia (discussed below and in Chapter 17). When the project ended, 81% of land parcels were registered jointly by men and women, 11% by women only, 6% by men and 2% by non-individualized institutions (RISD et al., 2017, citing, Government of Rwanda (2014)). This was a striking achievement by comparison with programs elsewhere in Africa and even many Asian programs.

Despite these successes, informed commentators on Rwanda's program have identified a number of issues that may in the future undermine the reform's policy objectives:

1. The extensive registration of husbands and wives as joint owners achieved in the first registration may not be sustained. The law does not require this inclusive approach in subsequent registration. The inheritance rights of women in civil unions are protected by law in the case of death or divorce. This is not the case for couples in consensual unions (including non-registered customary marriages), which are more prevalent than civil unions in rural areas (Brown & Hughes, 2017; Lawry et al., 2023, p. 173; Ali et al., 2014).
2. The haste with which the program was designed and implemented has given rise to concern on at least two points. First, good practice in a reform program is thought to require a solid policy process and consensus before moving forward

with drafting the legislation needed to implement it. In this case, the law was drafted before the policy was finalized, though the policy's main directions were clear. Second, the project devoted less than the usual attention to training staff in basic land administration skills necessary for the effective operation and maintenance of the registry system. Project implementation in the field ran ahead of the development of the administrative infrastructure needed for an effective land registration system. While no specific negative results have been attributed to this, some commentators express concern it may have a deleterious effect on the operations of the system (Ali et al., 2014).

3. The urgency with which the program sought to meet ambitious targets may have fueled resentment over its compulsory character, a feeling that is not uncommon among the "beneficiaries" of systematic titling and registration programs. I heard critics of the program speak of it as having "bulldozed" customary rights to replace them with leasehold certificates. Staff of other rural land programs operating at that time have attributed apparent broad enthusiasm for the project to suppression of opposition. One told me that government silenced critics with threats and barred foreign researchers from entry into the country. A donor had to suspend the research contract of one of their local counterparts when the counterpart received threats and had their vehicles vandalized. Such stories are heard frequently enough to suggest that they are not misleading, even if they are hearsay. If indeed demand for titles was superficial to a large extent, this may affect incentives for subsequent registration and therefore reform sustainability.[1]
4. Systematic titling itself was reasonably well received. Rwanda has struggled to implement two other reform measures that have proven thoroughly unpopular: minimum parcel sizes and land use consolidation. The former required that farmers not subdivide parcel sizes less than one hectare (Hughes & Kamatali, 2016). The latter directed small farmers to monocrop their parcels with adjacent farmers in an effort by the government to improve production efficiency (Huggins, 2019).
5. Given the experience of other such reforms in the region, it is hardly surprising that research by the World Bank found that during the first five years after first registration, 87% of transactions went unregistered (Ali et al., 2021). Lawry et al. (2023, p. 52) discuss possible reasons for this, including avoidance of a prohibition on parcel subdivision to less than one hectare and avoidance of high registration fees. They note that Brown and Hughes (2017) found that the unregistered transactions were within families and were handled by family and village authorities. While this makes the transactions more easily recalled, failure to register transactions does not do much to mitigate the deleterious effect on having a reliable system for proving rights and upholding security of tenure (Ali et al., 2021).

In an attempt to benefit from the experience to date, a new version of the land law was enacted and published in 2021. The changes:

1. Eliminate a periodic fee for the emphyteutic lease (Art. 2).
2. Provide that all Rwandans are entitled to freehold tenure if they apply and their land is developed for any of a broad range of purposes, but not agriculture (Art. 6).

3. Provide for automatic lease renewal in the case of Rwandans upon expiry of the term, while for non-citizens it is, as before, merely renewable (Art. 10).
4. Allow foreigners access to emphyteutic leases only for investments but remove a limitation on the term of emphyteutic leases for foreigners to 49 years and no longer require them to register their leases (Art. 15).
5. Remove a requirement that all landowners register their ownership, but retain a requirement that leases for agricultural purposes be registered (Arts. 26, 28).
6. No longer restrict sub-division of parcels (Art. 21).
7. Specifically assert state ownership of mineral resources (Arts. 42, 43), whereas the previous version asserted state ownership of "natural resources."
8. Expand the right of the state to terminate a lease based on a breach of any lease term (Art. 49), as opposed to the more specific grounds specified in the earlier version.

These are fundamental changes in some respects. Some are clearly responsive to grassroots reactions to the reform and positive, such as elimination of the minimum parcel size provisions. Experience elsewhere has shown that customary systems have the flexibility to avoid inheritance rules forcing the subdivision of parcels *ad infinitum*.[2] Land use consolidation reforms, created by a different statute but implemented in conjunction with systematic land titling and registration, likewise sought to deter fragmentation. While the measure did not involve the physical consolidation of parcels (a very complex process), it required holders of neighboring parcels to cultivate the same crop in an effort to induce greater production and marketing efficiencies. Its close supervision by government functionaries proved highly unpopular with farmers, who complained that they no longer felt their land belonged to them (Pritchard, 2013). This program is unaffected by the new land law. The expansion of government authority to terminate leases for failure to comply with all their conditions unfortunately is consistent with Rwanda's tendency to exert state management authority over privately owned land, a source of popular resentment.

Its drawbacks aside, the rate of Rwanda's implementation of tenure reform and its success in compelling registration of joint ownership for couples have generated a great deal of interest among those who assess different approaches to African land tenure reform. The experience is relatively recent, however, and it will be some time before we have a clear picture of its overall adequacy. Early evidence suggests that fundamental issues of maintenance of records and sustainability of the registry have not been addressed (Ali et al., 2021; Lawry et al., 2023).

## Côte d'Ivoire

Côte d'Ivoire became an autonomous colony of France in 1893, overseen by a governor who reported to the Ministry of Colonies in Paris. Its land was occupied by African communities of diverse ethnicities, holding land they farmed under their customary land tenure systems. Those customary claims were rejected by the colonists. The land of Côte d'Ivoire was deemed to belong to France by right of conquest. Like Kenya, Côte d'Ivoire entered the 20th century with a promising future as an export economy based on extensive plantings of tree crops, including coffee, cocoa and oil palms. These are crops which, in the commercial context, call for substantial investment and secure land tenure to protect the investment. Tree crops were common under customary land tenure, suggesting a reasonable degree of security of tenure, initially as rights not to land, but as rights to trees held by the person who planted them. Only 1–2% of the land was converted to private ownership, but Africans could obtain certificates for their customary landholdings. Rural land in Côte d'Ivoire, as in Senegal, was managed lightly through a decentralized system of land administration operated through the commune system, the local governance system for rural areas (Gagné, 2022).

The country's first president, Houphouët-Boigny (1960–1993), promoted expansion of commercial tree plantations into the country's forests. Early in his administration, he announced that, henceforth, the person who brought the land into production should own the land. This led to extensive invasions and clearing of forests. In 1998, Law No. 98–750 was enacted in reaction to his policies, creating a new regime for rural land. It reversed earlier policy so that an owner of undeveloped land could no longer be ousted from his right by someone else clearing that land (Gagné, 2022). It assigned land ownership to its registered holder, not necessarily its direct user. It also privileged Ivorians by relegating foreigners to long-term emphyteutic leases, rather than ownership (Gagné, 2022).

Customary land rights were recognized in the same law. Côte d'Ivoire, like virtually all Francophone countries, opted to retain state ownership of land after independence, though the very limited landholdings in private ownership were not affected and are still in that tenure. Customary rights, by contrast, are overlaid on the base of state ownership of land and are to be registered (Lestang et al., 2018). The registration involves two steps. First, any applicant(s) (individual or group) that can prove continuous and uncontested use of the land are issued transitional land certificates (certificat foncier [CF]). Second, Ivorian citizens who are individual certificate holders may apply for land titles within three years of certification. Non-Ivorians who hold certificates must register them with the state. The state can then issue a long-term lease to the non-Ivorian applicant (World Bank, 2018).

It effectively extinguishes customary rights and replaces them with statutory rights.

Law No. 98–750 prescribes that the certificate of customary land holding is valid for only three years. If issued in the name of a family, lineage or village, its holders must divide the land among themselves to obtain an individual title (Gagné, 2022, citing Kouamé, 2018). In 2017, a Declaration of Land Policy was issued extending the validity of customary certificates to ten years. Despite these measures, few Ivorians have sought to obtain land titles given the cost of the procedures and associated taxes (Gagné, 2022).

Prior to independence until 1989, land registration in Côte d'Ivoire was carried out sporadically, on application, expanding very slowly. Concurrently, those holding land under custom were affected by many of the same forces promoting monetization and tenure change in other African countries, though less intensively than in countries that had been settler colonies. Systematic titling and registration were piloted in some areas, but generalizing the system has proven difficult. Systematic land registration pilots began in Côte d'Ivoire in 1989 while Houphouët-Boigny was still in office. Bassett (2020) describes the World Bank's Côte d'Ivoire Rural Landholding Project as a US$3,800,000 project initiated in the absence of any local demand. He indicates it was first implemented in 1989 in five pilot zones, with the pilot phase ending in the spring of 1991 when the government began to extend the project more broadly in the country. Bassett notes that while the project presented itself as a neutral and unthreatening inventory of rights terms, it had some of the problems of earlier titling and registration work. He argues that rather than reflecting the indigenous land rights system, the photomaps presented an incomplete view of these tenure systems by their exclusive focus on the rights of agriculturalists and lineage heads. He describes an area in eastern Côte d'Ivoire with a fluid land use pattern, in which local landholders farm the same land for five to ten years and then leave it fallow for 10–20 years. The areas cultivated are different over time. The extent of plantings varies with a variety of factors including labor availability. There is a continually changing pattern of land use and property rights in which only the boundaries of villages and lineage landholdings are stable (not individual parcels), and even those are challenged from time to time. The rights recording process excluded many of those who had rights to use land of the community but were not there all the time: pastoralists with grazing rights, hunters, gatherers, wood cutters and emigrants who were absent at the time the survey was carried out (Bassett, 2020).

Expansion of the land registration system has been slow. It has had to address successive waves of widespread land disputes between local customary land users and waves of immigrants, many relatively recent, from Ghana and Burkina Faso. From the colonial period, groups of Ivorian internal migrants have held land under oral agreements with the local communities which originally settled and established ownership of the land there. The groups now often interpret the agreements differently and as populations in the areas concerned have grown, the rights of the more recent arrivals are challenged. Recently, large numbers of immigrants from neighboring countries entered Côte d'Ivoire seeking land from local communities and government and sometimes occupying land without permission. In 2014, 24.2% of the national population consisted of immigrants, mostly Burkinabe but also Ghanaians and Malians (Gagné, 2022).

The urgency of settling these disputes has become a critical justification for systematic titling and registration. As in many such projects, the registered title is based on unchallenged occupation for a prescribed period, rather than a customary right derived from lineage membership or other group affiliation. Reliance on occupation avoids the necessity of an inquiry into local customary land tenure, though when the issue of occupation is contested, it is difficult to resolve it without reference to how the land had been handled at custom. It also means that only the rights of claimants who are present on the land all year round are likely to be registered. Rights exercised seasonally or which do not require regular presence on the land, such as the exercise of a traditional right of way, are not recorded.

The World Bank involvement continued and in 1990–1996 provided support for the Plan Foncier, under which the government processed 20,000 parcels in 369 villages in five zones, surveying 500,000 hectares. The Rural Land Management and Community Infrastructure Project began in 1998. The World Bank and France's Caisse Francais de Developpement co-funded pilot work for implementation of the new law under a project called Plan Foncier Rural. Work under the project began very slowly. Political instability during 2000–2010 delayed implementation. During this period the government set up a Rural Land Agency to implement the program (Lestang et al., 2018). By 2016, the field work for 27,300 land parcels in 360 villages had been completed, though only 3,000 of those parcels were finally registered. It was estimated that the total number of land parcels nationally was 1,000,000. Migrants had been found to comprise between 5% and 70% of the populations of the zones surveyed. The Bank reported substantial demand for "tenure clarification" and indicated that the program had been extremely well received by villagers (Teyssier, 2017).

In 2016, a new Constitution affirmed that ownership of land is confined to citizens. In 2017, a new Land Policy Document set out a ten-year program for land registration reform: four years of institutional strengthening and piloting registration and six years of national implementation. In 2018, the World Bank loaned Côte d'Ivoire US$450,000,000 at a concessionary rate, making systematic registration possible on a much larger scale. The legal basis for the program's registration is still Law No. 98 of 1998. The program's purpose was to "register customary land rights" in selected rural areas and its primary activity was clarification of land tenure. The terminology is confusing given that the law being relied upon replaces customary rights with statutory rights (Gagné, 2022). By 2023, World Bank-financed systematic registration had issued over 33,000 land certificates with 22% of these including women on the certificate (World Bank Group, 2024).

Have increasing land rights and security in those rights increased productivity? The Ivorian program's planners have been careful not to promise too much, for example improved access to formal credit. But many of the fundamental problems of Kenya's experience seem likely to trouble the implementation, including that of sustainability. The program involves the same narrow focus on rights of individuals to the exclusion of community rights and so risks being seen as rejecting community claims to commons and other group-held land, refusing them the protection provided to individually held lands. As in Kenya, the project may find it is often registering and thus protecting land acquired illegally or illegitimately, and face reactions similar to those that generated the "Reform of the Reform" in Kenya.

As in most countries, the project model in Côte d'Ivoire has failed to improve women's access to land (Gagné, 2022). In practice, patrilineal customary land tenure systems rarely allow women to access land ownership, participate in land management or inherit land. Decision-making about land management is usually reserved for men (heads of family and lineage chiefs or village chiefs). Women have use rights as members of the family unit. Female children are excluded from inheritance. Issuing land certificates or titles for women is virtually impossible under the standards in the 1985 Land Law[3] and the rules of customary law, especially in patrilineal societies. As of June 2021, only 11% of land certificates issued have been granted to women. Some matrilineal societies in the south-east allow women to inherit land from their family of origin or allow men to bequeath land to their sisters' sons (Gagné, 2022). In matrilineal areas of the southeast, the number of land certificates obtained by women is higher than in the central-western and southwestern areas (Gagné, 2022). This program vests the primary right in the land in male heads of household, cutting off the modest protections of women's use rights under custom while leaving women, especially widowed or divorced women, exposed to loss of residence and fated to return to their natal family to beg a little land from their male relatives (Gagné, 2022).

Endemic land disputes between immigrants and local farmers in Côte d'Ivoire call for a more effective approach to addressing these during systematic registration. Registering titles has always necessitated resolving conflicting claims to land, whether through an administrative adjudication process, mediation or use of the courts. Some systematic land registration efforts, for instance the early registration work in Uganda and Sudan, dealt effectively with disorder in land right systems in post-conflict situations. Those programs were both remembered positively by those familiar with them when I visited, then later worked in the two countries (Sudan in the late 1970s and Uganda in the mid-1990s). These were *post-conflict* situations, which is not the case in Côte d'Ivoire where the rules for resolving disputes are not supported by a socio-political process and resultant consensus.

Pritchard (2016, pp. 247–248) concludes that Land Law no. 98–750, a tenure reform law whose purpose was to formalize and register all "customary" land rights, was not designed to deal with protracted land disputes in today's politically charged environment. He argues that the prevalence of land-related disputes and the unnecessarily complex nature of statutory reforms, dissociated from the socio-political and economic foundation of the "*tutorat*" system, are undermining the tenure security of rural households (Pritchard, 2016). Dealing with such conflicts using the processes under a systematic titling and registration law is not ideal. The fact that migrants do not have customary rights has politicized the registration process and made it much more difficult. Research on the impacts of the project have tended to focus on dispute resolution rather than the more standard indicators used to measure the impacts of such projects.

A key reason why the government has had to rely on the dispute resolution provisions of the land registration process is that the central government has no effective land governance presence at local level. There is potential for decentralization to rural commune level (village level), but there has been little government investment in the commune system for land administration. Local institutions had often been participants in the conflicts or advocates for one faction or another. The responsible institution also needed to deal with the challenge of implementation of registration decisions posed by the provision in the law for registered, but time-limited, rights to migrants in possession of land under customary land tenure (Lestang et al., 2018; Boone et al., 2021). Ultimately, the fate of the rural lands management depends on the government building local capacity in the commune system or some other institutional base.

## Ethiopia

Bank researchers admit that the results of early Bank programs in Africa have been disappointing (Deininger et al., 2008), but have been encouraged by the experience with a registration program in Ethiopia. The program was formally initiated after enactment of the region's land law. It was emulated by the other regions under their land laws, adjusted as needed, but limited in fundamentals by a federal land law, Proclamation No. 89/1997 (Ayano, 2018). The product of the program is a simple cadaster, useful for government and community purposes, but having little utility for developing large impersonal land markets, which the government in any case wishes to discourage. Its simplicity has made it relatively inexpensive to implement, capable of implementation by local high school graduates, and an efficient way of providing greater tenure security. Ironically, given how positively it has been received by Bank researchers (Holden et al., 2009; Deininger et al., 2011), it is so inexpensive that it does not require funding from the Bank to implement it. The government has declined offers of funds to integrate new technologies into its program.

The Ethiopian land titling and registration program grew out of an initiative by the Tigray Regional Government in response to tenure insecurity sown by the previous national government (the Derg), which outlawed customary land tenure and instituted periodic reallocations of land among households at village level. These tended to favor youthful recruits to the ruling party and resulted in loss of land by older men. It involved politicizing village level land management. Security of tenure suffered. To confirm land rights and reassure rural landholders, the Tigray Regional Government led an effort to certify individual land rights with the support of local government and villages.

The resultant certificates were simple, relying on sketch maps showing approximate boundaries and names of the holders of neighboring parcels. The government allows only inheritance, gifting and leasing of land. Land may not be sold. After a number of upgrades over the years based on field experience and with considerable community input, the system was adopted by other regions. As it spread throughout the country, local modifications were made by the regions. It is a system with relatively strong popular support and the support of local governments. There is significant local participation in implementation. Commentators have identified it as a best practice, inexpensive and built to be sustainable, community-based and provide simple security (Deininger et al., 2008). No major change in the land tenure reform supported by the government since the mid-1980s is contemplated, especially not in those elements that prohibit sales of land and allow, but regulate, tenancies.

## Notes

1 Interviews with land tenure experts living there at the time.
2 Hoben (1973) provides a thorough and revealing discussion of lineage systems of customary land tenure and fragmentation of landholdings and parcels in the crowded highland regions of northern Ethiopia. Hoben established a precedent in Ethiopia for anthropological researchers on land tenure in bringing their findings to bear on the land

tenure reform issues of the day and demonstrated how useful they can be. His work informed many subsequent studies, including my own study in Tigray.

3 An earlier statute to the 1998 Land Law concerning registration.

## References

Ali, D.A., Deininger, K., & Goldstein, M. (2014). *Environmental and gender impacts of land tenure regularization in Africa: Pilot evidence from Rwanda* (Policy Research Working Paper No. 5765). The World Bank Development Research Group.

Ali, D.A., Deininger, K., Mahofa, G., & Nyakulama, R. (2021). Sustaining land registration benefits by addressing the challenges of reversion to informality in Rwanda. *Land Use Policy*, *110*, 104317. https://doi.org/10.1016/j.landusepol.2019.104317

Ayano, M.F. (2018). Rural land registration in Ethiopia: Myths and realities. *Law & Society Review*, *52*(4), 1060–1097. https://doi.org/10.1111/lasr.12369

Bassett, T.J. (2020). Maps and mapping practices in Côte d'Ivoire's rural land reform. In African Natural Resources Centre, *Rethinking land reform in Africa: New ideas, opportunities and challenges* (pp. 142–155). African Development Bank Group.

Biraro, M., Khan, S., Konguka, G., Ngabo, V., Kanyiginya, V., Tumusherure, W., & Potel, J. (2015). *Final report of study on the access to the land tenure administration system in Rwanda and the outcomes of the system on ordinary citizens*. LAND Project, USAID, Kigali, Rwanda.

Boone, C., Bado, A.B., Dion, A.M., & Irigo, Z. (2021). Push, pull and push-back to land certification: Regional dynamics in pilot certification projects in Côte d'Ivoire. *The Journal of Modern African Studies*, *59*(3), 247–272. https://doi.org/10.1017/S0022278X21000124

Brown, M. & Hughes, A.K. (2017). Is land tenure "secure enough" in rural Rwanda? In *Annual World Bank conference on land and poverty*, Washington, DC.

Bruce, J.W. (2007). *Drawing a line under the crisis: Reconciling returnee land access and security in post conflict Rwanda* (Working Paper No. 11). Humanitarian Policy Group and Overseas Development Institute.

Deininger, K., Ali, D.A., Holden, S., & Zevenbergen, J. (2008). Rural land certification in Ethiopia: Process, initial impact, and implications for other African countries. *World Development*, *36*(10), 1786–1812. https://doi.org/10.1016/j.worlddev.2007.09.012

Deininger, K., Ali, D.A., & Alemu, T. (2011). Impacts of land certification on tenure security, investment, and land market participation: Evidence from Ethiopia. *Land Economics*, *87*(2), 312–334.

Gagné, M. (2022, July 28). *Côte d'Ivoire—Context and land governance*. Land Portal Foundation. https://landportal.org/book/narratives/2022/cote-d-ivoire.

Government of Rwanda (2014). *LTRP independent review*. Kigali, Rwanda.

Hoben, A. (1973). *Land tenure among the Amhara of Ethiopia: The dynamics of cognatic descent*. University of Chicago Press.

Holden, S., Deininger, K., & Ghebru, H. (2009). Impacts of low-cost land certification on investment and productivity. *American Journal of Agricultural Economics*, *91*(2), 359–373. https://doi.org/10.1111/j.1467-8276.2008.01241.x

Huggins, C. (2019). Curbs on land rights in Rwanda: The "bundle of rights" in context. *Gates Open Research*, *3*, Article 446.

Hughes, A.K. & Kamatali, J.M. (2016). *Implementation and outcomes of restrictions on agricultural land subdivision: An investigation of article 30 of the 2013 Land Law* (Policy Brief No. 8). USAID LAND Project.

Kouamé, G. (2018). La loi foncière rurale ivoirienne de 1998 à la croisée des chemins: vers un aménagement du cadre légal et des procédures?. Comité technique, foncier & développement, AFDI and MEAE. https://landportal.org/library/resources/la-loi-fonci%C3%A8re-rurale-ivoirienne-de-1998-%C3%A0-la-crois%C3%A9e-des-chemins-vers-un

Lawry, S., McLain, R., Rugadya, M., Alvarado, G., & Heidenrich, T. (2023). *Land tenure reform in sub-Saharan Africa: Interventions in Benin, Ethiopia, Rwanda, and Zimbabwe*. Taylor & Francis.

Lestang, J.P., Loue, D., Paillat, G., & Dabin, F.Y. (2018). *Ivory Coast: The implementation of the law relating to the rural land domain*. Annual World Bank Conference on Land and Poverty. www.oicrf.org/documents/40950/0/185_03-05-Lestang-818_paper.pdf/1e53f521-15a6-1255-7b95-0491c7cb8261?t=1562326470815

Payne, G. (2011). Land issues in the Rwanda's post conflict law reform. In R. Home (Ed.), *Local case studies in African land law* (pp. 21–38). Pretoria University Law Press.

Pritchard, M.F. (2013). Land, power, and peace: Tenure formalization, agricultural reform, and livelihood insecurity in rural Rwanda. *Land Use Policy*, *30*(1), 186–196. https://doi.org/10.1016/j.landusepol.2012.03.012

Pritchard, M.F. (2016). Contesting land rights in a post-conflict environment: Tenure reform and dispute resolution in the centre-West region of Côte d'Ivoire. *Land Use Policy*, *54*, 264–275. https://doi.org/10.1016/j.landusepol.2016.02.022

Republic of Rwanda Ministry of Lands, Environment, Forestry, Water and Mines (2008, February). *Strategic road map for land tenure reform*. https://landwise-production.s3.amazonaws.com/2022/03/Rwanda_Strategic-Roadmap-for-Land-Tenure-Reform_2008.pdf

RISD, GI-ESCR, & AAR (2017, February 13–March 3). *Parallel report to the United Nations Committee on the Elimination of Discrimination Against Women, Rwanda 66th Session*. www.ecoi.net/en/file/local/1401753/1930_1497428246_int-cedaw-css-rwa-26607-e.pdf

Teyssier, A. (2017) *Cote d'Ivoire: Land policy improvement and implementation project (English)*. World Bank Group. http://documents.worldbank.org/curated/en/847131516184821909

World Bank (2018). *International development association project appraisal document on a proposed credit in the amount of EUR 41.8 million (US$ 50 million equivalent) to Côte d'Ivoire for a Côte d'Ivoire land policy improvement and implementation project* (Report No. PAD2350). World Bank Group. https://documents.worldbank.org/curated/en/158861522699104205/pdf/COTE-DIVOIRE-PAD-NEW-03092018.pdf.

World Bank Group. (2024, March 8). *Scaling up customary land rights registration for inclusion and sustainability*.www.worldbank.org/en/results/2024/03/08/cote-ivoire-scaling-up-customary-land-rights-registration-for-inclusion and-sustainability

# 15 Confirmation Reforms that Recognize Custom as a Base Tenure

## Ghana, Uganda and Liberia

### Revival of Customary Tenure

In Ghana, customary land tenure has proven capable of evolving rapidly to meet new needs and has long been provided with quite strong legal protection, but Ghana doubled down on this protection when the new Land Act of 2020 (Act 1036) confirmed customary land tenure as a base tenure, along with private ownership and state ownership. In Uganda, a colonial era focus on systematic individualization and registration of customary land was flipped when President Idi Amin nationalized all land and abolished customary land tenure and private ownership in the mid-1970s. Then, in 1995, Uganda's new constitution under President Museveni denationalized land and restored both private ownership and customary ownership of land, and a new Land Act (1998) was legislated for the management of land under custom by Land Boards. In Liberia, custom was denigrated by its Libero-American leaders, who, after two civil wars and a growing fear of renewed ethnic strife, enacted a new Land Rights Act in 2018 that similarly gives full legal protection to customary land tenure. These three cases, plus a land tenure debate in South Africa that, although not yet finally resolved, seems to be taking the same direction, raises the question of whether the policy tide is turning after 50 years of consistent movement toward state ownership policies in the post-independence period.

### Ghana

Like most African countries, Ghana inherited a dualistic land tenure system. Ghana was not a settler colony, however, so there are only small amounts of freehold land remaining from colonial times. The vast majority of land is held under custom, including most urban land. At the same time, because of the widespread and early introduction of commercial tree crops in Ghana, land has seen more substantial evolution toward marketability under custom there than in many African countries (see Chapter 7).[1] The statutory law of colonial Ghana recognized customary land ownership as an allodial tenure,[2] either vested in traditional authorities in trust for their people or vested in families and clans. Neither land under custom nor land under private ownership was derived from or subject to any underlying ownership of land by the state. Later, in 1962, land held under custom was nationalized by

DOI: 10.4324/9781003476429-18

a socialist government, leading to a painful experience of grandiose planning and uncompensated expropriations. It was the 1979 Constitution that returned ownership of customary lands to traditional authorities.

"Customary land law"—commonly used to describe the body of judicial decisions and findings on the rules of indigenous custom concerning land, a version that often differs considerably from custom on the ground—was elaborated over a century ago through accumulation of a great many judicial decisions. It distinguished between two major categories of customary land tenure: (1) ownership of land by chiefs in trust for the community (referred to as "stool and "skin" lands,[3] in which the title is vested not in a person or a thing but in a symbol of authority); and (2) family and clan land (owned by families or clans descended from a first settler or other common ancestor). Until passage of the Ghana Land Act in 2020, this "common law of customary land tenure" was exclusively used to settle disputes on customary land that were filed with the courts.[4] This was the "customary law" critiqued heavily by Chanock (1985) and others as distorted by the land and governance priorities of colonial government.[5] Ghana was one of four or five countries, including Nigeria, Kenya, Malawi and Sudan, with a fairly substantial body of case law on customary land tenure, and it is in those case reports that one finds the "common law of customary land tenure."

Customary land tenure has seen a strong development in the years since independence. Customary rights have also become decidedly more marketable under Ghanaian law. The vesting of customary land ownership in traditional authorities combined with the increasing land values associated with increasing commodification of land, cocoa cultivation and urbanization have led to highly controversial practices of chiefs selling and leasing out land out from under communities to investors (Ubink, 2008; Hughes et al., 2019). Chiefs are powerful authority figures in Ghanaian culture, and controversial court decisions expanded their power over the customary land of their communities, including their power to sell that land to outsiders. The *de facto* marketability of land held by chiefs has permitted them to acquire substantial wealth, some of it derived from what are market-value sales of customary land, reported to government only as customary "drinks money" to formalize the transaction.[6]

Today, land in rural Ghana remains governed by customary land tenure, and the country even has significant areas of valuable urban land under custom. Government has invested and developed a complex administrative structure that interacts with traditional authorities rather than seeking to replace them, including the recent development of customary secretariats for chiefs. With the 2020 Land Act, the government reinforced its commitment to custom, recognizing private ownership, public ownership and customary ownership as three pillars of the land tenure system and harmonizing their application. The law confirms the legal status of customary land tenure as an allodial tenure.

The preamble of the Land Act, 2020, declares that its purpose is "to harmonize and consolidate the laws on land." It confirms customary titles as allodial and specifies that allodial title "may be held by the State or a stool or skin, or clan or family or an individual."[7] It also deals decisively with marketability of customary titles. Prior to this law, the leasing of land by customary owners had been legal, but sales were not. This was in spite of the fact that it was widely acknowledged that chiefs, who hold the allodial title to customary lands, regularly sold those lands and sometimes sold the same parcel several times over (Kasanga et al., 1996; Ubink, 2008). After persistent and increasingly unsuccessful attempts since independence to prohibit sales of land under customary land tenure, the 2020 Land Law explicitly sanctions the outright sale of customary tenure lands, including sales by chiefs.[8]

Rather than seeking to replace customary land tenure in Ghana, reform projects instead have focused on improving land administration. In 2003, the World Bank launched a land administration project in Ghana, which was followed by the Land Administration Project II (LAP II) in 2020. Unlike other World Bank land administration projects in Africa, it explicitly aimed to develop both civil and customary land administration and link the two together.[9] To achieve its aims, the project leveraged an existing practice under some chieftainships, the creation of modest administrative offices by chiefs to facilitate their work generally and sometimes their administration of land, including their interactions with the national Lands Commission and other government agencies. Building on that existing practice, the project provided funds for the establishment of several customary land secretariats (CLS) and negotiated work agendas with them that reflected local needs and interests that the Lands Commission saw as constructive. Technical assistance for the parties involved in this process was funded by Britain's Department for International Development (DFID), along with the Bank.

The project placed major emphasis on institution-building and training, and this dominated early negotiations with chiefs for establishment of CLS. The Land Commission proved quite flexible regarding activities of local interest which the secretariats might undertake in addition to regular dealings with central agencies of government. Better record-keeping on land transactions has been a consensus objective, and beyond that the secretariats have been given the leeway to work on a wide range of land and non-land-related problems and business.[10]

Whereas the Lands Commission staff saw the CLS as a local presence that would learn to work with them in bureaucratic mode and help them understand and deal with local practices and problems in the interest of more effective national land administration, chiefs saw the CLS as a means to enhance not only their capacity for local land administration, but their authority and power too. While the Commission has some sub-offices around the country, its authority on the ground is subservient to that of powerful traditional authorities in many areas. There has been a lack of systematic interaction between the Lands Commission and chiefs, and chiefs have resisted control by the Commission.

A final project evaluation of LAP II by an independent evaluation team confirmed that the setting up of the CLSs had been demand-driven by traditional authorities who wished to upgrade their land operations, but they also stressed the limitations of the secretariats (World Bank Independent Evaluation Group, 2019). The assessment and consultant reports mention: (1) the need to clarify the relationship between the CLS and the many land institutions of central government; (2) persistent problems with lack of transparency and rent-seeking on the part of chiefs; (3) poor messaging by state agencies on policy and programs; and (4) lack of clarity on the appropriate roles for the CLS as communicated to chiefs and their subjects.

If those concerned with the piloting of the CLS had some reservations about them earlier, the matter was legally resolved by the 2020 Land Act, which provides the legal basis for a national system of CLS that links customary land administration to civil land administration.[11] The Act requires every land-owning group to establish a CLS for management of its land and specifies the functions of a CLS (see Box 15.1).

**Box 15.1 CLS Functions, Ghana**

A Customary Land Secretariat shall, in relation to customary interests, rights and transactions, perform the following functions:

(a) Record the interests and rights in land and keep and maintain up to date accurate and up-to-date records of land transactions within their area of operation of the Customary Land Secretariat;
(b) Provide a list of existing customary interests and rights in land in the area of operations of the Customary Land Secretariat including indications of persons with the capacity to make grants of interests and rights in the area;
(c) Provide relevant (i) records on land, (ii) information on hierarchy of interests and rights in land and (iii) laid down processes for effective dispute resolution.
(d) Facilitate the settlement of land disputes through alternative dispute resolution;
(e) Facilitate the participatory preparation of local plans;
(f) Undertake community education, sensitization and awareness on land matters;
(g) Prepare periodic accounts of all revenue received at the Customary Land Secretariats in accordance with clause 8 of article 36 of the Constitution;
(h) Provide facilities for search to be conducted on records on land; and
(i) Perform any other functions in relation to land as determined by the landowning group.

Source: Article 15(1) Functions of the Customary Land Secretariat, Land Act 2020.

The Act provides joint roles for the Lands Commission and the Office of the Administrator of Stool Lands in creating and supporting the CLS. Each CLS is required to maintain adequate staff to carry out its functions. It may charge fees for services it provides the public. Taxes and fees on customary land generate considerable revenue. Ghana has a remarkably complicated system of handling that revenue. Taxes and fees are collected from the public by traditional authorities and remitted to central government institutions which allocate it to the budgets of districts and other local government activities, including those of the CLS. The funds to finance the operations of a CLS for areas of stool and skin lands are to be an (unspecified) proportion of the revenue paid to the land-owning stool or skin and the traditional authority by the Office of the Administrator of Stool Lands, and in the case of clan and family lands, an unspecified proportion of the revenue paid to the clan or family by the Lands Commission. The CLS experiment is nested within what is certainly one of the most complex sets of institutional arrangements for management of customary land anywhere in Africa.

The provisions of the 2020 Land Act reflect a muted, but very real, struggle for power over land between civil and traditional authorities. Traditional authorities in Ghana are powerful and adept in the politics of land. Government cannot manage to replace them overnight, especially given that popular support for customary arrangements remains strong, even if there is considerable criticism of the machinations of the chiefs who administer them. The CLS are seen by central government officials as a vehicle for decentralization of their work in the short run, but also a means to create a localized capacity that reduces central government's dependence on chiefs and could in the long run pave the way for the elimination of the role of traditional authorities in customary land management. The chiefs, on the other hand, see the CLS as a means of enhancing their capacity to manage their land more effectively and build out their own authority. They are not so naïve as to not see the long-term potential for their displacement. Central government and traditional authorities in Ghana have a long history of conflict and cooperation, and future rounds of that contest seem likely to play out in struggles for control of the CLS and its evolution as an institution.

## Uganda

Britain's Uganda Protectorate generally recognized customary land tenure and instituted freehold for settlers and in urban areas. A major exception was the former Kingdom of Buganda. Under the 1900 Buganda agreement, the British granted the Buganda Kingdom[12] statutory ownership of its land in a major replacement of a customary land tenure system. This was a political rather than an economic measure, designed to restore order to the Kingdom of Buganda, shore up the position of the Kabaka (the traditional ruler) and allow the peaceful imposition of British colonial rule. Members of the Buganda nobility were granted a tenure called *mailo* to large areas of land they had ruled, rights equivalent to private ownership. Their subjects became their tenants. However questionable this was from a policy standpoint, it established the first substantial competence in systematic land survey and titling in eastern Africa.[13]

The colonial government recognized customary rights in the rest of the country in the tradition of indirect rule. In the run-up to independence, it contemplated extending freehold to the remainder of the country. Systematic title registration of customary holdings was carried out in three pilots around the country in the early

1950s. The pilots had mixed results and were not expanded after independence in 1962 (Okec, 1969; Lawrance, 1960). Instead, after a 1971 coup d'état, all land was nationalized by President Idi Amin in his 1975 Land Reform Decree. As a matter of law, the decree abolished *mailo*, freehold and customary titles and replaced them with leaseholds from the state. The law was only spottily applied before it was repealed in 1979. Its arbitrary and corrupt implementation generated considerable resentment.[14]

Toppling Amin was followed by several years of instability and brutal conflict. In 1986, the National Resistance Movement, led by Yoweri Museveni, took control after a long insurgency. His new government provided the stability needed to chart a new direction in land policy. The donor community—principally the United States Agency for International Development (USAID) and DFID—was actively engaged in facilitating this process through applied research and provision of advisory services.[15] The policies which emerged were enacted in Chapter 150 of the 1995 Constitution and the 1998 Land Act.

The Constitution provided that: (1) the government no longer owned all land; (2) private ownership was reintroduced; and (3) land could be owned as freehold, *mailo*, customary land and leasehold. The 1995 Constitution gave ownership under customary land tenure the same legal recognition as freehold and *mailo*, effectively making customary tenure an allodial tenure, not a lesser tenure granted by the government as owner of the land. Non-citizens cannot own land but can rent land from citizens or the government. A Land Commission was created to manage public lands, including land housing government buildings, roads, project areas and other specified areas. Natural resources would be held in trust by the government for the people.

The 1998 Land Act directed that each District must have a District Land Board whose members are selected by the District Council. Land committees are to be established to help the Board decide whether customary land is held by individuals, families or communities. Boards are responsible for providing certificates of customary ownership to those who request them although the certified land would continue to be regulated by custom. Application for certificates is voluntary and customary rights are to be upheld by law whether or not a certificate has been obtained. Owners may convert their certified customary parcel to freehold if they wish. Communities which opt for collective ownership of customary land may form a communal land association to formalize this. The Constitution and Land Act left the power of traditional authorities largely intact.

Implementation of the law with respect to communities holding land under customary land tenure has been weak. Implementation is expensive, and, in my observation, donors tend to not come forward with assistance. It is not hard to find funds for the relatively brief task (3–5 years, ideally) of considering and recommending reforms. Where a policy reform requires a law to implement it, when that new law is enacted, the donor sometimes declares victory and abruptly withdraws from work in the land sector. This usually happens when the donor realizes that national implementation is likely to be the work of several decades. Support for the law's implementation has been slow to arrive and the scale of even piloting it modest.

The Uganda government had not prioritized resources for this purpose either; some Ugandan officials argued against denationalizing land and would have preferred to retain it in the hands of the state. District Land Boards have been established, but the funding available has been focused on building, equipping and staffing their offices, not training staff or funding ongoing operations. Few certificates of customary ownership have been applied for, few land committees set up and few communal land associations formed. Data is not available, but "few" is probably an overestimate.

Observers warn that at the same time, "internal" land-grabbing by elites is common and growing. State action is implicated in almost all the major land grabs. Under the Act, the state owns "natural resources" on behalf of the people, and large areas are so classified. The lack of demarcated community boundaries increases insecurity of tenure in these circumstances. Government is creating special areas for development, recreation and environmental purposes, effectively limiting community opportunities to develop those areas. The state often uses its authority over natural resources to take control of such land. Where such a claim is not available, expropriation is available to the state. The Land Act lacks clear standards regarding compensation for customary land, but there is a market in such land and market values for such land can be established to provide compensation.

The result is that while customary land tenure in Uganda has been recognized by national law as an allodial tenure alongside private and state ownership of land, has this in practice meant less to the communities and individuals holding customary land than might have been expected? Weak implementation provisions and lack of funding for implementation have meant that the customary system continues largely as it has, subject to pressures similar to those affecting customary tenure throughout much of Africa.

Implementation is the Achilles' heel of land tenure reform. Systematic land titling and registration, while open to many objections, offers a process that is clear about its objectives, has been implemented enough to have a basis for building a better process and is replicable in many circumstances.[16] At its best, it can be consultative and rely on community consensus to validate claims to land rights. What has been lacking is a model for a more localized process that empowers local communities to think through their tenure change paths and document their decisions, including an effective approach to enabling those communities to pursue a process that will make their aspirations legally effective. The 2010s have seen important efforts to develop and field test such a process, perhaps the most impressive being a program initiated by the International Labour Organization and then assumed by the non-governmental organization (NGO) Namati, which was developed and piloted in Mozambique, Uganda and Liberia. Some key points from those experiences are discussed below in the section on Liberia and in the section on Mozambique in the following chapter.

## Liberia

Liberia was colonized by Africans originally from a variety of African regions, notably the Congo, whose ancestors had been enslaved and transported to the United

States, then freed in the North as the Civil War approached. They began arriving in Liberia in the 1820s, their declared intention being to establish a colony for Africans like themselves. The Republic of Liberia was established in 1847. Those returning to Africa brought with them American land law and the idea of private individual ownership of land. Initially they purchased land from local people, but later, they simply took it. Americo-Liberians, as descendants of the settlers came to be known, established freehold tenure for the land they held. Initially, each settler received land and a deed describing the land in relation to physical features, which was later registered in a Deed Registry. By the early 20th century, settlements along the coast created a band of freehold land extending about 40 miles inland. Settlements initially expanded up the rivers from the coast and later along the roads built into the interior. In many cases, indigenous communities violently resisted colonization. The Liberian state fought several wars with various tribes as it gradually expanded into the interior. Land there was sold to settlers as freehold by the Office of the President. Before the sale could take place and the parcel surveyed and titled, the applicant was required to produce a "tribal certificate," a document signed by a chief and stating that there was land available that had been allocated for this applicant. When such sales took place, traditional authorities were required to select the land to be sold; they could not refuse to process such a sale (Stevens, 2014).

The Liberian state governed the country through traditional authorities in much the same manner as other colonial powers in Africa (Greene, 1936). Customary land tenure was accepted as governing the landholdings of local inhabitants residing in what became known as "the Interior." Customary land tenure remained in force and traditional authorities were responsible for administering it. While it was never provided with a clear legal status under national law, it continued to govern the bulk of the land in the country *de facto*. In time, members of important indigenous families who adopted the culture of the Americo-Liberians were able to acquire deeds to their land and even deeds to holdings of their communities. The result was patches of freehold in an ocean of customary land tenure, but this changed with time. Where the two tenure systems collided, a registered deed always trumped any customary claim. After a long period of legal uncertainty, Liberia in 1956 enacted the Aborigines Law, which provided that all land not registered in ownership belonged to the Liberian state. No clear legal status was provided for custom (Stevens, 2014).

In 2003, at the end of the Second Liberian Civil War, a United Nations (UN) peacekeeping mission was established that became the civil government of Liberia. Ethnic relations were tense, but the lines were not drawn as clearly as a century ago. A good deal of intermarriage between colonist and indigenous families had taken place. Some of the small corps of Liberian officials remaining in Monrovia recognized that there were land tenure issues generated by the long-standing abuse of the land rights of the indigenous peoples, issues with the potential to wreck the peace. In 2006, they began to talk with the new President Ellen Johnson Sirleaf about a reform. A group responsible for planning the reform was assembled informally and began meeting.

In 2009, a Land Commission was formally proposed by the president and created by a law passed by the Legislature. Its members led a long policy and legal reform process that resulted in enactment of a law that for the first time recognized customary land tenure: the 2018 Land Rights Act. The reform benefited from early awareness on the part of the party in power that reform was needed, ample if fragmented support from the international donor community, consistent support from the president and the capable leadership of Dr. Othello Brandy, a former Vice-Minister of Agriculture who had led the informal working group on land reform. While successful in achieving its aims, the process was nevertheless incredibly long, consisting of three years of very intensive work on policy formulation, after which it remained for several years before the legislature before enactment.

**Liberia's Journey from Policy to Law**

What does a competent "policy-to-law" reform process look like? Liberia's tenure reform journey, while hardly perfect, offers an example of good practice.

Liberia's tenure reform was led by a Land Commission between 2010 and 2018. While the process was extremely lengthy, it concerned the most fundamental land issue facing African nations: the fate of customary land rights. In spite of solid legal arguments to the contrary, Liberian officialdom had long treated land under customary land tenure as government land, available for sale to settlers and others. Public administration in the "Interior" was managed through a system of indirect rule by Americo-Liberian colonists, with traditional authorities paid to administer land.

But now the political and social dominance of the descendants of Americo-Liberian colonists was eroding. Many generations of intermarriage had produced many Liberians who belonged to both groups. When I visited Liberia in the early 1980s, Americo-Liberians tended not to mention their indigenous family connections. By the time I returned to Liberia in 2007, I found that they often volunteered that information. Much changed in those years, including the ousting from power of the Americo-Liberian elite by the Doe regime in 1980. The post-war return to civil authority in 2003 provided an opening for reconsidering the state's position on customary rights. Some influential Americo-Liberians in government recognized the potential explosiveness of this issue. At the same time, NGOs and civil society organizations (CSOs) were providing new opportunities for Liberians of indigenous ancestry to express their concerns regarding the land situation.

As Liberia came out of 20 years of mostly civil war and conflict and power gradually shifted back from the UN to civil authorities, the Johnson-Sirleaf government in 2007 appointed a Governance Commission to address the sad state of governance. That Commission recognized the importance of the "land situation" and recommended a national Land Commission. The Liberian officials involved in creating and leading the Commission got things right on a number of key points, things which enabled it to build a strong consensus for reform. They included:

1. In creating the Commission, government created an independent entity. Its chair reported directly to the Office of the President rather than to the minister of any one of the concerned ministries, which had particular and competing interests.

2. The government provided for a modest Secretariat for the Commission, recruited and hired by the Commission itself.
3. Government was sensitive to public concerns that the Commission not be composed of just "Monrovia people" and appointed commissioners from a variety of regional origins and other connections.
4. Confronted by the absence of a national land policy, the Commission decided it must develop such a policy, rather than moving directly to draft a reform law.
5. The Commission undertook a series of public consultations at the outset, exploring participants' immediate concerns regarding land, rather than assuming people saw the issues the way they did. The consultations were open-ended and the results were published, including summaries in local languages.
6. Having identified several themes from the consultation, the Commission created several working groups, each with representation of middle-level officials from relevant government agencies, staff of NGOs and CSOs working in rural development and persons knowledgeable on land tenure matters.
7. As these groups began work, a series of lectures were arranged for members of the groups, presented by both Liberian and international experts on land tenure conditions in Liberia and on international best practices on land policy and law. The working groups acquired a common set of concepts and a common terminology.
8. Each group was headed by a commissioner or other Commission staff member and had opportunities for further interactions with experts.
9. Early on, the Commission identified several areas in which it lacked information and contracted with consultants to carry out needed short-term studies.
10. Having obtained funding from several multilateral and bilateral donors, the Commission organized a Donor Coordinating Committee on Land Matters which helped reassure donors about where their money was going.
11. The work of the Commission on Land Rights was first presented in a substantial Land Rights Policy Paper, which recommended that customary land rights should be recognized by law as equivalent in legal status to private ownership and entitled to equal protection by the law. Its recommendations were quite detailed and provided a good basis for the drafting of a reform law.
12. A legal drafting team was selected by the Commission, composed of key actors from the Land Rights Working Group and other relevant working groups to ensure continuity in the transition from policy to law.
13. That drafting team was tasked with selecting, orienting and supervising the work of a respected Liberian attorney as legal drafter. The legal drafting was facilitated greatly by the highly specific recommendations of the Land Rights Policy Paper.
14. After preparation of a draft law acceptable to the Commission, summaries of the draft law were prepared and published together with the full draft. The draft received extended public commentary, including comments from the NGO and CSO communities and public meetings. Key legislators were briefed on the intention and substance of the law, and several international experts reviewed and commented upon the law.

15. After revisions based on those comments, the bill was submitted to the President for Cabinet review, with more revisions by the drafting team before submission to the Legislature in 2012.
16. After further and extended discussions between committees in the Legislature and the Commission, and a delay of nearly two years caused by a national election, the Land Rights Law was enacted in 2018.

While the process may seem alarmingly long, the political consensus it produced was sufficiently robust to survive the expiry of the Land Commission's term and its dissolution in 2016, as well as a general election in 2017 which brought an opposition party to power. The Commission's involvement of local environmental and rural NGOs in policy and legal discussions had prepared them to lobby effectively and stimulate a groundswell of public support for the bill. The Commission's proposals for a new land governance institution were also well received, and the Liberian Land Authority was created in 2017, moving principal authority for land out of the Ministry of Lands, Mines and Energy, which had not prioritized land matters.

### Legal Recognition of Customary Land Tenure

The Land Rights Act (No. 5 of 2018) recognizes customary land as a fundamental form of land ownership, defining it as "land owned by a community and managed in accordance with customary norms" (Art. 2), rights which can be proven by oral evidence. A "community" is "a self-identifying coherent social group or groups composed of Community Members" (Art. 2), and a community member is "a Liberian citizen irrespective of age, gender, belief or religious backgrounds who was (i) born in the Community or (ii) parent(s) was born within a Community; or (iii) who has lived continuously within the Community for at least seven years; or (iv) a spouse of a Community Member both of whom reside in the Community" (Art. 2). The Act places a positive duty on government to protect customary rights in land and provides for the registration of customary ownership at both community and household level.

The Act provides that "[c]ustomary land is acquired and owned by a community in accordance with its customary practices and norms based on a long period of occupancy and/or use" (Art. 32). This includes land deeded to the community prior to the Act, land held by the community for a minimum period of 50 years and land used for shorter terms where community consensus and neighboring communities confirm the customary right. It affirms the rights of communities to exclude others, to hold and use the land, and to transfer portions of the land by lease and other means consistent with the Act. It confers on communities the right to use their forests but preserves national government's ownership of minerals. These rights are provided whether the community is registered or not. While the Act does not invalidate existing concessions, it requires free, prior, informed consent for any future "interference" with customary land.

All members of the community have equal rights to land from the community, but there is a major exception with serious implications for gender equity.

Inequality in land rights is allowable where "It is in accordance with the customs and traditions of the Community and not in violation of this Act or the Constitution of Liberia" (Art. 34). Regardless of whether they register their land, each community is to prepare by-laws, develop a land use plan and elect a Community Land Development and Management Committee (CLDMC) with legal personality. The CLDMC's membership must consist of equal numbers of men, women and youth, democratically elected, with chiefs serving as ex-officio members. All CLDMC decisions must be made by consensus and "All decisions taken in respect of customary Land must be in accordance with the customs, traditions and practices of the Community" (Art. 35). However, the ultimate authority over land is the body of all community members acting collectively by a two-thirds vote. Decisions concerning sale and long-term leasing of customary land are specifically reserved to this body. In the case of concessions awarded on community land by the CLDMC, the community has a 5% interest in the concession and once the concession ends, the land reverts to the customary land of the community.

Limited transactions in customary land are allowed, including leasing, with CLDMC approval required for long-term leases. Sales are allowed for residential sites, but they are prohibited for all other categories of customary land for 50 years from the effective date of the Act. Customary land (along with state-owned land) cannot be lost through adverse possession, but is subject to the government's exercise of eminent domain for public purposes, even without the agreement of the owner. The Act sets out detailed provisions applicable to all ownership forms, protected areas, leases, easements, licenses, mortgages (limited to residential properties in the case of customary land) and transitional provisions.

The Act is notable for its: (1) recognition of customary land rights based on oral evidence without the necessity of documentation, such as titling, by the state;[17] (2) recognition of community ownership of customary land; (3) reliance on community self-identification to accommodate diverse customary land tenure structures and community priorities; (4) its provision that communities as registered owners are private, not public, entities; (5) creation of community-based democratic land governance structures; (6) its assertion of community ownership of forests; (7) its requirement of free, prior and informed consent from those affected in order to grant concessions; and (8) provisions to communities of a share in the profits from concessions and requirements that upon expiry of the concession, the land reverts to the customary community rather than to the state.

The law nevertheless falls seriously short in its treatment of women's land rights. The fact that Liberia's Constitution excludes women's land access from its equal protection provision prevents assertion of a constitutional right to gender equity. However, it does not prevent issues arising from women's lack of land rights being addressed in a statute, not as a matter of equal protection, but simply as a remedy for specific problems caused by excluding women from comparable land rights. The reform program sought such changes regarding women's access to land, but they ultimately did not survive the revisions of the draft law in the legislature.

## Implementation Challenges with Registering Community Land Rights

One of the challenging areas in application of the law is the issue of community self-identification. These should ideally be customary communities of residence or descent that Liberians holding their land under custom recognize as landholders for their members. We can imagine these units on a map, showing the territory of each community and the land rights of households within the community. However, these levels of societies are often part of a hierarchical social system, with a number of small communities subsidiary to a larger community and a number of those larger communities subsidiary to a still larger community. Often colonial governments forced these structures on indigenous societies for the convenience of administration and today these societies regard them as "traditional." The result in Liberia is often split authority structures with a "paramount" chief, exercising ultimate authority, primarily through resolving appeals of disputes over customary rules, and lower-level authorities overseeing the day-to-day management of the system.

The action research project led by Namati in Liberia's River Cess County had to grapple with these issues. The project was implemented by the Sustainable Development Institute (SDI), the local NGO partnering with Namati. The project was founded on a priority objective: to protect community lands from outsiders through recognition of property rights protected by national law, which outsiders would need to respect. It was planned and largely implemented before the Land Rights Act and prioritized community rather than individual or family rights both because those managing the project believed that a community would be more powerful and effective than individual families in defending land rights under threat by the rush for land for concessions. Such protection could be most quickly and most economically met by titling larger areas, i.e. those of communities. The researchers worked with interested communities to decide which of several levels of landholding "communities" might be best poised to go through the process of obtaining a deed for its customary holdings (Kaba, 2015).

**Box 15.2 Titling Communities in Liberia: Choice of Scale, Choice of Community**

The definition of "community" in Liberia needed to be made based on existing local governance structures. The customary land governance structure in Liberia has long been aligned with the national system of administration, with chiefs turned into salaried government functionaries. As in many other cases in Africa, lesser levels of authority are nested within greater levels of authority. There are: (1) Paramount Chiefs, designated by the state in the 1950s as paid government officials responsible for two to three clans, with general responsibility for seeing that customary and state law were observed;

(2) Clan Chiefs, also paid government employees, responsible for good governance of a clan, which consists of three to 30 towns closely related to one another by some combination of descent and history; (3) Town Chiefs, only lightly regulated by the state and with authority over a town, which can be small or quite large; and (4) Village, Section and Quarter Chiefs, not regulated by government and differing in authority and responsibilities from area to area. At each level, chiefs work with councils of elders in dealing with land matters, and the dynamics between chiefly power and the authority of elders differs from case to case (Kaba, 2015).

SDI and Namati had to decide at which level of community they should work. SDI researchers consulted with interested communities on factors potentially influencing the choice of community to be titled. They considered factors such as the capacity and potential of communities for participatory governance and decision-making. Titling to the Paramountcy had the advantage of permitting protection of a very large area and would assure that the community included relatively undeveloped land between villages, areas that might otherwise be left to the state. Selection of a lower level such as the town would enable a more localized, participatory form of land management, but risked legal identity obstacles regarding towns. Through an iterative consultation process, the research team worked with communities to evaluate pros and cons affecting the feasibility and appropriateness of community titling at the different levels. In the end, the clan level was agreed to be the level most likely to provide the needed protection. SDI researchers conducted similar consultative research in Lofa County, and again the clan level was found to be the most promising level for granting a community title, in part because it was the clan that had the principal customary authority over land (Kaba, 2015).[18]

The Namati/SDI effort has informed policy discussions in Liberia and provided useful experience and lessons for more empowering approaches to community-based land tenure reform. It also raised important issues about how best to go forward. In addition to its protection objective, the program sought to encourage uptake of participatory methods and social objectives, including gender equality in land matters.

## Protracted Implementation of Reforms

Implementation, as with many of the progressive reforms, has been slower and less coherent than expected, especially for indigenous communities waiting for the protection of their land rights. The law establishing the Liberia Land Authority was enacted in 2016, but the Land Rights Law itself was delayed until 2018 for a number of valid reasons. One was an intervening presidential election, in which the party that had sponsored the Land Commission was defeated. It is remarkable that the Land Rights Law survived. It did so only because the leadership of the Land

Commission had worked hard to maintain a non-partisan stance and build a broad national consensus in support of the reform. The Land Commission's mandate expired in 2016 when it had completed its assigned tasks, except for the Land Rights Law under consideration in the Legislature. Most of the commissioners and other key staff moved on to other jobs. The departing Sawyer administration could find only enough funds to maintain a core of two or three essential individuals, such as the Commission's chairman, to engage with the committees of the Legislature reviewing the Land Rights Bill. The time could have been used for training staff of the Authority, but donors were not at all sure that the law that was the justification for the Authority would ever be passed. The Lands Department in the Ministry of Lands, Mines and Energy had been a modest establishment. None of its staff had any background in land policy, but some promising staff had emerged in discussions of the policy and law. The Department had previously engaged largely in cadastral surveys in support of a sporadic program of work under a land registration law. Many of the staff moved into the new Authority, but others, primarily surveyors and technicians, left the government to benefit from the great number of survey contracts generated by the booming concession sector.

Following the enactment of the Land Rights Law, the Liberian Land Authority (LLA) worked on regulations for the registration and governance of customary land, which were promulgated in November 2022. Through two successive projects, the Integrated Land and Resource Governance program and the Land Management Activity, USAID has played a major role in supporting the LLA to implement the six-step process required for rural communities to obtain a deed. Initial pilot efforts generated important lessons learned about implementation and streamlined processes and templates adopted by the LLA as National Guidelines. Together, these projects have helped to strengthen communities' understanding of their rights as a community and as individuals, including women, youth, disabled and other marginalized groups. They also supported establishment of community governance structures for future decision-making on land and resource use and allocation. Training and awareness raising have strengthened communities' abilities to respond to investor interest in land and negotiate acquisition. As of early 2025, 14 communities had completed the full registration process and secured deeds. Several challenges remain. Fraudulent, backdated Tribal Certificates have continued to be issued to individuals on community land, a practice that was outlawed. As in other countries pursuing progressive reforms, some officials in the institution responsible for reform implementation can be seen to have been working at cross purposes with the reform. While the responsibilities for community land governance have been clarified and a process established for confirming community boundaries, there remains a need for the Land Authority to be more transparent on the community land registration process and the costs and requirements for their involvement in it (Huth, 2023; Gobewole, 2021).

There are some important lessons to be taken from these experiences with elevating the legal status of customary tenure. While on the surface they hold the promise of communities reverting to a more secure and legitimate tenure system that had been disrupted by prior reforms, the realities of implementation have made this path much more complicated. In Ghana, the increasing commodification of land and rising land values have enticed traditional authorities to act in their personal interests over the interests of their communities. In Uganda, which sought administration of customary land through state institutions rather than chiefs, the challenge has been a lack of capacity by the government to put these local land administration units in place and staff them, resulting in failures to register customary holdings. Whereas Liberia laid the foundation for strong recognition of customary rights in their 2018 land law, it also has fallen prey to protracted implementation, underfunding and malfeasance, with the result that most rural communities remain vulnerable to investor acquisitions of their land.

## Notes

1 Benneh (1989) and Migot-Adholla et al. (1994) examine the different rules and practices regarding sales of land by several ethnic groups in Ghana and their impact on investment in agriculture, which proved less significant than the impact of a right to inherit parental land.
2 In Ghana's new Land Act, customary land tenure is referred to as "allodial." Allodial tenure is an absolute ownership of land held entirely free of any obligation to the state. This would seem the maximal legal recognition for customary land tenure, a tenure that is free of any obligation to the state. But such ownership rarely exists, if it ever has, and the debate between attorneys as to the appropriate use of the term in the Ghanaian case suggests that the outcome would have few practical implications. See, for example, https://ghanalawhub.com/the-decline-of-allodial-title-in-ghana/.
3 "Skin" and "stool" are symbols of chieftainship and the role of such chiefs in customary land tenure systems. See Benneh (1968).
4 For a sense of the literature assessing this experience, see Allot (1957), Woodman (1969, 1985) and Kludze (1985).
5 Chanock (1985), regarding Malawi and Zambia, and Snyder (1981), in relation to Senegal, providing a more critical view of such endeavors.
6 "Drinks money" has its roots in a west African tradition of providing drinks to a chief in exchange for receiving a parcel of land, usually when land is given to someone from outside the community. Over time, drinks became monetized, first as a modest payment, later growing to the point of approximating the market value of much larger pieces of land. See Chauveau and Colin (2007).
7 Article 2 of the Land Act, 2020.
8 Article 2, Land Act 2020.
9 While the project included a pilot systematic land title registration, this affected only small areas and was implemented extraordinarily slowly (Alhassan & Manuh, 2005).
10 The diverse activities carried out by the first LAP project-sponsored CLSs are described in Yiri (2006), Larbi (2006), Antwi (2006), Siaw (2009) and World Bank (2013).
11 The provisions relating to the CLS are at Articles 14–18 of the Land Act 2020.
12 The kingdom of the traditional Baganda people. For more information see: https://en.wikipedia.org/wiki/Buganda.
13 West (1965, 1972).
14 The drafting of the law is obscure. I have been told that at President Idi Amin's request, Ethiopia's Marxist-Leninist President Mengistu Haile-Mariam had a bill drafted and flown to Kampala in his personal plane. The story is probably just a story, but I have not heard an alternate answer to the question of who drafted the law.
15 USAID funded an extensive program of collaboration between the University of Wisconsin-Madison's Land Tenure Center (LTC) and Makerere University's Institute

for Social Research (MISR), co-managed by MISR's Professor Dan Mudoola and the author. LTC's resident director of the program was Dr. Mark Marquardt. Tthe responsible senior research fellow in charge at MISR was Wilberforce Kisamba-Mugerwa, later Uganda's Minister of Agriculture. A series of workshops with the Ugandan government identified policy priorities. Later, DFID provided the government with the services of Patrick McAuslan, the distinguished expert on African land policy and legislation who drafted the legal basis for the new policies.

16 In a section labelled the "Land administration reform in Africa: An unfulfilled promise?", Deininger et al. (2008, pp. 1788–1789) detail the many contexts in Africa in which the anticipated benefits of land titling have not materialized or have been accompanied by countervailing negative impacts. They then remind us that this does not mean that there is no demand by African smallholders, then go on to review positively this low-cost program of certification of existing statutory rights (rather than replacing rights at custom) initiated by the Ethiopian government without international donor involvement or sophisticated technologies.

17 Mozambique was the first African country to recognize customary rights in this manner.

18 Knight et al. (2012, pp. 34–35) discusses the community self-selection process in all three country contexts in which studies were conducted.

## References

Alhassan, O. & Manuh, T. (2005). *Land registration in eastern and western regions, Ghana* (Research Report No. 5). IIED. www.iied.org/12522iied

Allot, A.N. (1957). The judicial ascertainment of customary law in British Africa. *The Modern Law Review*, *20*(3), 244–263. www.jstor.org/stable/1090609

Antwi, Y.A. (2006, March). Strengthening customary land administration: A DFID/World Bank sponsored project in Ghana. In *5th FIG regional conference: Promoting land administration and good governance*, Accra, Ghana.

Benneh, G. (1989). The dynamics of customary land tenure and agrarian systems in Ghana. In *The Dynamics of Land Tenure and Agrarian Systems in Africa: Case Studies from Ghana, Kenya, Madagascar and Togo*. Food and Agriculture Organization of the United Nations.

Chanock, M. (1985). *Law, custom and social order: The colonial experience in Malawi and Zambia*. Cambridge University Press.

Chauveau, J.P. & Colin, J.P. (2007). Changes in land transfer mechanisms: Evidence from West Africa. In L. Cotula (Ed.), *Changes in "customary" land tenure systems in Africa* (pp. 65–80). IIED.

Deininger, K., Ali, D.A., Holden, S., & Zevenbergen, J. (2008). Rural land certification in Ethiopia: Process, initial impact, and implications for other African countries. World *Development*, *36*(10), 1786–1812. doi:10.1016/j.worlddev.2007.09.012

Fifty-fourth legislature of the Republic of Liberia (2018). *An act to establish the land rights law of 2018, Republic of Liberia*. https://liblaw.org/wp-content/uploads/2022/10/Land-Rights-Act-2018.pdf

Gobewole, S.H. (2021). Land in Liberia: The initial source of antagonism between freed American Blacks and Indigenous Tribal people remains the cause of intense disputes. *Journal of Politics & Law*, *14*(4), Article 19. https://doi.org/10.5539/jpl.v14n4p19

Greene, G. (1936). *Journey without maps*. William Heinemann Ltd.

Hughes, A.K., Knox, A., & Jones-Casey, K. (2019). Customary leaders and conflicts of interest over land in Ghana. *Gates Open Research*, *3*, Article 684. https://doi.org/10.21955/gatesopenres.1115272.1

Huth, M. (2023). *Liberia final report: Integrated land and resource governance task order the Strengthening Tenure and Resource Rights II (STARR II IDIQ)*. Tetra Tech for USAID.

Kaba, A. (2015, August). *Community land protection: Lessons from the field. Complexities of community self-identification in Liberia.* Sustainable Development Institute for NAMATI.

Kasanga, R.K.B., Cochrane, J., King, R., & Roth, M. (1996). *Land markets and legal contradictions in the peri-urban areas of Accra, Ghana* (LTC Research Paper No. 127). Land Tenure Center, University of Wisconsin-Madison.

Kludze, A.K.P. (1985). Evolution of the different regimes of customary law in Ghana within the framework of the principle of stare decisis. In A. Allot & G.R. Woodman (Eds.), *People's law and state law: The Bellagio papers* (pp. 97–104). Foris Publications.

Knight, R., Adoko, J., Auma, T., Kaba, A., Salomao, A., Siakor, S., & Tankar, I. (2012). *Protecting community lands and resources: Evidence from Liberia, Mozambique and Uganda*. International Development Law Organization (IDLO) for NAMATI.

Larbi, W.O. (2006, March 8–11). *Land administration reform in a plural environment: The case of Ghana* [Conference presentation]. 5th FIG Regional Conference, Accra, Ghana. https://pdfs.semanticscholar.org/184a/2c27bd0f28c7dc5c19482330c910077d25a0.pdf

Lawrance, J.C.D. (1960). A pilot scheme for the grant of land titles in Uganda. *Journal of African Administration, 12*, 135–143.

Migot-Adholla, S.E., Benneh, G., Place, F., & Atsu, S. (1994). Land, security of tenure, and productivity in Ghana. In J.W. Bruce & S.E. Migot-Adholla (Eds.), *Searching for land tenure security in Africa* (pp. 97–118). The World Bank.

Okec, S. (1969). Pilot schemes for the registration of land titles in Uganda. In J. Obol-Ochola (Ed.), *Land law reform in East Africa* (pp. 255–264). Uganda Trust Press.

Parliament of the Republic of Ghana (2020). *Land Act, 2020*. https://ir.parliament.gh/handle/123456789/1875

Siaw, J.Y. (2009). *Draft report on enumeration of property owners in six Customary Land Secretariat (CLS) areas in the Ashanti Region*. Land Administration Project for the Ministry of Lands, Forestry and Mines, Republic of Ghana.

Snyder, F.G. (1981). Colonialism and legal form: The creation of "customary law" in Senegal. *The Journal of Legal Pluralism and Unofficial Law, 13*(19), 49–90. https://doi.org/10.1080/07329113.1981.10756258

Stevens, C.J. (2014). The legal history of public land in Liberia. *Journal of African Law, 58*(2), 250–265. https://doi.org/10.1017/S0021855314000059

Ubink, J.M. (2008). *In the land of the chiefs: Customary law, land conflicts, and the role of the state in peri-urban Ghana*. Leiden University Press.

Uganda Ministry of Lands, Housing & Urban Development (1998). *The Land Act, 1998*. https://mlhud.go.ug/wp-content/uploads/2019/03/Land-Act-Chapter_227.pdf

West, H.W. (1965). *The Mailo system in Buganda: A preliminary case study in African land tenure*. Government Printer.

West, H.W. (1972). *Land policy in Buganda*. Cambridge University Press.

Woodman, G.R. (1969). Some realism about customary law: The West African experience. *Wisconsin Law Review, 128*.

Woodman, G.R. (1985). Customary law, state law, and the notion of institutionalization of norms in Ghana and Nigeria. In A. Allot & G.R. Woodman (Eds.), *People's law and state law: The Bellagio papers* (pp. 145–165). Foris Publications.

World Bank (2013). *Project performance assessment report: Ghana land administration project* (Report No. 75084). Independent Evaluation Group (IEG) for The World Bank.

World Bank Independent Evaluation Group (2019). *Implementation completion report (ICR) Review. GH–land administration* (Report No. ICRR0021446). GH Land Administration Publications. https://documents1.worldbank.org/curated/en/849481553216957142/pdf/Ghana-GH-Land-Administration-2.pdf

Yiri, K. (2006, March 8–11). *Customary lands administration and good governance: The state and traditional rulers interface*. [Conference proceedings] 5th FIG Regional Conference, Accra, Ghana.

# 16 Conversion from Customary to Statutory Community-Based Systems

## Botswana, Tanzania and Mozambique

### The Rationale for Community-based Tenure

The decision by the governments of Botswana, Tanzania and Mozambique to uphold community-based tenure is driven by a number of factors having different weights in decisions by each country. In some, it is a practical recognition that for simple reasons of capacity, the state would have difficulty suppressing and replacing the customary arrangements. In others, it involves a desire to draw on communities' sense of common interest and legitimacy of custom. There may be an element of commitment to traditional values behind the decision, but it clearly does not extend to the role of traditional authority with respect to land. In all three, these reforms have deprived chiefs of their role in land management, a role expanded under colonial direct rule. Botswana and Tanzania both shifted the leadership of those communities away from traditional authorities to options comporting better with national governance preferences, for instance, democratically elected leaders or those preferred by the party in power. In these cases, differences between customary land tenure institutions and traditional authorities are clearly distinguished. The former are retained to some degree, but traditional authorities should withdraw from a role in land matters, whether implicitly or explicitly. The exception is reliance, often informal, on the most local level of traditional authority for their knowledge of landholding histories in their areas. In both countries, customary land tenure remains a source of law, though statutes continue to cut into its coverage.

These decisions to use existing institutions are not driven by nostalgia, but based on a calculated judgment of how fragile new states need to live with what are potential competitors for power. They reflect a policy of co-opting those institutions rather than seeking to suppress them, understanding that the latter might easily result in long, painful social and political conflict.

### Botswana

Botswana, like virtually all other African countries, came to independence with a dual land tenure system: one sector called "tribal lands" under customary land tenure and a sector governed by western land law that included both a small amount

DOI: 10.4324/9781003476429-19

of privately owned land and a larger area of state-owned land. Each sector took up roughly half the country. A protectorate of Great Britain, Botswana was not a settler colony, and only 4–5% of land was in private ownership. Immediately after independence, the government shifted considerable land from state ownership to tribal customary ownership, with the result that by 1998, 71% of the land in Botswana was tribal land. The remaining 24.8% was state land (Dickson, 1990).

In 1968, the government enacted the Tribal Land Act of 1968, an innovative law that embraced customary land tenure. Such innovation came relatively easily in Botswana because the country's first president, Sir Seretse Khama, was the son of the paramount chief of the politically influential Bamangwato clan of the Tswana and the grandson of their king. His government sought to provide a statutory legal basis for customary land tenure while at the same time developing Botswana's market economy. The Act was the first law in Africa to grant customary land tenure the same legal status as private ownership. The Act affirmed customary law as the governing law for "tribal land" and did not attempt to alter its rules. It restated some of the basic rules of customary tenure, including the requirement that in order to receive an allocation of tribal land, one must be a "tribesman." In most of Botswana, "customary land tenure" has in practice meant that of the numerically and politically dominant Tswana. The rules of customary land tenure, which continue in force, are enforced by the District Land Boards (formerly Tribal Land Boards) and Sub-District Land Boards, statutory, autonomous bodies created by the Act. Their linkage to central government is the Ministry of Land Management, Water and Sanitation (Adams et al., 2003). Another reform followed in 1975, the Tribal Land Grazing Policy, discussed in Box 16.1 and Chapter 6.

**Box 16.1 Tribal Land Grazing Policy**

The Tswana are pastoralists. Much of the tribal land consists of pasture. Grazing was historically managed by communities as commons, but the introduction of the borehole in the 1930s changed this. Proximity to boreholes was important. Grazing patterns changed as individuals established "cattle posts" in the commons, and new boundaries began to take shape. Introduction of the Tribal Grazing Land Policy (TGLP) in 1975 left the landscape even more changed. As the result of that well-meant, but ultimately very unfortunate, experiment in grazing area tenure reform, the government subdivided the range into large ranches allocated to large stockholders on long-term leases from the state. Under TGLP, the government re-zoned tribal land into four areas: commercial land (within which individuals and groups would be granted exclusive rights); communal land (allocated and managed according to customary principles); reserved areas (unallocated lands to be held as a safeguard for the poor's future land needs); and "wildlife management areas" (where cattle were permitted to graze, but which were primarily reserved for wildlife). Small stockholders grazed their cattle on the much-reduced communal grazing commons, having little incentive to sustainably manage them because each year, when good browse became scarce, the holders of the large ranches would turn their livestock out onto the commons, ensuring overuse and range degradation.

Sources: Peters (1994) and Cullis and Watson (2005).

The point has been made that land tenure systems have a normative side and an institutional, organizational side. The organizational issues become critical in cases such as Botswana, whose post-independence government decided to maintain a large part of its community-held land under customary land tenure. Few national governments in Africa have decided to trust administration of customary land entirely to traditional institutions, though Ghana has come close (see Chapter 15). In Botswana, traditional authorities initially played a role on Land Boards but later were barred from them because of the inappropriateness of chiefs as board members reviewing their own decisions in their other roles as traditional authorities, including resolution of land disputes (Mathuba, 2003).

The boards are hosted by district government, most districts being based on sub-tribes, each with its "major village" (more a town) as the district capital. Under the Act, the boards hold tribal land in trust for the people of Botswana and have broad discretion in administering that land. They administer tribal land and control land use planning, allocation of land for residential, commercial and agricultural uses, and the granting of water and pasture rights. They manage tribal land according to custom, as modified by the Tribal Land Act, but have also been given the power to grant common-law leases in areas under the boards' authority (Dickson, 1990). This provides unified management under a single administration of both land under customary tenure and land under statutory tenures on tribal land.

The boards are a blend of elected members, local officials and, at the outset, traditional authorities. Originally, the chief was an ex-officio member of each Land Board, and in some districts, the Chair. At first, the boards were given authority over land disputes. Later this was transferred to customary courts on the ground that land litigation sometimes challenged actions by a Land Board and it was inappropriate for board members to adjudicate disputes in which they were a party. As chiefs assumed greater responsibility for judicial roles, they were barred entirely from participation on the Land Boards. Of the 12 members of the District Land Board, five are selected by the Land Board Selection Committee, but must be confirmed by the Minister of Land. Another five are appointed by the Minister of Land, and the remaining two are representatives from the ministries of Agriculture, Commerce and Industry (Adams et al., 2003)

Botswana's Tribal Land Act, in addition to retaining customary land tenure and entrusting its implementation to Land Boards, vested authority in District Land Boards to manage land under statutory tenures (largely long-term leases, referred to in Botswana as "common law tenure") in rural areas. Key competences were reserved at national level in the Ministry, including control over freehold land and state land (the latter including urban land) and technical units such as survey and registration (Dickson, 1990).

It became clear that District Land Boards did not have the reach to be effective over such large areas. The Act was amended to establish 41 subordinate Land Boards, dealing exclusively with customary rights. Similar membership patterns apply to the subordinate Land Boards as in the District Land Boards. Chiefs, with one exception, now have little to do with management of tribal land but remain influential in political matters relating to land. The exception is the "ward chiefs," the lowest level of the traditional hierarchy, who preside over village sections and upon whom the Land Boards must rely for knowledge of land rights held by residents and for implementation of Land Board decisions (Mathuba, 2003).

The Land Boards' unique technocratic/governmental/community character has gained much attention as a model. It has enabled the boards to take on a broader range of responsibilities than normally expected. In tribal lands, the boards control both sides (customary and statutory) of the country's dualistic land tenure system, managing the boundary between the two systems. This was the result of the central government allowing land boards to begin handling common law leases on the tribal lands. Botswana has achieved a harmonization of its dualism through organizational reform. Since independence, land has been shifted between categories. A significant amount of privately owned land and state land have been acquired and converted to tribal land. Large areas of customary grazing land have been converted to "common law tenure" (in this case long-term leaseholds for commercial ranches). Limited amounts of customary tenure have been converted to leasehold for residential purposes (Mathuba, 2003; Bruce, 1988).

There are opportunities for improving the land board system. While normally the boards have substantial autonomy, it is limited by the Act's provision that the minister can order a land board to carry out an action. Ministers have used this provision to intervene in the work of the boards. Some of the interventions have been intended to restrain boards from acting in their personal interests. Others have been to impose the Ministry's opinion on the boards. The Ministry's powers are too broad and should either be removed or substantially narrowed to specify acceptable reasons for intervention. This power, if retained at all, should be vested in the president rather than the minister. There is a need to rethink the role and remuneration for the ward chiefs. They really know who holds what land where. They are ignored by the Act but are in practice essential to the system's functioning (Bruce, 1988).

The Tribal Land Act provides an alternative option to customary rights by providing that a tribesman can apply for a statutory "common law right," essentially a long-term lease administered by one's local land board. Leases can be for residential or commercial purposes, including commercial agricultural purposes. The leases are transferable and mortgageable and have been used primarily in urban and peri-urban areas. On tribal lands they have been used for large expensive residences built in the small home villages of notables (Bruce, 1981). The expansion of the use of these leases has not been as extensive as might have been expected due to the seriousness with which successive governments pursued reforms of customary land tenure. The most fundamental change, in recognition that growing numbers of non-tribesmen lived and worked in the major villages of Botswana, was amendment of the Act in 1993 to allow any citizen resident in a village to apply for land. What in the initial Act had been an entitlement to land for "tribesmen" became an entitlement for "citizens." By the mid-1990s, judicial decisions and administrative actions had confirmed the evolution of customary land tenure that had been underway for some time. Tribal land could be freely sold, mortgaged or left by will. It was, as one commentator suggested, "Tswana Freehold" (Kalabamu, 2021). Many of these changes were made by judicial decision. Even foreigners could acquire tribal land on long-term leases from the state. Custom, as evolved, remains the body of rules governing tribal land (Kalabamu, 2021).

Some ten years after the last government paper on land tenure policy and the amendments to the Tribal Land Act, the government launched a National Land Policy Review in 2002. This was a thorough and comprehensive review, involving consultants and stakeholder consultations. Two policy papers were prepared as the basis for a government paper. The review concluded that Botswana's 1983 strategy of careful change that responded to particular needs with specific tenure innovations had served the country well and would continue. The report, crowded with proposals for specific changes in land law, focused on moving from allowing land sales to the development of markets in land. Some changes were overdue. Departing from the Act's initial focus on individual rights, community-based property rights would be recognized and adequately provided for in the amended Act. Much of the land that might have profited from effective natural resource management was zoned for livestock under TGLP. The problems of women's land rights and strategies for protecting access to land for those outside the land board system, such as the San, were discussed at length (Kalabamu, 2021).

There are, nevertheless, many points on which the Botswana land tenure reform has come up short. Knight (2010) catalogues many of them:

1. Despite commitments to periodically amend the law to foster greater equity, sustainability and integrated development, political elites have instead sought to strengthen state control to their own benefit.
2. Although the Act intended for land boards to administer land according to custom, changes have been introduced to the law that significantly depart from custom.
3. The removal of traditional leaders from land boards and shifting from elected members to selection by the minister has weakened the downward accountability of boards to communities in favor of the central government, as has locating land boards away from communities.
4. Management of common property traditionally belonging to communities, especially grazing areas, has increasingly reflected the private investment priorities of central government with land boards allocating large tracts of communal grazing land to commercial ranchers.

5. As of 2010, the Act continued to ignore women's land rights by permitting customary land grant applications by male household heads alone with no provisions for joint or derivative rights for spouses or family members.
6. The Act effectively sanctions discrimination against non-Tswana tribes, which in some cases has led to their dispossession from land they claim.
7. Unregistered customary claims have lost protection as a result of case law and administrative decisions that favor leaseholders and amendments to the Act that allow land boards to determine if land is being used and developed appropriately.

Major system characteristics have continuity. Botswana has expanded land registration. It stayed with its deed registration system originating in Dutch cadaster law. It facilitates systematic registration and provides a level of security of tenure not available in English deed registration statutes. The Land Board system, criticized in recent times as being less efficient than hoped, is affirmed. No major changes have been made in the institutional setup. There has been no attempt to address the question of how and whether customary land tenure will evolve in the future. In the absence of such a consideration, it's likely that customary land tenure, having provided the basis for the national law on tribal land, will gradually cease to exist as custom and be changed through occasional amendments to the Act and judicial decisions as to the nature of customary law. The legislature and the courts should both draw on land board practice to understand how custom is changing and will need to consider whether to absorb new custom into the Act or the common law of Botswana (the decisions of the nation's courts). A customary land tenure system has been in the process of evolving into a national statutory land tenure system supplemented by judicial precedents through a process that might be called gradual codification through formalization. Is this model replicable elsewhere? Does the fact that Botswana has one ethnic group which composes a strong majority of the population have anything to do with this? Could the approach work in countries with many customary land laws?

### Tanzania

Botswana's approach to land tenure reform has from the outset had a pragmatic feel about it. Tanzania's reform at independence was firmly rooted in first president, Julius Nyerere's ideology of African Socialism. It had ambitious plans for restructuring rural Tanzania. At independence, most land in Tanzania was state-owned, held in trust for the people (Knight, 2010). A modest amount of freehold land existed. By 1970 it had been nationalized, the former owners remaining with only a weak right of occupancy.

In 1973, Tanzania's government launched Operation Vijiji, a program of land expropriation, villagization and collectivization. The program involved the relocation, sometimes forced, of many thousands rural Tanzanians to *Ujamaa* villages[1] in order to facilitate communal farming and service provision by the government. Incorporating the program into its five-year plan, the government sought to prove that increased agricultural yields were possible within socialist communal living.

Although hindered by poor planning and execution, the villages were built, but it proved difficult to convince families to leave their family holdings. Force was sometimes used. While many of the villages created have survived and are towns today, it failed as a demonstration of the virtues of collective production. It served instead to disrupt agricultural production. One of the biggest failings of Operation Vijiji was the creation of misinformation. Tanganyika African National Union officials would often record preexisting villages as newly formed *Ujamaa* villages to inflate success numbers. Tanzania under Nyerere made great strides in vital areas of social development, but Operation Vijiji led to decreased production, casting doubt on the program's ability to offer economic growth.

Nyerere retired in 1985 and was succeeded by less ideological presidents. In 1991, a National Commission on Land Matters was created, headed by Professor Issa Shivji of the University of Dar es Salaam. The Commission conducted a thorough assessment of the land tenure situation in Tanzania involving extensive public consultations. This resulted in a frank report, reflecting disillusionment with public land management and proposing a system of individual rights in land vested in the landholders (Tanzania Ministry of Lands, Housing, and Urban Development, 1994).

The 1995 National Land Policy retained state land ownership, vesting it in the president in trust for the people of Tanzania. A new tenure regime for rural Tanzania was introduced by the Village Land Act (No. 5 of 1999). The new law recognized customary land tenure as the governing law for rural land and allowed each ethnic group to retain its own tenure arrangements to the extent that they conformed to judicial and other written law.[2] It added that any custom that denies women, children or persons with disabilities access to land shall be void.[3] A process under the Act provides for identification of villages with the highest authority over land being the village assembly, consisting of all village residents. An elected village council provides day to day governance, including land governance. Traditional authorities lost their role in land administration under the new law but retained a role in settlement of disputes over land under custom.

The law called for documenting land rights through certification of village lands and issuance by a village council of certificates of individual or household landholdings to its residents. The rights of individuals and families are use rights, referred to as "rights of occupancy." In villages not yet certified, custom continues to be applied. The Village Land Act directs villages to apply custom, except where it contradicts national law (e.g. on women's land rights) (Wily, 2003).

## Certification Process

Certification is a two-stage process. Land rights are identified at village level and then household level. Household rights derive from the right of the village. To receive a certificate of village land, each village must first identify and describe its boundaries, which it may do by reference to physical features or through survey, then identify and demarcate its commons areas. The certificate of village land empowers the village council to administer village land, plan land use, manage village commons areas and allocate land to village members. Land use plans and land allocations must be approved by the village assembly. The village also has a role in land dispute resolution. Disputes over village land are resolved by a mediation team according to customary land rules. This committee is comprised of seven members (three of whom should be women), nominated by the Village Council and approved by the Village Assembly (Wily, 2003).

The certificate of village land provides less security of tenure than would be desirable. Prior to the 1999 Act, villages had the option to register their land in ownership and obtain a title deed. This is not legally possible under the Village Land Act (Wily, 2003). The Act gives the president the power to shift village land to another legal category (reserved or general), allowing the government to reallocate village lands to concessionaires, as happened during the great land grab by investors that began in 2003.

The tenure provided by the customary certificate of occupancy is reasonably secure. This is qualified by the fact that, according to the Act, the tenure is determined by custom, varying from place to place. Custom, in the case of Tanzania, means the custom of 120 ethnic/tribal groups living in an estimated 12,000 villages. They pursue a variety of land-based livelihoods in different environments and display a remarkable variety of customary land tenure practices. Recognition of custom is limited by the requirement that it not be in conflict with a statute. Extensive defining of the right of occupancy in the Act wipes out much of what was custom in the villages. It creates a right of occupancy which will, when the Act has been fully implemented, provide rural Tanzanians with much the same land rights.

That customary certificate of occupancy creates the right of a resident to village land that is perpetual and inheritable. It can be leased, mortgaged and bequeathed and even sold to other residents subject to spousal approval. Land can be sold to outsiders. Such sales must be approved by the village assembly. Direct allocations to outsiders are possible as well, but the Act sets out a complex application process and other requirements. The village can lease land to an investor if the investment meets certain requirements set out in the Act.

Land under customary certificates of occupancy can be taken by government for public purposes, the definition of which includes "investments of national interest." People whose land is taken are required to receive full, fair and prompt compensation for the loss of value caused by the taking.[4]

## Implementation of the Act

There has been an almost total lack of structured, careful monitoring needed to assess the progress of implementation of the Act, let alone studies on impact.[5] As of March 2016, 1,640 out of an estimated 12,788 villages had undergone land use planning, the first step in the process toward issuance of a certificate of village land, which must be done before the issuance of individual certificates of customary occupancy. At that time, 258,134 certificates of customary occupancy had been issued, 13% in the names of women.[6] Very few had been accepted by lenders as collateral for a loan, unsurprising and consistent with experiences elsewhere in Africa with registered readily marketable smallholder titles (Massay, 2016).

## Appropriateness of the Legal Model

Implementation of the Village Land Act has yet to be launched in many parts of Tanzania. The majority of rural Tanzanians continue to farm their land under the widely variable local custom of its many ethnic groups. Discussions of implementation have raised questions about the Village Land Act itself. It is 108 pages. Regulations under the Act are over 120 pages, the most detailed of any land law in Africa. The British legal expert who assisted with the drafting of the law, Patrick McAuslan, has argued that where government is the owner of the land, a detailed, administrative approach to land law is preferred, as it seeks to regulate process and ensure accountability of officials (McAuslan, 1998). Knight questions whether this is appropriate in societies where so few of those affected by the Act have legal skills necessary to absorb and interpret the law (Knight, 2010). There appears to have been a failure to prepare and disseminate materials that would have made the most relevant provisions of the Act more accessible and to deliver large-scale training programs that would be needed to facilitate expansion of implementation.

While the Act is excessively long and complex, it provides a fully elaborated example of a village-based tenure system seeking to embody some values of African systems of community-based customary land tenure. Limited implementation of the law, though common in other countries with less voluminous laws, raises questions about the complexity of the process under the Act, especially the slow village land certification process and the relative weakness of the protection provided to the village by its certificate. Twenty years of growing pressure for land for large-scale agricultural projects and the government's lackluster performance in implementation of the Act and rural development generally have encouraged the World Bank to fund activities aimed at expanding registration of land rights process,[7] initiated by government. This resulted in a national land conference and a new land law in 1997 (Tanner, 2002).

Mozambique's 1997 Land Law (Law 19/97) is perhaps the shortest land tenure reform law in Africa and one of the best known, in part because one can actually pick up a copy and easily read it. It is innovative in a number of respects. It leaves all land in state ownership but establishes a new property right in land, the DUAT,[8] a land use right which is inheritable and, in urban settings, transferable.

There are two types of DUATs, one acquired and one automatically recognized by the state. The first is a right of 50 years maximum duration and renewable. It is a private right in land, derived from the ownership of land by the state and legally, at least, available upon application to all Mozambicans using land.[9] DUATs acquired by application to government are initially provisional and subject to an approved plan of development, with non-compliance cause for revocation of the right.[10] The DUAT in its *state-granted* form is highly conditional and is not a very secure tenure.

## Mozambique

FRELIMO, the Marxist movement that had brought Mozambique to independence in 1975, nationalized all land, converted the large commercial farms of the Portuguese (who had in most cases left, abandoning their farms) to state farms and launched a collectivization of customary land. Insurgency developed under a movement, RENAMO, in 1976. Launched by white Rhodesian officers and later supported by the South African armed forces under Apartheid, much of the movement's support came from traditional authorities, who had been stripped of their power over land. The war ended in mutual exhaustion. Under the 1992 peace settlement, FRELIMO remained in power but RENAMO was brought into the government. The land sector at that point can only be described as chaotic. The government stirred alarm by beginning to allocate land to commercial operators, including several from South Africa. Most DUATs under Article 12 of the law are not acquired via application but come into being without official action. These DUATs are created either by prescription (acquiring land rights through good faith occupation of land for ten years) or by occupation "according to customary norms and practices."[11] Land use rights acquired by prescription or by customary occupation are not conditioned upon exploitation plans, they are not provisional but final and they are not required to be titled in order to be recognized.[12]

Automatically granting strong use rights to landholders by law, both under custom and based on simple occupation, has excited interest in other countries grappling with these issues. So have provisions in Articles 12 and 13 which recognize "local communities" as primary holders of land use rights. These rights may be held over substantial areas of land constituting their traditional territories. The definition of the areas of such communities in Article 1(1) of the law is extensive, and includes commons resources and "areas for expansion." Community claims are curbed by the stipulation that such a community must be no larger than the size of the "locality," the smallest official unit of local administration in Mozambique. The state is *de facto* the ultimate decider as to the extent of the territory recognized in the DUAT.

The DUAT is a western-style land right, without attached duties to a lineage or community. Unlike Tanzania and Botswana, the community is not a tenurial intermediary between individuals with their DUATs and the state as owner of the land. Individuals and communities alike derive their DUATs directly from the state and have the option to have them certified. The law protects the landholdings of those who have customary rights, but their customary rights are effectively replaced with rights derived from the state, even if they continue to be governed under custom.

In areas under custom in Mozambique, the primary holder of land is "the local community," even while individuals and families have customary rights to their parcels within these communities. In the face of intense, mounting pressures from international investors to acquire land in post-war Mozambique, those involved in the drafting of the law and other proponents were keen to provide a means by which whole communities could protect their land rights. While the law provided those with customary rights robust statutory recognition through DUATs, in the absence of documentation, they remained for all practical purposes invisible and vulnerable to exploitation. Part of the rationale for fast-tracking documentation of community DUATs was cost and expediency. Documenting the customary rights of every individual right-holder was the work of decades. Protection of rural families' land could be achieved more rapidly by delimiting the boundaries of large blocks of community land and certifying the community's rights to that land, rights that were already granted to them through the law.

Rather than worrying about the internal operations of communities and documentation of the rights of community members, custom would continue to regulate holdings within the community. Because of the diversity of customary land tenure systems, the law did not attempt to define further or standardize the concept of local community, instead leaving it up to communities to "self-identify," a process that, in the absence of facilitation, can impose an implementation barrier, but also opens up opportunities for customary governance reform (see Box 16.2). The law also leaves it to the community to apply for identification of its land and certification of the community as the owner of the land. It resembles sporadic registration, but on a community rather than an individual level. An annex to the law[13] lays out a process to assist communities in establishing their DUAT territories in preparation for delimiting their boundaries.[14] As part of the DUAT certification process, local communities must acquire a legal personality that can often pose a barrier. With a certified DUAT, a community can enter into contracts, including deals with outside investors to allow them to use community land.[15]

**Box 16.2 Supporting Community Acquisition of DUAT Certification**

During 2009–2011, international non-governmental organization (NGO) Namati conducted a program of participatory action research in selected rural communities on reform of customary land tenure and community DUAT certification. What was learned from that process and the experience with it suggest ways to improve the process.

Implemented through the local NGO Centro Terra Viva (CTV), the program pilots addressed the complex issue of community "self-identification." The Law did not identify any one level of community as the primary land administrator. The definition of a community in the 1997 law is in general terms, given the variety of their customary norms and governance systems for land. In rural Inhambane Province, where the pilots were carried out, several *zonas* made up a *povoado* and three or four *povoados* made up a *regulado*, headed by an official, the *regulo*. This structure is a "rationalization" of the colonial government's administrative organization, with most authority vested in the *regulo*. Three out of the four communities who applied for titling did so at the *povoado* level. Participation was a key value of the project. Potential for participation was considered important enough to justify relocating some land competences to the *povoado* level. Self-identification by communities is guided by consultation on the viability of performing the relevant function at a given level.

The law's flexibility also enabled the CTV implementers to promote important reform objectives, such as increased participation, improved land access and rights for women, thereby guiding communities through a process of reforming certain customs before moving on to acquisition of DUAT certificates.

Source: Knight et al. (2012)

In addition to community DUATs, individual/family holdings under custom are entitled to DUATs. A landholder may prove his/her customary right through oral evidence (e.g. testimony from neighbors) and are not required to prove "good faith" occupation nor obtain documentation of their rights. The law provides that community members can themselves acquire certificates to their individual DUATs on the land they use within the community territory.

Implementation remains quite limited. Most rural Mozambicans have not certified the DUATs granted to them by law. Thanks to an intensive civil society organization (CSO)-led campaign that almost immediately followed passage of the law, the law and its purpose are reasonably well understood throughout much of the country, although this is much less true of the necessary procedures for DUAT certification. While the law is very general in nature, it seems to this author to be appropriate in Mozambican circumstances. Greater specificity should come from regulations under the law, which can be framed specifically for different regions of the country. The Land Law Regulations Decree No. 1/2003 established new provisions for the National Land Registry and Real Estate Cadaster, procedures for registering inherited land use rights and secure rights to customary rights-of-way (Government of Mozambique, 2003). These meet some of the need but further regulations are needed (Norfolk & Tanner, 2007).

Without assistance from NGOs or donor-supported systematic registration programs, Mozambican smallholders face cost and complexity barriers when navigating the process to obtain individual DUAT certifications. This may explain why most certificate recipients for individual DUATs are not from rural communities. There has been development of good practices in some cases, including those in which funding was provided by donors for NGO assistance to communities in getting their DUATs surveyed and titled.[16]

Tanner (2005, pp. 28–29), a consultant from the Food and Agriculture Organization of the United Nations deeply involved in development of the 1997 Land Law and the training of court staff to deal with cases arising under it, wrote of implementation:

> The progressive mechanism of the community consultation is being applied, but in a way that does not bring real local benefits—instead it gives a veneer of respectability to what is more like a European style enclosure movement,

> aimed to rationalise land use and place resources in the hands of a class that sees itself as more capable and better able to use national resources than the peasant farmers whose rights are legally recognised but still unprotected in practice. The mid-1990s consensus on land policy is still in place, but under serious pressure to move towards a market in land rights.

Legal recognition of customary land rights is the first critical step in any reform strategy seeking to protect the land of rural communities in Africa, but legal recognition alone will not accomplish a great deal. When recognition is accompanied by a CSO-assisted campaign against further concessions and support for that position exists in at least some quarters of government, then legal recognition of customary land rights can have real power. Such assistance is not available in many areas and support by decision-makers is often thin. In Mozambique, this has allowed investors to take advantage of communities in return for large amounts of land while government representatives facilitating the deal fail to advocate for communities' interests. Investors are afforded such modes of "compensation" as contributions to local government development funds, which are simple and convenient for the concessionaire. They may create a more positive attitude toward the concession on the part of local officials. They do very little for people who have lost their customary land to the concession. This is unlikely to change until all the parties concerned acknowledge that a community property right is involved and merits official recognition (through identification, demarcation and registration of communities' land) before it can be considered for use by investors.

With some parameters established by government on the community titling process, it would seem from the Namati/CTV project experience that NGOs can partner with communities to carry out the work needed relatively effectively and economically. Whether state agents or NGO staff facilitate these processes could shape tenure futures quite differently. In the absence of a major role for NGOs, even well-planned self-identification and titling exercises seem likely to follow the path noted with alarm by Tanner (2005): investors partner with communities in schemes that obtain title for the community but give the investor access to the land on terms that hardly benefit the community.

While strong and documented property rights can grant communities the right to say no to an investor and even the government, such leverage is often weakened by the gap in knowledge and influence between rural communities and investors. Even with clear land rights, some rural communities will settle on surprisingly little to alienate large parts of their land for generations to come. A new roof for the school and a well for the village can resemble a golden egg for rural villagers whose government has neglected their development needs. Secure land rights are essential, but they need to be accompanied by: (1) firm government policy and dedicated budgets in support of key benefits for rural communities; (2) clear and specific regulations governing public consultations with communities concerning investments; and (3) pro-community advice and assistance in titling and investment negotiations, preferably provided by NGOs or other independent agencies backed by reliable and adequate donor support.

Technical problems with the law and existing regulations that impede implementation are secondary problems. The fundamental reason for slow implementation is that the public land agencies responsible for implementation as well as some major donors have prioritized fast-tracking corporate land use applications, which promise a more immediate return in production and revenue. Often, they also provide rent-seeking benefits to public officials that can facilitate expedient land acquisition for investors.

This issue is fundamental, for Mozambique and other African countries. How can government land administrators and land program implementers be motivated to focus on tenure reform programs that benefit communities, rather than their traditional land registration tasks? The colonial history of Africa almost guarantees two land tenure sectors at the national level. and programs to address the different needs of each. This is the case even if the duality is expressed in agricultural development plans in terms of smallholder agriculture and larger-scale "commercial" agriculture in agricultural development plans. Most people in the concerned offices and ministries have been trained to deal with land under the laws of the state, not community-based land tenure. Absent a powerful reorientation of the agency responsible for implementation, the concerned offices and staff tend to continue doing what they were trained to do, rather than tackling the challenges of implementing reforms. In the Mozambique case, this means working with firms both foreign and domestic that are applying for new DUATs for large commercial operations. Work in that sector is more rewarding in terms of career opportunities and in other ways, including bribes and kick-backs. The Ministry has concentrated its staff and budget on surveying and certifying DUATs for commercial operations, and only undertakes the work with customary communities where the community self-identification and application for DUAT certificates is facilitated by NGOs and CSOs, which are financially supported by foreign donors. It is a daunting problem, taken up in the final chapter of this book.

If the protective objective of the Land Act is to be achieved, there is a pressing need for an extensive program of systematic identification and certification for community DUATs. Such a program should build on learning from donor-funded community titling cases. It would require a major infusion of support from international donors, which may be looking at community DUAT certification in Mozambique in the rearview mirror.

**Similarities and Differences**

In both Botswana and Tanzania, the land farmed by customary users remains publicly owned by the village in trust for the people in Tanzania and in Botswana by the District Land Boards in trust for the tribes. Mozambique's law simply declares that land is state-owned. In Tanzania and Botswana, the governments have chosen to keep customary land tenure in effect but replace traditional authorities with a new statutory institution to manage the customary and statutory rights in the land they hold. Both are organized around communities. In Tanzania, they are small, village-level institutions. In Botswana, they correspond to the districts which were based on Tswana sub-tribes. In Botswana, these land boards are institutions of the district government. In Tanzania village assemblies and village councils derive from traditional communities but represent a new land governance arrangement. In both cases, government has been motivated by a desire for more democratic land governance as well as clearer lines of responsibility and potential for accountability. By contrast, Mozambique has opted not to exert governance authority over land within rural communities.

In Botswana and Tanzania alike, the role of traditional authorities in rural land administration has been reduced or eliminated, shifting them into dispute resolution roles. Both recognize and administer customary land tenure but also provide alternative tenures such leaseholds for investors. Rights provided for in the statutes deviate from many customary rights, including allowing for greater marketability of land within the community and, on a more restricted basis, with outsiders. In both cases, the land use rights of individuals are private, individual rights which can be bought and sold.

Botswana's District Land Boards were found to have jurisdiction over territories too large for them to manage customary land effectively. In response, sub-district boards were established. While the boards in Botswana have considerable power, they still have residual reliance on ward chiefs and reliance on the ex-officio members of the board for transport and facilities. They appear to be less independent from the central government than the village governance structures in Tanzania, which exhibit more democratic decision-making. Similar to both systems is their legal authority over tenure in land and the relationships created by it. The ability of both to change rules is limited by fairly specific statutory provisions on tenure. This does not appear to be the case in Mozambique, which leaves the administration of land within communities up to the communities, with the option for community members to acquire state-issued DUAT certificates at the household level.

Implementation of tenure reforms has been a challenge in Tanzania, Mozambique and to a lesser extent in Botswana. Admittedly, Tanzania's and Mozambique's reforms are more recent. Both Mozambique and Tanzania have had to contend with the sheer number of communities and lack of funds to implement the Land Law and Village Land Act, respectively. Botswana, a wealthier government with a much smaller task (less land, fewer villages and fewer people), moved quickly to set up and capacitate the new institutions at district then sub-district level, nationwide. It made significant investments in training for staff and members of the boards, a continuing task because of scheduled turnover in board members. The administrative boundaries of Botswana's districts (the entities in which the communities' land rights are vested) had already been established before implementation of the law. In Tanzania and Mozambique boundaries of most communities, many times the number in the Botswana case, remained to be done as the first step in creating a new community-based system of land tenure.

Another difference is that in Botswana, tribal land is managed by the land boards under a customary tenure significantly reformed by statute. In Tanzania and Mozambique the community and its institutions hold and manage the land, making customary tenure rules more flexible and less subject to statute, apart from restrictions that they not contradict national law. These institutions allocate land to community members. Their members have a right to land from the community, which has its own tenure. While both Tanzania and Mozambique administer customary tenure at the community level, the key difference between them is that Mozambique has not established statutory institutions for this purpose, but instead allowed customary institutions to continue in this role. This is not unlike the reform introduced by Liberia's Land Act of 2017, which recognized customary land tenure as the land tenure governing extensive areas of the country previously held under custom. Mozambique's, Liberia's and Tanzania's reforms were also motivated by the depredations of customary land tenure during the Great Land Grab, giving rise to an urgency to protect customary rights through recognition of community rights. These systems, together with customary land tenure systems, can be called "community-based systems," which is why the reforms this chapter addresses are called "conversion to statutory community-based systems."

## Notes

1 Highly controversial, the program was abandoned in the 1980s and was criticized heavily in the Report of the Presidential Commission of Inquiry into Land Matters (1994). Many people then attempted to return to their former homes, leading to widespread land disputes.
2 Article 20(2), Village Land Act.
3 Article 20(2), Village Land Act.
4 Village Land Act, Part II.
5 A notable exception is: www.land-links.org/wp-content/uploads/2021/03/LTA-IE-Endline-Report-FINAL-2–18–21_508.pdf.
6 A 2021 World Bank project appraisal document indicates that as of 2021, 864,000 CCROs had been issued of the approximate 6,000,000 rural households (World Bank, 2021).
7 The author first worked in Mozambique on a United States Agency for International Development project with the Land Tenure Center. Working with the Ministry of Agriculture and in particular the Ministry's monthly newsletter, the Center's project manager, Gregory Myers, managed to bring the land tenure issue from a topic that could not be publicly mentioned in Mozambique to the point where the Center could organize the national conference.
8 Direito de Uso e Aproveitamento dos Terras, in Portuguese, i.e. Right of Land Use and Benefit.
9 While this right is legally available to all under the Law, it is very difficult to imagine most smallholders applying for a DUAT. The lack of information and resources would make this difficult, as would the lack of government capacity at local level to process an application for a DUAT. Government has failed to systematically identify and record the vast majority of DUATs acquired by custom or occupation.
10 Law 19/97, Article 18(1)(a).
11 Law 19/97, Article 12(a).
12 Law 19/97, Article 13(2).
13 The process for identifying and recording the rights of local communities and good-faith occupants is governed by the 2000 Technical Annex to the Land Law Regulations Decree No. 1/2003.
14 On the consultation process, see Tanner and Baleira (2006).

15 To date, there seems to be little interest among investors in negotiating with communities holding certified DUATs to secure their land.
16 See, for example, MCA Mozambique Land Tenure Services Project and the World Bank-supported Terra Segura program.

## References


Adams, M., Kalabamu, F., & White, R. (2003). Land tenure policy and practice in Botswana: Governance lessons for southern Africa. *Journal Für Entwicklungspolitik, 19* (1), 55–74

Bruce, J.W. (1981). *Observations on land tenure and housing development in the major villages of Botswana.* University of Wisconsin-Madison Land Tenure Center, No. 75.

Bruce, J.W. (1988). Residential land tenure and housing development in the major villages of Botswana. *African Urban Quarterly, 3*(1–2), 100–111.

Cullis, A. & Watson, C. (2005). *Winner and losers: Privatizing the commons in Botswana.* IIED.

Dickson, W.L. (1990). *Land tenure and management in a developing country: The case of Botswana, 1966–1985.* National Institute of Development Research and Documentation, University of Botswana.

Government of Mozambique (2003). *Decree no. 1/2003 amending decree no. 66/98 regulating the Land Act.* Ecolex. www.ecolex.org/details/legislation/decree-no-12003-amending-decree-no-6698-regulating-the-land-act-lex-faoc052061/

Kalabamu, F.T. (2021). A commentary on Botswana's 2019 national land policy. *Land Use Policy, 108,* 105563. https://doi.org/10.1016/j.landusepol.2021.105563

Knight, R.S. (2010). *Statutory recognition of customary land rights in Africa: An investigation into best practices for lawmaking and implementation* (Legislative Study No. 105). FAO. www.fao.org/4/i1945e/i1945e01.pdf

Knight, R., Adoko, J., Teresa Auma, Kaba, A., Salomao, A., Siakor, S., & Tankar, I. (2012). *Protecting community land and resources: An investigation into best practices for community land documentation.* http://namati.org

Massay, G.E. (2016). Tanzania's village land act 15 years on. *International Journal of Rural Development, 50*(3), 18–19. www.rural21.com/fileadmin/downloads/2016/en-03/rural2016_03-S18-19.pdf

Mathuba, B.M. (2003, January 26–27). *Botswana land policy* [Conference proceedings]. International Workshop on Land Policies in Southern Africa, Berlin, Germany.

McAuslan, P. (1998). Making law work: Restructuring land relations in Africa. *Development and Change, 29*(3), 525–552. https://doi.org/10.1111/1467-7660.00088

Norfolk, S. & Tanner, C. (2007). *Improving tenure security for the rural poor: Mozambique—country case study* (CLEP Working Paper No. 5). FAO Workshop for Sub-Saharan Africa.

Peters, P.E. (1994). *Dividing the commons: Politics, policy and culture in Botswana.* University of Virginia Press

Tanner, C. (2002). *Law-making in an African context: The 1997 Mozambican land law* (Legal Paper No. 26). FAO. www.fao.org/fileadmin/user_upload/legal/docs/lpo26.pdf

Tanner, C. (2005, November 28–29). *Land rights and enclosures: Implementing the Mozambican land law in practice* [Paper presentation]. International Conference on the Changing Politics of Land in Africa: Domestic Policies, Crisis Management, and Regional Norms, Pretoria, South Africa.

Tanner, C. & Baleira, S. (2006). *Mozambique's legal framework for access to natural resources: The impact of new legal rights and community consultations on local livelihoods* (LSP Working Paper No. 28). FAO Access to Natural Resources Sub-Programme.

Tanzania Ministry of Lands, Housing, and Urban Development (1994). *Report of the presidential commission of inquiry into land matters, Vol. 1: Land policy and land tenure structure*.

Wily, L.A. (2003). *Community-based land tenure management: Questions and answers about Tanzania's new Village Land Act, 1999* (Issue Paper No. 120). IIED. https://core.ac.uk/download/pdf/79425296.pdf

World Bank (2021). *Tanzania land tenure improvement project*. World Bank. https://documents1.worldbank.org/curated/en/466181641925880285/pdf/Tanzania-Land-Tenure-Improvement-Project.pdf

# 17 Reforms to Improve Women's Land Access and Tenure

*Co-authored with Anna Knox*[1]

## Inheritance, Marriage and Women's Land Rights

Most groups in Africa pass land from generation to generation through patrilineal systems of inheritance, i.e. from fathers to sons, and practice patrilocal marriage, i.e. women move to the community belonging to her husband's lineage when they marry. Together, these systems exclude women from the most important means of acquiring land under custom—inheritance through one's lineage. Women suffer disadvantages under matrilineal systems when they practice patrilocal marriage. While land is passed through the female line under those systems, it is typically passed from a woman's brother to her son, i.e. from a man to his nephew, who moves to his uncle's community when he inherits. The land concerned is effectively managed and controlled by male relatives. Matrilineal systems, generally considered to provide better land access to women—or at least more of a say in the succession—than patrilineal systems, are a small minority of customary land tenure systems in Africa. A tiny fraction of matrilineal systems practices matrilocal marriage where men come to settle in their wives' communities and land is inherited by daughters. Even these are evolving toward patrilineal inheritance as the value of land and land-based natural resources increases (Hilhorst, 2000).

These systems of inheritance and marriage mean that during marriage, the majority of African women living under custom are dependent upon their husbands for access to farmland. During marriage, women may have somewhat robust rights to manage plots and decide on how harvests are used,[2] but are not considered owners of the land and lack rights to transact in it (Slavchevska et al., 2021). When the husband dies, the lineage—represented by their sons or their former husband's brothers, take control of the land and the widow's access to land is largely a matter of their discretion. She may, in some societies, retain use of land by marrying a brother of the deceased, or, if there are minor children (especially if there is a male child), to support the children until they are grown, after which her land access depends on her son's decision on whether to retain her in his household. In the case of divorce, she will need to leave her marital community and return to her family of birth. Here, she will have no land rights and may or may not be taken in and allowed to farm family land. Failing such land access, divorced women and younger

DOI: 10.4324/9781003476429-20

widows often go to cities, into irregular and exploitative relationships, to support themselves and sometimes their children.

### The Effects of Lineage, Markets and Colonialism

There is perhaps no other feature of customary land tenure more offensive to modern norms of human rights than denial of land rights to women. This does not affect a marginalized minority. Fully half the population is denied equal rights in land. Freedom from discrimination based upon gender is relatively recent and not honored with any consistency, including in the global north. There is no area in which reform of customary land tenure systems is more difficult than granting men and women equal land rights. This is because lineage systems' rules on inheritance and marriage are a fundamental organizing principle of rural societies, shaping how land and resources are governed.

The spread of commercial markets for agriculture and land and increased competition for land has likewise not dealt women any favors when it comes to asserting their land rights (Whitehead & Tsikata, 2003; Yngstrom, 2002). Over time, women's lineage-based rights to land in patrilineal systems have been eroded with the expansion of the cash economy as their brothers seek to take control of their shares, arguing that their sisters can access land in their husbands' communities (Yngstrom, 2002). Land's ability to generate wealth and cash has also led women to become increasingly vulnerable in their husbands' communities. If her husband dies or they divorce, she lacks a lineage-based right to land. The lineage retention of the household's land denies lineage members an opportunity to generate wealth from the land or at least improve their subsistence. The lineage owes its first obligation to other lineage members. Widows who have children, especially sons, stand a better chance of remaining on the land because of the customary obligation to provide land to and otherwise look after the interests of its lineage members. Women also face major economic and social barriers to access impartial forums to resolve land disputes, exacerbating their tenure insecurity (Henrysson & Joireman, 2009).

Colonial systems of governance were known to weaken women's land rights through their interpretations of them as subordinate to the rights of men (Cousins, 2007). The treatment of customary law by the colonial courts may have worsened the position of women. Decisions construing customary rules regarding women's access to land tend to state general rules and freeze them in time, depriving custom of the flexibility that has allowed it to adjust to social change and new needs. As the South African Constitutional Court related, women "were deprived of their opportunity to manipulate the rules to their advantage through the interplay of social norms, and at the same time, denied the protection of the formal legal order."[3] Some of the most destructive outcomes of these trends are their impact on gendered distributions of power and women's livelihood security. With the erosion of women's ability to control land and derive wealth from it, they lose a critical opportunity to achieve asset parity with men, one of the most fundamental levers of social and economic power. Faced with the prospect of being evicted from her husband's community, a woman's survival is at stake. In the absence of this power and steeped in a climate of extreme risk, many remain economically dependent on men and deprived of the capacity for self-determination, escape from which is impeded by the asset poverty cycle.

### International and National Norms

While international law provides little protection for property rights in any general sense, women and some other vulnerable groups have legal protection from international law against discrimination with respect to property, including land. Box 17.1 highlights key provisions of both legal and voluntary instruments for women's property rights.

**Box 17.1 Women's Land Rights under International Human Rights Law**

**Convention on the Elimination of All Forms of Discrimination against Women (1981)—CEDAW**

Article 14(2) State Parties shall take all appropriate measures to eliminate discrimination against women in rural areas in order to ensure, on a basis of equality of men and women, that they participate in and benefit from rural development and, in particular, shall ensure to such women the right (…) to enjoy adequate living conditions, particularly in relation to housing (…)

Article 15 2. States Parties (…) shall give women equal rights to conclude contracts and to administer property and shall treat them equally in all stages of procedure in courts and tribunals.

Article 16 1. States Parties... shall ensure: (…) The same rights for both spouses in respect of the ownership, acquisition, management, administration, enjoyment and disposition of property.

**Protocol to the African Charter on Human and Peoples' Rights on the Rights of Women in Africa (2005)**

Article 1 (k): 'Women' means persons of female gender, including girls;

Article 6 States Parties (…) shall enact appropriate national legislative measures to guarantee that:

(j) during her marriage, a woman shall have the right to acquire her own property and to administer and manage it freely.

Article 7: States Parties (…) shall ensure that:

(d) in case of separation, divorce or annulment of marriage women and men shall have the right to an equitable sharing of the joint property deriving from the marriage.

Article 19: States Parties shall take all appropriate measures to:

(c) promote women's access to and control over productive resources such as land and guarantee their right to property (…)

Article 21 1: A widow shall have the right to an equitable share in the inheritance of the property of her husband. A widow shall have the right to continue to live in the matrimonial house. In case of remarriage, she shall retain this right if the house belongs to her or she has inherited it.

2. Women and men shall have the right to inherit, in equitable shares, their parents' properties.

The revised 2022 version of the U.N.'s Voluntary Guidelines on the Responsible Governance of Tenure of Land, Fisheries and Forests in the Context of National Food Security provides:

3.B(4). Gender equality: (…) States should ensure the equal right of women and men to the enjoyment of all human rights, while acknowledging differences between women and men and taking specific measures aimed at accelerating de facto equality when necessary. States should ensure that women and girls have equal tenure rights and access to land, fisheries and forests independent of their civil and marital status.

4.6. States should remove and prohibit all forms of discrimination related to tenure rights, including those resulting from change of marital status, lack of legal capacity and lack of access to economic resources. In particular, States should ensure equal tenure rights for women and men, including the right to inherit and bequeath these rights.

These are powerful statements of intention, but some African governments have not ratified them. Even where ratified, they are rarely referenced by national courts or otherwise enforced. Most national constitutions simply prohibit discrimination based on sex or gender. While such general statements should be read as applicable to land, some constitutions (e.g. Lesotho, Uganda, Botswana and Liberia) include "claw-back clauses," which, after guaranteeing gender equality generally, withdraw that protection by exempting customary law or specifically women from the prohibition of discrimination with regard to land rights (Ezer, 2016). Even absent such caveats, there is often a failure to operationalize the gender equality concept even in modern and relatively progressive land legislation, as in the new Liberian Land Rights Act. Retrograde judicial rulings have thwarted the intention of equal rights provisions, as in Zimbabwe (Giovarelli, 2006). The South African Constitution contains a provision specifically intended to prevent such evasions. While culture and religion can be asserted against constitutional requirements, it is also provided that this cannot be done if it would violate South Africa's Bill of Rights (Ezer, 2016).

Advocates for gender equality in land rights have rarely advocated for laws granting women a right to as much land as men, or a wife a right to as much land as her husband. They have called for daughters to inherit shares of land equal to that of sons. Such a provision is by itself little help to a widow or a divorcee to land. Even where a portion of a deceased's estate is reserved by law specifically for spouses or children, regardless of sex, some countries provide limited to no restrictions on testamentary freedom. In such cases, a male landowner can provide by will that his land shall go exclusively to his sons. One finds such law not only in some African countries, but also in most countries in the global north like the United States where most states grant full testamentary freedom.[4]

## Approaches to Strengthen Women's Land Rights

There are a variety of different approaches to addressing gender inequality. The most direct is for the state to give women state-owned land. This can be done easily, but most women live under patrilocal custom, relocating to their husbands' communities when they marry. Projects have sought to advance gender equity by arranging for the allocation of customary land to women's groups—usually by a traditional authority—to implement project land development strategies, for example, reclamation of degraded land. If these groups have no established status under custom or statutory law, they are unlikely to retain the land after the project ends. The community or other local authority, when the contract is over, often takes the land from the women who have developed it and reassigns it, or requires the women to hand over control of the land to their husbands. This is likely where a firm legal basis for the women's landholding has not been established, requiring first forming a legal entity (e.g. an association or, in countries with simplified company laws, a company) that can hold rights in land and concluding a contract vesting the land in that entity.

Other approaches to addressing gender-based discrimination with respect to land access and security of tenure in African contexts include:

1. Reforms seeking to address gender inequities in the national, statutory law on land. An important example involves rights between husbands and wives. In several countries in southern Africa, colonial-period laws condemned women to a perpetual minority status and radically limited their ability to deal with land, requiring that a male relative represent them. Several countries have since repealed such provisions. Other offending provisions can be difficult politically to repeal and the effects on behavior change are often marginal (Englert & Daley, 2008). A study of 17 countries comparing legal frameworks governing women's rights in west Africa against actual practice revealed that most countries had incorporated gender equality provisions into their legal frameworks governing inheritance of assets, including land. In seven countries "only 43% of widows report inheriting any assets, and even fewer (27%) report inheriting the majority of assets" (Bouchama et al., 2018, p. 12).

2. Identifying and recognizing such limited rights as women may have under custom and obtaining their legal recognition. Ezer (2016, p. 73) suggests that "[e] ffectively navigating the complexities of customary law can turn it into an asset." She argues that codifying customary rules could be helpful if certain conditions were observed: compliance with human rights law; a process rooted in community engagement; a focus on core values and a process for customary law's ongoing development (Ezer, 2016).
3. In the land registration context, some title registration programs have sought to promote voluntary registration of household land in some form of joint ownership between the husband and wife. Where provisions have been made in African countries for the voluntary co-registration of land to couples, results have been disappointing. In Kenya approximately 5% of land is jointly registered by married spouses and only 1% is registered solely to women (Federation of Women Lawyers, Kenya, n.d., p. 1). In Uganda 16% of land is registered in the names of women (International Land Coalition, 2024). Creating the option for joint land ownership may not be enough to yield meaningful change unless it is accompanied by robust education and advocacy (Behr et al., 2023). In the few countries and projects requiring joint titling of land to married couples during systematic registration programs, impact may be short-lived if land registration authorities are not required and trained to ensure married couples register both spouses during land transfers. This is made more challenging by the proliferation of marriages that are not afforded legal recognition (e.g. traditional, religious or polygamous marriages) and consensual unions in sub-Saharan Africa. Joint land rights on paper also do not assure joint control rights over land in practice, but may be an important step toward influencing behavior change (Slavchevska et al., 2021).
4. Reforms that seek to specifically address the serious risk of loss of access to land when the husband sells the land, or when he dies and his kin seek to take the land.[5] This may be by creating a right of survivorship for widows, or laws that limit the power of the owner/husband to sell the land, i.e. laws that require that a wife co-sign or otherwise consent to any transaction by the husband regarding household land. It may be a law allowing a wife to raise an objection to an administrative or judicial authority to a sale on the grounds that it imposes a negative impact on the family. Kenya's Land Boards are a case in point.[6] Nevertheless, women who marry under custom or do not have their marriages registered are often not protected by these statutory provisions (Morrow-Richardson, 2004; Human Rights Watch, 2017; Oshodi, 2023).
5. Reforms that specifically legislate equality in inheritance and allocations of land by government. Rwanda and Ethiopia did so relatively recently. Their experience is discussed below.

### Ethiopia

One of the most widely implemented reforms to provide equality in land access to women began in Ethiopia's Tigray Region around 1980. It was carried out as pilots by a revolutionary movement in its "liberated areas." Box 17.2 provides background on and the effects of these reforms on women's land rights.

**Box 17.2 Early Reforms of Women's Land Rights in Tigray, Ethiopia**

The dominant form of customary land tenure in Tigray was *risti*, a system of land inheritance in both male and female lines. In this patriarchal society, land was largely held by men. Very few women had land of their own. Women did sometimes appear in a man's line of descent as presented in a land claim case. In 1980, an insurgent group called the Tigray People's Liberation Front (TPLF) began implementation of land reform in its "liberated areas." Customary practices prevailed in rural areas where the TPLF tested its reform. The reform confiscated monastery and church lands and the land of some nobles. It also reformed the customary land system. It gave all rural residents, both men and women, a right to their own land. In land allocation by village authorities women and men each received land equal in quality and amount, allocated by lottery. New inheritance rules specified that land should be inherited equally by male and female children. The impetus for change came directly from strong participation of women in the rebellion. In 1982, the TPLF indicated that 30% of its fighters were women. By the conclusion of implementation in 1985, the land of over 2,000,000 rural inhabitants had been redistributed. Land continued to be redistributed in adjustments through 1987, with many communities going through two or even three adjustments (as opposed to redistributions).

The impact of reform has been judged positive. World Bank-sponsored studies suggest significant welfare benefits for women, including strengthening women's power in their households and communities, giving them greater economic security and broader options for livelihoods. They were found to be excellent farmers given the needed inputs and access to plow animals. Fragmentation of holdings did not increase, as had been feared. There were more plots, but husbands and wives received contiguous land. They farmed their land together with the husband managing the land and marketing the crops. Divorces initiated by women increased, not surprisingly, given many women had been married in their early teens and domestic abuse was common. Divorces initiated by men decreased since women leaving their husbands took their land out of the marriage with them. Demands by female-headed households for legalization of tenancy grew and were accepted. Short-term rentals are now common between smallholders and often employed by female-headed households to get their land farmed.

Early economic studies and assessments by donor organizations suggest that reforms have been genuinely empowering for women. Factors limiting success of the policy are women's lack of plow oxen and other necessary implements and their generally lower community status making it difficult to enforce their land rights.

Source: Makonnen and Haile (1999).

What started in the Tigray Region, spread to the regions of Amhara, Oromia and the Southern Nations, Nationalities and Peoples' Region, later expanding to other regions (Tura, 2014). In all cases, regional constitutions, family codes and land laws prescribed equal treatment for women with respect to land. Implementation approaches have varied from region to region, as might be expected in a country of such geographic and ethnic diversity. In several regions, only female heads of household have been allocated land. In some cases, land certificates for family plots have been recorded in the names of both husband and wife. The program has had to grapple with difficult issues such as how to register women in informal unions and, in southern Ethiopia, how to register multiple legal wives. These women are provided little or no protection.[7]

The Ethiopian government has effectively developed national consciousness on gendered land issues and communicated demand for reform to regional governments which have been responsive. Actual progress is gradually occurring, especially in the more developed regions. Non-governmental organizations (NGOs) have played a lesser role than in many countries. Government-sponsored women's organizations have been active. State-led reform has been effective because of the organization of local governments and the culture of mobilizing rural people to address national priorities developed during the country's socialist period. Holden et al.'s (2011) study in Tigray using panel data found that following systematic land certification female-headed households rented out land with greater frequency than male-headed households partly because certification increased women's tenure security (and therefore willingness to rent out land) in a patrilineal society by reducing her risk of being evicted from her former husband's family land (Holden et al., 2011).

## Rwanda

In 2003, nine years after the genocide which caused shuffling people in successive waves of refugees and the displaced, Rwanda enacted a new Constitution. Article 26 declared that "parties to a marriage have equal rights and duties upon and during the subsistence of a marriage and at the time of divorce." Under the patrilineal customary system then, women had no right to own land and depended on husbands and male relatives for access to land (Kairaba & Simmons, 2010). In 1999, a law governing succession was passed, providing that daughters and sons were entitled to equal shares of inheritance. In 2004 a National Land Policy was approved that outlined an ambitious program of land policy and land tenure reform, calling for the replacement of customary land tenure by a statutory system founded on gender equity. Two land laws, in 2005 and 2013, have provided for implementation of those commitments.[8] Article 4 of the 2013 law provides for implementation of the constitutional priority of gender equity in landholding.

Implementation has largely taken place through the Land Tenure Regularization Program (LTRP), drawing on law requiring couples married in civil unions to jointly register their land. Initiated as a five-year program starting in 2009, the LTRP was implemented with technical and financial support of the British Department for International Development, with the aim of issuing a registered title to every landholder in Rwanda through a one-off, low-cost, community-based process of land tenure regularization. The program enabled women to own land individually or, in case of a civil marriage, as equal shareholders with their husbands. Under LTRP, 10,300,000 parcels of land were demarcated between 2009 and 2013, with 81% of land registered owned jointly by men and women, 11% owned by women only, 6% by men only and 2% by institutions (RISD et al., 2017, p. 3, citing Government of Rwanda, 2014). Despite the progress made, neither land nor family laws recognize property rights of women married under custom or in consensual unions with men (Jones-Casey et al., 2014). Women in these relationships often fail to have land they work with their husbands recorded in their names.

Following the implementation of the LTRP, there has been an increase in intra-household disputes over land, mainly relating to inheritance. These disputes have had a disproportionate impact on women. As women claim their statutory rights to own land jointly with their husbands and inherit land equally with their brothers, male family members (fathers, husbands and brothers) resist these changes. A young man quoted in an NGO report complained: "These new policies are distorting our culture. How can my sisters be granted to take away our land, which will end up in another family's hands" (RISD et al., 2017, p. 3).

Land disputes involving women are heard by their families, village authorities, administrative authorities and the local *Abunzi* committees. Although the *Abunzi* have their origins in custom, they were accorded statutory recognition and became regulated by statutory law and the Ministry of Justice. The membership of these committees must by law include 30% women.[9] Women often fail to have their cases reach the *Abunzi* and instead must present their cases to their families and then village authorities, who they often perceive as biased against them, before escalating them to official levels (Jones-Casey et al., 2014).

While the LTRP significantly increased the number of women accessing land titles alone or jointly with their husband (Gillingham & Buckle, 2014; Santos et al., 2014), challenges remain. Women in informal unions have no protection for their land rights. Women, especially widows, women in polygamous marriages and women in informal marriages and *de facto* unions and their children (especially orphans) are seriously disadvantaged and tenure insecure (Jones-Casey et al., 2014). Hopes that women would be able to borrow from banks once they had improved access to and security in land have been disappointed. This could be partially due to women's low general standing in society and partially to their reluctance to place land that feeds their family at risk. While those factors may be in play here, based on broad international experience there is little reason to expect that commercial banks will develop lending programs for smallholders, even male smallholders.

## What Have We Learned?

The Ethiopian and Rwandan cases discussed here involve governments with an exceptional commitment to gender equity. In both cases, post-conflict governments considered they owed a debt to women for either the role they played in armed struggles or the hand they were dealt as a result of them. Both were developmentally proactive governments with a commitment to radical change needed to achieve development. In one respect, they contrast. In Rwanda, civil society and NGOs have played important roles in supporting government's efforts and providing government valuable feedback. Government–civil society relationships have sometimes been tense and views on certain land issues have clashed. Civil society and NGOs have steadfastly supported the government's progressive stance on gender issues. In Ethiopia, a similarly proactive government took a decentralized approach under its federal system and benefited from strong village level institutions and their participation. The government was suspicious of NGOs, never giving them the opportunity to play the positive roles they played in Rwanda.

Regarding women's land rights, change on the ground requires more than a clear, well-considered law. Patrilineal inheritance combined with patrilocal marriage practices are key pillars of most customary governance systems in sub-Saharan Africa and are the means by which these systems reproduce themselves over time. It is the fundamental mechanism ensuring the lineage—in this case through the man—retains governance and control over land, moving family land from one male heir to the next, as described in Box 17.3.

**Box 17.3 A Rule or a Way of Life?**

Those who participate in donor-funded workshops on gender equity around Africa often sense that the exchanges of views are failing to connect. One official told me:

> They act as if we are talking about changing a rule. This is not about a rule but about the whole way we grow up and live. In my locked filing cabinet at home, in the bottom drawer, I have an old paper bag with sacred things in it, given to me by my father. I was given them in the initiation ceremony in the forest. I swore oaths that night in the forest and made a promise to my father. I live in Nairobi now and I am not sure what I should do with those things in the filing cabinet. Maybe I will take them back to our home village and give them to someone there. I am not sure about that but I do know I do not want to dishonor my oaths.

Since most legal reforms to women's land rights challenge centuries of patrilineal-based governance of land, the primary economic asset of rural communities, reform is a long-term struggle. The broader literature confirms the difficulty of persuading men that discriminatory customary practices are in some sense "wrong." Effective reform and reform implementation call for innovative approaches to advance women's land rights without undermining a central foundation of community-based land governance. This could mean putting stronger emphasis on ensuring daughters receive land in their lineage communities, efforts to shift customary norms for marriage to enable men to marry and settle in women's communities, providing daughters and sons equal value assets through gifts and inheritance such as higher education as a substitute for land and increased investments in sensitizing men about the benefits of women's land rights and a more gender-just society.

Measures gradually helping to reshape cultural norms include public education on gender and land issues, mobilization of external and internal support networks for reformers and building internal advocacy organizations, such as the national network of village-level paralegals trained by the Lesotho Federation of Women Lawyers.[10] The Federation provided key support for the Inheritance Act amendment of 1992 which gave married women the right to own land in their own name and helped enact the Legal Capacity of Married Persons Act 2006. Those supporting public education and advocacy efforts need to avoid pitfalls of their own gender biases. A woman lamenting how sensitization programs on women's land rights have been carried out in Rwanda frames the advice this way: "Men still have bad mindsets. People who train us on gender and land rights only train women, don't train men. We need to be trained together so that we both have a common understanding" (Jones-Casey et al., 2014).

## Notes

1 The author was a researcher at the Land Tenure Center, University of Wisconsin-Madison. She later worked at the Consortium of International Agricultural Research Centers, Landesa and for various United States Agency for International Development projects. She is now an independent researcher and contractor.

2 Analysis of data from six Sub-Saharan countries by Slavchevska et al. (2016) found that countries in east and southern Africa afforded more of these rights to women, while women's rights in all tenure categories were the weakest in the two west African countries studied (Niger and Nigeria).

3 Bhe and Others v. Khayelitsha Magistrate and Others (CCT 49/03) [2004] ZACC 17; 2005 (1) SA 580 (CC); 2005 (1) BCLR 1 (CC) (15 October 2004), quoting Nhlapo (1995). See: www.saflii.org/za/cases/ZACC/2004/17.html#:~:text=%5B68%5D%20I%20conclude%2C%20then,section%2036%20of%20our%20Constitution.&text=%5B69%5D%20Section%2036%20of%20the,human%20dignity%2C%20equality%20and%20freedom.&text=%5B71%5D%20The%20rights%20violated%20are,that%20include%20race%20and%20gender.

4 According to Gilmartin (2019), "The United States provides an extreme example of how testamentary autonomy has been bolstered in a way that offers a testator nearly unrestricted freedom to dispose of his or her property free of any obligation owed to dependents."

5 Examples include Ghana, Zambia, Zimbabwe, Nigeria, Malawi, Rwanda and Uganda (see Morrow-Richardson, 2004; Human Rights Watch, 2017; Oshodi, 2023; UN-Women, 2011; Andersson Dejurfeldt, 2020).

6 Kenya's land registration legislation provides an opportunity for women threatened by such a sale to object to Land Boards, an approach which seems to have been ineffective (Coldham, 1979; Migot-Adholla et al., 1994).

7 It is difficult to gauge the extent of implementation, While most sources judge it to have been impressive (Woldegiorgis, 1996), Tura (2014) questions this based on his study in Wolaita in southern Ethiopia.

8 Organic Land Law N° 08/2005 of 14/07/2005, determining the use and management of land in Rwanda, later revised to the current law N°43/2013 OF 16/06/2013.
9 Organic Law No. 02/2015/OL of 16/07/20.
10 The Lesotho Federation of Women Lawyers (FIDA) provides advice and information on women and children's rights so that they can achieve social justice. Current work focuses on property or land claims, domestic abuse, women's empowerment and children's rights. FIDA has trained and sustained a remarkable cadre of women paralegals, who remain in their villages after training and provide rural women with an unparalleled access to information and support.

## References

Andersson Dejurfeldt, A. (2020). Gendered land rights, legal reform and social norms in the context of land fragmentation: A review of the literature for Kenya, Rwanda and Uganda. *Land Use Policy*, *90*, 104305.

Behr, D.M., Grousssard, H., Khaitina, V., & Shen, L. (2023). Women's land rights in sub-Saharan Africa: Where do we stand in practice? *World Bank Group Global Indicators Brief* 23. http://documents.worldbank.org/curated/en/099432211092367495

Bhe and Others v. Khayelitsha Magistrate and Others, 49 CCT 3 (2004). www.saflii.org/za/cases/ZACC/2004/17.html

Bouchama, N., Ferrant, G., Fuiret, L., Meneses, A., & Thim, A. (2018). Gender inequality in West African social institutions. *OECD Publishing: West African Papers* 13. https://doi.org/10.1787/fe5ea0ca-en

Bruce, J. 2025.Written for this volume.

Coldham, S.F. (1979). Land-tenure reform in Kenya: The limits of law. *The Journal of Modern African Studies*, *17*(4), 615–627.

Cousins, B. (2007). More than socially embedded: The distinctive character of "communal tenure" regimes in South Africa and its implications for land policy. *Journal of Agrarian Change*, *7*(3), 281–315. https://doi.org/10.1111/j.1471-0366.2007.00147.x

Englert, B. & Daley, E. (Eds.) (2008). *Eastern Africa series: Women's land rights and privatization in eastern Africa*. James Currey.

Ezer, T. (2016). Forging a path for women's rights in customary law. *Hastings Women's Law Journal*, *27*, 65–86.

Federation of Women Lawyers, Kenya (n.d). *Women's land and property rights in Kenya: Training manual*. https://land.igad.int/index.php/documents-1/countries/kenya/gender-3/625-women-s-land-and-property-rights-in-kenya/file

Food and Agriculture Organization of the United Nations (2022). *Voluntary guidelines on the responsible governance of tenure of land, fisheries, and forests in the context of national food security* (1st rev.). FAO. https://doi.org/10.4060/i2801e

Gillingham, P. & Buckle, F. (2014). *Rwanda land tenure regularisation case study: Evidence on demand*. http://dx.doi.org/10.12774/eod_hd.march2014.gillingham

Gilmartin, B. (2019, July 29). How the United States shows us the potential consequences of holding testamentary authority to be a fundamental right. *WEL Newsletter*. https://welpartners.com/blog/2019/07/how-the-united-states-shows-us-the-potential-consequences-of-holding-testamentary-autonomy-to-be-a-fundamental-right/

Giovarelli, R. (2006). Overcoming gender biases in established and transitional property rights systems. In J.W. Bruce, R. Giovarelli, L. Rolfes Jr., D. Bledsoe, & R. Mitchell (Eds.), *Land law reform: Achieving development policy objectives* (pp. 67–105). The World Bank.

Government of Rwanda (2014). *LTRP independent review*. Kigali, Rwanda.
Henrysson, E. & Joireman, S.F. (2009). On the edge of the law: Women's property rights and dispute resolution in Kisii, Kenya. *Law & Society Review*, *43*(1), 39–59. https://doi.org/10.1111/j.1540-5893.2009.00366.x
Hilhorst, T. (2000). Women's land rights: Current developments in sub-Saharan Africa. In C. Toulmin & J. Quan (Eds.), *Evolving land rights, policy and tenure in Africa* (pp. 188–96). IIED Natural Resources Institute.
Holden, S.T., Deininger, K., & Ghebru, H. (2011). Tenure insecurity, gender, low-cost land certification and land rental market participation in Ethiopia. *The Journal of Development Studies*, *47*(1), 31–47.
Human Rights Watch (2017, January 24). "You will get nothing": Violations of property and inheritance rights of widows in Zimbabwe. www.hrw.org/report/2017/01/24/you-will-get-nothing/violations-property-and-inheritance-rights-widows-zimbabwe
International Land Coalition (2024, December 20). *Women's land rights in Uganda: Struggles and progress*. www.landcoalition.org/en/latest/womens-land-rights-in-uganda/
Jones-Casey, K., Dick, L., & Bizoza, A. (2014). *The gendered nature of land and property rights in post-reform Rwanda* (USAID LAND Project Report). https://genocideresearchhub.org.rw/wp-content/uploads/2022/11/policy-7.pdf
Kairaba, A. & Simmons, J.D. (Eds.) (2010). *Impact of the land reform on the land rights and economic poverty reduction of the majority rural especially women who depend on land for their livelihood: Rwanda case study*. Rwandan Initiative for Sustainable Development (RISD).
Makonnen, B. & Haile, M. (1999). *Impacts of the allocation of land to women in Tigray under the TPLF's land reform* [Research paper submitted for publication]. Institute of Development Research, Addis Ababa University.
Migot-Adholla, S.E., Place, F., & Olouch-Kosura, W. (1994). Security of tenure and land productivity in Kenya. In J. Bruce & S. Migot-Adholla (Eds.), *Searching for land tenure security in Africa* (pp. 119–140). The World Bank.
Morrow-Richardson, A. (2004). Women's inheritance rights in Africa: The need to integrate cultural understanding and legal reform. *Human Rights Brief*, *11*(2), 19–22.
Nhlapo, T. (1995). African customary law in the interim constitution. In S. Liebenberg (Ed.), *The constitution of South Africa from a gender perspective* (pp. 157–166). Community Law Centre at the University of Western Cape Town.
Organic Land Law No. 08/2005 of 14/07/2005 determining the use and management of land in Rwanda (Rwanda).
Oshodi, M. (2023, November 11). *The inheritance rights of women in Nigeria*. International Association of Women Judges. www.iawj.org/content.aspx?page_id=2507&club_id=882224&item_id=4986#:~:text=In%20conclusion%2C%20Nigeria's%20journey%20towards,the%20Federal%20Republic%20of%20Nigeria
RISD (Rwanda Initiative for Sustainable Development), GI-ESCR (Global Initiative for Economic, Social and Cultural Rights), & AAR (ActionAid Rwanda) (2017, February 13–March 3). *Parallel report to the United Nations Committee on the Elimination of Discrimination Against Women*. Rwanda 66th Session. www.ecoi.net/en/file/local/1401753/1930_1497428246_int-cedaw-css-rwa-26607-e.pdf
Santos, F., Fletschner, D., & Daconto, G. (2014). Enhancing inclusiveness of Rwanda's land tenure regularization program: Insights from early stages of its implementation. *World Development*, *62*(C), 30–41.
Slavchevska, V., Kaaria, S., & Taivalmaa, S.L. (2016). *Feminization of agriculture in the context of rural transformations*. World Bank.

Slavchevska,V., Doss, C.R., De La O Campos, A.P., & Brunelli, C. (2021). Beyond ownership: women's and men's land rights in Sub-Saharan Africa. *Oxford Development Studies*, *49*(1), 2–22.

Tura, H. (2014). Women's right to and control over rural land in Ethiopia: The law and the practice. *International Journal of Gender and Women's Studies*, *2*(2), 137–165.

UN-Women. (2011, February 27). *Inheritance laws*. www.endvawnow.org/en/articles/767-inheritance-laws.html

Whitehead, A. & Tsikata, D. (2003). Policy discourses on women's land rights in sub-Saharan Africa: The implications of the return to the customary. *Journal of Agrarian Change*, *3*(1–2), 67–112. https://doi.org/10.1111/1471-0366.00051

Woldegiorgis, O. (1996). *Gender and land access in Ethiopia: A report for the IFPRI*. Land Tenure Center, University of Wisconsin-Madison.

Yngstrom, I. (2002). Women, wives and land rights in Africa: Situating gender beyond the household in the debate over land policy and changing tenure systems. *Oxford Development Studies*, *30*(1), 21–40. https://doi.org/10.1080/136008101200114886

# 18 Assessing Land Tenure Reform

## Systematic Titling and Registration Reforms

Countries like Kenya, Rwanda, Côte d'Ivoire and Ethiopia have sought to replace customary tenure with individualized statutory land rights via systematic titling and registration, albeit providing different base tenures and bundles of rights. In Kenya, customary rights are replaced with freehold and the full breadth of rights associated with this tenure, including perpetuity and the right to permanently alienate land. The Rwandan model extends almost the full breadth of rights to landholders, except that allodial tenure belongs to the state, which provides landholders 99-year, renewable leaseholds. In Côte d'Ivoire, conversion of customary tenure to statutory tenure has involved granting a provisional tenure offering a more limited set of rights with the expectation that landholders should apply for fully marketable titles within ten years. Ethiopia has also opted for state ownership as the base tenure, but individual landholder rights are more restrictive. They are perpetual, but limitations have been imposed on their marketability.

These reforms confirm the rights of existing holders to land they occupy and provide them with secure tenure, or at least as secure as national policy allows. That alone should provide some protection against land-grabbing. The exception is in cases in which the government is the "grabber" and is acquiring the land for its own use or doing so for some private interest. In those circumstances, the compensation tends to be nominal, very modest and often nil, because the government concerned does not recognize customary rights on its land. Public consultation on implementation has improved. Field adjudication procedures have become less bureaucratic and more participatory. There is increasing flexibility regarding survey and mapping standards. Costs per hectare for these services have been reduced substantially. While misuse of the system by officials and local elites to their personal advantage does occur in the systematic registration context, it is modest compared to the grabbing of land that takes place using sporadic titling and registration. In systematic land registration all claims to land in an area are dealt with at the same time in a public manner, making opportunities for fraud much more limited (Loue, 2020).

As discussed in the preceding chapters, these reforms do not simply confirm customary rights as their promoters often imply. Instead, customary governance over

DOI: 10.4324/9781003476429-21

land administration is replaced with land administration by the state. Collective rights over community-held commons are typically excluded from rights recognition. Overlapping rights of secondary users such as pastoralists, hunter-gatherers and migrants are effectively erased, handing all rights to a single user, the farmer. Women's use rights under custom are often also put in jeopardy, especially if joint certification/titling is voluntary and where the law does not require subsequent joint registration of couples.

World Bank design teams for many systematic titling and registration (STR) projects have attempted to persuade governments to introduce mandatory joint titling of husbands and wives but have been unsuccessful. The Bank has agreed that such projects go ahead, posing a grave disservice to women. While endowing the registered holder with new rights, particularly the right to sell the land, with the same stroke of the pen, these new capacities expose them and their communities to risks of losing their land. By failing to register collectively or communally operated lands, they leave land these communities have claimed and historically relied on vulnerable to takings by the state. The Bank and other donors continue to invest vast amounts of resources year after year in STR, seemingly undeterred by its negative impacts.

Because land is so vital to livelihoods in rural Africa, farmers are often reluctant to accept risks that come with obtaining a marketable title. The governments involved must pay for the work, because the beneficiaries are not willing to do so and so the governments must borrow to fund implementation. Interest rates are waived to make these projects possible. The persistence of negative gendered impacts of these projects and their role in rendering community-held resources vulnerable to grabbing by the state suggests that aggregate impacts on tenure security may actually be negative. Registration involves destruction of all individual and community rights that do not fit into the individualized model of land tenure. Community rights and secondary rights of other private right-holders in the land—wives, children, neighbors—are stripped away. Communities lose rights that customary land tenure provided to natural resources in community commons. The community loses its territoriality and the potential for expansion into those areas. The reform tries to create a standardized, very simple form of land right that can move smoothly in commerce across political and cultural boundaries in impersonal land markets. The cost to landholders under custom is increased exposure to loss of a highly reliable transgenerational asset, the material basis of family and other social relationships, as well as a sense of community and a source of identity.

The economic foundation for these projects in Africa has been shaken by evidence from empirical studies that a registered title does not significantly increase the ability of former customary land tenure holders to secure commercial credit or increase yields (Place & Migot-Adholla, 1998; Bruce et al., 1994). Lenders pay more attention to socio-economic information on the borrower and the characteristics and location of one's parcels than to the nature of the title (Okoth-Ogendo, 1986). Studies carried out in the 1970s and 1980s raised other questions about the effectiveness of STR programs. In the 1970s, their lackluster performance threatened their support within the Bank, only to be saved by the enthusiasm rekindled by Hernando de Soto's restatement of these theories of economic development as a historical puzzle, solved by replacing "informal" customary land tenure with "clear" property rights and their titling and registration (de Soto, 2000). Further editions of these projects have been instituted in Madagascar, Rwanda, Côte d'Ivoire, Niger and Mali. Drawing on discussions with a wide range of discussions with African governments, the Bank's increasingly broader focus on land governance reform and needs assessments is a positive step toward a vision broader than simply STR programs (see Box 18.1). I've observed that the Bank's assessments and even critiques of STR usually produce recommendations that include some role for systematic titling and registration.[1]

**Box 18.1 The Changing Role of the World Bank**

The World Bank is the thought-leader and largest funder of land registration programs in the global south. The Bank's earlier programs of systematic replacement of customary tenure through titling and registration were in Kenya, and then southern Malawi. Both were criticized in the academic and development literature, generating more "push-back" than those in Asia because of the greater prominence and robustness of customary land tenure systems in Africa (Wangari, 1990).

After a hiatus of STR projects in Africa, the Bank re-engaged in them around 2000. The new energy behind them stemmed in part from the writings of Peruvian economist Hernando de Soto, an advocate for titles based on his experience with informal landholders in Lima, Peru. He became a fulsome advocate of the need to "formalize" not only urban land held informally but also land under customary land tenure. De Soto argued that if land cannot be sold, it cannot play the roles that land transfers play in mature market economies, such as mortgages, which can become a major source of domestic capital, something most countries in the global south are desperately short of. De Soto argued that formalization would increase land values, enriching and empowering poor landholders (de Soto, 2000). World Bank senior staff bought into these arguments, reinvigorating support for the Bank's land administration project portfolio.

Despite the market-oriented motivations for revival of replacement reforms, when the Bank took up these reforms in Ethiopia and Tanzania around 2000, it showed significant flexibility in responding to African policy makers' concerns about land sales leading to landlessness and concentrating land in the hands of a few. Prior to 2000, the Bank had made it a policy condition of these projects that national law allow the sale of registered parcels. When embarking on projects in Tanzania and Ethiopia, the Bank dropped its requirement that the registered title be freely marketable. The change could also have been influenced by lessons learned in earlier projects and criticisms raised by researchers.

Rather than embracing the de Soto argument, the rationale motivating the most recent major African registration projects (Ghana and Côte d'Ivoire) appears to be some combination of the assurance and incentive impacts of greater security of tenure, positive environmental impacts and the avoidance of land disputes and broader conflicts between individuals and between communities. While more realistic, they continue to assume customary landholders are tenure insecure, rather than substantiate it.

They also continue to ignore the problem of sustainability that seems so pervasive. The Kenyan land tenure expert, Shem Migot-Adholla, a Bank sociologist, looking back in 1997 at 40 years of rocky experience with systematic individualization and registration, concluded that it would have been better to rely on evolutionary processes and formalize results of that process only when there was real demand for formalization in the locality concerned. This would have been better than a forced march that left his country with dozens of "moribund" registers (Migot-Adholla et al., 1994, p. 116). It is clear today that many of these early projects were significantly premature, even if one approves of privatization as an objective.

The issue of effectiveness is receiving more attention due to the publication of two comprehensive reviews of empirical studies of the effects of titling and registration projects. The first of these studies, Lawry et al. (2017, p. 68), reports that:

> The evidence indicates clear benefits measured in terms of productivity and consumption expenditure or income, and suggests that long-term investment and increases in perceived tenure security are plausible channels through which tenure recognition may contribute to welfare.

Lawry's same review of the studies of African titling programs showed no support for the claim that a registered marketable title increases access to agricultural credit and enables investment to increase yields (Lawry et al., 2017, p. 68). This accounts for part of the disappointing results of these programs in increasing agricultural production. What improvement does take place is generally attributed to the "assurance effect." Increased security of tenure alone can increase farmer confidence and more substantial, longer-term investments. World Bank land projects are more cautious than in the past in their predictions of financial benefits to farmers from tenure reform. They tend to rely more on the relatively simple and defensible connection between tenure security and investment incentives, abandoning the fiction that a title would allow an African smallholder to access commercial credit.

With systematic registration projects in Africa, even these impacts have been weaker when compared with similar projects in Asia. Lawry and his team's explanation for this is the "Africa effect," a diminution of returns to government attempts to increase security of tenure because African customary land tenure systems have in most cases provided African farmers with tenure security they find adequate, so a registered title offers them nothing they feel they need (Lawry et al.,

2017). A second "study of studies" on the effects of land registration on agricultural productivity carried out by Singirankabo and Ersten (2020) reviews data from 85 studies. They find that: (1) there exists little data that clearly establishes that formal documents-based dealings in land leads to investment and increased production; (2) studies suggest that in some cases registration can threaten security in customary land tenure systems and even create generalized insecurity of tenure and conflict; and (3) present gendered implementation of land titling and registration seriously undermines women's access to land. The reviewers call for more research on the feasibility of programs of tenure securitization customized to meet local needs. It concludes: "Our results as well as those of the LTC (1990) suggest that large-scale land registration programs are unlikely to be economically worthwhile for much of sub-Saharan Africa at this stage of economic development" (Singirankabo & Ertsen, 2020).

Recent data collected under the Global Property Rights Index (Prindex), an endeavor to assess land tenure security globally, likewise finds that formal documentation of tenure is less associated with perceptions of secure tenure in Africa compared to other regions. Prindex and salient findings for its aggregated findings for countries in Africa are presented in Box 18.2.

**Box 18.2 Prindex**

Administered by the Overseas Development Institute and the Global Land Alliance, the Prindex database features a measure of perceived tenure (in) security of adult property-holders for 140 countries globally. It is based on a uniform survey that asks the question:

> *And in the next five years how likely or unlikely is it that you could lose the right to use this property or part of this property, against your will?*

Respondents are given the choice to select *very unlikely*, *unlikely*, *somewhat likely* or *very likely*.

The survey, delivered as part of the Gallup World Poll, is administered to a random sample of adults who either own or rent their residential property. Sample sizes are generally around 1,000 adults per country, somewhat larger for more populous countries to enable greater statistical integrity. In addition to demographic information, several additional questions are asked, including sources of tenure insecurity, confidence in land governance institutions and possession of tenure documentation (both formal and informal).

The survey is not directed exclusively to the head of household. Following random sampling of households, one person 18 years or older within the household is randomly selected, enabling Prindex to capture the tenure security perceptions of women, youth and older adults not identifying as head of household.

*What does Prindex tell us about the perceived security of tenure of Africans?* Prindex data reveal that, compared to other regions, the proportion of tenure insecurity is especially high in sub-Saharan Africa where 26% of sampled adults from 34 countries reported their tenure to be insecure (Prindex, 2022). Aggregate perceptions are lower in all other regions, except the Middle East and North Africa (Prindex, 2020). Contrary to expectations from the literature on women and land in Africa, perceptions of tenure insecurity among African women are not notably different from those of African men either regionally or within countries (Prindex, 2022). This changes when considering only married women, who are more tenure insecure than married men. Almost half of African women fear loss of land due to death of a spouse (Prindex, 2022).

*What can it tell us about the tenure security provided by customary institutions in Africa?* While Prindex offers insights about Africans' perceptions of their tenure security generally, the survey does not ask respondents to indicate if their land is under customary tenure or not. The fact that the survey is administered to urban, peri-urban and rural adults plus renters and owners alike narrows the slice of the sample that is likely to be governed by customary tenure. One could potentially exclusively examine rural landowners in Africa reporting on tenure security for a second parcel used for agriculture and assume they are governed under custom. Aside from the risk that the sample would be too small to report statistically robust findings, some of those sampled could be individuals who purchased rural land for farming or otherwise acquired it through non-customary means. The fact that sub-Saharan Africa shows the highest gap between urban adults reporting tenure insecurity (27%) versus rural adults (22%) (Prindex, 2020) may nod to *potential* tenure security enhancing effects of customary systems.[2]

*What can it tell us about the effects of formal documentation on tenure security in Africa?* The data suggest that formal documentation of tenure is less associated with perceptions of secure tenure in Africa compared to other regions. Hypotheses about what lies behind this trend include the so-called "Africa-effect," coined by Lawry et al. (2017) to explain the weak influence of formal tenure on agricultural productivity in Africa (Lawry et al., 2014, 2017). This theory suggests that the presence of (still) strong customary institutions in Africa may provide many landholders adequate tenure security, such that statutory documentation of rights does not generate substantial added benefit. There may be other explanations as well, such as whether the faith Africans have in the governance institutions of the state to protect their land rights may be particularly weak. The Prindex data show clear correlations between levels of reported tenure insecurity and countries' Corruption Perception Index and low rankings for World Governance Indicators non rule of law and government effectiveness. As such, there may be little trust in the protection afforded to documents backed by the state. The Prindex data are not equipped to say if either or both explanations for the weak effect of tenure documentation in Africa are correct. As their sponsors themselves admit, "Subsequent data collection efforts could help to illuminate why it is that documentation has not translated into improved security in these cases."[3]

When it comes to understanding the causes of tenure insecurity broadly, the Prindex data has limited explanatory power. Its major contribution has been to provide a host of valuable insights about tenure (in)security and its correlation with other factors which can then be used to inform field level research capable of reliably guiding policy decisions.

Source: Anna Knox (see Chapter 17, this volume).

Despite these aggregate findings, STR programs have not been wholly unsuccessful and in cases like Ethiopia and Rwanda have provided important tenure security benefits. Some explanations for their success may derive from the post-conflict realities that accompanied their reforms. Large areas of rural northern Ethiopia are densely populated, as is Rwanda. Population pressure on the land resource has been a concern in both countries for at least the last half-century. In both countries, many land users had been displaced during conflicts and customary land tenure systems were either terminated legally or badly disrupted on the ground. In Ethiopia customary land tenure had been legally nullified by the previous government, the Derg. In Rwanda, continuing to rely on customary land tenure was a non-starter. Rwanda had two major ethnic groups struggling with one another for power, a dynamic that also played out in the customary land tenure system (Bigagaza et al., 2002).

In both Rwanda and Ethiopia, post-conflict insecurity of tenure was strongly felt and articulated. Government support for the reforms was firm and public attitudes toward them were positive, in spite of both programs introducing important improvements in women's land rights (Deininger et al., 2008). Under the low-cost, locally based Ethiopian system, registered landholders seem to be successfully registering permitted transfers and successions. This is not so much the case in Rwanda, especially for rural land. Successes achieved in registering women's land rights appear to be eroding with subsequent transactions (Ali et al., 2021).

Individualization of tenure via systematic land registration programs will continue, as will support from the World Bank. The Bank will stress the opportunities provided for increased security of land tenure, farmer investment in their holdings, increased yields, benefits from leasehold markets, empowerment of the poor, conflict prevention and resolution, environmental benefits and other benefits for which they have little solid evidence. It is tempting to describe the history of STR as a tool wandering the world looking for a purpose. The spread of these projects remains motivated by donor confidence that the tool will ultimately facilitate the development of a market in land rights that will in turn spur economic development. They remain faithful to this conviction, largely ignoring many of the negative impacts from these projects that have been well documented for decades.

The African governments are happy to pursue these projects for the sake of objectives usually not articulated in project documents, such as nation-building and firmer political control achieved through imposition of a common statutory land tenure regime for the country. Another potential benefit to governments, which is sensitive and only obliquely mentioned in project documents, is the potential for land taxation when there is a centralized depository of land ownership records. Capacity constraints in governments have meant that this has largely not been realized. On a political level, there is also the power that goes with knowledge of who is holding land and where it is held. At the same time, and perhaps most important to those in government at national level, registration provides information on where land exists which is *not* titled or otherwise protected by national law, and so may be "available" for public and private appropriation by concessions or other development initiatives. Officials act on that knowledge in both their public and private capacities. Kenya has provided a case study of how manipulation of land issues for political purposes can undermine public order and development.

From the viewpoint of the national host institution, usually a ministry of lands, a multi-million-dollar land project generates a variety of benefits for staff and officials of the implementing government agency, from salary supplements (to ensure competent managers and technically competent staff are hired for the project) to vehicles with petrol and drivers, ample per diem for travel on agency business, international travel and training opportunities in the sophisticated technical skills required by the high-tech components of many of these projects. All these considerations are in play. In the end, I am convinced, national governments and their officials are drawn to these projects because they advance the agenda of the center to subdue and bring under its control the indigenous institutions and power structures of the rural areas.

At the right scale and place, these projects can be highly relevant and meaningful for development. They have been most appreciated in cases such as Uganda, Sudan, Ethiopia and Rwanda, where the reform assisted land sectors disordered by violence and natural disaster. Post-conflict situations will offer important opportunities. Land registration may also have a legitimate role as a capstone exercise, to confirm titles on an area which has largely accepted sale of land, typically on the edge of an urban area. There are also major opportunities to use the system constructively in urban contexts, especially in the vast peri-urban sprawls of shanty towns, often larger than the "concrete city" itself, with their lack of tenure security and their informal (but not customary) normative structures. In countries with recent violence and other post-conflict contexts, one finds land and structures at central locations in urban areas that are either occupied by former soldiers or other groups which exert influence and act to prevent the municipality from exercising its legitimate control. While the area may legally be state land, there may be actors occupying the land who have legal claims to it. In such situations, the potential for empowering the poor and generating national capital are huge compared to rural areas now being subjected to STR. The potential in these areas is discussed further in Part IV on futures. Essentially, one could say that systematic land registration projects have been poorly targeted. Indeed, there is something odd about the development of a major innovation that is taken to the countryside before it is proven in urban contexts.

**Preservation of Customary Tenure**

In contrast to the countries discussed above, Ghana, Botswana and Uganda have sought—at least initially—to preserve customary land tenure, while also confirming rights at the household or individual level. Nevertheless, their models of preservation are distinct in terms of the base tenure regime and the institutional arrangements selected to govern customary tenure. In Ghana, customary land secretariats created to administer customary land records are the subject of contested control by traditional authorities and the government's Land Commission. Vesting customary lands in chiefs in a climate of increasing demand for land for investment and urbanization has established a path for powerful traditional authorities to enrich themselves at the expense of community members who risk being dispossessed of their land.

In Botswana, the fact that its first president after independence was also a senior chief put him in a unique position to champion a land tenure reform rooted in preserving customary land rights. This was also facilitated by the existence of the numerically and politically dominant Tswana tribe, whose tenure norms became the basis for how newly created local land boards would administer customary tenure. Initially, traditional authorities occupied a role on these boards and lineage dominated who could be eligible to receive land. Reforms to the law now permit allocations of customary rights based on citizenship and residence, rather than tribal affiliation. Groups with very different land use practices such as the migratory San have been excluded from landholding or even well-protected use rights. The law has further been revised, so that district land boards may allocate statutory common law leases on tribal land once reserved exclusively for allocation of customary tenure. The result is an institutional arrangement still rare in Africa where both civil and customary rights are administered by boards applying both customary and civil law and consisting of both central government-appointed officials and elected members. Decades of revisions to the law have seen gradual weakening of protections for unregistered customary rights and the intervention of central government in the affairs and decisions of the land boards.

In Uganda, the situation is muddled. The 1996 constitution restored customary land tenure to a status equivalent to private and state ownership of land. State-created local land committees and the support system for that institutional structure have been underfunded and proven inadequate for the task. This was in part due to last-minute modifications in the reform legislation that reflected an unwillingness of government to commit the necessary resources to enable the viability of that institutional framework. If further steps are not taken to support that system, the reform may simply create a holding pattern while private ownership—which has a long history in Uganda and enthusiastic advocates—gradually expands at the expense of unprotected customary rights. This is even more probable owing to the fuzzy nature of customary ownership. The legal framework does not make it clear what happens if customary land is sought for a concession. While Uganda's 1965 Land Acquisition Act provides for compensation when land is expropriated (Article 2(2)), it does not require paying the market value of land acquired.

## Preservation of Community-based Customary Tenure and Governance

The third model of reforms is more recent and has largely sought to recognize tenure at the community level, while also providing opportunities for recognition of customary rights at individual and household levels within or outside of those communities. Reform models, as adopted by Tanzania, Mozambique and Liberia, are far from replicas.

Under the Village Land Act of 1999, Tanzania grants legal recognition to customary tenure and permits communities to exercise their customary tenure systems to the extent that they do not conflict with civil or common law, including instituting prohibitions against discrimination based on sex. The law shifts administration of customary tenure from traditional authorities to village assemblies (all adult village members) and elected village councils, relegating traditional authorities to settlement of disputes. The reforms call for lands claimed by villages to be demarcated and issued certificates by the state, after which village land councils may issue certificates for "rights of occupancy" to households within the village. Rights of occupancy may be leased, bequeathed, mortgaged and sold to other members of the village, or even outsiders with village assembly approval.

Implementation of Tanzania's model, often heralded as progressive not only for its recognition of customary tenure, but also governance by village level institutions, has been protracted and many communities have never had their land registered. Those communities whose land was registered remain vulnerable to having it appropriated. The president still has the power to redesignate village land to another legal category and reallocate it (e.g. to a concessionaire). Because land is state-owned, there is perhaps a greater tendency for the state to intervene. This is difficult to say for sure. Even in countries where customary tenure has been granted as a base tenure, akin to freehold, much depends on laws governing land acquisition, compensation and involuntary resettlement as well as on political economies surrounding investor demands for land.

Another barrier to implementation may be the law's sheer length and level of detail. Its primary author argued that this was necessary in order to minimize discretion in its application and thereby close off opportunities for abuse. Knight (2010) observed that its length and complexity posed barriers to understanding and implementing it. One wonders if Tanzania may have been better served by a shorter, broader law accompanied by regulations setting out specifics for its application?

In the case of Mozambique, all land rights are protected under a single tenure type, referred to as DUATs, and are only distinguished by their method of acquisition; they may be acquired from the state or automatically granted through occupation—either under good faith or by virtue of customary occupation. The latter do not need to be registered to have legal validity, and entire communities can claim to hold a DUAT based on customary occupation. Communities hold DUATs directly from the state and have the option to have their boundaries delimited and their DUATs certified. The law is not explicit on the subject of land governance within community DUATs. It is generally understood that customary authorities may continue to exercise governance authority within them.

Mozambique's 1997 Land Law is short and spelled out largely in layman's terms, in sharp contrast to the Tanzanian law. It omits any criteria for communities to identify their land claims and customary governance jurisdictions. This lack of parameters for how communities should self-identify may potentially be problematic by creating conflicts within communities and among its various levels of customary leadership. It also opens the door for powerful traditional leaders governing large areas to try to exert dominion to the detriment of meaningful community participation and decision-making, which would be more likely to emerge within smaller governance units. These types of risks perhaps explain why in Liberia the 2018 reforms, informed by considerable participatory research, established that community land rights be recognized at the (intermediate) clan level. The capacity for community member participation in decision-making was a key consideration.

Like Tanzania, Mozambique has suffered from stalled implementation of community DUAT certification, which largely relies on the support of non-governmental organizations and donor funding. Despite undocumented DUATs' legal strength, in practice these are vulnerable given such claims' lack of visibility. Certification is also required for communities to enter into deals with investors. Investors would often prefer the simplicity of not having to deal with negotiating with communities, a political economy reality that local governments are all too aware of and often seek to accommodate to the detriment of protecting community land rights.

Another lesson to be drawn from Mozambique is the futility of government efforts to suppress land markets. By law, land cannot be sold, although improvements on land can. In rural areas, people wishing to transfer their land and sell improvements to another party must secure the permission of local government authorities. Where there exists a strong demand for land and willing sellers, absent robust community governance structures that regulate land sales, an underground market develops with the value of land and improvements wrapped into the sales price.

Liberia's recognition of customary tenure came about through a lengthy, but highly inclusive political process seeking to overcome a history of major structural inequality that afforded the vast majority of customary communities no legal rights to their land. Even its reform period was plagued by contradictions with some of the same people pushing for reforms also doling out concessions to investors, giving rise to increasing disputes with local communities. Like Mozambique and Tanzania, implementation of reforms has been slow. Since passage of the 2018 Land Act, 14 communities have had their land formally certified thanks in large part to the support of successive United States Agency for International Development projects. The modest headway can partly be attributed to numerous steps communities need to pass through leading up to certification. Close observers have pointed to malfeasance by the leadership of the Liberian Land Authority and chronic underfunding of the authority as major reasons for the slow progress.

## Takeaways

Looking broadly at the experience of land tenure reform in sub-Saharan Africa, one begins to see certain patterns emerging that convey important understandings about what gives rise to their relative strengths and weaknesses, successes and failures.

Among countries that may opt to replace customary tenure with statutory certificates or titles, there are important lessons to be derived from the STR approach despite their many drawbacks. Rwanda, Kenya and Côte d'Ivoire have sought to replace rights under custom with a statutory right that is marketable. Ethiopia has embraced a simplified, inexpensive system of land registration whose primary objective is strengthening security of tenure as opposed to facilitating land markets. To support the growth of formal land markets, many STR reforms have embraced the promise of technological fixes and sophisticated electronic land information management systems requiring substantial training of land administration staff and are typically costly to maintain. This may lead to sustainability issues over time, especially as donor assistance phases out.

Most countries adopting the replacement model and even those that have otherwise leaned into registration of marketable individual land rights (e.g. Uganda) have struggled to put in place effective decentralized land administrative systems necessary to record subsequent transactions, and to make recording of such transactions affordable to small-scale landholders. These statutory systems involving registries, cadasters and land information systems, created at great cost, have often been left largely unused and even abandoned, raising an issue not adequately addressed in the research so far by the Bank or independent researchers.[4] This situation occurs not just due to community resistance or disinterest, but through reliance on overly sophisticated technologies and lack of administrative staff who possess the strong administrative skills necessary to operate them. Created using donor funding, operation of these costly systems is typically beyond the capacity of most cash-strapped African countries. Since new titleholders see little value in formally recording their land transactions, let alone paying for it, land administration units are unable to finance their own operation through fees for services, making these systems difficult to maintain. As a result, the registry rapidly loses validity. Since Ethiopia's system is much more low-cost and decentralized with fewer transactions to record, it may prove more feasible for both government and landholders to keep the system up to date and relevant.

There is remarkable consistency in external skepticism about these projects by outside experts, who have looked at the experience and found it disappointing for one of two reasons: (1) the registrations were premature in relation to development of a felt need for tenure change, which assumes that in time such a demand might or will develop; or (2) they are wasteful and unnecessary and should not be done at all, which assumes that no such demand will develop because people are not interested, being happy with their customary land tenure. Most worrying is that having provided a bureaucratic solution for maintaining a viable registry, there ends up being little for district land offices to do. The perpetual wave of customary land tenure and traditional authority has swept over these islands of supposedly privately owned land, leaving behind drawers of sandy files. This is the same phenomenon Migot-Adholla observed in Kenya and refers to as "'moribund' registers" (Migot-Adholla et al., 1994, p. 16; see also Place & Migot-Adholla, 1998; Lawry et al., 2017). There is a need for a multi-country research program assessing the viability of district land registries several decades after implementation of systematic land registration to examine what is left of the system and the extent to which the intended changes in land tenure (e.g. individualization and alienability) have been sustained. One might expect the experience to be quite different between rural communities and those near urban centers where lineage-based customary tenure has lost its relevance.

Reform models seeking to preserve custom are promising in that they provide a means by which governance of customary tenure is not replaced outright with statutory tenure. In Botswana, replacement of customary authorities with selected and Ministry-appointed land board members to administer both customary and statutory tenure on tribal land has put the country on a replacement path, however gradually. Tanzania's model of locally elected councils and Mozambique's model that refrains from interference with customary land governance seem better poised to preserve the evolution of customary tenure. Whether their governments have the incentives and resources to implement them seems questionable. The same concern might also apply to Liberia, which continues to face considerable demand for land from investors.

While countries like Uganda, Ghana and Liberia have afforded allodial tenure status to customary land tenure, customary land rights in these countries face many of the same vulnerabilities that they face in tenure regimes where they are subservient to state ownership, including failures in implementing registration programs that, through recording and making land rights visible, provide landholders with greater protection against land-grabbing. This points to a major failing on the part of both governments and donors, which tend to be drawn to the relatively swift and inexpensive process of reforming laws and less prepared to invest in undertaking lengthy reforms on the ground. Ghana stands apart with long-standing political power wielded by traditional authorities. The law's vesting of land rights in chiefs poses a major threat to tenure security of customary landholders. In all three cases, opportunities for wealthy interests to acquire land and for those who administer land to benefit from such transactions appear to underpin both failures of implementation and abuses of authority.

There are certainly no easy legal fixes for achieving gender equity in land rights given the predominance of patrilineal inheritance and patrilocal marriage systems, which also act as key pillars of community-based governance in sub-Saharan Africa. While STR programs can require or strongly encourage registration of joint land rights among spouses, such tenures seem unlikely to endure when land is passed down to children or otherwise transferred. In cases of inheritance, jointly registered land will continue to be passed along to sons, who, if they register the land at all, are not likely to register it jointly with their spouses. More creative solutions considering how women's land rights can be strengthened without disrupting the foundations of community-based governance and tenure are worthy of consideration, including avenues for strengthening the claims of daughters to land in their natal communities. Legal and technical solutions also need to be accompanied by effective socio-behavioral change approaches that resonate with men, tackle stigmas surrounding masculinity and overcome men's fears of sharing control over land with women.

While many of these conclusions might appear to paint a negative outlook for the potential for reforms to protect customary land rights and do so equitably, this is not my intention. Rather, by raising the myriad complex issues that often accompany or ensue from reforms, it should equip us with a better understanding of challenging realities and give rise to locally relevant innovations that can move countries from point A to point B in a quest to provide improved tenure security to their citizens. Tenure reforms are important. Land plays so many different functions, economic, political and social. If land tenure is simply treated as a variable that can be manipulated to achieve other national objectives, the result is often a slew of unintended consequences that may ultimately undermine the value of the reforms.

When there are not a huge number of tenure reforms in sub-Saharan Africa, the contexts in which they operate are often quite varied and unique. This makes it hard to generalize about what is likely to work and what isn't. Even among STR programs, there are differences. Some offer tenures that are fully marketable while others have restrictions on transactability; they often have different priorities, such as managing disputes and preventing violent conflict, increasing investment and productivity or creating a basis for increased public revenue generation. In sorting out which technical approaches provide the best results in different reform models, it is easy to imagine that these will determine the success or failure of land registration. What matters more is whether the project responds to a felt need of government and intended beneficiaries.

Because context plays a major role in the success of tenure reforms, serious studies and frank analysis of the legal, socio-political and economic contexts of a suggested program area need to precede detailed project design, choice of indicators to measure success and decisions on implementation approaches. Development agencies have some staff who have, through experience, developed good instincts for such issues, but they are no substitute for careful, structured studies and consultation with locals to explore the often delicate political and cultural issues involved.

## Notes

1 See, for example, Lamb et al. (2016).
2 However, the data also reveal renters to be more tenure insecure than owners, and renters are much more common in urban areas; this likely accounts for the largest share of the urban–rural tenure insecurity gap.

3 See Frequently Asked Questions (FAQs) about Prindex methodology. www.prindex.net/about/faqs/.
4 I know of no attempt to assess, whether for a single project or on a national basis, the amount of land registered under STR programs for which the registration systems have largely ceased to be used by the beneficiaries and have as a result become hopelessly out of date. I have repeatedly observed this outcome in my own field visits to registries, and suspect the situation is more widespread than is generally realized.

## References


Ali, D.A., Deininger, K., Mahofa, G., & Nyakulama, R. (2021). Sustaining land registration benefits by addressing the challenges of reversion to informality in Rwanda. *Land Use Policy*, *110*, 104317. https://doi.org/10.1016/j.landusepol.2019.104317.

Bigagaza, J., Abong, C., & Mukarubuga, C. (2002). Land scarcity, distribution and conflict in Rwanda. In J. Lind & K. Sturman (Eds.), *Scarcity and surfeit: The ecology of Africa's conflicts* (pp. 50–82). Institute for Security Studies.

Bruce, J.W., Migot-Adholla, S.E., & Atherton, J. (1994). The findings and their policy implications: Institutional adaptation or replacement. In J. Bruce & S.E. Migot-Adholla (Eds.), *Searching for land tenure security in Africa* (pp. 251–265). The World Bank.

de Soto, H. (2000). *The mystery of capital: Why capitalism triumphs in the west and fails everywhere else*. Basic Books.

Deininger, K., Ali, D.A., & Alemu, T. (2008). *Impacts of land certification on tenure security, investment, and land markets: Evidence from Ethiopia* (Policy Research Working Paper No. 4764). The World Bank.

Knight, R.S. (2010). *Statutory recognition of customary land rights in Africa: An investigation into best practices for lawmaking and implementation* (Legislative Study No. 105). Food and Agriculture Organisation of the United Nations. www.fao.org/4/i1945e/i1945e01.pdf

Lamb, T., Endo, V., & Stanley, V. (2016). *Systematic property registration: Risks and remedies*. The World Bank. May. https://documents1.worldbank.org/curated/en/163361485942263162/pdf/112345-WP-P148874-PUBLIC-FirstRegistrationproblemsFINAL.pdf

Lawry, S., Samii, R., Hall, A., Leopold, D.H., & Mtero, F. (2014). The impact of land property rights interventions on investment and agricultural productivity in developing countries: A systematic review. *Campbell Systematic Reviews*, *10*(1), 1–104. https://doi.org/10.4073/csr.2014.1

Loue, D. (2020). *Cote d'Ivoire -AFRICA- P157206- Cote d'Ivoire land policy improvement and implementation project – procurement plan* (Report No. STEP30300). The World Bank. http://documents1.worldbank.org/curated/en/146791582533829011/pdf/Cote-dIvoire-AFRICA-P157206-Cote-dIvoire-Land-Policy-Improvement-and-Implementation-Project-Procurement-Plan.pdf

Migot-Adholla, S.E., Benneh, G., Place, F., & Atsu, S. (1994). Land, security of tenure and productivity in Ghana. In J. Bruce & S. Migot-Adholla (Eds.), *Searching for land tenure security in Africa* (pp. 97–118). The World Bank.

Okoth-Ogendo, H.W.O. (1986). *The perils of land tenure reform: The case of Kenya*. University of Nairobi digital repository. https://erepository.uonbi.ac.ke/bitstream/handle/11295/35689/059_The%20perils%20of%20land%20tenure%20reform-%20the%20case%20of%20Kenya.pdf?sequence=1&isAllowed=y

Place, F. & Migot-Adholla, S.E. (1998). The economic effects of land registration on smallholder farms in Kenya: Evidence from Nyeri and Kakamega districts. *Land Economics, 74*(3), 360–373. https://doi.org/10.2307/3147118

Prindex (2020, July). *A global assessment of perceived tenure security from 140 countries* (Comparative Report). https://prindex-dev-bucket.s3.eu-west-2.amazonaws.com/documents/PRINDEX-Comparative-2020-DIGITAL_3.pdf

Prindex (2022, December). *Land indicators and the land rights agenda in sub-Saharan Africa's development challenges: Insights and issues from Prindex survey results* (Working Paper). https://prindex-dev-bucket.s3.eu-west-2.amazonaws.com/documents/Prindex-Land_rights_in_Sub-Saharan_Africa.pdf

Singirankabo, U.A. & Ertsen, M.W. (2020). Relations between land tenure security and agricultural productivity: Exploring the effect of land registration. *Land, 9*(5), Article 138. https://doi.org/10.3390/land9050138

Wangari, E. (1990). *Effects of land registration on small-scale farming in Kenya: The case of Mbeere in Embu District* [Unpublished PhD dissertation]. New School for Social Research.

Part IV

# Land Tenure Futures

# 19 Conclusions

## The Land Tenure Situation

The cardinal fact of post-colonial land tenure in Africa is the state's insistence that it owns all or most of its land and other natural resources. The new, independence-era governments considered that Africa's farmers and herders needed to be protected against the anticipated negative impacts of a land market, and this could best be achieved through the state owning all land. The reforms prioritized by African governments in the years after independence were reforms of customary land tenure. Almost all of the land tenure reforms in the years since independence have sought to take the management of farmland from African communities and vest it in individuals and their households, usually, in the case of farmland, in the households who had already been using them under customary land rights. In some cases, individualization is also privatization of ownership, in that, as in Kenya, the ownership as well as the right to use and manage the land was vested in private individuals, usually a household head. In most reforms there was no privatization of ownership. Land was either vested in or retained by the state and only a limited use right, often not alienable by the holder, was provided to the individual holder. In both cases, the new title came from the state, no longer from the community, and the titleholder had to depend on the state for protection of that right.

Most land in Africa is legally owned by the state. That state-owned land is the land that, during the colonial period, was left for the African people and in most cases is still occupied by their descendants under customary tenure. With a few exceptions (Kenya, Tanzania, Rwanda and a few others), the tenure reforms legislated after independence were only implemented in limited areas in the new states. If custom was left *de facto* as the operating system of land tenure, this was not true of the role of traditional authorities with respect to customary land. Most independent African governments, led by western-educated new elites, feared the power of traditional authorities and so eliminated or reduced the role of those authorities in governance of land under customary land tenure. They saw control of land, the essential resource in an agrarian society, as the source of that power. New governments usually failed to establish an effective national system of land governance and administration. They enacted tenure reform laws which they lacked the ability to implement. In most countries an effective system of land management and

DOI: 10.4324/9781003476429-23

administration would have required a political accommodation between the new national political elite and local, traditional elites. The new elites rejected this path. As a result, customary land tenure still actually controls the use and allocation of land in most of rural Africa. Despite traditional authorities being substantially disempowered by the state under national law, in practice, they retain considerable authority among their own people.

Instead of creating a unified national tenure for all land, the policy of state ownership for all or most rural land created a reality gap between the *de jure* government ownership of land and *de facto* customary land tenure as the normative reality on the ground. While custom continued in force, traditional authorities' enforcement of prohibitions or limitations on sales of land gradually weakened, resulting in an increasingly contentious and extensive grabbing of relatively inexpensive land by outsiders using both market mechanisms and state appropriation. As they became conscious of the growing value of that land, traditional authorities, most of whom perceived the damage being done to their customary social system by loss of land to outsiders, initially resisted land sales. As pressures on their land have grown, however, and with their authority undermined by the state, some traditional authorities are turning into middlemen between local sellers and outside buyers or are themselves selling land traditionally regarded as held in trust by them for their communities. The net result has been that in these nation states, weak national governments largely lost or failed to attain effective control of evolving patterns of land tenure and landholding in their rural areas.

The state has in most cases proved a poor custodian of the land resource. Most land loss by African farmers and herders in the years since independence have been the result of actions by state agencies and their employees, either for public or (often) their own private purposes. Custom itself has evolved under the influence of the national economies, which are predominantly market economies. Growing demand for land from outsiders to the traditional tenure systems has given rise to significant numbers of often illegal sales of customary land. Black and grey markets in land rights have developed in peri-urban areas and along roads. In some cases, custom has embraced outright sales of land. They have sometimes flourished even where land sales are prohibited by both custom and national law. Land values and markets are not dependent on law for their existence, and the ability of governments to create them or prevent their operation by legal fiat is limited.

Most western development economists assumed that such sales would involve more efficient local farmers buying land from less efficient farmers. But efficient farmers have been unable to access the credit they needed to expand their owned holdings and often had to rely on leasing additional land. Even with registered titles, commercial credit was not available to smallholders, and it has instead been outsiders who have acquired large areas of land in an illegal or illegitimate fashion, often for land speculation rather than productive investment. Traditional authorities, the most effective barrier to sales of customary land, have had their legal authority over customary land undermined or are being co-opted into selling customary land to outsiders, usually from commons or other land not yet allocated to local households. In the absence of effective state regulation of transactions in customary land, national and local officials along with local traditional authorities often collude to facilitate irregular transactions to their mutual personal financial advantage. Staff of land ministries are in an especially strong position to act as intermediaries in such irregular transactions. Registration of an ownership or user right in the name of the purchaser provides legal validation for a transaction. Such processes are becoming new *de facto* land administration systems in some countries.

Africa's rural communities and people have been subjected to a chaotic competition of different values, the values of community protection and control over land versus the values of individualism and profit-making from land. Governments, by undermining the traditional institutions but failing to create the institutions necessary to implement the new values, have failed in most cases to provide security of tenure to the continent's smallholders and herders. Individuals are confronted by conflicting expectations, involving real risks if they choose incorrectly. African governments have also largely failed to establish a land-based system of revenue generation to capture a significant part of the growth in land value.

There are important exceptions to this rather grim picture. A few countries, notably Kenya, Uganda and South Africa, have major areas of land under freehold ownership. Only Kenya has expanded this substantially. All three still have areas under customary tenure and a few countries, notably Mozambique, Botswana, Liberia and Ghana, have conferred legal recognition of customary land tenure comparable to that of state or private ownership. But throughout the continent, and even in these countries, tenure security of African smallholders and herders remains weak. Throughout Africa, it has been dramatically undermined by the appropriation of customary holdings in the Great Land Grab.

Administrative and financial weakness of most African governments, corrupt practices that are all too common in their land management and administration, and the role of ethnicity and custom in land matters and the consequent political fragility of many of these states were evident prior to the Land Grab. The enthusiastic concession-granting by African governments in the Grab was an assertion of state ownership of land by weak governments who had so far failed to take control of this national asset and use it to generate revenue. They took advantage of the rising world demand for land to mobilize the support of powerful interests, both foreign and urban-based investors, wresting land from African smallholders and their communities, attempting to direct a portion of the income generated by the concessions to government coffers. It was a policy path offering not only revenue for governments, but also opportunities for personal enrichment to those in government and in some cases local elites who have been involved in identifying land for and negotiating concessions.

Today, African policy makers must deal with increasingly diverse tenure landscapes, with areas of land under a variety of different tenures, often associated with different farm sizes, production technologies, crops, supply chains and marketing strategies. Some of these tenures are legal under national law. Others lack clear legal recognition and protection or are illegal under national law. These different tenure domains include:

1. Areas of smallholder and herder agriculture in which customary land tenure remains largely in force, with traditional authorities still effectively in charge of land allocation and management, but with little or no effective protection under national law.
2. Areas in which government has used its legal ownership of land to take that land from traditional users and allocate it to larger-scale producers, foreign and domestic, on long-term contractual instruments such leases and concessions.
3. Areas in which customary land tenure systems have evolved and continue to evolve under pressures from the larger market economy, with land acquiring market value and being bought and sold, with or without legal recognition of the new right.
4. Areas in which customary land rights have received legal recognition and legal protection, either as customary rights, rights of ownership or statutory use rights conferred by the state on smallholders/herders using legally government-owned land.

In most countries all these tenure categories are present, but in widely differing amounts and in different geographical configurations reshaping the structural landscape of African agriculture and augmenting both collaborative and competitive interactions between concessionaires and customary landholders.

This is a rapidly developing situation with much unknown. We have a good deal of public information regarding the terms of concession contracts but much less on their actual operations and only fragmentary information on how they are affecting those whose land became part of the concession and those occupying areas surrounding concessions. Such major gaps in knowledge exist for those areas in which customary law continues in force and even those in which reform programs have been implemented. My own observations suggest that some areas subjected to systematic titling and registration have, through failure to update registers for transactions and especially successions, led to a virtual abandonment of the new system and a reversion to a modified customary tenure. Full or partial abandonment of replacement tenure exists, but we have no clear idea how common it may be. I suspect it is more extensive than acknowledged by supporters of systematic titling and registration programs. There is an important need for more and better research on these issues, research that tracks the embrace or rejection by registered holders of opportunities to document land transactions over time, the different incentives affecting their decisions and winners and losers in this process. Policy makers need to know more to plan for the future.

## The Ongoing Land Grab and the Response

In the context of the Global Land Grab, we must ask not only how far the land takings have met asserted government objectives (e.g. jobs for local farmers and social infrastructure construction), but how much harm has been done to the viability of smallholder agriculture by the takings of the last decade. This question can only be answered for a particular country or regions within a country. It will depend on how much land held under custom has been taken, what it was used for by the customary holders, and the quality and extent of the land remaining with them. In assessing harm to communities, one also needs to examine the rate of expansion of clearing the concessions' lands and bringing them under cultivation. As a general rule, new concessions take longer than expected—in some cases decades longer than expected—to start cultivation on most or even a major part of the concession and meet initial production targets. Different concessions may pursue different policies regarding continued use by customary users of land not yet under production.

In some countries it is only now coming to light how much land has been committed to concessions. In the heyday of concession-issuing, concession-granting was not well organized and systems for tracking how much land was being issued to whom and where did not exist. Some communities find that considerably more of their land than expected has been included or more has been taken than was contracted. Researchers and those in government whose responsibilities include rural livelihoods worry about the uncertain future of rural food security, increased rates of rural–urban migration, unsustainable intensification of farming in what land remains to smallholders and herders, new pressures for overuse and degradation of forests and pastures, and more conflict over and politicization of disputes over land issues, including conflicts with ethnic dimensions.

It is important that every effort be made to avoid worsening this situation in countries that have experienced major land takings for outside interests, while also urging a fairer and more careful consideration of applications for concessions in countries less seriously affected. While the majority of farmed land in Africa is still farmed by small farmers under customary land tenure (Chimhowu, 2019; citing Wily, 2017, p. 468), this may change as more concessions are granted and more land already under concession is put into production. I see no reason why we should not expect new waves of demand from the world economy for land from Africa to grow food crops. Given that most land held under custom remains poorly protected under national law and insecure, what can be done to ensure communities do not endure further uncompensated takings?

Although the explosion of land acquisitions for large-scale farming by foreign investors since 2000 has slowed for now, the full implications of these acquisitions for land policy in Africa will only become clear in time. Remarkably little has been published on their long-term impact on the larger tenure situation. Future analyses of country land tenure situations will need to track changes both on concession holdings and their use as well as on the land still being used under customary tenure. I'm concerned that the backfire from the impact of these concessions will be more serious than is being assumed. Note that the Grab in the early 2000s set off a secondary wave of domestic investment in land through leases or local concessions.

The Great Land Grab was not part of African countries' development plans before it began. While many countries already welcomed foreign investment and made land available to investors, there was little investment and usually modest areas of land allocated to them. There were painful precedents to the huge appropriations of land during the Grab. The major funding and the amounts of land demanded combined with the response of African governments to that demand created the Grab. It was a response on a scale that has changed or is changing how fundamental tenure issues are seen by governments. Most importantly for our purposes, it has broadly undermined security of tenure of African smallholders and herders.

From relatively early stages, there were critical or at least cautionary responses to the Grab from elements in the development community. The most concrete and substantive response to the ongoing appropriation of land under custom was the Voluntary Guidelines on the Responsible Governance of Tenure of Land, Fisheries and Forests in the Context of National Food Security (the "VGs") approved by the UN Committee on World Food Security (CFS) and governments in 2013. Key provisions on customary land rights are provided in Box 19.1. As their name implies, the VGs are voluntary and not enforceable, but with their endorsement by the CFS they provide an authoritative source on agreed-upon "good practice" for governments. Implementation of the VGs as well as enforcement of International Labour Organization (ILO) Convention 169 in the case of Indigenous Peoples are potentially important tools for protecting rural communities from land acquisitions and restoring a waning sense of security of tenure among customary landholders. But to be effective, powerful actors, especially governments, wealthy donors and highly organized civil society, would be needed to compel their uptake by governments and the private sector.

**Box 19.1 Customary Land Rights in the Voluntary Guidelines**

The VGs recommend in provision 5.4:

> States should ensure that policy, legal and organizational frameworks for tenure governance recognize and respect, in accordance with national laws, legitimate tenure rights including legitimate customary tenure rights that are not currently protected by law; and facilitate, promote and protect the exercise of tenure rights. Frameworks should reflect the social, cultural, economic and environmental significance of land, *fisheries and forests.*

Other provisions of the VGs provide similarly:

- 9.1 urges acknowledgement that land has "social, cultural, spiritual, economic, environmental and political value to indigenous peoples and other communities with customary tenure systems."
- 9.4 calls for states to provide "appropriate recognition and protection of the legitimate tenure rights of indigenous peoples and other communities with customary tenure systems."

- 9.5 provides that where indigenous peoples and other communities with customary tenure systems have legitimate tenure rights to the ancestral lands on which they live, states should recognize and protect these rights. Indigenous peoples and other communities with customary tenure systems should not be forcibly evicted from such ancestral lands.
- 9.6 calls on states to consider adapting their policy, legal and organizational frameworks to recognize tenure systems of indigenous peoples and other communities with customary tenure systems.
- 7.1 calls on states, when they recognize or allocate tenure rights to land, they should establish safeguards to avoid infringing on or extinguishing tenure rights of others, including "legitimate tenure rights that are not currently protected by law."
- 9.11 provides that states should respect and promote customary approaches used by indigenous peoples and other communities with customary tenure systems to resolving tenure conflicts within communities, and that for land used by more than one community, means of resolving conflict between communities should be strengthened or developed.
- In 14.1, it is provided that where appropriate considering the national context, states should consider restitution for the loss of legitimate tenure rights.

Other provisions call for recognition of sale and leasehold markets in land rights (11.1), and urges, in some detail, that where possible, "legal recognition and allocation of tenure rights of individuals, families and communities should be done systematically, progressing area by area in accordance with national priorities, in order to provide the poor and vulnerable with full opportunities to acquire legal recognition of their tenure rights" (7.4).

The word "legitimate" recurs regularly in the VG provisions. While a definition is not provided, "legitimate" customary rights are by no means limited to those customary rights already legally recognized by the national law of the country concerned. Paragraph 5.4, which calls upon governments to protect "legitimate customary tenure rights that are not currently protected by law," makes it abundantly clear that that customary land tenure and land tenure more broadly can be "legitimate" without being recognized and protected by national law.

In 2016, legal guidance prepared by the Food and Agriculture Organization of the United Nations (FAO) on the VGs sought to clarify the meaning of "legitimate" tenure rights. It emphasizes that they include not only rights recognized by national law, but also those enjoying broad social acceptance by local communities, such as customary land rights, even when they are not recognized in formal law (Cotula et al., 2016). The VGs call on states to recognize and respect legitimate tenure rights and to incorporate into law those not currently included. Provision 4.4 of the VGs leaves it up to states to define categories of legitimate rights to be incorporated into formal law. Cotula et al. (2016) point out the challenges of accommodating competing views of which rights enjoy social legitimacy and the potential for powerful groups to hold sway over determinations of legitimacy. In 2021, the FAO provided further legal guidance on implementation of the VGs, confirming that "legitimate tenure rights" refers to both legal and *social* legitimacy as prescribed by communities themselves, including customary rights to land held as commons of communities (Cotula & Knight, 2021). While the VGs urge states to legally recognize socially legitimate tenure rights not reflected in law, the voluntary nature of the guidelines means that it is up to the states to decide which socially legitimate rights—including customary tenure rights—merit official recognition, if any. The real questions, it seems to me, is whether donors will use willingness to adhere to the VGs to condition their support for a country's land sector and whether they will offer countries a robust set of proposals for which socially legitimate rights could be recognized in law and how this can best be done.

The VGs are not the only guidelines governing land tenure in Africa. Over the past several years, the African Union (AU) has embarked on various efforts to strengthen land policy and governance by its member states with the understanding that they play an essential role in countries' ability to achieve their broader development goals. Two important ones are the Framework and Guidelines on Land Policy in Africa (F&G) and the African Union Land Governance Strategy, 2023–2032 (LGS). Box 19.2 points to how these policies serve distinct purposes and how they treat recognition of customary tenure and women's land rights.

While the FAO continues to actively promote VG good practices on the protection of customary land rights, their uptake by African countries is slow and their impact is as yet unclear (Myers & Sanjak, 2022). The vast majority of land takings for concessions in Africa appear to have violated the terms of the VGs with regard to how they should treat customary landholders. This has serious implications regarding the future implementation of the VGs, making the rollout of the VGs an uphill struggle. They are only advisory advice to governments with considerable incentives to simply pay "lip service" to their principles. Adequate protection of customary land will ultimately depend not just on restraint on the part of governments in response to the VGs, but also on their acceptance of a requirement that a taking only be allowed with the free and informed consent of communities and their adoption of tenure reforms that create real rights for communities.

**Box 19.2 Framework and Guidelines on Land Policy in Africa (F&G) and the African Union Land Governance Strategy, 2023–2032 (LGS)**

Published in 2010, the F&G establishes a set of principles and recommendations for AU member states to embark on land policy reforms and successfully implement them. Preparation of the F&G was led by the African Union Commission (AUC), the United Nations Economic Commission for Africa and the African Development Bank via the Steering Committee of the Land Policy Initiative and with the support of FAO, the Fund for Agricultural Development, Swedish International Development Cooperation Agency, the

Rockefeller Foundation, UN-Habitat, the United Nations Development Programme and the World Bank.

The LGS was developed by the AUC's Department of Agriculture, Rural Development, Blue Economy and Sustainable Environment and the African Land Policy Centre—formerly the Land Policy Initiative—to further the realization of land-related objectives outlined in the African Union Agenda 2063. Responsible land governance is also seen as critical to accelerate implementation of the African Continental Free Trade Area to advance intra-Africa trade, a major goal of AU member states. The LGS was formally launched in November 2023 at the biennial Conference on Land Policy in Africa organized by the United Nations Economic Commission for Africa, the AUC and African Development Bank. As of this writing, only the 2021 draft of the strategy could be accessed online.

The two documents serve distinct purposes. The F&G focuses much more on recommending *processes* for developing and implementing land policy. Emphasis is laid on: (1) these processes being participatory with a high level of engagement by those impacted by land policy, including women; (2) ensuring adequate budget and capacity for implementation with decreased reliance on donor support; (3) decentralization of governance authority; (4) garnering the necessary political will to enable implementation; and (5) sequencing the steps in land policy development and implementation and allocation of adequate time to the process in order to secure buy-in. By contract the draft LGS offers a much more prescriptive road map for achieving specific land policy goals within the region. Its overarching goals are centered on responsible and equitable land governance, tenure security and environmental sustainability. The draft places emphasis on four major technical approaches for its member states to achieve these aims: (1) land rights formalization and administration; (2) promoting equitable land access and security of tenure for women, youth, pastoralists and other vulnerable groups; (3) land use planning that is responsive to climate change and disaster management; and (4) responsible land investments.

Both documents relay stances on different policy issues, some of which are not entirely consistent. Perhaps the most striking difference is in how they regard customary tenure and statutory registration of land. The F&G is explicit about the importance of recognition of customary land tenure while also acknowledging the need to reform them to improve women's land rights. It argues, "land policies should seek to remove age-old rigidities in traditional structures and systems which tend to discriminate against women while at the same time building on and thereby improving indigenous tenure arrangements." It calls for recognition of community-based and local land governance institutions and their interface with statutory systems. The LGS, on the other hand, regards customary tenure and the dearth of recorded and registered statutory land rights as major sources of tenure insecurity in

Africa. Moreover, the LGS frames documented land rights as necessary for investment and access to credit, stating:

> In other countries where the community enjoys the usufruct rights, farmers feel some insecurity of tenure due to lack of landownership proof and do not effectively carry out the investments in land as they do not have opportunities to access the bank loans.

Another major distinction in how the two documents frame women's land rights. The F&G emphasizes strengthening women's rights to documented land claims, and less so their rights within customary systems, where they are typically undocumented. Specifically, the F&G calls for "legislation that allows women to enforce documented claims to land within and outside marriage" and provision of "equal rights for women to inherit and bequeath land, co-ownership of registered land by spouses and the promotion of women's participation in land administration structures." The LGS, by contrast, places much stronger emphasis on broader social inclusion, with one of the five Strategic Objectives of the strategy centered on "Enhancing the security of land tenure and access to land and other productive resources for women, youth, persons with disabilities, pastoralists and other vulnerable groups in Africa."

Nevertheless, they are limited to carrying out assessments and advocating for women's representation on land management committees. Specific measures to strengthen women's statutory land rights—such as joint land titling and reforms to matrimonial property regimes are not prescribed.

Source: Anna Knox (see Chapter 17, this volume).

The major western donors have likewise not reacted as strongly to the Grab as might have been expected, given their involvement in the development of the VGs. There has been unease in the development community with the rate and extent of large-scale land acquisitions, but major donors often politely express these as "concerns." It seems doubtful that major western donors will take a meaningful stance against what some critics have called a "recolonization of Africa by wealthy private interests" from outside Africa.

## The Future of Land Tenure Reform

Africa's experience with tenure reform has not been encouraging, but this does not mean that governments can turn away from the issues involved. Problems remain unresolved. Mistakes made in earlier reforms need to be corrected. There will be new ideas emerging requiring legal changes to implement them.

***The Concession Sector***

While there has been some excellent research on the nature and extent of the Grab, we need to understand its immediate impacts far better than we do now. We have some notion of the land-related processes going on within and around these new and hastily established commercial farms, but many of our ideas about what is happening depend too much on the contracts and do not necessarily reflect reality. The following list points to where economic data is needed to assess the success or failure of concessions:

1. Information on the amounts of land actually brought under cultivation or used for other purposes (e.g. herding, timber clearing and sale) and by whom; where use has been initiated but later abandoned and the reasons for this; and by whom and for what purpose the land had been used earlier and the community it belonged to under custom.
2. Assessment of the extent of customary landholders' loss of land including gender-disaggregated data on communities that have lost land and the extent to which their members remain there or have moved. If they have relocated, where did they go? Urban or rural destinations? Are they gaining access to land in the new location, and if so, how? If they remain in their affected communities, are they still farming, and how do they access land? Is it the same land they used before or different lands? Are new forms of land management developing on the concession, such as smallholder tenancy, contract farming or patterns of land use reminiscent of latifundia–minifundia relationships in Latin America?
3. Analyses of the uses of surrounding lands remaining under customary land tenure. Have pressures on rural land in these areas increased? Is that pressure resulting in changes in land use patterns and new farming practices? Are the new practices environmentally sustainable?
4. Examination of government programs to support smallholder agriculture. Have policies regarding smallholder agriculture been changed on paper and/or in practice? What steps is government taking to provide education, training and direct support for farmers? Have the support programs for these farmers been enhanced and adjusted to meet new needs of smallholders or have resources for such programs been reduced? To what extent has development of private sector supply and marketing services for large farmers had benefits for smallholders?
5. An appraisal of popular reaction to land acquisitions, including patterns of resistance. What is the extent and frequency of expressions of resentment, such as crop burning, sabotage, sniping, labor disputes and land disputes? What is the extent of support for popular resistance by national political parties, foreign non-governmental organizations (NGOs), national and community-based civil society organizations (CSOs) and NGOs, traditional authorities and concession labor forces? What is the response of concessionaires and government authorities to resistance? What mechanisms, if any, are used to resolve disputes, and how effective are they?

My expectations regarding the future of concessions are colored by my experience in Liberia, a particularly extreme case of appropriation of customary land for concessions. Is there a legal basis for regaining the land lost? The VGs refer to restitution and litigation challenging concessions, which may be possible. But as in the case of Liberia, it would probably take a regime truly committed to indigenous rural people's interests for this to happen. There may be opportunities to attempt to force termination of concessions that are failing and the return of land to customary owners as provided for in Liberia's 2018 Land Rights Act. Litigation might also be appropriate to restore land to communities who held them under old aboriginal or other titles that may have been trampled in the rush to establish concessions.

Disputes and conflict between concessionaires and local people were deeply worrisome during the lifetime of Liberia's Land Commission. In much of Africa, there is growing conflict over land. That conflict is due in large part to the failure in many countries to recognize custom and harmonize the operation of the state and customary systems. Adding a layer of conflicts involving government/investor takings of customary land could make this situation worse. It is bitter to have to work as hired labor on land that was until very recently owned by one's family and governed by one's community. Takings at scale can also impact the shape of national politics and further inflame an already volatile political issue. This is materializing in Liberia and seems likely to do so in other countries, especially in areas heavily affected by concessions.

***Resources for Reform***

Those discussing the future of customary land tenure and future tenure reforms today have resources that did not exist a few decades ago:

1. A more nuanced understanding of customary land tenure and especially why the members of groups holding land under custom value those systems.
2. A better appreciation of the capacity and limitations of central government in addressing the needs of rural populations.
3. A better understanding of the power relations in traditional authority structures and the patterns of informal interactions that have developed between them and central and local government land administrators with respect to land.
4. A body of documented experience on prior land tenure reforms from African contexts, rather than just those from European or other countries in the global south.
5. A body of experience with different systematic land titling and registration approaches, and replacement reforms more broadly.
6. A strengthened appreciation of the need for institutional innovations of local land administration and management that would allow for integrated management of land under diverse tenures.
7. A body of experience with participatory approaches to tenure reform, including the roles that can be played by NGOs and private contractors.
8. A realization that competition for land and the power it confers are at the heart of much of the growing violent conflict in Africa, its increasing number of failed states and post-conflict contexts.

***Possible Tenure Futures***

This book does not propose an overall reform strategy with regard to customary land tenure. That would contradict a point made repeatedly throughout the book: the details of local contexts matter greatly in planning any reform of customary land tenure. Instead, it suggests a number of possible approaches, some more novel than others, that might be worthy of consideration by those with a solid understanding of a particular reform context.

***Land Titling and Registration Programs***

In most contexts around the world, land registration programs and land administration systems have been developed first in urban contexts with respect to potentially high-value land, from which such systems are expanded to rural areas. In Africa, systematic land registration has often been initiated in remote, rural areas. The country studies of reforms in Part II of this book suggest that this has resulted in disappointing economic impacts, been more disruptive of social systems and values than would have been likely in urban areas, and—because the rural landholders were not willing to pay for this "service"—has left government covering most of the costs of establishing and maintaining these systems.

At same time, Africa's urban areas have rapidly grown to include vast informal settlements that exist beyond the systems of land administration and public services of formal cities. In most cases, government (often the municipality) claims ownership of informally settled land and considers the settlers to be illegal "squatters." Often the municipality does not wish to regularize the land to assign tenure to its occupants but also cannot take the risk of violence or political repercussions involved in forced removals of residents. This creates a deadlock in some instances and frequently failure by government to accept responsibility for the provision of basic public services to informal settlement areas.

The potential of these areas lies in their value due to their location and in the substantial increases in value that would accompany a registered title, the security it would provide and in some cases a replanning of land use. The challenge would be to convene an interactive process to explore the investment required, potential benefits from such a program, and what would be a reasonable process and fair allocation of land to occupants and government. The World Bank or another major donor with experience with land registration might, through its provision of the needed investment funding, convince the interested parties of the feasibility and mutual benefits (secure access to land, more efficient land use, improved public services and rental or tax revenue) from such a project. This model might be helpful depending on context. In many cases mistrust of government will be difficult to overcome. This would require a neutral third party, performing fact-finding, mediation, facilitation and monitoring roles.

***Managing Change in Customary Land Tenure***

Many governments in Africa have lost control of land tenure change in the customary tenure sector. A shift in custom to allow sales in land is taking place, driven less by reforms than by the largely market economy context in which these customary systems now exist. Informal land administration arrangements among local officials, traditional authorities and central government officials have developed to manage and allocate the benefits of such transactions. (See discussion and sources in Chapter 13.) If the state attempts again to impose a uniform national tenure system, it seems unlikely to succeed. Concession-granting in recent years can be seen as an expression of frustration with such an approach.

Some degree of control by central governments might instead be re-established by showing more flexibility and greater tolerance for a diversity of land tenures in the short and medium term. One option would be to formalize informal arrangements, accepting and legalizing those *de facto* processes. Such arrangements, while they leave much to be desired, at least may reflect local realities of legitimacy and power better than some other options.

Alternatively, governments might employ a reform strategy allowing local communities to make important decisions about their land tenure, placing those decisions in their own hands and restoring their sense of agency. Communities could choose to remain under an evolving customary tenure. If they did, they could manage their land under their local, village-level traditional authorities. The role of the upper levels of traditional hierarchies, such as paramount chiefs, should remain minimized, depending upon the circumstances of the community as provided by law and custom. A community could decide if it wished instead to manage its land through a local committee periodically elected by all adult residents, male and female. The land committee should be empowered to alter and restate customary rules, including basics such as entitlements to land and transactions in and inheritance of land, effective when such changes are conveyed formally to the responsible ministry for government land. For the longer term, governments might facilitate changes in desired reform direction through involvement of NGOs and CSOs as facilitators of community-based reform. This has been pursued to some extent by the NGO Namati in Uganda, Mozambique and Liberia. That program involved working with local communities to document, reform and formalize community practice under national law. See Chapters 15 and 16 for details.

Another variation of tenure reform would allow the landholding community to decide when and how their land should move onto the market. See Box 19.3 for such a tenure reform experience in rural China.

**Box 19.3 Timing Conversion of Community-Held Land to a Marketable Right**

Teaching at Renmin University in Beijing in 2014–2015, I observed that Chinese municipal governments captured most of the rapid increase in land value taking place when municipalities expanded through expropriation of rural land on their borders. They initially paid very little compensation to the communities because under Chinese law, the land was owned by the rural collectives and could not be sold. Once expropriated it became state-owned municipal land. The land was then sold by the municipality to urban residents or real estate development companies as long-term capitalized and marketable leaseholds. These can be sold and so are very expensive. The difference between what the municipalities paid for the rural land and what the municipalities received when they sold it was a major windfall for the cities, the source of much of the growth of urban infrastructure in those years. For at least two decades this was an off-budget source of funding, but by 2015 farmers were demanding more for rural land. Municipalities had also begun to embark on ultimately disastrous "land banking" practices in which they acquired but held onto land as valuable "banked" leaseholds, assets against which they could borrow funds from public and private credit institutions. When the housing market and the market for leaseholds collapsed some years later, the overleveraging of those assets left many municipalities deeply in debt.

During my three years in China, a major reform of rural land tenure took place. Rural collectives, who owned rural collective land, were now permitted to lease out large pieces of their land for agricultural or other purposes. This land had been held and farmed by household members of the collectives since the early 1980s when the Chinese system of large-scale collective production collapsed. As indicated above, rural collective land could not be sold. Now, because the land had not been sold piecemeal by household members of the collectives, the collectives could first replan and densify the use of some parts of their community land for improved housing and residences with garden plots for their members. Then they would lease most of their farmland in large units on long-term leases (with substantial payments up front) to private investors or state enterprises in large units, for impressive rentals. The rural collectives invested the money from the rents in town businesses owned by the collective, both small industries and shops.

In both cases, the ability of the Chinese government to adapt tenure to exploit site-specific market opportunities had a major impact on benefit distribution by converting land rights that had not been marketable before to ones that were marketable. In the first instance, the main beneficiaries were the municipalities, while in the second, they were the landholding rural community. These offer useful experiences for those considering options for future tenure reforms in sub-Saharan Africa.

Source: Bruce (2017).

If a government could recognize an African traditional land holding community as the owner of its land and allow the governance structure for that community to sell that land—not now but at some point in the future—this might have the same potential of directing a good deal of the sudden growth in the value of that land to the benefit of the local community. Even if the government did not want to recognize ownership by the community, one option might be to recognize a right less than ownership, say a long-term leasehold right to their land. In this way, the community could sell part of that leasehold right as part of its transition to marketability. This would allow the state to retain ownership of the land and the community to use the rental revenue for its own development, perhaps subject to a tax. That process would need to be managed by a community institution with a clear legal status, the right mandate and the capacity to implement it. Community members should decide when and if their land should be leased out. While there are dramatic differences between the Chinese and African context, the fundamental need being addressed is the same: how the transition from non-marketable to marketable land rights can be managed so as to give the current landholders a major part of the new value created in that transition, as many of them exit agriculture and join the migration to towns and cities. As in the case of other reform options discussed here, it could only be utilized in a limited number of contexts and then with important adjustments.

Leaving behind this option inspired by the Chinese experience, it is important that the expansion of formal titles and replacement of customary tenure by them should be limited to circumstances in which there is a strong demonstrated demand for titling by the local landholders under custom and only implemented with their informed and voluntary consent. While Chimhowu (2019) suggests that sales of land have become sufficiently common to allow a general, national legalization of land sales, I would suggest a more graduated approach, led by communities in most cases, or perhaps through a zonal approach. Where there is such a demand, any tenure conversion should involve a land use planning exercise that would identify community and state land as well as individually and family-owned land, to be registered in individual and community titles, or both in a mixed system. Household tenure could be leasehold from the state, or ownership, or whatever formal tenures are recognized in national law. Importantly, any community-led decision-making process should meaningfully take account of the priorities of women, youth and minority groups in these communities and ensure that community elites—typically older men—do not steer the decision-making in their favor. There is potentially a role for local NGOs in this regard.

Another strategy for reform, more narrowly focused than those above, can be seen in efforts to provide protection under international conventions for the land rights of groups subject to discriminatory land policies and laws, such as women (see Chapter 17), or groups which are particularly vulnerable, such as indigenous peoples under ILO Convention 169. The ILO Convention provides protection to customary land tenure only in situations where the community can meet requirements, including self-identification and following a largely traditional way of life dependent on access to land and natural resources. This might sound as if it applies to many rural Africans, but it has generally been treated by most African governments as intended to benefit ethnic minorities, such as forest dwellers, traditional hunter-gatherers and other historically marginalized groups (see Box 19.4).

**Box 19.4 Protection of the Customary Land Rights of Indigenous Peoples**

The Indigenous and Tribal Peoples Convention, 1989 (No. 169), commonly referred to ILO Convention 169, is an international treaty that prescribes rights afforded to indigenous peoples, including rights to land. The Convention aims to safeguard the human rights and fundamental freedoms of indigenous and tribal peoples, foster the full realization of their social, economic and cultural rights, close the socio-economic gap between them and other members of the national population and provide measures to protect indigenous and tribal institutions, environment, land, resource labor and culture. In the tenure domain, it establishes rights of ownership and possession over traditionally occupied lands, along with rights to use land not exclusively occupied by the community for subsistence or traditional practices. Rights to use, manage and conserve natural resources are afforded protection. It further requires governments to identify land of indigenous peoples and protect their rights of ownership and possession.

The treaty covers two classes of peoples: indigenous and tribal. Article 1 describes *indigenous peoples* as: (1) "[descended] from the populations which inhabited the country, or a geographical region to which the country belongs, at the time of conquest or colonisation or the establishment of present state boundaries"; (2) those who, "irrespective of their legal status, retain some or all of their own social, economic, cultural and political institutions"; and (3) those who self-identify as belonging to indigenous people. *Tribal peoples* are defined as persons: (1) "whose social, cultural and economic conditions distinguish them from other sections of the national community"; (2) "whose status is regulated wholly or partially by their own customs or traditions or by special laws or regulations"; and (3) who self-identify as tribal peoples. For both cases, all three criteria must be met.

The treaty is legally binding on countries that ratify it, which now stands at 24, most of which are Latin American or European. Apart from the Central African Republic, no other African country has signed on to the convention. African states have argued that all African peoples, being descended from those who occupied their countries prior to colonization, can be considered indigenous. They have also expressed concern that the "peoples" terminology could lead to exacerbating ethnic tensions, while references to "self-determination" could undermine national unity and territorial integrity.

The first argument is somewhat misleading, because not all African people meet the full definition of indigenous peoples, which includes, in addition to self-identification, include retention of "some or all of their own social, economic, cultural and political institutions."

Applying this criterion would narrow the scope of application primarily to rural communities that substantially govern themselves through customary institutions. The second argument essentially casts a spotlight on the concerns of African political elites with loss of hegemony over these same communities.

Despite continued failures to achieve widespread ratification of the Convention, it has exerted substantial influence over subsequent international instruments aiming to afford special protections to indigenous peoples—notably the United Nations Declaration on the Rights of Indigenous Peoples (UNDRIP) and the VGs, both of which are legally non-binding—and made its way into African jurisprudence. Convinced by advocacy efforts accompanying efforts to seek endorsement by African states of the UNDRIP, the African Commission on Human and People's Rights concluded that the African Charter on Human and People's Rights already embodied several of the UNDRIP principles, including the rights of "peoples" to "self-determination" and to land, whether individual or collective rights. This has led the African Commission on Human and People's Rights to uphold the ancestral land rights of the Endorois and declaring their eviction by the Kenyan government to create a national reserve to be illegal under the African Charter. Also in Kenya, the African Court of Human and Peoples' Rights in 2017 ruled that the Ogiek, as a self-identified indigenous people, could not be evicted from their ancestral lands in the Mau Forest by the government on the grounds of conservation.

Source: Anna Knox (see Chapter 17, this volume), drawing on NORMLEX (nd) and Minority Rights Group (nda, ndb).

***Rural Situations where Systematic Titling may be Appropriate***

Systematic and effectively compulsory land titling by the state should be limited to situations of natural or man-made disasters or war and major population displacement, such that evidence of land rights have been destroyed and such rights have become so confused as to require an allocative approach replacing customary rights. In any case of systematic titling and registration of land under custom, the law governing such programs should be amended to eliminate or minimize negative impacts expected based on earlier experience with this model. The amendments should: provide for registration of women's land rights under custom and statute; mandate joint registration of couples; require a wife's permission for any alienation of land used by the household; recognize secondary in addition to primary rights; and prevent rectification of the registry where land has been acquired illegally, fraudulently or otherwise unfairly. A good starting point for considering needed changes in land registration law are the legal and administrative changes made as a part of Kenya's "reform of the reform" (see Box 19.5).

**Box 19.5 Reforming Land Law: The Case of Kenya**

Kenya's 2012–2016 land law reforms included amendments to its registration law that include:

1. A provision that systematic land titling and registration shall be implemented only with the voluntary, informed consent of the community.
2. A provision that awarding title to a landholder in the context of systematic land titling and registration shall be based not primarily on his/her physical occupation of the land but upon the appropriateness of the title award under customary land tenure.
3. Elimination of provisions that customary interests in a registered parcel not noted on the register at the time of registration are extinguished by registration, instead providing that only customary interests specifically altered by the law shall be affected by the law.
4. A provision that no landholding shall be excluded from titling and registration on the grounds that such persons who are in regular occupation of that land cannot hold that land under the land custom of the community by virtue of occupation, religion, gender or sexual orientation.
5. Elimination of the provision that made a title conferred under the Act indefeasible, which has allowed those officials and others to misappropriate land and then shield it by registration of the title; it was replaced with a specific provision regarding restitution.
6. A provision for the co-ownership of registered land by husband and wife during a marriage and inheritance by a surviving spouse of the same share received by a son of the deceased; and that any transfer of ownership or other legal right that would frustrate the intention of this provision shall be invalid, except if consented to by the spouse in writing.
7. A provision should be made to require registration to the community of all land and natural resources used collectively by the community as a matter of right and under its effective control.

## Tenure Diversity and Bridging Institutions

The institutional forms and processes discussed here have sought to create more effective local land management. They seek, at the local level, to coordinate and harmonize administration of customary and statutory land tenure. They are designed to serve the needs of a specific national land tenure system and are not necessarily transferable between country systems. They can certainly stimulate thinking about what might work in a given context.

One example is the Tribal Land Boards in Botswana. Botswana's land board model is remarkable for its integration of both customary and state land administrators in one institution, and second, for its nationwide implementation, which has functioned reasonably effectively for more than 50 years. It has a democratic or at least participatory character, even if the civil government side in the current version of the model seems to have a greater influence over outcomes than the citizen side. That could be fixed without losing the expertise the ex-officio members bring to the boards.

Whatever the flaws of the Botswana land boards, we have more than a half-century of experience with them suggesting a number of lessons. Customary land tenure does not require chiefs to administer it. It can be done by citizens if they are properly chosen. There is a significant cost of effective participation by citizens: the continuing need for training for members who are replaced by others from time to time. This training has appropriately been focused on the statutory system and the Tribal Land Act itself. This need was greatest when the boards were new. I dealt with several boards in the 1970s. It was clear that the government had made a serious effort to train and that it had been effective. The most important lesson is that the presence of officials and citizen representatives at the same table, discussing land-related issues on a continuing basis and making the decisions required together, has made the operation of this dual land tenure system relatively smooth and efficient, reducing conflict and confusion in landholding. While much of the contemporary commentary on African land tenure these days concerns growing conflict over land, Botswana does not figure to any significant extent in those discussions.

Ghana's Customary Land Secretariats represent a very different response, turning over the local land roles of government to an essentially customary institution, the chieftaincy Secretariat, with unpredictable results. Ghana has chosen to double down not just on customary rules but also traditional authorities. The land boards of Uganda and Kenya are essentially decentralized civil institutions created out of customary cloth to manage customary land and only to manage that land. Chiefs have no formal role in them, though they are not excluded from the boards as in Botswana and could continue to exercise influence in land matters as well as more generally.

## Final Reflections

I am convinced that African policy makers do not need a "best" reform model, but far more ideas about reform options. There are, however, some basic and often cautionary principles that they, and those who advise them, should regularly revisit in thinking about the next generation of land tenure reforms:

1. Land tenure is not about a relationship between people and land. It defines social relationships among people over land.
2. Land tenure is as much about institutions and authorities and their power base as it is about rules and titles.
3. Land tenure, as provided for in law, often reflects the aspirations of an enacting government, rarely reflecting normative realities on the ground. In Africa, they often diverge significantly.

4. There is no ideal land tenure system. The right tenure system is the system that best serves the interests of a particular society and does so equitably.
5. Land tenure is constantly changing, often in response to powerful forces of climate and markets, so reforms need to be regularly revisited and adapted.
6. Land tenure reform can be wielded as a tool for change. Land tenure systems are also the glue that holds traditional communities together and a key element in the identity of communities and individuals.
7. One must be clear on the difference between land law reform and land tenure reform. Land tenure reform may change land law but ultimately seeks to alter the normative reality on the ground.
8. No land tenure reform is without both winners and losers. Enduring reforms prioritize equity and seek to prevent or overcome social conflict.

Legal advisors in particular must take care. Professor Robert Seidman (University of Wisconsin-Madison Law School) taught students in his African Law course that while laws from one western country may usefully provide models for other countries with similar societies and economies, this is not the situation in Africa. Laws provoke different responses from individuals and groups that are differently situated. If a law from a European country seems to have elements that seem useful, that law needs to be disassembled, the different provisions examined, the rationale for each understood, the relationship between them considered, and, when available, the experience in implementing them assessed. Then, "try them on." That is, think through how particular elements and institutions might work together in the distinctive political, economic and cultural-ethnic context for which one is seeking a way to move forward. Other reform models are resources to be mined for ideas and elements which may be useful in another context. An issue that often arises is whether one can "put new wine in old bottles," that is, to what extent can an existing institution handle new tasks or needs to be modified or replaced? Ask "If these elements need to change, what elements need to remain the same?" My experience has convinced me that change and development come more easily and sustainably when they take advantage of the values and useful characteristics of an existing system. A "guided evolution" approach may often serve best, though even in that case there will be winners and losers. After all, evolution involves selection and is not always kind.

The discussion in this book has to a significant extent been informed by the concept of legal and tenurial dualism. Dualism is not simply a holdover from colonial notions of private property or state control but rather a tool that can be used to promote political hegemony, attain policy goals and serve elite interests. In China, it took me some time to recognize dualism. It surprised me to find it operating there, half a world away, in a very different cultural and political context. While both instances involve the use of land tenure to exploit one group for the benefit of another, it seems to me that land tenure can also be used in more benign ways and deserves more thought by those who work on land policy and law.

There are three areas I have found particularly difficult to reach conclusions. One concerns the tension between state building and decentralization. Ethnic federalism has failed in Ethiopia. Tribalism casts its shadow over efforts to decentralize.

Decentralization, while clearly essential, must be approached with care; it may be managed without too much difficulty in some contexts but is very risky in others. A second difficult area concerns how to carry forward custom into the future. The codification solution clearly sacrifices flexibility. If reform is not urgent, absorption through the courts by incorporation in a nation's common law, where this legal option is present as in Common Law countries, can work reasonably well. Will the resultant "customary law" of the state reflect to some extent the priorities of the state and even the government of the day, rather than a "pure" custom as it exists in the minds of people "on the ground?" Certainly, but this seems to me less objectionable today than under a colonial government. A third such area is that of the destination and beneficiaries of the growth of value in land as land becomes marketable. My general preference would be to let value accrue to rural small farmers and herders. The state, whose investment in infrastructure and land-related services is responsible for part of that rise in value, has a legitimate claim to some of it. Simultaneously, Africa's fragile and failing states badly need to develop lines of land-based revenue (taxes, rents, etc.). Concessions seem to me a particularly unfortunate way of doing this, certainly from the point of view of small farmers and herders.

In Africa today, one finds growing levels of tenure insecurity, misappropriation, dispossession and conflict with respect to land. While the landless and land-poor around the world struggle to obtain the land they need, governments in Africa, blessed with a relatively broad distribution of land among its people, are in danger of squandering an important resource for political stability and economic development. At the same time, one finds encouraging changes and new change agents, though hardly as many as might be wished. It is encouraging that several countries have given new recognition and protection to customary land tenure in the last two decades. Even in countries where there has been no breakthrough at the rural land policy level, there have been positive developments in narrower fields, such as programs that expand access by rural communities to state-owned natural resources. Among the most positive developments are growing numbers of NGOs and CSOs engaging in land tenure issues. They are generally better attuned to the needs of rural communities than governments. They can bring into play international NGOs, which can provide funding and ideas and training in land tenure advocacy, and bilateral donors, which can provide funding even where advocates of change are engaged in a frankly political struggle. Among the larger bilateral and multilateral donors, the FAO stands out for its work on the Voluntary Guidelines and its consistent attention to land tenure issues over the years.

Africa is experiencing an unprecedented growth in conflict directly related to control of land. Peters addresses this phenomenon in a remarkable series of articles (Peters, 2004, 2013a, 2013b, 2018). She states tenure dualism is an important root of this struggle, because of its lack of recognition of customary land rights, a policy adopted by the new governing elites in most countries after independence as part of their effort to disempower traditional authorities. If new governments had been able to establish effective governance of land under custom, the situation might not have developed on problematic lines. They did not. Without controls over land markets under colonialism and traditional authorities, outsiders moved to acquire cheap customary land. A variety of forms of land-grabbing developed, some through quasi-market and often illegal land transactions. Others involved abuse by authorities of the great power implicit in the states' claim to own all land under custom, often driven by elite interests and with their participation in these processes. This has led to endemic conflict involving inconsistent claims to land based on custom and the law of the state, complicated by the existence of multiple fora applying different rules, and resulting in normative confusion and undermining rule of law and land tenure security.

Land registration programs, seen by some as the solution to tenure insecurity, have had disappointing results. Sporadic registration is often used to protect those who have acquired the land illegally or unfairly, engendering anger and conflict. Systematic land registration has proven unsustainable in perhaps most rural communities, with unregistered transactions creating an ever-widening gap between right-holders shown on the register and those actually holding the land. As Lawry et al. (2023) document, these programs increase tenure insecurity for some land users as they increase tenure security for others. Registration is not neutral but creates winners and losers.

Peters expresses concern that, accustomed as scholars are to the flexibility and negotiability in customary tenure systems, they may fail to fully appreciate that such levels of conflict indicate. Processes of exclusion and class differentiation are underway that limit or end negotiation for certain social groups (2004, 2013a, 2013b).

While land tenure policies have played important roles in the creation of Africa's troubled situation, the problem is larger than land tenure. We need to think more in terms of land governance as part of an overall governance strategy and land tenure as one way to implement that strategy. The displacement of African smallholders and herders by large land concessions to foreign investors can be seen as an attempt by governments, having failed to develop smallholder agriculture, to outsource land governance in extensive areas to foreign, private firms. African policy makers need to find ways to reorient development policy and land policy to support their rural citizens through the difficult transitions ahead, easing those transitions rather than turning them into "surplus people."

There is reason to be hopeful that some of the lessons learned from Africa's experience with land tenure reform will be absorbed by today's African policy makers. A new generation of African researchers on land tenure is emerging. Hopefully they can avoid capture by the disciplinary and ideological perspectives developed by a generation of well-meaning foreign scholars and bring to this work an authenticity informed by personal experience of the various cultures and tenure systems of the continent. Perhaps they will be able to reframe the debate in important ways. There are new challenges on the horizon. As climate change becomes an increasingly ominous part of Africa's future, a basic question arises: many of the tenure policies put forward since the colonial period have stressed the need for settled agriculture, stable and with tenure secure. Migratory pastoralism has been increasingly marginalized. In the future, if changing weather patterns no longer allow more settled forms of rainfed farming, or make it much more difficult over large areas, might rural and herders be better served by tenure systems that incorporate rotating seasonal use, as did the tenure systems of pastoralists in the *dars* (tribal territories) of western Sudan or the Tigrean peasant communities in highland Ethiopia and Eritrea a century ago?

## References

Bruce, J.W. (2017, March 20–24). *Land tenure dualism in China: How the dichotomy between state and collective ownership of land has shaped urbanization and driven the emergence of wealth inequality* [Conference presentation]. Land and Poverty Conference, Washington, DC, The World Bank.

Chimhowu, A. (2019). The "new" African customary land tenure: Characteristics, features and policy implications of a new paradigm. *Land Use Policy*, *81*, 897–903. https://doi.org/10.1016/j.landusepol.2018.04.014

Cotula, L. & Knight, R. (2021). *Protecting legitimate tenure rights: From concepts to practice* (Legal Brief No. 2). FAO. https://openknowledge.fao.org/items/563db4fe-7b88-4afa-b309-9721e049d874

Cotula, L., Berger, T., Knight, R., McInerney, T., Vidar, M., & Deupmann, P. (2016). *Responsible governance of tenure and the law: A guide for lawyers and other legal service providers* (Governance of Tenure Technical Guide No. 5). FAO. https://openknowledge.fao.org/server/api/core/bitstreams/62029425-d044-4a47-8295-15ad62222b3a/content#:~:text=This%20technical%20guide%2C%20Responsible%20governance,and%20all%20those%20who%20are

Lawry, S., McLain, R., Rugadya, M., Alvarado, G., & Heidenrich, T. (2023). *Land tenure reform in Sub-Saharan Africa: Interventions in Benin, Ethiopia, Rwanda, and Zimbabwe*. Routledge.

Minority Rights Group (nda). Landmark ruling provides major victory to Kenya's indigenous Endorois. https://minorityrights.org/landmark-ruling-provides-major-victory-to-kenyas-indigenous-endorois/

Minority Rights Group (ndb). Victory for Kenya's Ogiek as African Court sets major precendent for indigenous peoples' land rights. https://minorityrights.org/landmark-ruling-provides-major-victory-to-kenyas-indigenous-endorois/

Myers, G. & Sanjak, J. (2022). Reflections on the limited impact of the VGGT in sub Saharan and opportunities for its future with lessons from Nigeria and Sierra Leone. *Land Use Policy*, *113*. https://doi.org/10.1016/j.landusepol.2021.105870

NORMLEX (nd). Information System on International Labour Standards. https://normlex.ilo.org/

Peters, P.E. (2004). Inequality and social conflict over land in Africa. *Journal of Agrarian Change*, *4*(3), 269–314.

Peters, P.E. (2013a). Conflicts over land and threats to customary tenure in Africa. *African Affairs*, *112*(449), 543–562.

Peters, P.E. (2013b). Land appropriation, surplus people and a battle over visions of agrarian futures in Africa. *Journal of Peasant Studies*, *40*(3), 537–562.

Peters, P.E. (2018). Land grabs: The politics of the land rush across Africa. In N. Cheeseman (Ed.), *Oxford research encyclopedia of politics* (pp. 139–149). Oxford University Press. doi.org/10.1093/acrefore/9780190228637.013.825

Wily, L.A. (2017). Customary tenure: Remaking property for the 21st century. In M. Graziadei & L. Smith (Eds.), *Comparative property law: Global perspectives* (pp. 458–477). Elgar. https://doi.org/10.4337/9781785369162.00030

# Index

Note: **Bold** page numbers refer to tables and *italic* page numbers refer to figures.

For Product Safety Concerns and Information please contact our EU
representative GPSR@taylorandfrancis.com
Taylor & Francis Verlag GmbH, Kaufingerstraße 24, 80331 München, Germany

www.ingramcontent.com/pod-product-compliance
Ingram Content Group UK Ltd.
Pitfield, Milton Keynes, MK11 3LW, UK
UKHW020153200926
475702UK00016B/2688
* 9 7 8 1 0 3 2 7 5 9 6 9 2 *